www.letsgo.com

NEW YORK CITY

researcher-writers
Davida Fernandez-Barkan
Daniel Normandin

staff writers
Mark Warren
Sara Joe Wolansky
Qichen Zhang

research manager
Matthew Whitaker

editor
Meagan Michelson

managing editor
Daniel C. Barbero

CONTENTS

RESEARCHER-WRITERS

DAVIDA FERNANDEZ-BARKAN. This Milwaukee native fearlessly held her own among New York's wildest characters, from skateboarders in Queens to queens in Chelsea. An art history major, Davida soaked in the city's great masterpieces at MoMA and the Met while still finding time to write hilarious listings—and capture her adventures on video.

DANIEL NORMANDIN. A *Let's Go* veteran of Belize and Guatemala, Dan was more than ready to take on the concrete jungle of New York City. From stuffing himself in Chinatown to hitting the clubs in Brooklyn, this recent college graduate had a personal investment in learning the ins and outs of the Big Apple—he was about to move there.

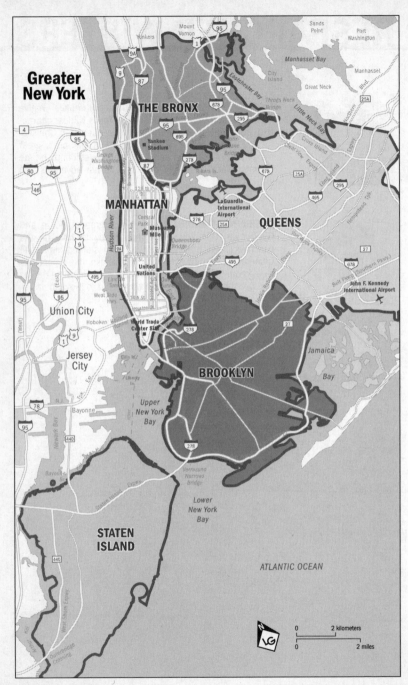

Greater New York

DISCOVER

NEW YORK CITY

"Take me back to **Manhattan.** Take me back to New York. How I'm longing to see once more my little home on the hundredth floor."
—composer and songwriter Cole Porter

"I don't need bodyguards. I'm from the South **Bronx.**"
—Al Pacino

"The road to Tomorrow leads through the chimney pots of **Queens.**"
—writer E.B. White

"Yeah, Yeah, I'mma up at **Brooklyn,** now I'm down in Tribeca, right next to DeNiro, But I'll be hood forever."
—rapper Jay Z

"Um, hello?!"
—resident of **Staten Island**, Angelina of MTV's *Jersey Shore*

when to go

Start spreading the news—you're leavin' today. But what kind of conditions should you expect? Regular floods of tourists head to New York City year-round, but fall and spring are by far the most temperate seasons in which to visit the "Big Apple." In winter, be ready for temperamental northeastern weather (they don't call 'em "Noreasters" for nothing). The city is often blanketed in heavy snowfall throughout the winter months and sometimes later. Still, despite potentially grim weather, NYC's holiday hoopla makes a December visit worthwhile. The summer months in the city can be hot, humid, and unpleasant—especially when you're forced to rub elbows (at the very least) with droves of people on the street. Hotels tend to be cheaper in the summer and more expensive in the riveting, Rockette-riddled winter months. Note that accommodations in NYC are often tailored to businesspeople, and so they may have reduced weekend rates.

top five places to give a "standing O"

- **RADIO CITY MUSIC HALL.** Don't miss the *Christmas Spectacular* at this midtown Manhattan landmark.

- **MADISON SQUARE GARDEN.** This arena is a must-see, whether you go gaga for Gaga or get your kicks from the Knicks.

- **YANKEE STADIUM.** This Bronx ballpark is home to the 27-time World Series champions. For those who care less about the sport itself, it's the stomping ground of that cutie patootie Derek Jeter.

- **STUDIO 54.** Though no longer host to debauched parties boasting the likes of Liza, Elton John, and Andy Warhol, this legendary venue has proven that—like disco diva Gloria Gaynor—it will, in fact, survive. In its current incarnation, Studio 54 acts as the resident venue for Roundabout Theatre Company.

- **LINCOLN CENTER.** From arias to scat, this 16.3-acre complex hosts countless theatrical and musical performances and is home to the 🎭**Metropolitan Opera.**

what to do

NOCTURNAL NEW YORK

"Old Blue Eyes" wasn't joshing when he told us this city "never sleeps." Whether you prefer a laid-back lounge in Greenwich Village, transvestite karaoke in Chelsea, a cheap beer joint on the Upper East Side (yes, it exists), or a veritable libation festival in Queens, NYC is a land of endless possibility.

- **GREENWICH VILLAGE.** The **Fat Black Pussycat** (p. 146) is a plush student paradise, while the charmingly aged **Corner Bistro** (p. 147) serves up delectable burgers to match their brew.

- **CHELSEA.** For perhaps the best falsetto renditions of Whitney Houston and Tina Turner in town, head to karaoke at the gay bar **Barracuda** (p. 152).

- **QUEENS.** Sip on the innovative elixirs at prohibition-style bar **Dutch Kills** (p. 161).

- **UPPER EAST SIDE.** From Beantown jollity at **Pat O'Brien's** (p. 154) to $2 pints at the **Stumble Inn** (p. 154), the Upper East Side offers nighttime fun ideal for a college crowd.

- **UPPER WEST SIDE.** At **The Dead Poet** (p. 155), Lord Byron gives you his blessing for getting wasted.

- **LOWER EAST SIDE.** **200 Orchard Street** (p. 144) boasts obscenely cheap grub and booze, while **Barramundi** (p. 145) serves sangria with a side of laughs.

PLAYBILL

New York City is the theatrical capital of the world; from the mainstream to the small-scale, theaters and performance venues of all types are dotted throughout the city. Don't forget to keep your eyes peeled for the hidden gems off the Great White Way.

- **GIVE MY REGARDS TO BROADWAY, OFF-BROADWAY, AND OFF-OFF BROADWAY.** From ❧**belting green witches** to sultry female jailbirds to William Shakespeare, legendary Broadway is the theater capital of the world (p. 174). **Off-Broadway,** patrons will find slightly less mainstream, more off-the-wall productions. Many of the best off-Broadway houses can be found in the Sheridan Sq. area of the West Village. Others are located to the west of Times Square. Occasionally, off-Broadway productions make the leap to Broadway; you may have heard of a little production called *Rent.* And yes, **off-off Broadway** is a thing. It refers to theaters that seat less than 100, but we at *Let's Go* are proponents of quality over quantity. Off-off Broadway houses are sprinkled throughout the city and are particularly prevalent in Brooklyn.

- **WHO WEARS SHORT SHORTS?** The Rockettes, of course. Their annual *Radio City Christmas Spectacular* is an event that just screams American tradition...and Nair (p. 172).

- **'TIL THE FAT LADY SINGS:** Music and theater aficionados flock to events at the **Lincoln Center** (p. 77), home to 12 resident arts organization including the **Metropolitan Opera.** It's a veritable orgy of the performing arts.

- **COOL CAT SKAT.** If you're more bebop than Broadway, not to fear. New York City boasts jazz clubs galore, including **Birdland** (p. 170), **Lenox Lounge** (p. 157), and the **Apollo Theatre** (p. 80) where ❧**Ella Fitzgerald** made her singing debut.

PLAY BALL

New Yorkers are known for a few things: distinctive accents, world-class bagels, and die-hard sports fanaticism. The Big Apple's teams are some of the most famous in the world...or, rather, "infamous" if you're in Boston.

- **AN UMPIRE'S EMPIRE.** Good ol' American baseball is a favorite pastime of New Yorkers. Of course, it's easy to be a fan when your home team has won so many damn championships. Throughout history, the **New York Yankees' roster** has included the likes of **Mickey Mantle, Joe DiMaggio,** and **Babe Ruth.** While the Yanks spearhead the American League, New York's National League baseball team is the **Mets.** The "Amazin's" performance was less than Met-iculous, until they won the 1969 World Series. Today they continue to be the most successful expansion team in the MLB and have a fiercely enthusiastic fan base.

- **THE KNICKERBOCKERS.** Founded in 1946, the NBA's New York **Knicks** call **Madison Square Garden** (p. 63) their home turf. Though their history—with a total of 2483 wins and 2516 losses—may not be stellar, they have a pretty star-studded fan base, spearheaded by **Spike Lee.**

- **RANGERS ON ICE.** New York's 83-year-old hockey team, the **Rangers,** plays in the

Atlantic Division of the Eastern Conference of the NHL and was part of the "Original Six" national hockey teams in America. The Rangers, who have captured five Stanley Cups, share their home venue with the Knicks. The team was lucky enough to acquire hockey legend Wayne Gretzky for the final years of his career. Ice, ice baby.

student superlatives

- **BEST PLACE TO NOT BE A RED SOX FAN:** Yankee Stadium.
- **BEST PLACE TO GET A BLINGED OUT BIG MAC:** McDonald's in Times Square.
- **BEST PLACE TO HIGH KICK:** Radio City Music Hall.
- **BEST PLACE TO GET A SUGAR HIGH:** Dylan's Candy Bar.
- **BEST PLACE TO IMPERSONATE LIZ LEMON:** 30 Rock.
- **BEST PLACE TO BOOGIE DOWN:** the "Boogie Down" Bronx.
- **BEST PLACE TO FLY IN STYLE:** Queens, home to both LaGuardia and JFK Airports.
- **BEST PLACE TO BE A BATHING BEAUTY:** Orchard Beach in the Bronx.
- **BEST PLACE TO BE MALL RAT:** The mall at Columbus Circle.

'TIL YOU DROP

From ritzy-ditzy to pseudo-designer, any item you could possibly want is surely for sale in New York. Whether you're looking to drop the Benjamins on some Manolo Blahniks or finagle for that trinket you just *have to have*, you're set in the City.

- **IT'S VINTAGE.** Ring the buzzer and enter the magical vintage world of **Encore** (p. 187), a hidden surprise amidst the pricey shops of Madison Ave. on the Upper East Side. Be sure to head to Williamsburg in Brooklyn, a neighborhood abounding with vintage shops like **Viceversa** (p. 188) and **Beacon's Closet** (p. 188).
- **NIFTY THRIFTY.** Head to **Unique Boutique** (p. 189), located between Greenwich and East Villages, for some quality thrift-shopping for both dolls and guys.
- **ANTIQUE CHOTCHKIES. Ugly Luggage** (p. 189) in Williamsburg and—this is a mouthful—**Las Venus Lounge 20th Century Pop Culture** (p. 189) on the Lower East Side are among the best places in the city to buy those antique knick-knacks and armchairs you've been lusting after.
- **NO TOUCHY. Bloomingdale's** and **Barney's** in Manhattan are two New York's most famous upper-echelon department stores—ideal for budget travelers who can handle looking without the touching.

BEYOND TOURISM

- **STUDY.** At New York City's premier institutions like **Columbia** (p. 79) and **New York University** (p. 54), students can hit the books *and* hit the stage. Many of the city's universities also offer summer and extension programs—but only if you bring a big apple for teacher (yeah, we went there).
- **VOLUNTEER.** NYC's urban environment offers an abundance of volunteer opportunities, from combating homelessness and hunger to inspiring at-risk youth through art projects (p. 229).

what to do · beyond tourism

- **WORK.** If you want to rake in any kind of dough during your time in New York City, you should plan ahead. With the right qualifications, you may be able to find a teaching gig through an organization like **Teach NYC** (p. 233). A popular option for short-term work is being a film or television extra. Of course, to bring in anything substantial, you may have to take one, take two, or even three.

suggested itineraries

THE BEST OF NEW YORK CITY (1 WEEK)

MANHATTAN (3 DAYS): When Cole Porter wrote "Take Me Back to Manhattan," he knew exactly what he was talking about. The most famous borough of the city, Manhattan houses most of the quintessentially "New York" sights, beginning with **Central Park,** home to Strawberry Fields, "Shakespeare in the Park," and the most exotic flora and fauna in the city (well, that last part is debatable). If you've got the fortitude to merely window-shop, stop by ritzy **Upper East Side** classics Barney's and Bloomingdale's. Catch some of the city's most mellifluous performances at **Lincoln Center** on the Upper West Side, before practicing your chasse step down **Shubert Alley,** the sparkling center of the **Broadway Theater District,** Experience a totally worthwhile sensory overload in frenetic **Times Square.** Home to NBC Studios, Radio City Music Hall, and a totally baller Christmas tree, **Rockefeller Center** is an NYC highlight. Next, channel your inner art aficionado and tackle the astounding **Museum Mile.** Test your vertical *chutzpah* with a trek up to the top of the **Empire State Building.** Then—because what good is sitting alone in your room?—head to **Chelsea,** and its famous Piers and Studios. From there, saunter over to the artsy **East Village** and the gritty **Lower East Side.** Mosey on down to **Chinatown** for a meal or a faux Louis Vuitton. And who could visit NYC without catching a glimpse of the Statue of Liberty, that lady who'll take just about anyone? Head to the famous **Liberty Island,** and then hop over to neighboring **Ellis Island.**

BRONX (1 DAY): Get into some monkey business at the **Bronx Zoo** before getting a good whiff of the **New York Botanical Garden.** Finally, take yourself out to the ballgame at the new **Yankee Stadium.**

QUEENS (1 DAY): Pick up some scrumptious souvlaki in **Astoria,** and then walk it off in nearby **Flushing Meadows Corona Park.** You may want to take a jaunt to **Citi Field Park,** the new home of the New York Mets. And if a less-than-championship game leaves a bad taste in your mouth, make up for it with some Korean grub in **Flushing.**

BROOKLYN (1 DAY): Escape from Lower Manhattan's cluster of skyscrapers by crossing **Brooklyn Bridge.** Take a romantic stroll along the **Brooklyn Heights Promendade,** before picnicking on the **Long Meadow** in **Prospect Park.** Take an afternoon tour of the **Brooklyn Brewery** and let the free samples make the galleries in DUMBO seem particularly creative. As the day winds down, enjoy the dining and upbeat nightlife of **Park Slope.**

STATEN ISLAND (1 DAY): From Manhattan, hop aboard the **Staten Island Ferry** for some stunning views of the Big Apple. Once in Staten Island, make your way to the **Snug Harbor Cultural Center** where the **Staten Island Botanical Gardens** offer a veritable olfactory orgy. Finally, time travel with a visit to the 100 acre **Historic Richmond Town.**

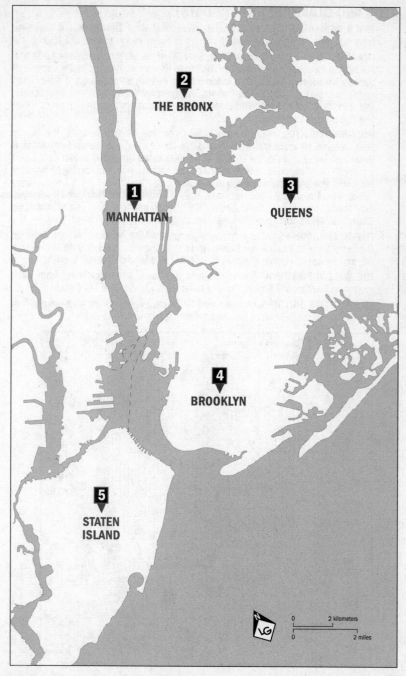

MANHATTAN

THE BRONX

QUEENS

BROOKLYN

STATEN ISLAND

0   2 kilometers
0   2 miles

GLITZ AND GLAMOUR TOUR (2 DAYS)

TOM'S RESTAURANT. It's been slightly remodeled since ⬛**Kramer** and his posse hung out here, but this joint made a cameo in nearly every episode of *Seinfeld*.

IMAGINE. Head over to **Central Park,** a staple of the silver screen since 1908 and the setting for scenes from *Borat* to *Tootsie* to *Kramer vs. Kramer.* In the park, stroll through **Strawberry Fields,** that landmark the Beatles immortalized in song. From there, Beatles fans can visit **The Dakota,** the apartment complex where John Lennon was assassinated in 1980. The exterior was also used in Roman Polanski's 1968 film *Rosemary's Baby.*

HOLY MONEY. NYC's most powerful comb-over; the conference table; the "You're fired" gesture. All quintessentially Trump. Be sure to visit the **Trump International Hotel and Tower** at 1 Central Park West. As you saunter through Midtown East, catch a glimpse of Tiffany's (as in *Breakfast At...*) on Fifth Avenue. You can't get eggs over easy, and you probably can't afford the jewels on display, but you'll be humming "Moon River" all day. As you approach The New York Palace Hotel, you'll wish you were loaded like those kids on *Gossip Girl.* Bypass the hotel and visit **St. Patrick's Cathedral,** where you'll pray that you, too, might one day be a rich girl. XOXO.

FIERCE FOURSOMES. After catching a glimpse of Matt, Meredith, Al, and Anne on *The Today Show* at **Rockefeller Center,** you can channel the fab four from *Sex and the City* and breeze by Manolo Blahnik (31 W. 54th) and Monkey Bar (60 E. 54th).

THE WALDORF-ASTORIA. You'll recognize this fancy-schmancy hotel from such movies as *The Out-of-Towners, Coming to America,* and *Maid in Manhattan.*

EMPIRE STATE BUILDING. A Hollywood landmark, everyone from King Kong to Tom Hanks *(Sleepless in Seattle)* has had a defining moment at its top.

A MUSIC LOVER'S TOUR (2 DAYS)

LENOX LOUNGE. This offbeat Harlem lounge and jazz venue is just as chill as it was in 1939.

LINCOLN CENTER. The Metropolitan Opera Company—the "Met"—is North America's premiere opera, with a performance venue the size of a football field. Also at Lincoln Center, New York Philharmonic is an orchestra that has been directed by Leonard Bernstein and Arturo Toscanini. No biggie. And as if Lincoln Center didn't offer enough musical variety, every summer the masses shake it at Midsummer Night's Swing. Outdoors in Josie Robertson Plaza, this summer event has boasted jazz, swing, Latin, and big band greats. Zoot suit optional.

CARNEGIE HALL. The New York Philharmonic used to live here. Now, the venue hosts premiere visiting orchestras and kick-ass soloists.

RADIO CITY MUSIC HALL. If high kicks and sequins aren't your bag, not to worry. This famed auditorium hosts artists besides the Rockettes.

BIRDLAND. The Cajun food is as delicious as the music menu at this dinner-and-jazz club which features Broadway Mondays and Dixieland Wednesdays.

MERCURY LOUNGE. Indie punk and rock dominate, but other types of music are also featured at this club. Oh, and there's a tombstone embedded in the bar. Talk about rock.

KNITTING FACTORY. Head to the Brooklyn branch of this popular bar and concert venue; you'll find lots to do, and it definitely *won't* involve knitting.

www.letsgo.com

how to use this book

CHAPTERS

In the next few pages, the travel coverage chapters—the meat of any *Let's Go* book—begin with **Orientation**. Once you feel situated within the five boroughs, we'll show you the best **Accommodations, Sights, Food, Nightlife, Arts and Culture,** and **Shopping** spots in New York. We'll then take you on some of the best **Excursions** available for visitors who want a day away from the busy city.

But that's not all, folks. We also have a few extra chapters for you to peruse:

CHAPTER	DESCRIPTION
Discover NYC	Discover tells you what to do, when to do it, and where to go for it. The absolute coolest things about any destination get highlighted in this chapter at the front of all *Let's Go* books.
Essentials	Essentials contains the practical info you need before, during, and after your trip–visas, regional transportation, health and safety, phrasebooks, and more.
NYC 101	NYC 101 is just what it sounds like–a crash course in where you're traveling. This short chapter on New York's history and culture makes great reading on a long plane ride.
Beyond Tourism	As students ourselves, we at *Let's Go* encourage studying abroad, or going beyond tourism more generally, every chance we get. This chapter lists ideas for how to study, volunteer, or work abroad with other young travelers in NYC to get more out of your trip.

LISTINGS

Listings—a.k.a. reviews of individual establishments—constitute a majority of *Let's Go* coverage. Our Researcher-Writers list establishments in order from **best to worst value**—not necessarily quality. (Obviously a five-star hotel is nicer than a hostel, but it would probably be ranked lower because it's not as good a value.) Listings pack in a lot of information, but it's easy to digest if you know how they're constructed:

ESTABLISHMENT NAME 💳💵♿⊘📶🍸❄⛅▼ type of establishment ❶
Address ☎phone number 🖥website
Editorial review goes here.
⇄ Directions to the establishment. ℹ Other practical information about the establishment, like age restrictions at a club or whether breakfast is included at a hostel. $ Prices for goods or services. ⏰ Hours or schedules.

ICONS

First things first: places and things that we absolutely love, sappily cherish, generally obsess over, and wholeheartedly endorse are denoted by the all-empowering 👍**Let's Go thumbs-up.** In addition, the icons scattered throughout a listing (as you saw in the sample above) can tell you a lot about an establishment. The following icons answer a series of yes-no questions about a place:

💳	Credit cards accepted	💵	Cash only	♿	Wheelchair-accessible
⊘	Not wheelchair-accessible	📶	Internet access available	🍸	Alcohol served
❄	Air-conditioned	⛅	Outdoor seating available	▼	GLBT or GLBT-friendly

The rest are visual cues to help you navigate each listing:

☎	Phone numbers	🖥	Websites	⇄	Directions
ℹ	Other hard info	$	Prices	⏰	Hours

OTHER USEFUL STUFF

Area codes for each destination appear opposite the name of the city and are denoted by the ☎ icon. Finally, in order to pack the book with as much information as possible, we have used a few **standard abbreviations.**

PRICE DIVERSITY

A final set of icons corresponds to what we call our "price diversity" scale, which approximates how much money you can expect to spend at a given establishment. For **accommodations,** we base our range on the cheapest price for which a single traveler can stay for one night. For **food,** we estimate the average amount one traveler will spend in one sitting. The table below tells you what you'll *typically* find in New York City at the corresponding price range, but keep in mind that no system can allow for the quirks of individual establishments.

ACCOMMODATIONS	RANGE	WHAT YOU'RE LIKELY TO FIND
❶	under $75	Dorm rooms or dorm-style rooms. Expect bunk beds and a communal bath. You may have to provide or rent towels and sheets.
❷	$75-120	Upper-end hostels or lower-end hotels. You may have a private bathroom, or there may be a sink in your room and a communal shower in the hall.
❸	$120-200	A small room with a private bath. Should have decent amenities, such as phone and TV. Breakfast may be included.
❹	$200-300	Should have bigger rooms than a 3, with more amenities or in a more convenient location. Breakfast probably included.
❺	over $300	Large hotels or upscale chains. If it's a 5 and it doesn't have the perks you want (and more), you've paid too much.

FOOD	RANGE	WHAT YOU'RE LIKELY TO FIND
❶	under $8	Probably street food or a fast-food joint, but also university cafeterias and bakeries (yum). Usually takeout, but you may have the option of sitting down.
❷	$8-15	Sandwiches, pizza, appetizers at a bar, or low-priced entrees. Most ethnic eateries are a 2. Either takeout or a sit-down meal, but only slightly more fashionable decor.
❸	$15-25	Mid-priced entrees, seafood, and exotic pasta dishes. More upscale ethnic eateries. Since you'll have the luxury of a waiter, tip will set you back a little extra.
❹	$25-40	A somewhat fancy restaurant. Entrees tend to be heartier or more elaborate, but you're really paying for decor and ambience. Few restaurants in this range have a dress code, but some may look down on T-shirts and sandals.
❺	over $40	Your meal might cost more than your room, but there's a reason—it's something fabulous, famous, or both. Slacks and dress shirts may be expected. Offers foreign-sounding food and a decent wine list. Don't order a PB and J!

ORIENTATION

manhattan

LOWER MANHATTAN

Not only is Lower Manhattan the most densely-populated area in the United States (and one of the wealthiest), it is also where the whole New York party got started. Comprising a roughly triangular area with the **Hudson River** to the west, the **East River** to the east, and **Chambers Street** and the **Brooklyn Bridge** to the north, this was where the Dutch set up shop when they founded **New Amsterdam** in 1624. Many of the streets are laid out exactly as they were 400 years ago, and some have not even changed names. You'll soak up this old world feel if you hit the cobblestoned **Stone Street** for a meal or a drink. **Broadway** cuts the neighborhood in half, and the area's most famous (or infamous...) street is **Wall Street**, which runs East and West from Broadway to **FDR Drive.** In addition to being home of the **New York Stock Exchange,** Wall St. is the site of **Federal Hall,** which was home of the country's first National Government from 1789-1790. Other sights that draw visitors are Battery Park, where millions of immigrants passed through **Castle Clinton** on their way into the country, the majestic buildings at **Civic Center** on the Northern border, and the **World Trade Center Site,** one of the targets of terrorist attacks on September 11, 2001. **Lower Manhattan** has played a key part of New York history for almost four centuries and definitely should not be missed.

SOHO AND TRIBECA

The great thing about SoHo and Tribeca is that you can tell their locations just from their names. "Tribeca" stands for **"Triangle Below Canal"** and sets up shop between **Houston Street** to the north, **West Street** to the west, **Canal Street** to the south, and **Broadway** to the east. "SoHo" stands for **"South of Houston"** and occupies roughly the area bounded by Houston to the north, **Varick Street** to the west, Canal St. to the south, and **Lafayette Street** to the east. Tribeca became a residential area during colonial times and then a center of commerce in the mid-19th century. Examples of architecture from hundreds of years ago can be spotted along the picturesque Tribeca streets; check out **Harrison Street** if you're itching to see some classic Federalist row houses. It has recently become the richest precinct in all of New York City, according to both *Forbes* and *New York Magazine.* SoHo can be thought of as Tribeca's wild and crazy younger sister. At one point crawling with pubs and prostitutes, the neighborhood is now a shopper's paradise. **Broadway** is the center of this commercial Mecca, holding every brand you could possibly imagine: **Gap, Victoria's Secret, H and M, UNIQLO**—you get the picture. The side streets are filled with some of the higher-end designers such as **Calvin Klein** and **Vera Wang.** SoHo is also home to a ton of galleries, both on the upper floors of the buildings on Broadway and on some of the streets that run parallel to it, such as **Mercer Street** and **Greene Street.** When you hit SoHo and Tribeca, prepare to look at art and majestic old buildings to your heart's content and to shop 'til you drop.

CHINATOWN, LITTLE ITALY, AND NOLITA

Surrounded by neighborhoods that have succumbed to the dreaded pressures of gentrification over the last few decades, Chinatown stubbornly (and thankfully) maintains its well-established restaurants, open-air markets hawking everything from knockoff designer bags to fresh eel, and straight-faced local crowds who cut through clusters of tourists. Its ever-expanding boundaries are nearly impossible to define (though its center is still between **Canal Street, Worth Street, Baxter Street,** and the **Bowery**). It's a budget traveler's dream: the food and shopping is dirt-cheap, the streets vibrant with the sense of real community, and the area is close to other downtown hotspots.

Chinatown's takeover of Little Italy is old news by now, but the former Italian immigrant enclave—which covered over 50 blocks a century ago—maintains its hold on a few blocks of **Mulberry Street** between Broome and Canal St. The strip is little more than an Epcot-like memorialization of its former self, with brass bands and brash signs struggling to connect with tourists despite the scarcity of an actual neighborhood. It's best seen as a museum celebrating a fascinating past, well worth a visit for those interested in immigrant history or just seeking unbeatable gelato, or the image of old Chinese vendors hawking "Fuhgeddaboutit" T-shirts and large Tony Soprano posters.

Over the past 20 years, the northern sections of former Little Italy (enclosed by Broome St., East Houston St., Lafayette St., and the Bowery) have become the pleasantly bland Nolita, "North of Little Italy"(a term created by real estate investors in the 1990s to lure new residents and spur gentrification). Cafes and boutique shops line the tree-shaded sidewalk, making it a peaceful spot to visit—even though SoHo to the west, the Lower East Side to the east, and the East Village to the north present more exciting destinations.

LOWER EAST SIDE

The Lower East Side is a tiny neighborhood packed between **Chinatown, Little Italy,** the **East Village,** and the **East River,** making its street boundaries **Grand Street** to the south, **Bowery** to the west, and **Houston Street** to the north. The main thoroughfare is **Delancey Street,** which runs east from Bowery and eventually becomes the **Williamsburg Bridge** leading to Brooklyn. The neighborhood has a history of providing a first home to immigrants, with many of the tenement buildings from the turn of the 20th century still intact. You can see a fully restored version of a tenement first used in 1863 at the **Lower East Side Tenement Museum.** Descendents of some of the early immigrants, especially Eastern European Jews, still rock the area, and you would do well to stop into **Kossar's Bialys** or **Yonah Schimmel Knishery** for a piece of doughy goodness. Immigrants from all over the world continue to find a home on the Lower East Side, so expect to find several sub-neighborhoods with large Asian and Latino populations. Rounding out the crowd is an ever-increasing hipster population who, though they sometimes dress oddly, contribute to cafe and nightlife culture.

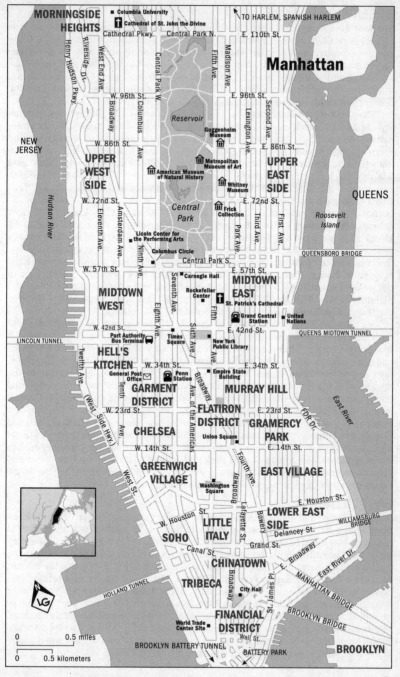

MORNINGSIDE HEIGHTS

■ Columbia University
✝ Cathedral of St. John the Divine

Cathedral Pkwy.   Central Park N.

TO HARLEM, SPANISH HARLEM

E. 110th St.

Manhattan

NEW JERSEY

W. 96th St.   E. 96th St.

Reservoir

Guggenheim Museum

W. 86th St.   E. 86th St.

UPPER WEST SIDE

Metropolitan Museum of Art

American Museum of Natural History

Whitney Museum

UPPER EAST SIDE

W. 72nd St.   E. 72nd St.

Central Park

Frick Collection

QUEENS

Roosevelt Island

Licoln Center for the Performing Arts

Columbus Circle

QUEENSBORO BRIDGE

W. 57th St.   Central Park S.

E. 57th St.

Carnegie Hall

MIDTOWN EAST

MIDTOWN WEST

Rockefeller Center

✝ St. Patrick's Cathedral

Grand Central Station

United Nations

W. 42nd St.   E. 42nd St.

LINCOLN TUNNEL

Port Authority Bus Terminal

Times Square

New York Public Library

QUEENS MIDTOWN TUNNEL

HELL'S KITCHEN

W. 34th St.   E. 34th St.

General Post Office

Penn Station

Empire State Building

GARMENT DISTRICT

MURRAY HILL

W. 23rd St.   E. 23rd St.

FLATIRON DISTRICT

GRAMERCY PARK

CHELSEA

Union Square

W. 14th St.   E. 14th St.

GREENWICH VILLAGE

EAST VILLAGE

Washington Square

E. Houston St.

LOWER EAST SIDE

W. Houston St.

LITTLE ITALY

Delancey St.

WILLIAMSBURG BRIDGE

SOHO

Grand St.

Canal St.

CHINATOWN

TRIBECA

City Hall

MANHATTAN BRIDGE

BROOKLYN BRIDGE

World Trade Center Site

FINANCIAL DISTRICT

Wall St.

BROOKLYN

BROOKLYN BATTERY TUNNEL

BATTERY PARK

HOLLAND TUNNEL

Hudson River

East River

FDR Dr.

(West Side Hwy.)

0   0.5 miles

0   0.5 kilometers

GREENWICH VILLAGE

For well over a century Greenwich Village embodied the simple, famed openness of New York City. Known nationally as a hotbed of political radicalism, social activism, and creative intensity, the Village has been home to seemingly every famous American author and their mothers, all of whom were famous American musicians, and their painter siblings, as well. The neighborhood's cool mix of cosmopolitanism, tolerance, and bohemianism once attracted everyone who wanted to start a revolution (or just sing a folk song about it) to its quaint, leafy streets.

The area's long history can be perceived in its many early 19th-century Federal-style buildings (which can make any walk an architectural tour in itself) to the street names west of Sixth Ave., many of which denote the owners of local farms and estates in days of yore. By the late 19th century, the area was already known as an intellectual and artistic center: **Herman Melville** and **Mark Twain** lived here, and **Henry James** analyzed the local culture in his novel *Washington Square*. The first half of the 20th century saw a deluge of radicals, communists, socialists, and authors, among them **Ernest Hemingway, e.e. cummings, John Dos Passos,** and **Willa Cather,** flock to the neighborhood. As if the similarities to your high school American Lit class weren't clear enough, **Allen Ginsburg, William S. Burroughs,** and **Jack Kerouac** soon moved in, making the Village a center of the **Beat Generation.** Quick on their tails were hordes of folk singers who made the **Cafe Wha?** and the **Kettle of Fish** famous, turning the neighborhood into the center of the folk revival movement. In June 1969, riots erupted after a police raid on **The Stonewall Inn,** a gay hangout on **Christopher Street,** essentially giving rise to the modern gay rights movement. Christopher St. is still a center of gay culture and nightlife. In the 1960s and 1970s, adventurous pilgrims moved east, called the area the **"East Village,"** and turned it into a center of the 1970s punk movement.

It's a loaded history, but today Greenwich Village seems to have left its wilder days behind. Constant creativity feels like more of a memory now, and over the last few decades upscale families have moved into many of the handsome townhouses and apartment buildings. It's hard to imagine many bohemians living in the gilded area above **Washington Square Park,** while the **West Village** (usually referring to the area west of 6th Ave. to the Hudson River) is mostly a quaint and quiet residential community (not to mention the setting for *Friends* and *Sex and the City*). But it hasn't turned into some stale museum piece yet; nightlife here is still among the best in the city, live music and theater performances take place on a nightly basis, and Washington Square Park remains a hangout for the offbeat. **New York University** pumps a constant stream of young blood into the area (student hangouts are clustered in the area below Washington Square Park and east of 6th Ave.). If you're pining too strongly over the neighborhood's arts scene of yore, just remember that the future 🎤**Lady Gaga** was playing the clubs here just a few years ago.

EAST VILLAGE

Attention ladies and gentlemen! You are now entering Boho Heaven. The neighborhood known as the East Village, bounded by Houston St. to the south, the **Bowery** to the west, **14th Street** to the north, and the East River to the east, is chock full of artsy types, and the coffee shops, bookstores, theaters, and poetry clubs that go with them. The **Astor Place** junction at Lafayette Ave., 4th Ave, and 8th St. is home to the famous **Astor Place Theatre** and **Joseph Papp Public Theater.** The East Village neighborhood also boasts an impressive number of tattoo and piercing establishments per capita, most densely concentrated along **St. Mark's Place.** In addition to the alternative East Village crowd, Ukrainian and Polish immigrants have a long history of inhabiting the area, to the neighborhood's great gastronomic benefit. Strongly consider a pierogi while you're here. One piece of final advice: make sure you have a lot of cash when you're in the East Village, as many restaurants don't take credit cards.

CHELSEA

The neighborhood of Chelsea stretches out in all its trendiness from 14th St. to 30th St. between Broadway and the Hudson River. Once an industrial hub (not to mention the birthplace of the **Oreo cookie**), since the mid-1990s Chelsea has morphed into one of New York's most important art centers. Around 300 galleries hang their canvases here, most of them concentrated between 10th and 11th Ave. Chelsea is also the heart of New York's gay community, with a GLBT nightlife scene that would satisfy even the most adventurous of clubbers. That said, everyone is welcome in Chelsea. You especially. Enjoy!

UNION SQUARE, FLATIRON DISTRICT, AND MURRAY HILL

The area just east of **Sixth Avenue** and north of **East 14th Street** includes some of the most stunning reminders of old New York. Towering landmarks like the **Flatiron Building, New York Life Building,** and the **Metropolitan Life Tower** stand as tributes to the city's ambition in its growing days. At the region's heart, the green space of Union Square is throbbing with activity and popular open-air markets. The Flatiron District west of it is a heavily commercial region dotted with loft apartment buildings, while the quiet streets of **Gramercy** (the neighborhood north and east of the square) are lined with the brownstones and mansions that once housed New York's upper crust in the Gilded Age. The swankiness continues to the north in the placid neighborhood of **Murray Hill** above **East 34th St.**

awfully lawful

With 10 million plus residents to govern on a regular basis, the city's police force depends on an unsurprising number of comprehensive laws to keep New Yorkers in line, some of them baffling additives to the legal system.

- **FINED FOR FLIRTING.** To this day, a $25 fine apparently still holds if men are caught turning around on the street to look "at a woman in that way." We're unsure how men with a facial twitch predisposition should proceed.

- **SUICIDAL SENTENCE.** The punishment for jumping off a building is death. Redundantly yours, the New York City Council.

- **SINFUL SUNDAYS.** A person is not allowed to walk around in public on God's day with an ice cream cone in his or her pocket. Save us, Father!

- **WATERED DOWN.** On Staten Island, a home owner can only water his or her lawn holding a hose in his or her hand. Those sprinklers are a bad influence on the kids.

- **RARELY BARE.** Women can be topless in public as long as their nudity is not associated with a business venture. All the Calvin Klein Jeans billboards in Times Square probably don't apply.

- **GOT THE BALLS.** Throwing a ball at someone's head for amusement is a specific offense. Hopefully, the Yankees pitch elsewhere.

- **ELEVATOR ETIQUETTE.** The law states that a passenger riding in an elevator must fold his or her hands and stay silent while looking toward the door. When was awkwardness written into the city constitution?

MIDTOWN WEST

Midtown West, from **29th** to **59th Streets** and from **Central Park West** to the **Hudson River,** is New York City at its most unapologetically touristy and commercial. This is the realm of **Times Square** (at the intersection of 42nd St., Seventh Ave., and Broadway), that 24hr. neon-lit shrine to capitalism, with M and M stores the size of supermarkets and Toys "R" Us stores gigantic enough to have their own Ferris Wheels. Midtown West is also home of the **Theater District,** the area boxed within Sixth and Eighth Ave. and 42nd to 53rd St. The 40 **Broadway theaters** in this neighborhood are the most famous, but the smaller theaters in the vicinity (called "Off Broadway" and "Off-Off-Broadway") offer countless possibilities for tourists willing to dish out some dough for a show. The neighborhood south of Times Square on the eastern portion of Midtown West is loosely referred to as **Herald Square** (the actual Herald Square is a triangle formed by Sixth Ave., Eighth Ave, and W. 34th St.). This area contains some of the major Manhattan sights, including **Madison Square Garden** and the **Empire State Building.** The **Garment District,** comprised of the streets from 30th to 42nd and between Broadway and Eighth Ave., is home to the showrooms, warehouses, and offices of the biggest names in fashion. The **Fashion Walk of Fame** which stretches up the sidewalks of Seventh Ave., contains 26 plaques paying tribute to these big-name designers. For a break from the shopping mayhem (and for some tasty, inexpensive restaurant options), head to **Hell's Kitchen,** encapsulated by 30th and 59th St. between Eighth Ave. and the Hudson River). The neighborhood was at one point a favorite locale of the Irish Mafia and also served as inspiration for **West Side Story.** There's a lot packed into this little region of the Big Apple. Whatever your experience here may be, rest assured that it will not be dull.

MIDTOWN EAST

The pocket of Manhattan from **29th Street** through **59th Street** and east of Central Park is occupied mostly by businesspeople, tourists, and others who don't actually live in the area. **St. Patrick's Cathedral,** the **Chrysler Building, Grand Central Terminal,** and other such sights draw visitors from miles around, as do the high-end retail stores on **Fifth Avenue.** The **New York Public Library** and **Bryant Park** are favorite study and lunch spots (respectively) for New York residents. The quieter **Turtle Bay** neighborhood in the eastern part of Midtown East is home to the ▓**United Nations** and is filled with international visitors. Put on your sightseeing glasses and get ready to take in some of New York's most iconic landmarks.

ROOSEVELT ISLAND

This long, thin strip of land between Manhattan and Queens (and directly beneath the Queensborough Bridge) has long been eclipsed by the presence of its two huge, world-famous neighbors. As a mostly residential community, it's really not worth too much of a visitor's time. Still, the island's fascinating history and stunning views of the Manhattan skyline make it worth a quick stop on the F train.

UPPER EAST SIDE

The Upper East Side is known for being high-class and high-priced. With one of the highest costs per square foot in American real estate, many of New York's most prosperous residents have resided here: **Audrey Hepburn, Bill Murray,** and **Katie Couric,** to name just a few. Although the cost of living is high, touring the Upper East Side can be affordable and fun. When visiting the Upper East Side, look forward to beautiful, tree-lined streets, gourmet food, exciting nightlife, and internationally regarded museums (some of them free, with only a "suggested" minimum donation).

UPPER WEST SIDE

Where can you see people jamming to Caribbean beats on the street corner? Shops selling "Jewish Souvenirs"? Restaurants advertising "Chinese-Spanish" food? The answer is New York's Upper West Side, ranging from 59th St. to 110th St. and bordered by the Hudson River to the West and Central Park West to the East. More residential than its East Side counterpart, the Upper West Side is a rainbow of cultures, ages, and lifestyles. A certain type of New Yorker wouldn't dream of living anywhere else. **Broadway,** lined with restaurants and shops, bisects the neighborhood, while the bar-packed **Amsterdam Avenue** brings the party. The Upper West Side is also the sight of the famed **American Museum of Natural History.** For performing arts enthusiasts, a visit to **Lincoln Center** is obligatory. Get ready for the city's most residential neighborhoods.

MORNINGSIDE HEIGHTS

Spreading from 110th St. to 125th St. and bordered by **St. Nicholas Avenue** to the east and the **Hudson River** to the West, Morningside Heights is dominated by **Columbia University.** The school sprawls over 36 acres from 114th to 120th St, between Broadway and Amsterdam Ave. of what was once farmland. The neighborhood is also home to two outstanding examples of Gothic-inspired architecture, **Riverside Church** and **St. John's Cathedral.** If completed, the cathedral would be the largest in the world. Morningside Heights is additionally the home of **Tom's Restaurant** (a.k.a. **Monk's Diner from Seinfeld**).

HARLEM

Manhattan's largest neighborhood is also one of its most storied and renowned. Though designed in the 19th century to house elite members of the upper class, the neighborhood gave way to poor European immigrants in the late 1800s before a huge influx of African-Americans in the early 20th century created the country's most recognizable, enduring, and celebrated black urban community. The neighborhood reached a cultural zenith in the Harlem Renaissance of the 1920s and 1930s, when writers like Langston Hughes and Zora Neale Hurston thrived in the midst of a frenetic jazz and art scene. A postwar slump followed, followed by rising crime, the rise of the Black Power movement, and the many artistic campaigns associated with it. Over the past 20 years, crime has plummeted and rents have skyrocketed. Now Bill Clinton has the headquarters to his foundation on famous 125th St., Harlem's main drag.

Its ongoing gentrification is hardly fatal to the neighborhood. Now 125th St. may be lined with countless franchises, but the black community that has traditionally defined Harlem still maintains a strong presence. Adventurous walkers can wander up to **Hamilton Heights** in the neighborhood's northwest corner between the Hudson River, Edgecomb Ave., 135th St., and 155th St., where a bustling Hispanic community keeps things moving by the Riverbank State Park. Further north, the distinctive architecture of **Strivers' Row,** between 8th Ave., Frederick Douglass Blvd., 135th St., and 138th St., dates from 1891 (you can still see a directive to "walk your horses" on one gate). The area got its nickname from the successful professionals who settled there once the buildings were opened to African-Americans in 1919. The same story applies to **Sugar Hill** even farther north, (between Edgecomb Ave., Amsterdam Ave., 145th St., and 155th St. "Sugar" meant money, and apartments in Sugar Hill were affordable only to the affluent. W.E.B. DuBois, Duke Ellington, Ralph Ellison, and Thurgood Marshall all once called the area home.

To the east, between East 96th St., Fifth Ave., and the Harlem and East Rivers, **East Harlem**—also called Spanish Harlem or El Barrio—is home to an historic and thriving Mexican and Puerto Rican population. Known as Italian Harlem in the years before World War II, the area has maintained a widespread Hispanic population for abut 60 years now. The neighborhood has emerged from decades of drug- and gang-fueled crime to emerge as a proud Hispanic center and Manhattan's best spot for Mexican and Puerto Rican food.

brooklyn

WILLIAMSBURG

For decades, a large part of Williamsburg was an industrial wasteland, home of Domino's Sugar Factory, abandoned riverside warehouses, and *A Tree Grows in Brooklyn*. A vanguard of artists began to make their way to the neighborhood throughout the '80s and early '90s, searching for that ever-elusive cheap loft space. The trickle became a flood in the late '90s and early 2000s; within a few years the neighborhood was being described as the site of a cultural renaissance and the American capital of a new species of hipster. By 2003, however, *The New York Times* had begun publishing articles about the neighborhood's cultural decline. There are signs of weariness now that the droves of hippie pilgrims have hit their thirties and forties. A steady stream of young parents with strollers patrols McCarren Park; the once underground, semi-illegal music scene that congregated in abandoned factories has given way to established venues and big names (Snoop!). The art scene moves deeper into Brooklyn; there are now dozens (hundreds?) of work spaces and galleries in Bushwick alone. Towering condo buildings rise above the humble industrial spaces and three-floor walk-ups. Many now see the neighborhood as an obnoxious conglomeration of like-minded and like-dressed young things subsisting on trust funds and the vaguest promise of artistic talent.

Still, Williamsburg remains a hub of artistic activity; its gallery scene continues to provoke and engage, and its nightspots and concert venues manage to reconcile quality and distinctiveness with popularity. The main thoroughfare is **Bedford Avenue**, lined with cafes, shops, and restaurants. Metropolitan Ave. is also bustling.

To the south, below Broadway and Division Ave., a large and vibrant Hasidic Jewish community has called this area home since the late 1940s: expect much Orthodox wear and many toddlers. The area roughly south of Metropolitan and east of Rodney St. is home to the neighborhood's sizable Puerto Rican community, whose flags hang proudly along streets lined with small eateries.

PARK SLOPE

Park Slope's iconic brownstones and leafy streets have attracted an increasingly privileged community over the decades. Half a century ago, a diverse mix of classes rubbed shoulders in this parkside neighborhood. Today, townhouses go for millions and a mostly professional group, youthful and mildly progressive, has settled in.

Park Slope is defined above all by its young families. Strollers, pushed by hired nannies and parents alike, are everywhere, as are countless kid-catering shops that line seemingly every block. It can get cloying, but the place actually feels like a neighborhood and is worth visiting while you're exploring the vastness of Prospect Park just to the east. The numbered grid system makes navigating the area a cinch. Most of the restaurants, shops, and bars line bustling **5th and 7th Avenues,** while the area becomes more residential south of 9th St. The eclectic mix of restaurants, low-key nightlife, and beautiful architecture more than make up for the baby and toddler crowds. And who doesn't like cute kids?

BROOKLYN HEIGHTS

Brooklyn's stateliest neighborhood is also its most scenic. Each street is gorgeous in its own way, with much of the architecture dating back to the early- to mid-19th century. The quiet, pristine atmosphere is perfect for daytime walks. The price for this beauty is a notable dearth of affordable restaurants and a virtually nonexistent nightlife scene (though Brooklyn's best collection of Middle Eastern restaurants stretches along Atlantic Ave., on the border with Cobble Hill). No matter: you came here for history, not hops. Best of all is the promenade by the East River to the west, where you can catch some of the best views of Manhattan and the Brooklyn and Manhattan Bridges. Two busy streets, **Atlantic Avenue** and **Court Street,** shelter the neighborhood from the rest of Brooklyn to the southeast. **Montague Street**—where ▧**Bob Dylan** "lived in a basement down the stairs" in "Tangled Up in Blue"—is a busy central nerve line. Things are quietest to the north along the fruit basket of **Pineapple, Orange,** and **Cranberry Streets.**

the nanny fad

Park Slope's fame as a family-friendly haven has spawned a book (or five) about women juggling men and children while enjoying the young professional life. Parents hustle their strollers through these brownstone-lined streets with a proud determination, as if they all got together and made a blood oath to enforce the neighborhood stereotype.

Luckily, they don't have to carry their burden themselves; the phenomena of the Park Slope nanny hit home when I was walking up Prospect Park West, passing bench by bench, each one claimed by the same group: one nanny, one young child, one baby.

Dan Normandin

DUMBO

In one of New York's most dramatic (if, by now, familiar) neighborhood evolutions, this tiny riverside area beneath the Brooklyn and Manhattan Bridges went from a mostly abandoned industrial wasteland in the 1970s to the bustling trendsetter it is today. The change was spearheaded by a group of artists and developers who built the neighborhood's many galleries and turned factory spaces into airy lofts.

DUMBO (short for Down Under the Manhattan Bridge Overpass) also draws its fair share of tourists disembarking from the Brooklyn Bridge or from the ferry landing just south of it. Back in the day, that service was rendered by **Fulton's Ferry,** which connected Brooklyn to Manhattan and shuttled many old-time stockbrokers from the "suburbs" to Wall Street. The old ferry station was also the site of the American army's secret nighttime retreat from the British in the 1776 Battle of Brooklyn.

Today, everyone's flocking here, creating a mini-SoHo by the river. Enjoy iconic food at Grimaldi's and the Brooklyn Ice Cream Factory, roam the quiet, historic streets of Vinegar Hill to the north, and then treat yourself to some freaky performance art at St. Ann's or Galapagos.

FORT GREENE

Yet more brownstones line the blocks of Fort Greene, once home to the Victorian upper class (and, most famously, ▧**Walt Whitman.** Today the scene is far more diverse, with an integrated community living in striking, preserved historic homes.

To take a break from staring at people's private residences, head to Fort Greene Park. It's a hilly, shady haven of green space, baseball and soccer fields, meadows, and benches great for chilling or reading.

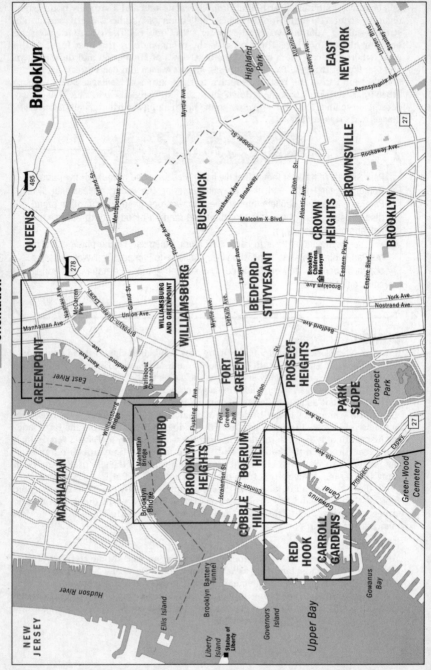

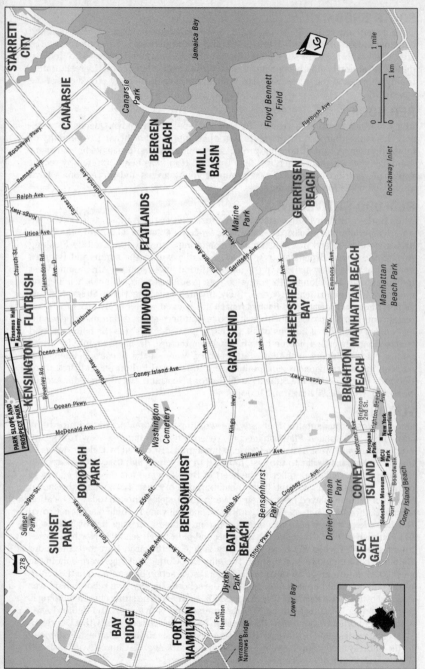

brooklyn . fort greene

SOUTH BROOKLYN

Once generically called South Brooklyn, now obnoxiously nicknamed BoCoCa, the conglomeration of **Boerum Hill, Cobble Hill,** and **Carroll Gardens** is a mostly residential area filled with pleasant streets and the even more pleasant families who flock to them. The action is mostly concentrated on **Smith Street,** a hub for quirky restaurants, trendy shops, and the occasional bar. It all draws a young, trendy crowd out of the woodwork.

RED HOOK

Red Hook lies south and west of the teeming, six-lane Brooklyn-Queens Expressway. It's still dominated by the piers that once supported a thriving community of longshoremen. A mix of housing projects, warehouses, and ramshackle apartment buildings give it a distinctly gritty feel. But Red Hook has been buffeted by recent waves of gentrification, and a new group of young artists and professionals have already gained a foothold in the area.

BEDFORD-STUYVESANT

After Harlem, Bedford-Stuyvesant is New York's largest and most famous African-American community. **Spike Lee, Chris Rock, Jay-Z,** the **Notorious B.I.G.,** and other luminaries were all raised in this expansive community roughly bordered by Flushing Ave. to the north, Broadway to the east, Atlantic Ave. to the south, and Bedford Ave. to the west. New arrivals in the neighborhood have included African and West Indian immigrants, along with young college graduates who are spearheading the much-dreaded gentrification trend. Busy throughways like **Fulton Street, Nostrand Avenue, Stuyvesant Avenue,** and **Bedford Avenue** are packed with a lively mix of African restaurants and shops, Caribbean fruit stands, southern-style restaurants, and countless corner delis. Most famous of all, perhaps, is "Bed-Stuy's" (as the neighborhood is affectionately called) iconic brownstone architecture, designed mainly for white middle-class residents in the late 19th century. Many of the finest specimens can be seen in the triangular region bounded by Halsey and Fulton St. and Broadway. Bed-Stuy is serviced by the Subway at Ⓢ Bedford/Nostrand Ave., Ⓢ Franklin Ave., Ⓢ Nostrand Ave., and Ⓢ Kingston/Throop Ave.

FLATBUSH

Once a prosperous suburb, then a white working-class area populated mostly by Jews, Irish, and Italians, Flatbush has only recently become home to New York's largest community of West Indian and African immigrants. Bordered by **Parkside Avenue** to the north, **Nostrand Avenue** to the east, **Avenue H** to the south, and **Coney Island Avenue** to the west, the neighborhood lies at the heart of Brooklyn and has the street energy to prove it. Fittingly, this was the home neighborhood of **Ebbets Field,** where the fabled Brooklyn Dodgers played before their move to Los Angeles (though today its location west of Bedford Ave. between Montgomery St. and Sullivan Pl. would place it in Crown Heights, where a huge housing complex currently stands). **Erasmus Hall High School** at 911 Flatbush Ave. (at Church Ave.), is the second-oldest high school in North America, founded in 1786 when Flatbush was just a village. Both Aaron Burr and Alexander Hamilton contributed to its founding. The imposing Gothic buildings were built in the early 20th century, however the original Federal-style schoolhouse stands in the center of the courtyard and houses a museum on the school's history. The school's land was donated by the **Dutch Reformed Church** across Flatbush Ave. The stone church building is itself a landmark, dating from 1796. At the intersection of Avenue H and Bedford Ave., at the neighborhood's southern edge, **Brooklyn College** campus soothes with a Georgian-style campus designed in the early 1930s centered on a small quad. Flatbush is serviced by the Subway at Ⓢ Church Ave./E. 18th St. or Newkirk Ave., Ⓢ Church Ave./Nostrand Ave., and Ⓢ Flatbush Ave./Brooklyn College.

SUNSET PARK AND GREEN-WOOD CEMETERY

Once home to New York's largest Scandinavian community, diverse Sunset Park, bordered by 36th St., Ninth Ave., 65th St., and the Upper Bay, is today witnessing the rapid growth of a Chinatown that may soon eclipse Manhattan's. The original Cantonese settlers of the 1980s have given way to an influx of Fuzhou immigrants from China's Fujian province and a more recent wave of Mandarin-speakers. From 36th St. down to 65th St., Fourth Ave., Fifth Ave., and Eighth Ave. are some of the busiest stretches of town, lined with Chinese restaurants, shops, and businesses. But an older, still sizable Hispanic community also makes its presence known through its own restaurants that commingle with those of the newer citizens. Sunset Park itself, between 5th and 7th Ave. and 41st and 44th St., provides views of the surrounding neighborhoods and lower Manhattan from its elevated position. Sunset Park is serviced by the Subway at S 36th St., S 45th St., or S 53rd St.

BENSONHURST AND BOROUGH PARK

With an Italian-speaking population that still numbered over 20,000 in 2000, Bensonhurst, bordered by 60th St., MacDonald St., 86th St., and 13th Ave., remains a proud Italian and Italian-American community that hasn't yet gone the totally commercialized way of Manhattan's **Little Italy**. The main drag here is **18th Avenue**, a.k.a. **Cristoforo Columbo Boulevard,** predictably lined with a steady stream of Italian restaurants, meat and cheese shops, and bakeries. Away from the busy avenues on tree-lined streets of stand-alone houses, the neighborhood has a distinctly residential and suburban feel. The Italian presence has recently been mixed with that of incoming immigrants from China and the former Soviet Union; the resulting melting pot can best be seen along 18th Ave. and 86th St. to the south. Bensonhurst is serviced by the Subway at S 62nd St., S 71st St., S 79th St., S 18th Ave.,S 20th Ave., and S 16th Ave./64th St.

Just to the north, bordered by 40th St., 18th Av., 60th St., and 11th Ave., Borough Park is home to the city's largest population of Hasidic Jews (South Williamsburg and the Lubavitchers of Crown Heights are strong contenders). It's the headquarters of the Bobov community, who maintain strict observance of Orthodox law. Almost all children attend yeshivas rather than public schools, and most stores sell kosher food only. Borough Park is serviced by the Subway at S Ft. Hamilton Parkway, S 50th St., S 55th St., and S 62nd St.

BAY RIDGE

Immortalized in the film *Saturday Night Fever*, Bay Ridge is a residential, middle-class neighborhood tucked away in Brooklyn's southwestern corner and enclosed by the Gowanus Expressway and the Belt Pkwy. There's little to see here: the **69th Street Pier** at Shore Rd. provides benches and views of Manhattan and New Jersey, while **Fort Hamilton** to the south is still an active military base. The **Verrazano-Narrows Bridge** stretches grandly to Staten Island by the neighborhood's southern edge, a landmark you can't miss when walking around the area's coast. **Shore Road**, at Bay Ridge's western edge by the water, is lined with gorgeous homes boasting spectacular views. Bay Ridge is serviced by the Subway at S Bay Ridge Ave./4th Ave.

CONEY ISLAND AND BRIGHTON BEACH

Ever since it first began attracting New York's lower classes in the late 19th century, **Coney Island** has been a national landmark. Though its early 20th-century days as a massive playground that drew all classes to its teeming shores are long gone, you can still find just about all types amid the aging rides and countless boardwalk eateries. Back in the day the three main parks that called the island home—Steeplechase Park, Luna Park, and Dreamland—were enormous, palatial constructions of grandeur at the cutting edge of technology. On certain days over 1,000,000 people would converge on the beaches and parks. With Steeplechase's closing in 1965, Coney

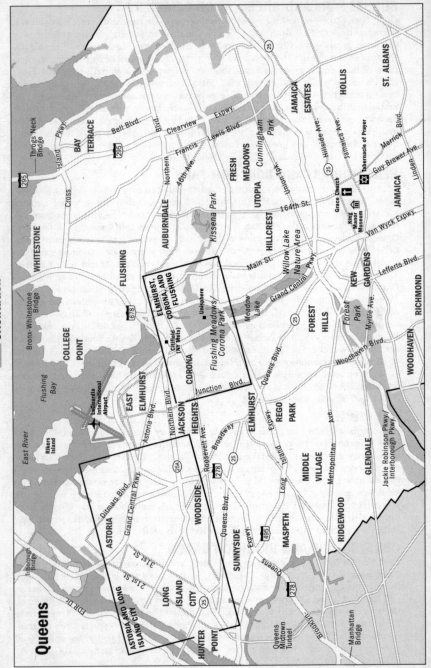

Queens

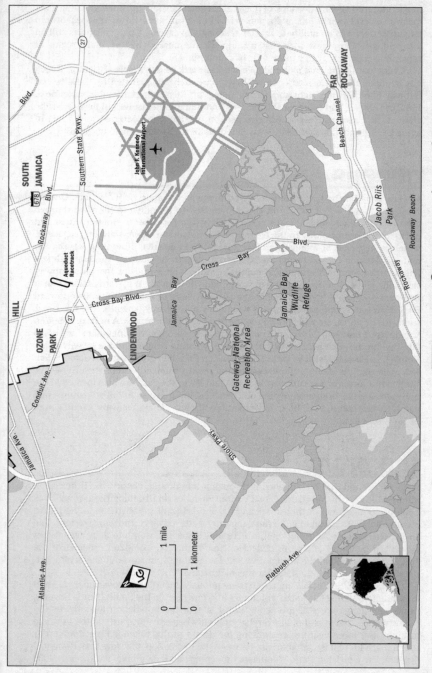

Island endured several decades of decline. It's been cleaned up, but signs of neglect exist in several vacant lots and a general feel of scruffiness. From its sideshows to its garish decor to its ability to attract seemingly everyone, Coney Island is still an integral part of any New York visit, a landmark in America's history, and a region of remaining eccentricity in a place of urban amnesia.

Lying just to the east along **Riegelmann Boardwalk** or **Surf Avenue,** Brighton Beach has become a firm Russian enclave. Brighton Beach Ave., shaded by the elevated Subway line that runs right above it, is lined with Russian restaurants, bookstores, furniture stores, and more establishments announcing themselves in proud Cyrillic characters. Cases of Russian pastries beckon outside small eateries, and a mix of aging immigrants mingles easily with American-born, Russian-speaking youths.

queens

Queens is by far the largest of the five boroughs in the area. At 109 sq. mi., Queens occupies about 35% of New York City. Connected to Brooklyn to the west through the town of Ridgewood, Queens is bordered by the **East River** to the northwest and north and Nassau County to the east. Both Brooklyn and Queens are on **Long Island,** which is just east of Manhattan. The Rockaway Peninsula, straddling **Jamaica Bay** and the Atlantic Ocean, forms the southernmost part of Queens. The borough is a patchwork of distinct ethnic and cultural groups, and a four- or five-stop Subway ride will yield a completely different world. Ride the **N** or the **W** towards **Astoria Ditmar Boulevard** and you'll find yourself in the Greek village of **Astoria.** The **A train** toward **Far Rockaway** in southeastern Queens will take you to sleepy beaches. The **F, E, J,** or **Z** trains to the northeast will take you to the pan-Caribbean **Jamaica.** A northeast-bound trip on the **7 train** will take you (from west to east) through the Bohemian **Long Island City,** the South Asian **Jackson Heights,** the largely Latino **Corona,** and the heavily Asian **Flushing.** In **Flushing Meadows Corona Park** you can find **Citi Field,** where the famous **New York Mets** play, as well as the **Unisphere,** the most prominent landmark of Queens. Both major airports, **Laguardia** to the North and **JFK** to the east, are also located in the borough. Queens is an intimidating place indeed, but it is also full of adventures just waiting to be taken. Gear up to have the time of your life in this lively, exciting area of New York City.

the bronx

A neighborhood that has toughed it through a tumultuous history, the Bronx is an unmissable part of New York City. For four decades and running the borough has been the boogeyman of the American city, and it is still synonymous in the public imagination with urban blight, crime, the drug trade, poverty, and gang warfare. The Bronx was literally "burning" in the 1970s and 1980s as post-white-flight tenants set unwanted buildings aflame to collect on the insurance. The 42nd Precinct of the NYPD, who patrolled the string of vacant lots and ugly, burned-out shells of apartment buildings in the South Bronx, was nicknamed "Fort Apache."

Today the situation has improved tremendously. An influx of government aid and community building has led to a plummet in crime rates in the South Bronx. Poverty, crime and gangs are still problems (some 50% of the population lives below the poverty line), and you should exercise caution when traveling around the borough at night. But more visitors are noticing the draws of this much-maligned area. For one thing, a lot of it isn't that urban; between the Bronx Zoo, the New York Botanical Garden, Van Cortlandt Park, Woodlawn Cemetery, and Pelham Bay Park, nearly 4000

The Bronx

RIVERDALE

WOODLAWN

Wave Hill ■

Van Cortlandt
Park

Palisade Ave.

Independence Ave.

Fieldstone Rd.

Waldo Ave.

Manhattan
■ College

Van Cortlandt
House

WOODLAWN
4

Woodlawn
Cemetery ■

Riverdale
Park

242 ST
1

231 ST
1

Broadway

SPUYTEN DUYVIL

230th St.

Riverdale Ave.

Mosholu Pkwy.

W. Gun Hill Rd.

Bronx River Pkwy.

MOSHOLU
PKWY

BUN
HILL RD
2,5

Hudson River

Henry
Hudson
Bridge

MARBLE
HILL

MARBLE HILL
1

BEDFORD PAR K &
LEHMAN COLLEGE
4

BEDFORD PARK
BLVD
B,D

NORWOOD
205 ST
D

BURKE AV
2,5

Inwood
Hill
Park

(MANH.)

Herbert H.
Lehman
College

Edgar Allan
Poe Cottage
House

KINGS
BRIDGE

ALERTON AV
2,5

Timiroff Blvd.

KINGSBRIDGE
RD 4

Kingsbridge Rd.

KINGSBRIDGE RD
B,D

NY
Botanical
Garden

White Plains Rd.

University
Heights
Bridge

FORDHAM

FORDHAM RD
4

FORDHAM RD
B,D

Fordham Rd.

Fordham
University

PELHAM
PKWY
2,5

9

Broadway

183 ST
4

182-183 STS
B,D

E. 187th St.

1

BRONX PARK
EAST
2,5

Alexander
Hamilton
Bridge

UNIVERSITY
HEIGHTS

BURNSIDE AV
4

Webster Ave.

Bronx
Zoo

White Plains Pkwy.

Bronx River Pkwy.

1   9

Washington
Bridge

Major Deegan Expwy.

Harlem River

Martin Luther King Jr. Blvd.

TREMONT AV
B,D

176 ST
4

Jerome Ave.

TREMONT

174-175 STS
B,D

Belmont Ave.

Arthur Ave.

BELMONT

TO
NEW JERSEY

95   1

MT EDEN AV
4

Cross Bronx Expwy.

WEST FARMS SQ
E TREMON AV
2,5

E 180 ST
2,5

E. Tremont Ave.

HIGH BRIDGE

170 ST
4

Crotona
Park

174 ST
2,5

95

George
Washington
Bridge

167 ST
4

Concourse

THE BRONX

169th St.

895

PARKCHESTER

Henry Hudson Pkwy.

87

167 ST
B,D

Grand

River Ave.

FREEMAN ST
2,5

Southern Blvd.

ST LAWRENCE AV
6

Macombs Dam
Bridge

161 ST
YANKEE
STADIUM
4,B,D

MORRISANIA

ELDER AV
6

MORRISON-
SOUNDVIEW AVS
6

Yankee ■
Stadium

The Bronx Museum
of the Arts

161st St.

SIMPSON ST
2,5

WHITLOCK AV
6

Westchester Ave.

Bruckner   Expwy.

River Ave.

MELROSE

INTERVALE AV
2,5

HUNT'S
POINT AV
6

Sound View
Park

149 ST
GRAND CONCOURSE
2,4,5

PROSPECT AV
2,5

3 AV-149 ST
2,5

JACKSON AV
2,5

Longwood Ave.

Garrison Ave.

LONGWOOD
6

Harlem River Dr.

138 ST
GRAND CONCOURSE
4,5,6

E. 149th St.

■ The Hub

3RD AV
138 ST
6

MOTT HAVEN

E 149 ST

278

Hunts Point Ave.

BROOK AV
6

E 143 ST
ST MARY'S

HUNTS POINT

MANHATTAN

Major Deegan Expwy.

CYPRESS AV
6

E. 138th St.

Bruckner Expwy.

Triborough
Bridge

PORT
MORRIS

East River

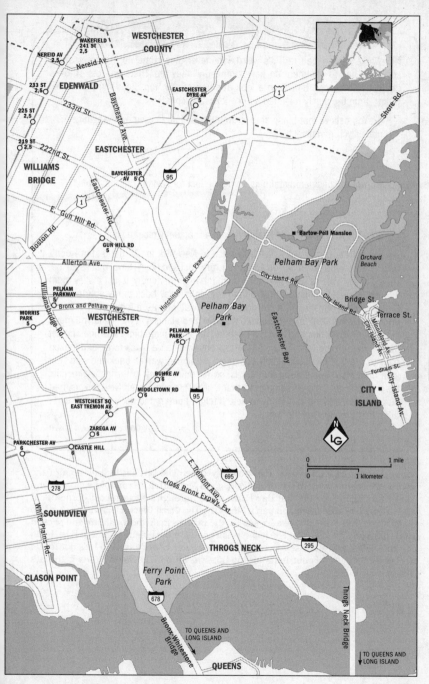

new yorkers are not mean

New Yorkers get a bad rap. It's weird. Whenever they come up in conversation, someone has to comment on how "unfriendly" they are. There are lots of jokes about this infamous trait. Take a look at some of the "Top Signs You are a New Yorker" from the highly-regarded source jokes2go.com:

4. You believe that being able to swear at people in their own language makes you multilingual.

...or

6. You've considered stabbing someone just for saying "The Big Apple."

...or even

27. You're suspicious of strangers who are actually nice to you.

You get the picture. Well, I've only been in New York for 24 hours, but I don't buy it. New Yorkers, as far as I can tell, are focused. They have places to be. Things to do. But this does not make them mean or unfriendly; it just makes them intense. Today, for instance, I got a little lost on my way back to my apartment in Queens. OK, I got a lot lost. A guy donning high-water pants, a fedora, and a tattoo on his neck that said "sweet," noticed my panicked glances at the signs and maps in the Subway station and asked if I needed help. I assured him I was fine and set out to climb to the top of the stairs. Homeboy was half a block away, and looked back to see that I was still visibly confused. He quickly walked back and said "You look mad lost." I confessed that I was, so he pointed me in the right direction. He promptly left before I could even thank him. This guy, like all New Yorkers, had places to be. Still, he was ready to help a fellow human find her way home, and I think that's really what matters.

Davida Fernandez-Barkan

acres of green space liven up the gray cityscape. The tiny Little Italy area of the Bronx in Belmont, west of the Bronx Zoo, gives Manhattan's a run for its money (and food). City Island, by Pelham Bay Park in the borough's easternmost corner, is at once a small seaside town and part of the city. The **Grand Concourse,** running south to north along the borough's western side, is the Bronx's main thoroughfare and packed with shops and restaurants. The **Hub,** a retail center at the meeting point of East 149th St., 3rd, Willis, and Melrose Ave., is a bustling center of activity. And let's not forget the borough's cultural contributions: hip-hop was born in the South Bronx in the late '70s and early '80s.

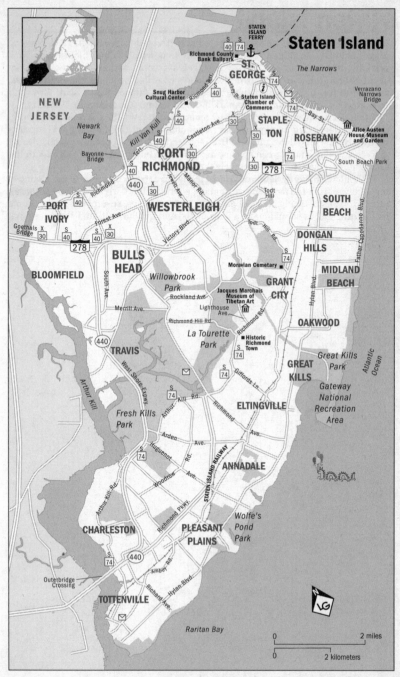

STATEN
ISLAND
FERRY

Richmond County
Bank Ballpark

Staten Island

The Narrows

**ST.
GEORGE**

Snug Harbor
Cultural Center

Staten Island
Chamber of
Commerce

Verrazano
Narrows
Bridge

NEW
JERSEY

Newark
Bay

Kill Van Kull

Castleton Ave.

**STAPLE-
TON**

Bay St.

ROSEBANK

Alice Austen
House Museum
and Garden

Bayonne
Bridge

**PORT
RICHMOND**

Manor Rd.

South Beach Park

278

Todt
Hill

**SOUTH
BEACH**

**PORT
IVORY**

Richmond

WESTERLEIGH

Forest Ave.

Victory Blvd.

Todt Hill Rd.

**DONGAN
HILLS**

Father Capodanno Blvd.

Goethals
Bridge

278

BLOOMFIELD

**BULLS
HEAD**

*Willowbrook
Park*

Rockland Ave.

Moravian Cemetary

**MIDLAND
BEACH**

South Ave.

Merrill Ave.

Jacques Marchais
Museum of
Tibetan Art

Lighthouse
Ave.

Richmond Hill Rd.

**GRANT
CITY**

Hylan Blvd.

OAKWOOD

440

*La Tourette
Park*

Historic
Richmond
Town

Richmond Rd.

TRAVIS

West Shore Expwy.

Great Kills
Park

Atlantic Ocean

**GREAT
KILLS**

*Gateway
National
Recreation
Area*

Arthur Kill

*Fresh Kills
Park*

Arthur Kill Rd.

Richmond

ELTINGVILLE

Arden
Ave.

Ave.

Huguenot
Ave.

Woodrow
Ave.

STATEN ISLAND RAILWAY

ANNADALE

Arthur Kill Rd.

Richmond Pkwy.

*Wolfe's
Pond
Park*

CHARLESTON

**PLEASANT
PLAINS**

Amber
Rd.

Outerbridge
Crossing

440

Richard Ave.

Hylan Blvd.

TOTTENVILLE

Raritan Bay

the bronx

| 0 | | 2 miles |
| 0 | | 2 kilometers |

staten island

The "forgotten borough" felt so neglected that it voted to secede in 1993. Nothing doing, obviously, so Staten Island remains a somewhat oddball inclusion in New York City. It's closer to New Jersey and feels it—you'd be hard-pressed to distinguish between the two, what with the island's crowded beaches, cluttered homes, and general feel of intensified suburbia. Though the famous **Staten Island Ferry** (still the borough's most famous "landmark") began linking the island to Manhattan in 1713, this black sheep of the city wasn't incorporated until 1898. It remained a fairly isolated, undeveloped immigrant-heavy community until 1964, when the Verrazano-Narrows Bridge linked the island to Brooklyn and sparked a population and housing explosion. Today, many green spaces, including the enormous **Fresh Kills Park** to the east, fight for space with crowded neighborhoods.

Without a Subway system, you'll most likely have to rely on buses to get around—they all leave from the **ferry terminal,** making coordination fairly easy. Though there's nothing too aesthetically pleasant about the surroundings, several unique museums and cultural spaces should make a journey beyond the Staten Island Ferry terminal worth your while.

orientation

ACCOMMODATIONS

They say this is the city that never sleeps, but that doesn't mean you shouldn't. While New York is host to some of the world's most legendary hotels, we bet you're not trying to pay Plaza prices. Still, just like the city's real estate, hotel rates are expensive and unavoidable. If you're willing to be a bit further from the party scene, uptown Manhattan has some of the cheapest hostels in the city. Prices get higher as you move further downtown, but we've got some suggestions for less expensive places to crash.

greatest hits

- **DREAM IN COLOR.** Sleep in the brightly decorated rooms of the Carlton Arms Hotel (p.39).
- **PATIO PREGAME.** The Pod Hotel (p.40) serves guests beer and wine outdoors from 4-9pm daily.
- **TO SLEEP, PERCHANCE TO DREAM.** Stay in the Shakespeare Room at the Chelsea Star Hotel (p.38).
- **GOLDEN SLUMBERS.** Visit the beautifully gilded Hotel Wolcott (p.40).

student life

Staying in New York City is hard on the wallet. Since hotels downtown can be very expensive, we recommend students look at hostels uptown. The **New York International HI-AYH Hostel** and **Jazz on the Park** are two great West Side options. Plus, they're just blocks away from the Columbia campus.

greenwich village

Housing in the Village isn't exactly the cheapest option around, but those who want to truly soak up the neighborhood's unique ambience can find some mid-range choices.

LARCHMONT HOTEL 💳🚫♿❄📶 HOTEL [2]

27 W. 11th St. ☎212-989-9333 💻www.larchmonthotel.com

Located in the tiny northern regions of Greenwich Village, the Larchmont is surely one of the quietest housing options in the city. Bathrooms are shared, but you receive slippers and the usual hotel amenities in plain but spacious rooms.

➡ [S] F, L, V to 6th Ave.-14th St. ℹ Continental breakfast included. $ Singles $90-109; doubles $119-129; family suite $219.

WASHINGTON SQUARE HOTEL 💳♿❄📶 HOTEL [3]

103 Waverly Pl. ☎212-777-9515 💻www.washingtonsquarehotel.com

True to Village form, the Washington Square Hotel does its best to be European. There's a healthy dose of classic Hollywood Americana, though, with pictures of famous movie stars from the Golden Age above nearly every bed. A sumptuous lobby complete with bar and a swanky eating area is the perfect introduction to sleek, Art Deco-inspired rooms that manage not to be too ostentatious.

➡ [S] A, B, C, D, E, F, V to West 4th St. ℹ Breakfast included. All rooms with bathrobe. $ Rooms with double bed $220-270; with queen bed $250-280; with 2 twin beds $250-280.

east village

JAZZ ON THE TOWN 🚫♿💳📶 HOSTEL [1]

307 E. 14th St. ☎212-228-2780 💻www.jazzhostels.com

This brightly-colored hostel does everything in its power to maximize the fun factor of your trip to New York. They go above and beyond the call of hostel duty by offering free pancake breakfasts *(Tu and Th 9-11am)* and organizing excursions such as trips to ★**MoMA** and walks across the Brooklyn Bridge.

➡ [S] 4, 5, 6, N,.Q to Union Square; or L to 3rd Ave.; or L to 1st Ave. ℹ Linens, towels, and lockers included. Free Wi-Fi in lounge. $ 8-bed dorms $41-53; 6-bed $45-56; 4-bed $47-58.

ST. MARK'S HOTEL 🚫💳🚫♿ HOTEL [2]

2 St. Mark's Pl., at 3rd Ave. ☎212-674-0100 💻www.stmarkshotel.net

The rooms are small and simple, but you'll be conveniently located among the shops and restaurants of hip St. Mark's Pl. Rooms have bath and TVs, but the hotel is more proud of its historic building.

➡ [S] 6 to Astor Pl. $ 1 full bed $120-140; 1 queen bed $130-150; 2 twin beds $130-160; 2 full beds $150-170, tax included.

chelsea

CHELSEA STAR HOTEL
HOTEL, HOSTEL ❶

300 W. 30th St., at 8th Ave. ☎212-244-7827 ✉www.starhotelny.com

Don't let the humdrum exterior fool you; on the inside, this economy-priced hostel and hotel is bright, lively, and fun. If possible, try staying in one of the custom-painted themed rooms, such as the **Shakespeare Room** where the bard will watch over you as you sleep. In the summer, the patio area is a great place to read, work on a computer, or just hang out. The lounge downstairs has computers, laundry facilities, and coffee and tea 7-11am.

✦ Ⓢ *A, C, E to 34th St./PennStation/8th Ave.* ⓘ *Free Wi-Fi.* Ⓢ *4-bed dorms $35 per person; singles with shared bath $79; doubles $99, with bath $169.*

HOTEL CHELSEA
HOTEL ❸

222 W. 23rd St., at 8th Ave. ☎212-243-3700 ✉www.hotelchelsea.com

Upon your visit to the **Hotel Chelsea,** you will be greeted by a woman on a swing high above your head—or a sculpture of a woman, anyway. Built in 1883 and opened as a hotel in 1905, this place is an artist's dream. In addition to a massive collection of art pieces, the hotel boasts an extensive guest list of artists who have called it home for a brief or extended period: Jasper Johns, Claes Oldenburg, Willem de Kooning, and Frida Kahlo rank among the most notable. It was also featured in Andy Warhol's 1966 film **The Chelsea Girls.** Your room itself will be a work of art; each room is beautifully decorated, and no two are the same.

✦ Ⓢ *C, E to 23rd St.; 1 to 23rd St.* Ⓢ *1-2 people $129; 1-2 people with bath from $179, 1-4 people with bath from $199, suites from $259.*

CHELSEA PINES INN
HOTEL ❸

317 W. 14th St., between 8th and 9th Ave. ☎212-929-1023 ✉www.chelseapinesinn.org

A small but classy hotel where they have a fascination with old movies. Classic posters decorate all of the rooms, and photographs of Audrey Hepburn and similarly classy celebs grace the walls. The breakfast area extends into a lovely garden so that guests may enjoy their complimentary breakfast alfresco.

✦ Ⓢ *A, C, E to 14th St.; L to 8th Ave. Free Wi-Fi and refrigerators. Business center available.* Ⓢ *Double rooms $199-299; deluxe rooms $189-350.*

CHELSEA SAVOY HOTEL
HOTEL ❷

204 W. 23rd St., at 7th Ave. ☎212-929-1023 ✉www.chelseasavoy.com

A more vanilla option than other hotels in Chelsea, the **Chelsea Savoy Hotel** is still a conveniently located, tastefully decorated place to crash. Amenities include cable television in every room and a complimentary continental breakfast in the morning.

✦ Ⓢ *1 to 23rd St./7th Ave.; C, E to 23rd St./8th Ave.* Ⓢ *Single room with double bed $99-145, with queen bed $125-$295, with king bed $165-350; quads with 2 double beds $145-325.*

COLONIAL HOUSE INN
BED AND BREAKFAST ❹

318 W. 22nd St., between 8th and 9th Ave. ☎212-243-9669 ✉www.colonialhouseinn.com

A unique opportunity to rent a room in a swanky townhouse so saturated with modern art it almost makes walking toward the place a nerve-racking experience. The Rothko-esque painting in the lobby was actually executed by Mel Cheren (as in "The Godfather of Disco"), who ran the establishment for 20 years. A climb to the deck on the roof, though taxing, is rendered completely worthwhile by the breathtaking view of New York City.

✦ Ⓢ *C, E to 23rd St.* ⓘ *Breakfast included. Free Wi-Fi in rooms with bath, $3 in economy rooms. Direct TV ensuite.* Ⓢ *Economy rooms with shared bath $130-180; rooms with bath $180-$300; suites from $300. Prices vary with season.*

accommodations

union sq., flatiron district, murray hill

Near the heart of Manhattan, the several affordable options in this area provide ideal bases for explorations of both the downtown and midtown/uptown neighborhoods. The area itself is full of beautiful architecture, bustling city parks, quiet streets, and decent restaurants.

CARLTON ARMS HOTEL
HOTEL ❷

180 E. 20th St. ☎212-679-0680 🖳www.carltonarms.com

A riot of painted walls sets this mid-scale hotel apart from just about any of its competitors. Each room has a unique variation on quirkiness: one is adorned with enormous caricatures of mug shots, another with a wall-to-wall Seussian landscape, another with abstract designs from a psychedelic fantasy. Individual artists' contributions (the famous graffiti artist Banksy painted one stairwell) give the entire interior a constantly changing, endlessly fascinating look. The rooms themselves are smallish but cozy—just be prepared to spend the night surrounded by very colorful and unavoidable wall paintings.

✦ Ⓢ 6 to 23rd St. Ⓢ Singles with shared bath $80, with bath $110; doubles $110/130; triples $140/155; quads with bath $180.

GERSHWIN HOTEL
HOSTEL, HOTEL ❸

7 E. 27th St. ☎212-545-8000 🖳www.gershwinhotel.com

Right next to the attention-grabbing **Museum of Sex**, the Gershwin strives for some public notice itself with several unique, curved glass sculptures adorning the facade. It's a welcome reprieve from the monotony that can mark this area of town. The indoor options are similarly enticing, with a spacious lobby attached to an in-house cafe and sleek, modern, but otherwise spare rooms with plenty of roaming space. Best of all is the wide range of options at hand, from "bunkers" lined with cheap dorm beds to pricey suites.

✦ Ⓢ 6, R to 28th St. *i* Wi-Fi $10 per day. Ⓢ Dorms $30-50; "economy" doubles $110-130; "standard" doubles $150-190; "superior" doubles $200-250; "suite" doubles $250-300.

AMERICAN DREAM HOSTEL
HOSTEL, BED AND BREAKFAST ❷

168 East 24th St. ☎917-883-6191 🖳www.americandreamhostel.com

Don't expect amazing digs at this plain Gramercy. Do expect comfort and a general atmosphere of hominess. Stairways and corridors lined with soft blue carpet lead to small, mostly unadorned rooms on three floors.

✦ Ⓢ 6 to 23rd St. Ⓢ Singles $75; doubles $105.

midtown west

HOTEL STANFORD
HOTEL ❸

43 W. 32nd St., between 5th Ave. and Broadway ☎212-563-1500 🖳www.hotelstanford.com

Stanford is a comfortable, convenient hotel with an air of Asian luxury that becomes evident in the miniature garden and fountain in the front lobby. Asian charm also permeates the wine, coffee and tea lounge on the second floor, which provides complimentary coffee, tea, cookies, and Wi-Fi from 7am-3pm.

✦ Ⓢ B, D, F, N, Q, R, M to 34th St./Herald Sq. *i* Continental breakfast at Café Ele next door 7:30-10am. Wine is available for purchase 50% off in lounge Su-W 6pm-2am, Th-Sa 6pm-3am. Ⓢ Singles $179-399; twins/queens $189-459; doubles $209-489; deluxe king $229-509; junior suite $249-539.

midtown west

▨ HOTEL WOLCOTT
◔♿ HOTEL ❸

4 W. 31st St., between 5th Ave. and Broadway　　☎212-268-2900 🖳www.wolcott.com

The **Hotel Wolcott's** ornate, gilded lobby, complete with high-ceilings and stunning chandeliers, may make it the most attractive hotel you've ever seen. The reasonable room prices include access to a fitness center and complimentary coffee and muffins in the morning.

✦ Ⓢ 1, 2, 3, 7, N, Q, R, S. *i* Internet $5 per 30min., $10 per day. ATM and vending machines in basement. Ⓢ Singles/doubles $140-220; triples $160-240; junior suite $150-230.

BIG APPLE HOSTEL
◔⊗ HOSTEL ❶

119 W. 45 St., between 6th and 7th Ave.　　☎212-302-2603 🖳www.bigapplehostel.com

If you're dying to stay in the middle of the Manhattan action, you can't beat this hostel's location. Don't expect many frills, though. There's nothing big about these Big Apple rooms, and not much exciting, either. For a pleasant break from the city, sit outside on the first level patio.

✦ Ⓢ 1, 2, 3, 7, N, Q, R, S to 42nd St./Times Sq. *i* Laundry and kitchen facilities. Free Internet in common room. Ⓢ 4-person dorms $37-$54; private rooms $110-154.

midtown east

▨ POD HOTEL
◔♿⊿ HOTEL ❷

230 E. 51st St., between 2nd and 3rd Ave.　　☎212-355-0300 🖳www.thepodhotel.com

If Andy Warhol had decided to go to a Japanese architecture school (and become an architect), he probably would have designed a hotel that looked like this. Big comic book-like graphics and ball-of-twine lights dominate the lobby, and the rooms are sophisticatedly compact. When the weather is pleasant, the **Pod Cafe** sells breakfast 7am-1pm and wine and beer 4-9pm on the picturesque patio.

✦ Ⓢ 6 to 51st St., E, M to 53rd St./Lexington Ave. *i* Free Wi-Fi. Ⓢ Singles $129-$199, with bath $199; 2 people $129-199, with bath $189-299.

VANDERBILT YMCA
◔♿⟨ɪ⟩ YMCA ❷

224 E. 47th St., between 2nd and 3rd Ave.　　☎212-756-9600

One of a dying breed of YMCAs that let out simple, clean rooms to cash-conscious travelers, the Vanderbilt has rooms that are small but they include TVs, A/C, and refrigerators. Guests also receive access to fitness and swimming facilities.

✦ Ⓢ 6 to 51st St.; E, M to Lexington Ave./53rd St. *i* All rooms with shared bath. Ⓢ Singles $105; doubles $115; quads $160.

DYLAN HOTEL
◔♿⟨ɪ⟩ HOTEL ❸

52 E. 41st St., between Park and Madison Ave.　　☎212-338-0500 🖳www.dylanhotel.com

For an enormous room smack-dab in the middle of Midtown East, the Dylan Hotel is the way to go. The rooms could not be more convenient or comfortable, and amenities include a fitness center and free Wi-Fi.

✦ Ⓢ 4, 5, 6 to 42nd St./Grand Central; 7 to Grand Central. Ⓢ Queen/king $249; executive king $299; executive junior suite $349.

upper east side

DE HIRSCH RESIDENCE
♿⟨ɪ⟩❄ YMCA ❸

1365 Lexington Ave. at 92nd St.　　☎212-415-5650 🖳www.dehirsch.com

Rooms are small and Spartan but famous for their cleanliness. Residents receive discounted access to the cafeteria and the 92nd St. Y Fitness Center as well as free tickets to tons of lectures, performances, and concerts (which the little old

accommodations

ladies at the desk gladly pay large sums to see). Amenities include fully-equipped kitchens on every floor, free Wi-Fi, and a free weekly housekeeping and linen service. Interested parties apply months in advance for residency, so plan ahead! ‡ Ⓢ *6 to 96th St.* *i* *30-day min. stay. Geared mostly toward students and young interns. Potential residents must apply.* Ⓢ *Monthly rates $1150-1800. Both singles and doubles available.* ⓩ *Reception M-Th 9am-7pm, F 9am-5pm, Su 10am-5pm, closed most legal and Jewish holidays.*

upper west side

NEW YORK INTERNATIONAL HI-AYH HOSTEL

HOSTEL ❶

891 Amsterdam Ave., at 103rd St. ☎212-932-2300 ◫www.hinewyork.org

These people have travel and fun down to a science. Whether you're looking to get down in the City or you'd rather stay in for the night, the folks at this hostel will show you a good time without making you break the bank. Information about free tours, clubbing, and movie nights is available at reception. Several large, comfortable common rooms offer the chance to relax and mingle with other travelers. ‡ Ⓢ *1 to 103rd St./Broadway.* *i* *Breakfast and shower sandals included.* Ⓢ *10- to 12-bed dorms $30-40; 8-bed dorms $35-45; 4- to 6-bed dorms $44-54; family rooms (up to 4 people) $130-140; private room (up to 4 people with bath) $145-155.* ⓩ *Reception 24hr.*

JAZZ ON THE PARK

HOSTEL ❶

36 W 106th St./Duke Ellington Blvd. ☎212-932-1600 ◫www.jazzhostels.com

If you're looking for an artsy, social hostel with a laid-back atmosphere, Jazz on the Park is your jam. No alcohol is served at the free comedy shows at the coffee bar on Thursday and Sunday nights, but luckily, shows are B.Y.O.B. The lounge in the basement is perfect for playing a game of pool or just hanging out. ‡ Ⓢ *B, C, to 103rd St./Central Park W.* *i* *Breakfast and linens included.* Ⓢ *Dorm $18-40; private rooms $100-195.* ⓩ *Reception 24hr.*

CENTRAL PARK HOSTEL

HOSTEL ❷

19 W 103rd St. ☎212-678-0491 ◫www.centralparkhostel.com

Central Park is a comfortable, affordable hostel without all of the commotion and craziness of some youth hostels. A large number of reasonably priced private rooms allow a degree of privacy, though a lounge with TVs, computers, and a well-equipped kitchen is available if you are feeling social. ‡ Ⓢ *B, C to 103rd St./Central Park W. Walk down 103rd St. between Central Park W. and Manhattan Ave.* Ⓢ *2-bed dorms (co-ed) $38-45, private rooms $99-109 with shared bath, $129-159 with bath.* ⓩ *Reception 24hr.*

HOTEL BELLECLAIRE

HOTEL ❺

250 W. 77th St., at Broadway ☎212-362-7700 ◫www.hotelbelleclaire.com

Steps away from some of the Upper West Side's best shopping and sights, the Hotel Belleclaire's amenities include free Wi-Fi and flat-screen televisions in every room as well as a fitness center. ‡ Ⓢ *1 to 79th St.* Ⓢ *Private rooms $129-199 with shared bath, $179-$359 with bath.* ⓩ *Reception 24hr.*

HOTEL NEWTON

HOTEL ❺

2528 Broadway at 95th St. ☎212-678-6500 ◫www.thehotelnewton.com

A perfectly nice, mid-priced New York hotel made from a cookie-cutter at the factory of perfectly nice mid-priced New York hotels. A granite counter and floor, friendly staff, that velvety, gold floral wallpaper, all the standard elements are here. Good location? Check. ‡ Ⓢ *1, 2, 3 to 96th St./Broadway.* Ⓢ *4-person private room $200-425; 2-person private room $150-275, a few with shared bathroom.* ⓩ *Reception 24hr.*

harlem

Harlem may be an inconvenient distance uptown from many points of interest and sites of action, but it's still a vibrant community and a fun place to rest your head. Luckily, both of these listings are in the heart of the neighborhood.

JAZZ ON LENOX
●▲(ᵗᵖ)🔊 HOSTEL ❷

104 West 128th St.   ☎212-222-5773◼www.jazzhostels.com/jazzonthelenox.php

The Jazz chain's northernmost outlet is a reliable choice smack dab in the middle of Harlem. Be aware, however, that it is an inconvenient distance away from other areas of the city—especially when compared to other Jazz hostels. Communal areas for eating, web-surfing, and TV-watching—plus the always valuable kitchen—sweeten the deal. Rooms are clean and plainly decorated. A free light breakfast is served every morning, but take note of the seven-night minimum.

✚ Ⓢ 2, 3 to 125th St. *i* 7-night min. stay. Ⓢ 8-bed dorms $21, with bath $23; room with 1 double and 1 twin $95, with bath $105.

HARLEM YMCA—CLAUDE MCCKAY RESIDENCE
● HOSTEL ❹

180 West 135th St.   ☎212-912-2100

Privacy is not on offer here—though all bathrooms are shared, only singles and doubles with bunks are available. The rooms are smallish and spare, some featuring minimal accessories like small desks. The perks are spiffy nonetheless, including use of the YMCA's gym, swimming pool, and lounge. And the building itself is an official city landmark; it dates from the early 1930s and is named after a famous author of the Harlem Renaissance.

✚ Ⓢ 2,3 to 135th St. Ⓢ Prices vary by season. High-season singles $63; doubles $75.

brooklyn

PACIFIC LOFT GUESTHOUSE
●Ⓧ(ᵗᵖ)❄ HOSTEL ❶

1082 Pacific St.   ☎323-286-7315

The name suggests an oceanside retreat, but this brand-new hostel sits among a desolate area of chop shops, abandoned factory buildings, and vacant lots. Still, the two open lofts here, each holding ten simple bunk beds and a small kitchen, are spacious and communal, and Prospect Park is just a 15min. walk away. A small common room downstairs has a TV and international guests enjoying these ultra-cheap digs.

✚ Ⓢ C to Franklin Ave., then walk down Franklin Ave. across Atlantic Ave. and turn right onto Pacific St. and walk 0.1 mi. The hostel stands next to the green funeral home on your left. *i* Online reservations required at ◼hostelbookers.com. Ⓢ Dorms $25.

ZIP112 HOSTEL
●●Ⓧ❄(ᵗᵖ) HOSTEL ❶

112 N. 6th St. (at Berry St.)   ☎347-403-0577◼www.zip112.com

This unmarked hostel—look for the yoga sign by the Sweet William store, then climb up five flights of stairs to the top floor—provides views of the Manhattan skyline from its open roof. The loft rooms themselves may seem just as open; high ceilings and an abundance of space leave plenty of room to move around. Same goes for the communal kitchen, dining table included. The decor here is spare, but the interior feels clean and welcoming. There are only a few rooms, so you'll probably get to know your neighbors.

✚ Ⓢ L to Bedford Ave. *i* Breakfast included. 2-night min. stay. Ⓢ Dorms (women-only) $50; doubles $120.

queens

▧ FLUSHING YMCA ●占 HOSTEL ❶

138-46 Northern Blvd., between Union and Bowne St.   ☎718-961-6880 ▣www.ymcanyc.org

Quiet and clean, this YMCA truly feels like a home. Rooms include refrigerators and small TV sets, and guests receive free access to the fitness center and pool.

⌗ Ⓢ 7 to Flushing/Main St.   *i* Breakfast included. Ⓢ Singles $65; doubles $85. All shared bathrooms. ⓠ Reception 24hr.

CLARION HOTEL JAMAICA ●(ᵗ) HOTEL❸

138-05 Jamaica Ave.   ☎718-523-3100 ▣www.choicehotels.com

A luxurious oasis among the thrift stores, bars, and El Salvadorian bakeries of Jamaica. If you're willing to shell out a bit of extra cash, you can live like a king in Queens.

⌗ Ⓢ E to Jamaica-Van Wyck.   *i* Breakfast included. All rooms include refrigerators, TV, and free Wi-Fi. Ⓢ $130-300. All rooms with bath. ⓠ Reception 24hr.

accommodations

SIGHTS

liberty and ellis islands

STATUE OF LIBERTY
Liberty Island

✎ NATIONAL MONUMENT
☎212-363-3200 ▣www.nps.gov/stli

In 1865, a group of French intellectuals began scheming about a 100th birthday present for the United States, celebrating liberty. **Eduoard de Laboulaye** was the driving force behind the operation and **Frederic-Auguste Bartholdi** and **Gustave Eiffel** (yes, *that* Eiffel) laid out the details. The statue was presented to the US ambassador to France on July 4, 1884, and subsequently disassembled and sent across the Atlantic in 220 crates.

But there was a slight problem—no pedestal. Richard Morris Hunt's pedestal design required money, and there simply was not enough for its execution. Enter tycoon *New York World* publisher **Joseph Pulitzer,** who conducted a massive, nation-wide fundraising effort. In 1886, the statue was finally reassembled, dedicated, and adorned with **Emma Lazarus'** famous "The New Colossus."

You can purchase tickets to see this 151ft., 1in. copper wonder online or in person at **Castle Clinton** in Battery Park. If you want to enter the statue, be sure to reserve your free tickets before you get on the ferry (usually about one

greatest hits

- **SPEND A DOLLAR** and an entire day wandering through The Metropolitan Museum of Art (p.71) on Fifth Ave.
- **SHH!** Don't make a peep as you tiptoe through the New York Public Library (p.67) to see the Declaration of Independence.
- **TAKE A STEP CLOSER TO WORLD PEACE** at the United Nations (p.67).
- **DISCOVER STYLE SECRETS** during a visit to the Museum at the Fashion Institute of Technology (p.57).

The most obvious New York tourist destinations are in Manhattan, but some of the best sights for students are in the outer boroughs. Here are a few worth hopping on the Subway for.

- **P.S.1 CONTEMPORARY ART CENTER** is MoMA's rebellious child in Long Island City. There's nothing elementary about the education you'll get in installation, video and performance art.

- **MAKE MOVES TO THE AMERICAL MUSEUM OF THE MOVING IMAGE** in Astoria. This Mecca for film junkies is doubling in size in early 2011, so there's now twice as much to look at.

- **BEER BUFFS** can take free tours of the **Brooklyn Brewery** on weekends. The factory in Williamsburg produces New York's finest lager and hosts Friday night happy hours.

week in advance), because you will be out of luck once you get to the island. If you want to go up to the crown, it will cost you $3 and you should plan way ahead—we're talking up to two months in advance during the high season. Even if you can't get into the monument, you can gaze at and take pictures with Lady Liberty from the ground, lounge in turn-of-the-century-inspired outdoor furniture, and take in the view of the Manhattan skyline. If you are content to admire the Lady from a distance, take the free **Staten Island Ferry** (🖳www.siferry.com) which leaves from **Whitehall Terminal** near the **South Ferry** Subway stop at frequent intervals.

✈ Ⓢ 4, 5 to Bowling Green; R, W to Whitehall St.; 1, 9 to South Ferry. *i* Buy ferry tickets online at 🖳www.statuecruises.com, by phone at ☎1-877-523-9849, or at the ticket kiosk at Castle Clinton at Battery Park. You must have tickets to enter the statue before arriving on Liberty Island. Tickets should be ordered at least a week in advance for statue entry and up to 2 months in advance for crown entry. Ⓢ Ferry passage $12, seniors $10, children $5. Audio tours $8. Additional fee for crown ticket $3. ☒ Ferries run from Battery Park to Liberty and Ellis Islands 8:30am-4:30pm. The last ferry leaves from Liberty Island at 6:15pm. Ferry times vary; check schedule on website for specific information; free ranger-led tours of Liberty Island every hr.; meet at the flagpole.

⬛ ELLIS ISLAND MUSEUM
✦⬥ MUSEUM

Ellis Island ☎212-363-3200 🖳www.ellisisland.org

The Ellis Island Museum operates within the main building of the immigration processing center that questioned, inspected, and approved for US entry 12 million immigrants from 1892 to 1954. If you are one of the more than 100 million Americans with ancestors who passed through Ellis Island, you can search for them at one of the computers at the **American Family Immigration History Center.** ($5 per 30min.) The first floor also holds informative exhibitions about immigration to the current United States from 1600 to the present. On the second floor, check out the enormous registry room that processed up to 5000 newcomers each day! The room has been restored to the way it appeared circa 1918-1924. The most poignant display may be the "Treasures from Home" exhibition on the third floor, showcasing clothing, instruments, religious articles, and other cherished items brought by immigrants to their new home. While on the island, you can also check out a handful of other buildings, including the contagious disease wards, a dormitory, and a ferry terminal from the 1930s.

✈ Ⓢ 4, 5 to Bowling Green; R, W to Whitehall St.; 1, 9 to South Ferry. *i* Buy ferry tickets online at 🖳www.statuecruises.com, by phone at ☎1-877-523-9849, or at ticket kiosk at Castle Clinton at

sights

Battery Park. $ Ferry passage $12, seniors $10, children $5. Audio tours $8. ⏰ Ferries run from Battery Park to Liberty and Ellis Islands 8:30am-4:30pm. Ellis Island Museum closes at 6pm, and the last ferry leaves from Ellis Island at 6:30pm. Ferry times vary; check schedule on website for specific information; free 45min. guided tours on the hour; free daily ferry terminal tours also available.

lower manhattan

At every stage in New York's 400-year history, Lower Manhattan has been at the center of the action. You can see layers upon layers of history wherever you go. If you pay a visit to **Wall Street** in the **Financial District,** you'll see **Federal Hall,** which was the national capital from 1789 to 1790. Now the area is considered the world's financial capital. Just south of Wall St., the **US Custom House,** finished in 1907, is situated on a site that first served as a trading center for Native Americans, then for European settlers. The building now houses the New York branch of the **National Museum of the American Indian.** South of that is **Battery Park,** a former artillery battery used by the Dutch and the British. **Castle Clinton,** within the park, was used as a fort, then as a public theater, then as an immigrant checkpoint, then as an aquarium, and is now a National Monument. Millions of tourists come to Battery Park to see the monuments and purchase tickets to see the **Statue of Liberty.** The **Civic Center** area in the north of Lower Manhattan is no less of a historical center. George Washington prayed at **St. Paul's Chapel** on his Inauguration Day in 1789, and the church withstood the terrorist attacks of 9/11, which covered it with debris. The former **World Trade Center** is just steps away. Just north of St. Paul's are **Tweed Courthouse,** the building that allowed Boss Tweed to embezzle huge sums of money (it is now home to the New York Department of Education), and **City Hall,** one of the oldest city halls still used for its intended purpose in the country. At this sight, as with so many in Lower Manhattan, it is eerie to see how history continues to resurface within its walls.

FINANCIAL DISTRICT

NATIONAL MUSEUM OF THE AMERICAN INDIAN ♿ MUSEUM

1 Bowling Green ☎212-514-3700 💻www.AmericanIndian.si.edu

In New York City, history has an strange way of layering itself. The **Alexander Hamilton US Custom House** was finished in 1907 on the site of what had been a trading center for hundreds of years, first for American Indians and next for merchants exchanging currency. In 1994, the Custom House became the home of the New York branch of the Smithsonian's **National Museum of the American Indian.** The museum's collection is based on 800,000 original artifacts from all over the Americas, assembled by New Yorker George Gustav Heye (1874-1957). The objects in the exhibitions, which celebrate American Indian culture of the past and present, stand in moving discord with the murals by Reginald Marsh, depicting ships and and maritime explorers, including several figures responsible for Indian annihilation and displacement on the 140-ton skylight in the rotunda. But, as museum director W. Richard West Junior (Southern Cheyenne) remarks, "NMAI is not just about the past and certainly not about the dead or dying. It is about the living." The museum lives up to this promise of showcasing vibrant, live American Indian culture through performances, talks, film screenings, and shows of works by contemporary American Indian artists.

[S] 4, 5 to Bowling Green; 1 to South Ferry. $ Free. ⏰ Open M-W 10am-5pm, Th 10am-8pm, F-Su 10am-5pm. Tours M-Th 1pm, F 1, 3pm, Sa 1pm.

TRINITY CHURCH CHURCH

Broadway, at Wall ☎212-602-0800 💻www.trinitywallstreet.org

Trinity Church has existed in several different incarnations since it was founded in 1697. King William III's charter compelled the vestry at Trinity to pay him an annual rent of "one peppercorn." When Her Majesty Queen Elizabeth II visited in 1976 for the US Bicentennial, she was ceremoniously presented with 279 peppercorns in back payment. The current mid-19th-century building was designed by Richard Upjohn in the style of, as Trinity Parish would have it, an "idyllic English Gothic country church." The church, with its floral and grisaille-latticed stained-glass windows, white walls, and surrounding Colonial graveyard is indeed an "idyllic" oasis amid the biggest rat race in the world. Be sure to check out the **Astor Memorial Doors** at the entrance of the church, and the **Soldiers' Memorial,** dedicated to Revolutionary War vets in the North Churchyard.

✚ Ⓢ 1, 2, 4, 5 to Wall St./Broadway. Ⓢ Free. Ⓠ Open M-F 7am-6pm, Sa 8am-4pm, Su 7am-4pm; yard closes 4pm on weekdays and 3pm on weekends. Holy Eucharist M-F 12:05pm, Su 9am and 11:15am. Morning Prayers M-F 8:15am; Evening Prayers 5:15pm; Contemplative Prayer Th 8:30am; Evensong Th 5:15pm. Free tours meet at the pulpit M-F 2pm.

FEDERAL HALL NATIONAL MEMORIAL
                                                       ♿ MEMORIAL

26 Wall St., between Nassau and William St.   ☎212-825-6990 ▣www.nps.gov/feha

Over the past 300-some years, **Federal Hall** has been just about everything an official hall can be. A City Hall from 1703-1788, the original building became Federal Hall and housed the first National Government under the Constitution from 1789-1790. The current building opened in 1842 and has served as US Custom House (1842-1862) and US Sub-Treasury (1862-1920). A gigantic statue of George Washington stands where he took his oath of office on April 30th, 1789. You can see the actual rock on which he stood inside! Inside the memorial are temporary and relatively permanent exhibitions about New York's role in American history. To commemorate momentous events in US history, the memorial hosts several ceremonies throughout the year (check website for special events). If you're lucky, you may even see people in Colonial garb reading the Declaration of Independence or playing the piccolo.

✚ Ⓢ 1, R, W to Rector St.; or 2, 3 to Wall ST./William St.; or 4, 5 to Wall St./Broadway; or J, M, Z to Broad St. Ⓢ Free. Ⓠ Open M-F 9am-5pm. Ranger-guided tours M-F 10, 11am, 1, 2, 3pm.

BATTERY PARK
                                                      ♿ PARK, MEMORIALS

Southern tip of Manhattan   ☎212-344-349 ▣www.thebattery.org

Battery Park is filled to capacity with monuments, tourists, and Statue of Liberty impersonators. You could run from statue to plaque all day long, but here are some of the greatest hits, roughly from east to west: the **East Coast Memorial** consists of a giant American Eagle staring down eight enormous slabs inscribed with the names of those who died in World War II and who "sleep in the American Coastal Water of the Atlantic Ocean." **Castle Clinton** was built in 1811 as a port from which to defend the New York Harbor. From 1823 to 1855, it had a stint as a public theater before assuming its most famous role as an immigrant depot. Between seven and eight million immigrants passed through the sturdy, D-shaped walls of this "Gateway to the New World." Home of the New York City Aquarium from 1896 to 1941, Castle Clinton became a National Monument in 1950. It now acts as a "reverse" gateway, since it is a popular place to buy tickets to visit Ellis Island and the Statue of Liberty. Behind the monument is a plaque dedicated to **Emma Lazarus,** who rose to fame for crafting the words at the base of the Statue of Liberty ("Give me your tired, your poor. Your huddled masses yearning to breathe free...") Just in front of Castle Clinton, a statue shows a huddled mass of six immigrants entering the country (aptly titled *The Immigrants*). Just West of Castle Clinton is Mac Adams's 1991 **Korean War Memorial,** with a stainless steel cutout of a soldier atop a collection of mosaic flags. On the ground, carved into the stones, are the numbers of dead, missing, and wounded from the 22 countries that took part in the war. **Pier A,** once a fireboat station, and Pier A Plaza form the Southwestern edge of the park.

🚶 Ⓢ *4, 5 to Bowling Green; or R, W to Whitehall St.* Ⓢ *Free.* 🕐 *Park open daily dawn-dusk. Castle Clinton open daily 8:30am-5pm.*

BOWLING GREEN
♿ PARK

Broadway and Whitehall ☎212-NEW-YORK 🖥www.nycgovparks.org

This tiny, triangular park has a special place in New York City lore. Established in 1733 as the City's first public park, it supposedly occupies the site where Manhattan was sold to Peter Minuit in 1626. The park was intended for the "Beauty and Ornament" of Broadway, and for the "Recreation and delight of the Inhabitants of this City." Almost 300 years later, the park and its flower-surrounded fountain continue to bring recreation and delight to hundreds of lunchers, resters, and web surfers.

🚶 Ⓢ *4, 5 to Bowling Green.* Ⓢ *Free.* 🕐 *Open daily dawn-dusk.*

NATIONAL SEPTEMBER 11 MEMORIAL
♿ MEMORIAL, MUSEUM

20 Vesey St., at Church St. ☎212-267-2047 🖥www.national911memorial.org

On September 11, 2011, a memorial will open at the site of the original World Trade Center (corner of Liberty and West St.), with two pools of water and 30 ft. waterfalls where the Twin Towers once stood. The waterfall edges will be inscribed with the identities of the 2980 people killed in the attacks 10 years earlier. The following September 11th (2012), a museum dedicated to education about the events of 9/11 is scheduled to open. In the meantime, visitors can view artifacts from the attacks, listen to oral histories, watch videotaped testimonials, and see a scale model of the future memorial and museum at the preview site at 20 Vesey St.

🚶 Ⓢ *4, 5, J, M, Z to Fulton St.; or A, C to Broadway-Nassau; or E to World Trade Center; or 2, 3 to Park Place; or R, W to City Hall.* Ⓢ *Free.* 🕐 *Open M-Sa 10am-7pm, Su 10am-6pm.*

MUSEUM OF JEWISH HERITAGE
♿➖ MUSEUM

36 Battery Pl., at Battery Park City ☎646-437-4200 🖥www.mjhnyc.com

Opened in 2007 as a "living memorial to the Holocaust," the Museum of Jewish Heritage remembers Holocaust victims through the display of photographs, artifacts, documents, film, and audio footage from their 25,000-object collection. The central exhibition is divided into three sections by time period: "Jewish Life a Century Ago," "The War Against the Jews," and "Jewish Renewal." The museum also hosts special exhibitions about all aspects of Jewish history and culture.

🚶 Ⓢ *4, 5 to Bowling Green; or R, W to Whitehall St.; or J, M, Z to Broad St.; or R, W to South Ferry.* Ⓢ *$12, students $7, seniors $10, under 12 free.* 🕐 *Open M-Tu 10am-5:45pm, W 10am-8pm, Th 10am-5:45pm, F and eves of Jewish Holidays 10am-5pm, Su 10am-5:45pm.*

THE SKYSCRAPER MUSEUM
➖♿ MUSEUM

39 Battery Pl., between 1st P. and Little W. Pl. ☎212-968-1961 🖥www.skyscraper.org

A museum to honor and explain those modern castles of steel and stone, the emphasis here is on the Wall Street area: its history is illustrated, diagrammed, documented, and scale-modeled. A corner dedicated to the Twin Towers of the World Trade Center includes videos, models, and information elucidating the engineering innovations that made them possible. The museum also tips its hat to the best and brightest of international buildings, including the 2683 ft. **Burj Dubai** and the 2070 ft. **Shanghai Tower,** scheduled to open in 2014. Be aware that when the museum uses the terms "Jumbo" and "Super Jumbo," they are not talking about hot dogs. Jumbo skyscrapers have twice the area of the average high-rise from the period, and Super Jumbo skyscrapers have four times the area.

🚶 Ⓢ *4, 5 to Bowling Green; or R, W to Whitehall St.; or J, M, Z to Broad St.; or R, W to South Ferry.* Ⓢ *$5, seniors and students $2.50.* 🕐 *Open W-Su noon-6pm.*

CIVIC CENTER

AFRICAN BURIAL GROUND — ♿ MEMORIAL, MUSEUM

Corner of Duane St. and Elk St., ☎212-637-2019 💻www.nps.gov/afbg

In the 17th and 18th centuries, when colonial laws prohibited the burial of Africans in officially consecrated sites, an estimated 15,000 Africans were buried by their loved ones in what was once a 6.6-acre plot beyond the city wall (now Chambers St.). In 1991 and 1992, the site was excavated, and in 2005 a design for a memorial was selected. The monument, conceived by Rodney Leon, consists chiefly of a 24 ft. Ancestral Chamber and a Circle of the Diaspora, covered with spiritual and cultural symbols from Africa, the Caribbean, and Latin America. The visitor center, a vast resource of information about the burial ground and slavery in New York, is well equipped with knowledgeable guides. The center also displays replicas of artifacts from the excavations and shows a 25min. documentary about the burial ground.

[S] 4, 5, 6, R, W, J, M, Z to Brooklyn Bridge/City Hall; or A, C, E to Chambers St.; or 2, 3 to Park Place. Visitor's Center at 290 Broadway. $ Free. ⏰ Memorial open daily 9am-5pm. Visitors center open M-F 9am-5pm.

SAINT PAUL'S CHAPEL — ♿ CHURCH

209 Broadway, between Fulton and Vesey ☎212-233-4164 💻www.saintpaulschapel.org

Saint Paul's Chapel is laden with American history. **George Washington** prayed here on his Inauguration Day in 1789, and the Chapel and 18th-century churchyard were covered with debris after the attacks on the World Trade Center in September of 2001. Both Washington and the victims of 9/11 (and countless people in between) are memorialized within the church; you can see the pew where the President prayed, now surrounded by myriad handmade tributes to those lost to the attacks. Look for the **Memorial Altar** and Deborah Fell's quilt, **Tuesday's Child: Does God Have Enough Hands?** In a similar combination of memorials to those recently and long ago departed, the churchyard, among tombs from over 200 years ago, contains a **Bell of Hope,** presented to the people of New York by the Bishop of Canterbury and Lord Mayor of London on September 11th, 2002.

[S] E to World Trade Center; or 4, 5, J, M, Z to Fulton St.; or A, C to Broadway-Nassau St.; or 2, 3 to Park Place. $ Free. ⏰ Open M-F 10am-6pm, Sa 10am-4pm, Su 7am-4pm; Holy Eucharist Su 8, 10am, Daily Prayers for Peace 12:30pm.

CITY HALL — ♿ LANDMARK

Broadway at Murray St., off Park Row ☎212-NEW-YORK 💻www.nyc.gov/designcommission

Completed in 1812 under the direction of the dynamic architectural duo **Joseph François Mangin** and **John McComb Jr.,** City Hall is one of the oldest city halls in the country. Generally closed to the public, this French-influenced, Federal-style feat of engineering can be accessed for free through a guided tour (call or visit website to book). When you visit the **Governor's Room,** which holds a museum of civic history and a gallery of American portraiture and furniture, you'll be joining the ranks of **Albert Einstein** and the **Marquis de Lafayette.** The picturesque **City Hall Park** outside of City Hall once housed a jail, public execution ground, and barracks for British soldiers. Now equipped with free Wi-Fi, the park is a popular lunch, study, and make out destination.

[S] R, W to City Hall; or 2, 3 to Park Place. $ Free. ⏰ Call or visit website for tour times; tours last approximately 1hr.

TWEED COURTHOUSE — LANDMARK

Chambers St. ☎212-NEW-YORK 💻www.nyc.gov/designcommission

The breathtaking Neoclassical and Romanesque designs of **John Kellum** and **Leopold Eidlitz** would be reason enough to book a free tour of the courthouse, but the real reason people come to see the Old New York County Courthouse, a.k.a. Tweed Courthouse, is its role in one of the greatest scandal stories in New York history. In the 1860s, Tammany Hall political machine boss **William Tweed** became president of the board overseeing the courthouse's construction and used the project to embezzle absurd quantities of money. In an ironic turn of fate, Tweed was tried and convicted in the very same building. Restored in 1999, Tweed Courthouse is now the locus for the New York Department of Education, which, hopefully, takes no lessons from the Boss.

♯ Ⓢ R, W to City Hall; or 4, 5, 6 to Brooklyn Bridge/City Hall. Between Centre St. and Broadway. *i* Accessible only through guided tour. Ⓢ Free. 🕐 Call or visit website for tour times.

SURROGATE'S COURT   ♿ LANDMARK
31 Chambers St., near Centre St.   ☎212-374-8244 📧www.nycourts.gov/courts/nyc/surrogates
Probate, estate proceedings, and other dull affairs take place in this stunning turn-of-the-century Beaux-Arts building, designed by James R. Thomas and Horgan and Slattery. The interior is constructed of exquisite marble and granite, and the lobby ceiling is covered with figures from ancient Egyptian and classical mythology. Although the building is generally closed to the public, you can usually sign in to take a quick peek at the marvelous interior. You can also gain entry if you have the urge to look at the old birth, death, and marriage records in the archives on the ground floor.

♯ Ⓢ J, M, Z to Brooklyn Bridge Station. Ⓢ Free. 🕐 Operating hours M-F 9am-5pm. Closed to the public.

soho and tribeca

🏛 NEW YORK CITY FIRE MUSEUM   ♠♿ MUSEUM
278 Spring St.   ☎212-691-1303 📧www.nycfiremuseum.org
Housed in a renovated 1904 stone firehouse, the museum displays impressive fire-fighting memorabilia, like a hand-pulled truck from George Washington's days as a volunteer New York City firefighter. The permanent September 11th exhibit, *If They Could Speak*, displays photos and artifacts from Ground Zero and has a searchable database of the city firefighters and police killed during the attacks.

♯ Ⓢ 1 to Houston St.; C, E to Spring St, between Varick and Hudson St. Ⓢ $7, students, children, and seniors $5. 🕐 Open Tu-Sa 10am-5pm, Su 10am-4pm.

🏛 THE DRAWING CENTER   GALLERY
35 Wooster St.   ☎212-219-2166 📧www.drawingcenter.org
What do **Michelangelo, Victor Hugo,** and **Sergei Eisenstein** all have in common? You can see the answer on the walls of **The Drawing Center,** which celebrates the importance of drawing to a wide variety of disciplines, including literature, science, dance, film, politics, and architecture. Exhibitions cover both contemporary and historical territory and feature both famous draughtsmen (and draughtswomen) and those who are not particularly notorious for taking pencil to paper.

♯ Ⓢ 1 to Canal St./Varich St.; A, C, E to Canal St./Ave. of the Americas (6th Ave.). Walk to Wooster St., between Grand and Broome St. Ⓢ Free. 🕐 Open W noon-6pm, Th noon-6pm, F-Su noon-6pm.

🏛 BROADWAY GALLERIES   ♿ GALLERIES
560-568 Broadway
As you walk down Broadway in SoHo, you will be bombarded with retail shops; Banana Republic, H and M, Victoria's Secret, The Gap, the works. But the hidden treasures of Broadway are the galleries located on the upper levels of these antique buildings. Worthwhile galleries include **Peter Freeman** *(560 Broadway, #602),*

which specializes in Minimalist and Pop Art, **Sous les Etoiles** *(560 Broadway, #205)*, which shows mainly fine art photography, **Susan Teller Gallery** *(568 Broadway, #502 A)*, which fills a 1930s-40s American Urban Modernist niche, and **⚑Westwood Gallery** which focuses on contemporary photography, but really shows a little of everything.

✈ Ⓢ *N, Q, R to Prince St.; B, D, F, M to Broadway/Lafayette St. Broadway between Spring and E. Houston St.* Ⓢ *Free.* 🕐 *Hours vary; Tu-Sa 11am-6pm are typical gallery hours.*

⚑ ANIMAZING GALLERY
⊗ GALLERY

54 Greene St., at Broome St.   ☎212-226-7374 ▣www.animazing.com

Let your imagination run away with you at this fanciful gallery, which displays works by illustrators such as Charles Addams **(The Addams Family)**, Matt Groening **(⚑The Simpsons)**, Maurice Sendak **(Where the Wild Things Are)**, and **Dr. Seuss** (you've probably got that one). This is your chance to own, or daydream about owning, a storyboard piece from **The Nightmare Before Christmas.**

✈ Ⓢ *N, Q, R to Canal St.* Ⓢ *Free.* 🕐 *Open M-Sa 10am-7pm, Su 11am-6pm.*

HARRISON ROW
ARCHITECTURE

Harrison St.

These red-brick, Federal-style houses, though built between 1796 and 1827, have only stood at their current location since 1975, when they nearly became casualties of gentrification. The land they now occupy was part of Annetje Jan's farm during the 17th century, then became the site of Harrison's Brewery, which served as the namesake for the street. **John McComb Jr.**, who also showed off his Federal skills by designing City Hall, was the architect of numbers 25, 37, 39, and 41. New York merchant Jacob Ruckle lived in number 31 in the early 18th century, and the house is characteristic of the merchant-class abodes from that period.

✈ Ⓢ *1 to Franklin St.; 1, 2, 3 to Chambers St. Walk to Harrison St., between Greenwich St. and New York 9A.*

HAUGHWOUT BUILDING
ARCHITECTURE

488-492 Broadway

When **John P. Gaynor** designed the building that would house E.V. Haughwout's fancy chinaware business in 1857, he had the arcades and columns of the **Sanvosino Library** in Venice on his mind. Haughwout's customers included **Mary Todd Lincoln** and **Czar Alexander II** of Russia. One hundred and fifty years later, the building houses a **Bebe** patronized by teenage girls with little to no interest in chinaware or Renaissance revival architecture. The building also holds the world's oldest successful passenger elevator (a designated landmark since 1857).

✈ Ⓢ *6 to Spring St.; N, Q, R to Canal St.; N, R to Prince St.*

RONALD FELDMAN ARTS
♿ GALLERY

31 Mercer St.   ☎212-226-3232 ▣www.feldmangallery.com

When you walk into this gallery, the sound of a woman reciting medical terminology might be the only human interaction you receive until you arrive at an administration desk two rooms later. Until then, you will be immersed in all manner of art: audio art, video art, installation art, mixed media—the most experimental and innovative of its kind.

✈ Ⓢ *N, Q, R to Prince St. Walk to Mercer St., between Canal and Grand St.* *i* *Shows generally change every 5-6 weeks.* Ⓢ *Free.* 🕐 *Open M-Th 10am-6pm, F 10am-3pm.*

ARTISTS SPACE
♿ GALLERY

38 Greene St., 3rd fl.   ☎212-226-3970 ▣www.artistsspace.com

Since its foundation in 1972, this gallery has been shaking up the art world. They've provided a forum for feisty young artists such as **Jeff Koons, Louise Lawler,** and **Barbara Kruger,** as well as exhibited the works of older artists largely ignored by New York's art establishment.

✦ Ⓢ 1 to Canal St./Varick St.; A,C,E to Canal St./Ave. of the Americas. Ⓢ Free. ⏰ Open W-Su noon-6pm.

"LITTLE SINGER" BUILDING   ARCHITECTURAL SIGHT
561 Broadway

This 12-story building was designed by architect Ernest Flagg in 1902 for the **Singer Corporation** and was nicknamed the "Little Singer" in order to distinguish it from the 41-story Singer Headquarters, also designed by Flagg, that was briefly the tallest building in the world. You can see Flagg's Beaux-Arts training in the intricate, forest-green, wrought-iron designs on the facade. Occupied by many residents and offices, the building's most prominent inhabitant is **MANGO** on the ground floor. In an amusing juxtaposition of old and new, the original "Singer Manufacturing Company" sign still hangs above the MANGO models on the Prince St. side of the building.

✦ Ⓢ N, Q, R to Prince St.; or B, D, F, M to Broadway/Lafayette St.

TRIBECA CINEMAS   ♿ THEATER
54 Varick St.   ☎212-941-2001 ▣www.tribecacinemas.com

Home of the annual **Tribeca Film Festival,** founded in 2001 by Robert DeNiro, Jane Rosenthal, and Craig Hatkoff in an attempt to resuscitate the Tribeca neighborhood after the attacks of 9/11. The festival includes premieres of movies from around the globe, talks with directors and actors, a street fair, and a slew of free events. Throughout the year, the theater hosts a **Tribeca Cinemas Presents: Doc Series,** which comprises a diverse assortment of new documentaries, as well as several other film festivals, such as the New York Surf Film Festival, the Russian Documentary Film Festival, and the New York Horror Film Festival.

✦ Ⓢ 1, A, C, E, N, Q, R to Canal St. Ⓢ Prices vary. ⏰ Hours vary; check website for schedule information.

chinatown

The colorful, vibrant mosaic of Chinatown is sight enough for most tourists, and there are plenty of cheap restaurants and eclectic ultra-discount shops to last you a few days. Explore a bit further, though, and you'll find fascinating museums and memorials evoking a very distant past.

MUSEUM OF CHINESE IN AMERICA (MOCA)   MUSEUM
215 Centre St.   ☎212-619-4785 ▣www.mocanyc.org

This sleek, small museum traces the history of Chinese immigrants throughout the United States, not merely New York City. Video installations, hundreds of reproduced and displayed documents, and a handful of artifacts all contribute to a study of discrimination, stereotyping, and inequality. Try lifting the 8-pound iron used by immigrants while laundering.

✦ Ⓢ N, R, Q, W, J, M, Z, or 6 to Canal St. Ⓢ $7, students $4, Th free. ⏰ Open M 11am-5pm, Th 11am-9pm, F 11am-5pm, Sa-Su 10am-5pm.

MAHAYANA BUDDHIST TEMPLE   RELIGIOUS SITE
133 Canal St.   ☎212-925-8787

Once a porn theater, this massive building by the Manhattan Bridge now houses one of Chinatown's most sacred spaces. Twin lions guard a red door, beyond which incense and calm prevail. A huge 20 ft. Buddha (said to be the largest in the city) adorns the auditorium, which is usually scattered with worshipers. It's a mind-bending change to the city bustle outside; in fact you can make it your first or last stop, as the Fung Wah bus stops just outside the doors.

✈ Ⓢ B, D to Grand St.; N, R, Q, W, J, M, Z, 6 to Canal St. *i* No shorts or sleeveless shirts. ⓩ
Open daily 10am-6pm.

FIRST SHEARITH ISRAEL GRAVEYARD

MEMORIAL

South side of Chatham Sq. on St. James Pl.

The Spanish-Portuguese Shearith Israel Synagogue was founded here in 1654, serving some of the city's first immigrants. It was the only synagogue in the city until 1825 and so served all of the young city's Jews for almost two centuries. Its graveyard is all that remains, and it's fascinating even though you have to stand on tiptoe to peer through its perpetually closed gate. Some graves date back to the 1600s--a reminder that the neighborhood's current vivacity hides a rich and surprisingly long history.

✈ Ⓢ N, R, Q, W, J, M, Z, 6 to Canal St. Between James and Oliver St.

greenwich village

WASHINGTON SQUARE PARK

        ♿ PARK

Between MacDougall St., Washington Sq. N., Washington Sq. E., and Washington Sq. S.

The heart of Greenwich Village is always packed—with tourists snapping photos of the Washington Square Arch built in 1889 to commemorate the 100th anniversary of Washington's first inauguration, locals sitting by the fountain to catch some spray, NYU students hanging out, working, or filming, a range of performers banging on buckets or playing a sophisticated jazz piece, and on, and on. One of the best places to simply people-watch in the city, **Washington Square** still attracts a constant onslaught of the offbeat and the interesting (and, as always, the homeless). The bustle can mask the long history of the place; Native Americans knew the area as a marsh, but it soon became a public burial ground for the downtown poor in the late 1700s. True to form, then, public hangings were staged here during the Revolutionary War. Soon the area was attracting a more genteel crowd who flocked to "the Row" just above the park (poorer residents lived south of it). Drug traffic and crime became problems in New York's dark days of the 1970s and early 1980s, but the square has been significantly cleaned up—though thankfully not to the point of cultural oblivion.

✈ Ⓢ A, B, C, D, E, F, V to West 4th St.

NEW YORK UNIVERSITY (NYU)

        ♿ UNIVERSITY CAMPUS

Information: 50 West 4th St.   ☎212-998-4636 ▉www.nyu.edu

Almost 50,000 students attend NYU's 14 schools, but it's hard to keep track of them in the general, all-encompassing bustle of the Washington Square Park area. Still, the influence of the university is always palpable, from the blocks of student hangouts and cafes south of the park to the purple NYU flags hanging from every other building. There is no enclosed campus: the school is open to the city and holds its commencement ceremonies in the park itself. Some architectural highlights include the Georgian-style **Law School** building just south of the park, whose courtyard provides a little oasis from the noise outside, and the massive **Elmer Holmes Bobst Library,** one of the largest in the country. NYU is famous worldwide for its communication and film departments. The latter fostered **Martin Scorsese** and **Spike Lee** among many other modern luminaries. The department is now housed in the **Tisch School of the Arts,** a few blocks north of the park on Broadway. If you're interested in exploring the university's other buildings, consult the campus maps around the Washington Square Park area.

✈ Ⓢ A, B, C, D, E, F, V to W 4th St. or 6 to Astor Pl.

sights

FORBES MAGAZINE GALLERIES

🍴♿❄ GALLERY

62 5th Ave. (at W. 12th St.) ☎212-206-5548 💻www.forbesgalleries.com

Yes, this tall, stately building is the headquarters of the powerful *Forbes* magazine. And yes, those are toys you are looking at on the first floor. These galleries are packed with old Monopoly games (and their forgotten cousins), figurines of historical personages like George Washington, countless toy soldiers, and even antique toy boats (say that ten times fast). Check online for their temporary exhibits, which have included JFK's documents and Lincoln's last pair of glasses.

🍴 Ⓢ 4, 5, 6, N, R, Q, W, L to 14th St.-Union Square. Ⓢ Free. ⓐ Open Tu-Sa 10am-4pm. Reservations required for Th.

NEW SCHOOL FOR LIBERAL ARTS (EUGENE LANG COLLEGE)

♿❄ UNIVERSITY

65 W. 11th St. ☎212-229-5600 💻www.newschool.edu

The New School was founded as a progressive educational institution in 1917; its founders hoped that a commitment to social change would inspire students to avoid calamities like World War I. Its reputation was bolstered during World War II, when it offered a safe haven and positions to exiled or displaced European academics. Since then, the school has become known for its liberal politics and radical approach to education, its reputation divided between its public policy and arts schools such as the Actors Studio and the Parsons School of Design. Eugene Lang College, Building B, is the steely undergraduate building. You can consult maps here for the school's other buildings.

🍴 Ⓢ 1, 2, 3, to 14th St. or F, V, L to 6th Ave.-14th St. ⓐ Building open M-Th 8am-11pm, F 8am-6pm, Sa 9am-6pm.

JEFFERSON MARKET LIBRARY

♿❄ HISTORIC BUILDING

425 6th Ave. (at W 10th St.) ☎212-243-4334 💻www.nypl.org/locations/jefferson-market

This behemoth on Sixth Ave. has become a Village landmark, not least because of its strange and multi-faceted history. It was built in 1877 as a courthouse, became a women's prison, and was only saved from demolition in the 1960s by its restoration and conversion to a public library in 1967. Its design suggests a Victorian-medieval style on acid: red brick, dotted with stained-glass windows, and topped by a turreted clock tower.

🍴 Ⓢ 1 to Christopher St. Ⓢ Free. ⓐ Open M noon-8pm, Tu noon-6pm, W noon-8pm, Th noon-6pm, F 1-6pm, Sa 10am-5pm.

CHRISTOPHER PARK

♿♿ PARK

At Christopher St., 7th Ave., and W. 4th St.

This small, shady, triangular green space near the eastern edge of the West Village is a quiet-ish resting spot for locals. Two sculptures adorn the park: one of the Civil War general Sheridan, the other, George Segal's *Gay Liberation*, depicting two same-sex couples embracing. Both can be linked to some tumultuous events in the park's history. In 1863, the area was one of the centers of the bloody draft riots that rocked the city during the Civil War, and in June 1969, the modern gay rights movement was born at the Stonewall Inn across the street when the bar's homosexual patrons refused to be arrested during a police raid. The standoff and riots that followed spurred an entire movement: one year later, the first **Gay Pride Parade** left from the park and progressed up Fifth Ave. This section of Christopher St. is also known as Stonewall Place in honor of these events.

🍴 Ⓢ 1 to Christopher St.

75½ BEDFORD ST.

HISTORIC BUILDING

75½ Bedford St.

This diminutive but very cute West Village building is on record as New York's thinnest, measuring only 9 ft. across. Its red-brick facade is also a stand-out, as are its former residents. The poet **Edna St. Vincent Millay** wrote her Pulitzer Prize-winning "Ballad of Harp Weaver" here while founding the Cherry Lane Theatre around the corner. Famous anthropologist **Margaret Mead** followed close after her, as did two icons of Hollywood's classic era: **Lionel Barrymore** and **Cary Grant.**

⇄ [S] *1 to Christopher St.*

MEATPACKING DISTRICT NEIGHBORHOOD

Bordered by W. 15th St., Hudson St., Little W. 12th St., and the Hudson River

One of New York's most glamorous nightspot centers was once a center for the processing and packaging of meat. In the 19th century, the area saw the rise of many markets and warehouses (their legacy lives on in the low-lying buildings fronted by steel canopies that once protected the loading docks). The outrage over unsanitary practices in the meatpacking industry, sparked by Upton Sinclair's 1906 novel *The Jungle*, couldn't stop the area from remaining a center of the industry until well into the 20th century. The neighborhood saw dark days in the 1970s and 1980s after the industry's decline and the citywide spike in crime. With cleanup, though, came some of New York's most intense gentrification. The area has long since transformed into a region of upscale restaurants, expensive boutique shops, high-priced hotels, and, most famously, glitzy nightlife taking up space in former packing plants and warehouses. On weekend nights, the streets teem with beautiful people in beautiful clothing, often exiting their beautiful limos. For some views of the action, climb up to the **High Line,** a former elevated railway that's been converted to a walkway, much of it deliberately covered with vegetation.

⇄ [S] *A, C, E, L, 1, 2, 3, 9 to W 14th St.*

east village

TOMPKINS SQUARE PARK ♿ PARK

Between Ave. A and B, and E. 7th and 10th St. ☎212-387-7685 💻www.nycgovparks.org/parks

With beautiful, gated gardens and tons of playgrounds, this park is filled with people sunbathing, reading, picnicking, and playing chess on tables with built-in boards. Dogs are hardly left out of the fun, and can generally be found at the **Tompkins Square Dog Run.** In the summer, performances and events occasionally take place on the **Old Bandshell Lawn,** and the **Tompkin Square Greenmarket** happens Sundays year-round from 8am to 6pm.

⇄ [S] *6 to Astor Pl. or N, R, W to 8th St.* $ *Free.* ⏰ *Open dawn-dusk.*

ST. MARK'S CHURCH IN-THE-BOWERY CHURCH

131 E. 10th St., at 2nd Ave. ☎212-674-6377 💻www.stmarkschurch-in-the-bowery.com

Built on the site of the chapel **Peter Stuyvesant** built in 1660, this late-19th century Georgian church is the oldest Christian worship site in New York. A bust of Governor-General Stuy, who is buried in the churchyard, crosses its arms authoritatively at the building's entrance. He also appears in one of the large stained-glass windows, many of which are at eye level. The interior is pew-free, with carpeted risers and chairs situated around the perimeter for worship. The church also hosts performances by a handful of experimental artistic companies, such as the **Incubator Arts Project** *(💻www.incubatorarts.org)* the **Danspace Project,** *(💻www.danspaceproject.org)* and **Poetry Project** *(💻www.poetryproject.org).* **Reverend Billy and the Stop Shopping Gospel Choir** also calls this church home.

⇄ [S] *6 to Astor Pl.* $ *Free.* ⏰ *Holy Eucharist Su 11am, W 6:30pm, F noon.*

ST. MARK'S PLACE ♿ STREET

Where 8th St. would be, between Cooper Sq. E and Ave. A

If you take a stroll down this street, you will have your pick of pashminas, fedoras, sunglasses, jewelry, tattoos, and piercings. Exotic items from Africa and

Tibet also make appearances on the street. Entertainment? You have more than one karaoke option. When you need sustenance, there are is plenty of Asian fusion and frozen yogurt to be found. St. Mark's place is also prime bong-buying territory for legal tobacco use only, of course.

⚡ Ⓢ 6 to Astor Pl.

ASTOR PLACE
                                                                    HISTORIC SITE

At the junction of Lafayette Ave., 4th Ave., and 8th St.

This junction predating the Manhattan grid plan is named after **John Jacob Astor** (1763-1848), who became the richest man in the United States by trading beaver pelts. Those beavers are honored in the **Astor Place** Subway station, with a large number of beaver plaques made by the Grueby Faience Company in 1904. Large geometric porcelain enamel and steel murals by Milton Glaser are also located in the Subway station. Above ground, you won't be able to miss Tony Rosenthal's enormous metal cube, entitled **The Alamo.** The piece was supposedly an anonymous gift to the city of New York in 1967. (Maybe it was left on a doorstep somewhere?) The All Too Flat squad created quite a spectacle in 2003 when they used cardboard panels to transform the work into a Rubik's Cube. The Astor Place area is known for its theaters: the **Astor Place Theater** *(434 Lafayette St.)* and **Joseph Papp Public Theater** *(425 Lafayette St)* are located nearby.

⚡ Ⓢ 6 to Astor Pl. Ⓢ Free. ☾ Subway station open 24hr. Junction also accessible daily 24 hr.

THE COOPER UNION FOUNDATION BUILDING
                                              ♿ HISTORIC SITE

7 E. 7th St., at Cooper Sq., off Astor Pl.   ☎212-353-4203; tours of New Academic Building
☎212-353-4100 ▣www.cooper.edu

Despite having finished just one year of formal schooling, New York industrialist Peter Cooper invented the first transatlantic telephone cable, the first functioning steam engine, and, with the help of his wife Sarah, ▣**Jell-o.** Cooper went on to found the free technical and design school in 1859. Both the **American Red Cross** and the **NAACP** got their starts at Cooper Union. The pillared **Great Hall** has been a forum for the speeches of eventual presidents from **Abe Lincoln** to **Teddy Roosevelt** to **Barack Obama.** The **Arthur A. Houghton Jr. Gallery** on the second floor has rotating exhibits of student work. The ultra modern **New Academic Building** is across Third Ave. and offers tours Tuesdays at 12:30pm.

⚡ Ⓢ 6 to Astor Pl. *i* For tours of New Academic Building call ☎212-353-4100. Ⓢ Free. ☾ Open M-Th 9am-5pm. Houghton Gallery open 11am-7pm.

chelsea

▧ **THE MUSEUM AT THE FASHION INSTITUTE OF TECHNOLOGY**   ♿ MUSEUM

7th Ave., at 27th St.   ☎212-217-5800 ▣www.fitnyc.edu/museum

The Museum at FIT provides a free history of fashion and textiles. The collection includes dresses from as far back as 1750, all the way up to the most cutting edge Nina Valenti purple hemp- and tencel-blend dresses of today. The collection also provides interesting fashion trivia. Did you know, for example, that the green dyes used in dresses in the mid-nineteenth century often contained arsenic and posed a health threat to both manufacturers and wearers? Learn all this and more at the Museum at the Fashion Institute of Technology!

⚡ Ⓢ 1 to 18th St. Ⓢ Free. ☾ Open Tu-F noon-8pm.

▧ **CHELSEA MARKET**   ⬦♿ SHOPPING CENTER

75 9th Ave., between 15th and 16th St.   ▣www.chelseamarket.com

Housed in the building that was once the Nabisco plant, Chelsea Market is now an indoor collection of shops, boutiques, and restaurants that meet the public's every need. And in Chelsea, people generally seem to need fine wine, gourmet cheeses, and handcrafted baskets. The famous **Chelsea Wine Vault** *(🖥www.chelseawinevault.com; M-Sa 10am-8pm, Su noon-7pm)* sometimes offers free samples. Throughout the market the **Chelsea Art Market Collective** displays rotating exhibitions of original, often quirky art.

🚇 [S] A, C, E, L to 14th St./8th Ave. $ Upscale market prices vary with store. ⏰ Open M-F 7am-9pm, Sa 7am-8pm, Su 10am-7pm.

★ GAGOSIAN GALLERY ♿ GALLERY

555 W. 24th St. ☎212-741-1111 🖥www.gagosian.com

Chelsea gallery pioneer Larry Gagosian owns exhibition spaces on three continents and five countries. Two of his three NYC galleries are located in Chelsea. Though the galleries mostly show art from the 20th century and later, the W. 21st St. location *(522 W. 21st St. ☎212-741-1717)* has dabbled in the dark arts of Impressionism. Past shows at the W. 24th St. location have included such jaw-droppers as David Smith, Roy Lichtenstein, and Yayoi Kusama.

🚇 [S] C, E to 23rd St. $ Free. ⏰ Open Tu-Sa 10am-6pm.

CHELSEA PIERS 🎟 INDOOR SPORTS

23rd St. and Hudson River Park ☎212-336-6666 🖥www.chelseapiers.com

In New York City, they don't tend to do things half-heartedly. If you're going to open an athletic center in Manhattan, why not make it an athletic center that spans six city blocks along the Hudson River? One that has golf, basketball, batting, bowling, martial arts, dancing, year-round ice skating, and a **trapeze school,** not to mention restaurants, boat cruises, and a spa? That was the logic of the **Chelsea Piers** developers in 1995, and the center has been a non-stop hit ever since.

🚇 [S] C, E to 23rd St. $ Chelsea Piers Lanes $11 per person per game, $6 shoes; Chelsea Trapeze School $70 per class; Chelsea Golf Club balls $25. ⏰ Chelsea Piers Lanes open M-Tu 9am-11pm, W 9am-midnight, Th 9am-1am, F-Sa 9am-2am. F-Sa after 9pm persons under 21 must be accompanied by someone 25 or older, Su 9am-11pm.

CHELSEA ART MUSEUM 🎟♿ MUSEUM

160 11th Ave., at 22nd St. ☎212-255-0719 🖥www.chelseaartmuseum.org

The Chelsea Art Museum hosts temporary exhibitions of work by contemporary artists. Home to the **Miotte Foundation,** the museum's permanent collection is constructed entirely of the work of the **Art Informel** artist **Jean Miotte.** Incidentally, Miotte lives above the museum, giving museum employees cause to stay on their toes!

🚇 [S] C, E to 23rd St. $ $8, students $4, seniors $4, Th free. ⏰ Open Tu-Sa 11am-6pm.

GENERAL THEOLOGICAL SEMINARY ♿ SEMINARY

175 9th Ave., between 20th and 21st St. ☎212-243-5150 🖥www.gts.com

Founded in 1817, the General Theological Seminary is listed on the National Register of Historical Places. Perhaps more importantly, the land on which the school is built was donated by **Clement C. Moore** (of *'Twas the Night Before Christmas* fame), who also served as the schools first professor of Hebrew and Greek literature from 1821 to 1850. The peaceful garden, containing some of the only elm trees in New York City, is open to the public every day except Sunday, and visitors are welcome at the gorgeous **Chapel of the Good Shepherd** for services.

🚇 [S] C, E to 23rd St./8th Ave. $ Free. ⏰ Gardens open M-Sa 10am-3pm; Morning prayer M-F 8am, Sa 10:30am; Holy Communion M 11:15am, Tu 6pm, W 11:15am, F 11:15am, Spanish-language 11:30am.

DIA ART FOUNDATION 🎭♿ ART EDUCATION

535 W. 22nd St., between 10th and 11th ☎212-989-5566 🖥www.diaart.org

Ready for some **Artist on Artist** action? You can get it on the 5th floor of 535 W. 22nd St., where the Dia Art Foundation hosts a series of lectures featuring a

sights

contemporary artist interpreting the work of an older artist. Highlights from the past have included **Sharon Hayes** on **Merce Cunningham** and **Luis Camnitzer** on **Blinky Palermo.**

🚻 Ⓢ *C, E to 23rd St.* Ⓢ *Lectures $6, students and seniors $3.* 🕐 *Lectures generally at 6:30pm.*

CUSHMAN ROW   ♿ ARCHITECTURAL SIGHT
406-418 W. 20th St., between 9th and 10th Ave.

After checking out the **General Theological Seminary,** be sure to pass by Cushman Row, the line of houses on the eastern end of 20th St. Built in 1840 by Don Alonzo Cushman, who also founded the Greenwich Savings Bank, they are an excellent example of **Greek Revival** architecture.

🚻 Ⓢ *C, E to 23rd St.* Ⓢ *Free.* 🕐 *Open daily 24hr.*

ANTON KERN   ♿ GALLERY
532 W. 20th St.   ☎212-367-9663 ◾www.antonkerngallery.com

Chelsea is home to over 200 galleries, most specializing in modern and contemporary art. A large portion of them are located between 10th and 11th Ave., from 20th and 27th St. For a fun and inexpensive day, unless you're looking to buy, start at 20th St. and work your way up. A good start is the Anton Kern Gallery, owned by the son of post-war German painter **Georg Baselitz.**

🚻 Ⓢ *A, C, E, L to 14th St./8th Ave.; or C, E to 23rd St./8th Ave.* Ⓢ *Free.* 🕐 *Open Tu-Sa 10am-6pm.*

529 W. 20TH ST.   ♿ GALLERY
529 W. 20th St.

A microcosm of the Chelsea art scene, this 11-floor colossus is home to over 30 different galleries. You can see contemporary African art, modern European and American art, and photography, without ever leaving the building.

🚻 Ⓢ *A, C, E, L to 14th St./8th Ave.; or C, E to 23rd St./8th Ave.* Ⓢ *Free.* 🕐 *Open Tu-Sa 10am-6pm.*

union square and murray hill

You can think of the area around Union Sq., Gramercy Park, and Madison Square Park as a museum in itself. A center of New York culture and upper-class residential life in the late 19th and early 20th centuries, the area still packs an architectural wallop. Huge *fin de siècle* landmarks rise above brownstones and former mansions. Exclusive parks are surrounded by even more exclusive social clubs. And the legacy of a long-gone aristocracy remains in the preserved homes and collections of some of America's most famous historical figures.

◼ THE MORGAN LIBRARY AND MUSEUM   ♨♿❀ MUSEUM
225 Madison Ave. (at 36th St.)   ☎212-685-0008 ◾www.themorgan.org

J.P. Morgan, Jr. donated his father's extensive collection of rare books, documents, and artwork to the public as a museum in 1924. It soon grew to encompass a complex of nearby buildings, and today they're packed with a surprisingly rich array of manuscripts, drawings, maps, paintings, and books. Treasures include an original, autographed 🎵**Mozart** score, a *Gutenberg Bible*, numerous medieval manuscripts, examples of the earliest writing in the Near East, and works by Old Masters like Rubens and Rembrandt. It's worth visiting as an insight into Morgan's behind-the-scenes life—the library itself was built in 1906 in Renaissance *palazzo* style—and as another priceless museum, complete with a varied rotating set of special exhibits.

🚻 Ⓢ *6 to 33rd St.* Ⓢ *$12, students $8.* 🕐 *Open Tu-Th 10:30am-5pm, F 10:30am-9pm, Sa 10am-6pm, Su 11am-6pm.*

FLATIRON BUILDING — LANDMARK/HISTORIC BUILDING

175 5th Ave. (at Broadway)

This striking, much-photographed landmark—New York's first skyscraper—stridently stands at the branching-off point of Broadway and Fifth Ave. Revolutionary in its day, the structure still impressed with an unusual triangular shape that seems to test the limits of architecture—it's only 6 ft. wide at its narrowest point. Originally called the Fuller Building, it derived its current name from its resemblance to a certain pressing instrument used in laundry rooms. The unique shape created wind tunnels that would lift women's skirts in the early 20th century; police dispersed gawkers with the soon famous phrase **"23 skidoo"** (after neighboring 23rd St.).

[S] R, W to 23rd St.

THE THEODORE ROOSEVELT BIRTHPLACE — HISTORIC BUILDING

28 E. 20th St. ☎212-260-1616 www.nps.gov/thrb

Despite his reputation as a fierce outdoor adventurer and steward of America's national parks, Teddy Roosevelt was the only US president born in New York City. He was born and raised in this luxurious brownstone until the age of 15. Though the building was torn down in the early 20th century, a group of businessmen and other admirers rebuilt the building down to the exact details, and the current museum opened in 1923. It's run by the National Park Service, so you can have an actual ranger take you on the informative tours. You can't see the upper floors otherwise; they include the library, the dining hall, the nursery (check out Teddy's crib), and the front bedroom where the future president was born. There's an added room filled with some of his hunting conquests—a stuffed lion, various heads on walls—while the floor level features chronologically arranged exhibits on TR's life illustrated by the flotsam of his adventures: clothes, letters, dinnerware, and more. A final impetus: admission and the tours are free.

[S] 6 to 23rd St. $ Free. Open Tu-Su 9am-5pm. Tours at 10, 11am, 1, 2, 3, 4pm.

UNION SQUARE — PARK, SQUARE

17th to 14th St., Park Ave. to Broadway ☎212-460-1200 www.unionsquarenyc.org

A center of downtown activity since the early 19th century, Union Square is one of Manhattan's most active hubs. It used to be the power center of the city; Tammany Hall, Gothamite aristocrats, and a host of cultural organizations once called the center home. The park, opened in 1839 and redesigned by Central Park masterminds Frederick Law Olmsted and Calvin Vaux in the 1870s, is deliberately modeled on London's green public spaces. Paths cut through public art exhibits and floral displays, while statues of George Washington, Abraham Lincoln, and Gandhi punctuate the scene. The **James Fountain** is a standout, with Charity emptying a jug of water in the center.

As the old aristocrats left their mansions and moved uptown in the late 19th century, the square became a center for socialist and radical activity. The first Labor Day parade marched from here up Broadway in 1882, while the park also became home to annual May Day festivities. As the dark 1970s fell, disrepair and drug dealing made the area unwholesome and dangerous. The revitalization effort included the introduction of the **Union Square Greenmarket** *(M 8am-6pm, W 8am-6pm, F-Sa 8am-6pm)*, New York's most popular open-air market and an ideal place to snatch up some pastries, breads, cheeses, jams, vegetables, and fruits. Impromptu music performances in the southern half, meanwhile, keep things interesting. Take a look (you can't help it) at the **Metronome,** a huge, controversial, multi-million public art project whose digits count down the day in simultaneous forward and backward motion (the left seven digits display military time, the right seven the amount of time left in each day). Next to it, smoke occasionally pours from a large hole surrounded by circular ripples.

[S] 4, 5, 6, L, N, Q, R to 14th St.-Union Sq.

STUYVESANT SQUARE
                                         ♿☃ PARK, SQUARE
Between E. 17th St., Perlman Pl., E. 15th St. and Rutherford Pl.
Designed in the 1840s on farmland owned by legendary New Netherlands Governor Peter Stuyvesant, this quiet but sprawling square is an ideal resting place, with far more space and serenity than nearby Union Sq. Divided by Second Ave., the park features several fountains, floral gardens, and a statue of Peter himself—complete with peg leg. The cast-iron fence surrounding the park is the second oldest in the city, dating from 1847. The old prestigious neighborhood that surrounded the square can be seen in nearby landmarks like **St. George's Church** (1848-1856), a striking Romanesque Revival structure where J.P. Morgan and other luminaries worshiped, the red-brick **Friends Meeting House and Seminary** (1861), and several row houses that date back to the 1850s.
⚓ Ⓢ *L to 1st Ave. or 3rd Ave.* ⓩ *Park closes at 11pm.*

MADISON SQUARE PARK
                                       ♿☃ PARK, SQUARE
Between E. 26th St. and E. 23rd St.   ☎212-538-5058 ▉www.madisonsquarepark.org
Surrounded by some of New York's most recognized buildings, Madison Square Park does its best to provide a bit of calm in the midst of a very busy area. Back in the day, it was an empty lot where the New York Knickerbockers, one of the first professional baseball teams, practiced. The park opened in 1847 at the center of an upper-class neighborhood of brownstones and mansions. The first versions of the **Madison Square Garden** were built next to the park. By the late 20th century a revitalization effort helped upgrade the disheveled park, and today the space is a clean, though crowded, center dotted with statues of 19th-century New York generals and luminaries, art exhibits, the occasional outdoor concert, and the always-popular Shake Shack (see **Food,** p. 99).
⚓ Ⓢ *R, W to 23rd St. Between E. 26th St., Madison Ave., E. 23rd St., Broadway, and 5th Ave.* ⓩ *Open daily 6am-midnight.*

METROPOLITAN LIFE TOWER
                               LANDMARK, HISTORIC BUILDING
1 Madison Ave. (at E. 24th St.)
The world's tallest building for three years until the Woolworth building stole its title in 1913, the still-intimidating MetLife tower soars into the sky above Madison Square Park. Designed after Venice's *campanile*, the tower was added to a preexisting office structure in an ambitious bid for maximal phallic power. At night, a constant light illuminates the cupola at the top.
⚓ Ⓢ *6, R, W to 23rd St.*

NEW YORK LIFE INSURANCE BUILDING
                         LANDMARK, HISTORIC BUILDING
51 Madison Ave. (at E. 26th and E. 27th St.)
Though not as tall as the MetLife Tower or as sleek as the Flatiron Building, the enormous New York Life Building outweighs both with its heavy stateliness. Designed by Cass Gilbert in 1926—and partly inspired by Salisbury Cathedral—the building is supported by a broad base covering the entire block. A gold-topped tower rises above, adorned with gargoyles and other modern Gothic touches.
⚓ Ⓢ *6, R, W to 23rd St.*

GRAMERCY PARK
                                        ♿☃ PARK, SQUARE
Between E. 21st St., Gramercy Park E., E. 20th St., and Gramercy Park W.
You can look, but you can't touch. New York's only private park is a doozy, dripping with impossibly manicured exclusivity and majestically surrounded by an 8 ft. iron fence keeping the commoners out. The park and surrounding neighborhood were designed above marshland in 1831 to cater to the city's aristocracy. The air of privilege is still palpable today in the beautiful, stately Victorian-era structures surrounding the park. It's all terribly lovely.
⚓ Ⓢ *6 to 23rd St.* ⓘ *Private park; no entry.*

union square and murray hill

NATIONAL ARTS CLUB

&❁ HISTORIC BUILDING, GALLERY SPACE

15 Gramercy Park S. ☎212-674-8824 ▦www.nationalartsclub.org

A gorgeous, sprawling 19th-century brownstone, the National Arts Club building is one of Gramercy's architectural highlights. Designed by Calvert Vaux, co-designer of Central Park, the home once belonged to New York governor, and winner of the popular vote in 1876's presidential election, Samuel J. Tilden. The National Arts Club bought the building in 1906. Members have included Gramercy local Theodore Roosevelt, Woodrow Wilson, Robert Redford, Martin Scorsese, and Uma Thurman. Most of the building is members-only, but there are a few free gallery spaces open to the public.

✦ Ⓢ 6 to 23rd St. Ⓢ Exhibits free. Ⓩ Open daily noon-5pm.

THE PLAYERS CLUB

&❁ HISTORIC BUILDING, PERFORMANCE SPACE

16 Gramercy Park S. ☎212-475-6116 ▦www.theplayersnyc.org

Next door to the National Arts Club, this other old and prestigious club for the creative was founded in 1888 by none other than Edwin Booth, brother of John Wilkes. Booth lived on the top floor and died there in 1893—they haven't changed his bed since. The 1845 brownstone, fronted by impressive columns, is a sight in itself. Members have included Laurence Olivier, Frank Sinatra, and Richard Gere.

✦ Ⓢ 6 to 23rd St.

CHURCH OF THE TRANSFIGURATION

&❁⌂ CHURCH

1 E. 29th St. ☎212-684-6770 ▦www.littlechurch.org

The attention-grabbing Church of the Transfiguration has more than distinctive courtyards and sprawling, anomalous architecture. It's acquired a reputation as an "actors' church," stemming chiefly from an 1870 incident. Friends of a recently departed Shakespearean actor were unable to arrange funeral services at posh, thespian-phobic churches nearby—but they were told that "there's a little church around the corner where that sort of thing is done." Today the "little church around the corner" is home to the Episcopal Actors' Guild, features scenes from *Hamlet* in its stained-glass windows, and has held the funerals of artistic celebs like Edwin Booth and O. Henry. The cottage-like exterior is graced by a gentle fountain and shaded benches.

✦ Ⓢ R, W to 28th St. Ⓩ Services M-F 8:40am, 12:10, and 5:10pm; Su 8, 8:30, and 11am.

69TH REGIMENT ARMORY

HISTORIC BUILDING

68 Lexington Ave. (at E. 26th St.)

Hard to believe, but this hulking structure was the site of modern art's first true introduction to American culture. The 1913 Armory show displayed works by Picasso, Matisse, Gauguin, and Duchamp, among others; locals were appropriately shocked and dizzied. On September 11, the space was used as a command center and gathering point for family and friends of the missing. Today, it's a recruiting center for the Army National Guard—you might see some young men and women in uniform lounging outside.

✦ Ⓢ R, W to 28th St. Ⓩ Not open to the public.

MUSEUM OF SEX

✒&❁ MUSEUM

233 5th Ave. (at 27th St.) ☎212-689-6337 ▦www.museumofsex.com

New York's most salacious museum takes an alternatively playful and scholarly look at sex. Two permanent exhibits, "Spotlight" and "Action," display sex objects and documents (incredibly painful-looking, Victorian-era anti-stimulation devices and scientific pamphlets, for example) and video excerpts of the media's representation of sex throughout the decades. The pornography from the 1920s and 30s is especially interesting; the clips from *American Pie*, not so much. These are complemented by rotating exhibits focusing on such topics as strange

American fetishes, the history of condoms, and the sex lives of animals. The admission fees are exorbitant, but you're guaranteed to acquire some unforgettable knowledge. The museum store sells books, dolls, bondage masks, and other sex toys.

[S] R, W to 28th St. $ $16.75, students $15.25. Open M-Th 10am-8pm, F-Sa 10am-9pm, Su 10am-8pm.

MURRAY HILL NEIGHBORHOOD

Between E. 42th St., the East River, E. 34th St., and Madison Ave.

Before the Upper East Side, there was Murray Hill and Gramercy. These neighborhoods were chock-full of stately brownstones and mansions in the late 19th and early 20th centuries, and a quiet, privileged atmosphere remains in these still-upscale neighborhoods. Murray Hill is especially quiet—there's not much to see here besides the excellent **Morgan Museum,** but admirers of classy architecture will probably get very excited on a stroll through here. Lovers of Indian and Pakistani food should also flock to **"Curry Hill,"** a conglomeration of South Asian shops and restaurants clustered around the upper 20s and lower 30s along Lexington and Third Ave.

[S] 6 to 33rd St.

midtown west

Midtown West holds some of the sights that first come to mind for people when they think of New York City: **Times Square, Broadway,** The **Empire State Building, Madison Square Garden,** and so on. Although (as you know from reading this guide) there is much more to New York than the sights that fit in this tiny area, the spectacle of the crowds frantically pursuing shopping and entertainment in Midtown West can be exciting. In all the bustle, don't miss the **Museum of Modern Art.** In the end, you'll want to check out these standby Manhattan sights, but don't feel guilty about leaving when the crowds and commercialism become overwhelming. There's much more to see elsewhere!

HERALD SQUARE AND THE GARMENT DISTRICT

GARMENT DISTRICT ♿ NEIGHBORHOOD

West 30s, between Broadway and 8th Ave.

This neighborhood may be home to big-name designers like **Ralph Lauren** and **Calvin Klein,** the likes of whom are honored by the circular plaques on the **Fashion Walk of Fame** along Broadway. But the real charm lies on the neighborhood's side streets, lined with stores selling wholesale fabrics and tacky dresses. The Fashion Center Business Improvement District's Information Kiosk, with the notorious **Needle Threading a Button** on top, is a good place to go for quick information about locations and events. Next to the kiosk is Judith Weller's 1984 bronze sculpture **The Garment Worker.** Depicting a man at a sewing machine, it's difficult to photograph because pedestrians somehow frequently mistake it for a bench.

[S] 1, 2, 3, 7, Q, R, S to 42nd St.

MADISON SQUARE GARDEN 🎟 ♿ ALL-PURPOSE VENUE

Between 31st and 34 St., 7th and 8th Ave. ☎212-465-5800 www.thegarden.com

The Garden, as it is casually called, hosts about 320 events every year in its 20,976 sq. ft. arena. "Gardeners" (those who run the Garden) apparently do not discriminate when it comes to picking those events either. Home to the NBA's **New York Knicks,** WNBA's **New York Liberty,** and NHL's **New York Rangers,** the arena also regularly hosts concerts, boxing, the **WWE,** the **Ringling Brothers Barnum and Bailey Circus,** and the **Westminster Kennel Club Dog Show** (among a slew of other regular events). In a recent Garden-sponsored poll **Michael Jackson's Bad World Tour** was voted greatest concert ever held at Madison Square Garden (the runner-up was his own 2001 30th Anniversary Tour).

[S] 1, 2, 3 to 34th St./Penn Station/7th Ave.; A, C, E to 34th St./Penn Station/8th Ave. $ Tour prices: $18.50, ages 12 and under $12, 62 and over $18.50. ⏰ Tours daily 11am-3pm, every 30min. Box office open daily 9am-6pm.

PENN STATION

TRAIN STATION

Between 31st and 34th St., 7th and 8th Ave. 🖳www.mta.info

Pennsylvania Station, New York's mothership of underground transportation, is filled with people on the go: going to **Jones Beach** for the day, going to Boston on a work trip, going to work (far, far away) from New Jersey...it's packed with news stores and restaurants designed for people with an average of 13min. to kill before they have to catch their elected form of transport. Penn Station is home to the **Long Island Railroad, Amtrak,** and **New Jersey Transit,** so if you do any East-Coast traveling through New York, chances are that you will join this mob of go-ers.

[S] 1, 2, 3 to 34th St./Penn Station/7th Ave.; A, C, E, to 34th St./Penn Station/8th Ave. i Serves LIRR, Amtrak, New Jersey Transit, MTA, and a wide range of buses including Boltbus, Megabus, Vamoos, Greyhound, and Eastern Shuttle. $ Admission free; train prices vary. ⏰ Open 24hr.

MACY'S

DEPARTMENT STORE

151 W. 34th Street ☎212-695-4400 🖳www.macys.com

You know a department store is big when it has four Starbucks within it. This particular department store, covering more than one million sq. ft. in 14 floors, happens to be the largest department store in the world. To name everything here would be useless; just assume Macy's has everything. In addition to being a shopping heaven, **Macy's** provides New York with some of its most beloved seasonal traditions: the **Macy's Thanksgiving Day Parade, Fourth of July Fireworks,** and amazing holiday window displays.

[S] 1, 2, 3 to 34th St./Penn Station/7th Ave.; A, C, E to 34th St./Penn Station/8th Ave. $ Admission free. Prices of items vary. ⏰ Open M-Sa 10am-9:30pm, Su 11am-8:30pm.

EMPIRE STATE BUILDING

SIGHT

350 5th Ave., at 34th St. ☎212-279-9999 🖳www.esbnyc.com

Ever since King Kong climbed to its spire for the first time in 1933, the Empire State Building has attracted scores of tourists—Queen Elizabeth, Fidel Castro, and Lassie among the most famous and unexpected. The skyscraper's observatories welcome nearly four million visitors every year. Built on the site of the original **Waldorf-Astoria Hotel** and completed in 1931, the structure stretches 1454 ft. into the sky and contains two mi. of elevator shafts containing 73 cars. When first completed, it included a docking platform for what was then thought to be the next frontier of modern transportation: the dirigible. Just one moored to the building before it was deemed too dangerous. Of course, you could always walk or run up the 1576 stairs to the 86th-floor observatory, as over 100 arguably sadistic individuals do every February during the **Empire State Building Run-Up.** The lobby is a gleaming shrine to Art Deco, all the way down to its stylized mail drops and elevator doors, and it contains vaulted panels depicting the seven wonders of the ancient world. Follow the arrows on the wall to find the escalator to the concourse level, where you can purchase tickets to the observatory. Note the sign indicating the visibility level—a day with perfect visibility offers views for 80 miles in any direction. The second floor houses the **Skyride** and an **IMAX** aerial virtual tour narrated by Kevin Bacon. Who can resist that?

[S] F, N, W, R, M to 34th St./Herald Square. i All visitors must pass through security before entering the observatory. $ $20, ages under 6, 6-12 $14, over 62 $18, military members $18. Skyride: $36, ages 6-12 $25, seniors $29. ⏰ Open daily 8am-2am; last elevator 45min. before close.

HELL'S KITCHEN

HELL'S KITCHEN   ♿ NEIGHBORHOOD

30th to 59th St., between 8th Ave. and the Hudson River

Hell's Kitchen was once an Irish Mafia hotspot infamous for general sketchiness. The neighborhood has become much safer and hipper (and the rents have risen correspondingly), though it still isn't exactly a PTA meeting. Strip clubs and peep shows abound in this lively, energetic place. Despite vestiges of seediness, the area is a terrific lunch and nightlife spot. Ninth Ave. and the surrounding streets especially are a cache of inexpensive, independently owned eateries.

⚥ Ⓢ *1, 2, 3 to 34th St./Penn Station/7th Ave.; A, C, E to 34th St./Penn Station/8th Ave.*

TIMES SQUARE AND THE THEATER DISTRICT

▨ MUSEUM OF MODERN ART   ♥♿ MUSEUM

11 W. 53rd St., between 5th and 6th Ave.   ☎212-621-6800 ▧www.moma.org

In the 1920s, the conservative Metropolitan Museum refused to display Modernist work. Scholar Alfred Barr, rebel that he was, responded by holding the first exhibit of the eventual MoMA, featuring Cézanne, Gaugin, Seurat, and van Gogh in a Fifth Ave. office building. As the great works of the 20th century transitioned from shockers into masterpieces, MoMA has grown into one of the most important modern art collections in the world. Be extra careful when walking through the galleries lest you trip over the dropped jaw or genuflecting body post-1880. Holy relics of Modernism not to be missed are Picasso's **Demoiselles d'Avignon** (the painting that paved the way to ▨**Cubism**) on the fifth floor, Andy Warhol's **32 Campbell's Soup Cans** on the fourth floor, and a room with several Pollock drip paintings (also on the fourth floor). The beautiful, canyon-like **Abby Aldrich Rockefeller Sculpture Garden** is another must-see. The $20 price tag for a visit may seem steep, but it's definitely worth every dime. With more than 100,000 paintings, 2000 videos, and 25,000 photographs, MoMA has more art than it could ever have a chance to display. Admission to the contemporary **P.S.1** (p.89) in Queens is also included. And, if all else fails, visit on **Target Free Fridays** (*4-8pm on F, free admission*).

⚥ Ⓢ *E, M to 5th Ave./53rd St.; B, D, F to 47-50 St. Rockefeller Ctr.* ⓢ *$20, 65 and over $16,*

the condé nast building

As one of the many looming architectural monsters in midtown Manhattan, the Condé Nast building has been brushed off as another high-end, high-stress office space for corporate minions hoping to make it in the City of Dreams. But standing at over 800 ft. and housing all Condé Nast publications including the *New Yorker* and *Vanity Fair,* the third largest structure in New York City became famous in the recent past due to a multitude of media attention, mostly attributable to *Vogue.* Lauren Weisberger's book *The Devil Wears Prada* came lashing out at a fictional Anna Wintour, and the author supposedly based the story's Manhattan skyscraper office on the Condé Nast tower. In 2007, R.J. Cutler's documentary on the making of Vogue featured the icy editor-in-chief's office and headquarters where she didn't help her already less-than-friendly reputation. Those in the science fiction world have also taken a liking to the building that received an American Institute of Architects award for its solar technology—*Battlestar Galactica* producers used an exact replica of the tower to decorate the skyline of Caprica City. Not bad for a steel phallus.

students $12, 16 and under free. F 4-8pm Free; free jazz and classical concerts in the garden dur-
ing July and Aug. Open M 10:30am-5:30pm, W-Th 10:30am-5:30pm (open until 8:45pm Th in
July and Aug), F 10:30am-8pm, Sa 10:30am-5:30pm.

INTERNATIONAL CENTER OF PHOTOGRAPHY
⌐& MUSEUM

1133 Ave. of the Americas at 43rd St. ☎212-857-0000 🖳www.icp.org

The center hosts exhibitions focused on both the history of the medium and
the work of contemporary artists. Curators have a refreshingly loosey-goosey
sense of what qualifies as a photographic exhibition, extending their focus to
many other forms of culture. A recent exhibition on visual culture of the Civil
Rights movement included television clips of **Richard Pryor** and **Tina Turner** while
an exhibition of current photography included installation art featuring books
with photographic images.

⌗ S B, D, F, M to 42nd St./Ave. of the Americas. $ $12, students and seniors $8, under 12
free. Open Tu-Th 10am-6pm, F 10am-8pm, Sa-Su 10am-6pm.

STUDIO 54
⌐& THEATER

254 W. 54th St. ☎212-719-1300 🖳www.roundabouttheatre.org

Built in 1927 as an opera house, the theater changed identities several times
before assuming its most famous (and scandalous) form as the hard-partying
Studio 54 nightclub in 1976. For a decade, the club was the hottest place in town,
frequented by stars of the **Madonna** and **Michael Jackson** variety. In 1986, it was
closed on account of too much sex, drugs, and rock n' roll. Things have come
full circle, and **Studio 54** is a theater once more, inhabited by the acclaimed
Roundabout Theatre Company.

⌗ S B, D, E to 7th Ave. Studio 54 is between Broadway and 8th Ave. $ Tickets $67-117. Box
office open Tu-Sa 10am-8pm, Su 10am-6pm.

PALEY CENTER FOR MEDIA
& ARCHIVE

25 W. 52nd St., between 5th and 6th Ave. ☎212-621-6600 🖳www.paleycenter.org

If you are a TV junkie or are rabid for the radio, the Paley Center for Media is
not to be missed. The center's crown jewel is a 150,000-program media archive,
which you can peruse in the Paley Center Library. Additionally, the center hosts
talks and panels with all of the biggest names in sitcoms, news, and drama as
well as media experts from around the world. Paley Center guests have included
Sarah Jessica Parker, Chris Rock, Christiane Amanpour, and the cast of **Glee.**

⌗ S B, D, F, M to 47th-50th St./Rockefeller Center/6th Ave. or E, M to 5th Ave./53rd St. i Cash
only when purchasing tickets at door. $ Admission to archives $10, students and seniors $8.
Event prices vary. Open W noon-6pm, Th noon-8pm, F-Su noon-6pm.

ST. MALACHY'S CHURCH (THE ACTORS' CHAPEL)
CHURCH

239 W. 49th St. ☎212-489-1340 🖳www.actorschapel.org

From the early '20s to the late '60s, **St. Malachy's** was packed with pious thespians.
If you come to mass here, you'll be praying in the same place where **Douglass
Fairbanks** and **Joan Crawford** were married and **Tennessee Williams** was blessed for
the final time. Since around 1968, the percentage of actors worshipping here has
declined, but there is still a mass for actors and stagehands at 11pm on Saturday
night. Come and maybe you'll catch a cast member from the show you just saw.

⌗ S C, E, 1 to 50th St. $ Free. Mass M-F 8am and 12:15pm; Sa 5 and 11pm for Actors and
Stagehands. Su 9, 11am, and 6pm; Confession W, F noon; Sa 4:45pm.

INTREPID SEA-AIR-SPACE MUSEUM
⌐& MUSEUM

Pier 86, at 46th St. and 12th Ave. ☎212-245-0072 🖳www.intrepidmuseum.com

An astonishing adventure into the mysteries of aquatics and aviation, the
museum is home to the **USS Intrepid,** which served as warship from 1943 until
its retirement in 1974. Having survived bomb attacks, kamikaze assaults, and
a torpedo strike, the Intrepid is essentially the Rasputin of aircraft carriers.

The museum also exhibits the **British Airways Concorde** that holds the record for fastest pond-crossing (2hr. 52min. and 59sec.). Guests enjoy tours, simulations, and exhibitions. Commemorate your visit with a ⊠**Space Suit** from the gift shop *(available in youth sizes, $50).*

✦ Ⓢ *A, C, E to 42nd St./Port Authority. Take the M41 west to 42nd St. and Hudson River (12th Ave.) Walk north to the museum.* Ⓢ *$22, US college students and seniors $18, 3-17 years old and vets $17, active and retired military and children under 3 free.* ☼ *Open Apr-Sep M-F 10am-5pm, Sa-Su 10am-6pm; Oct-Mar Tu-Su 10am-5pm. Last entry 1hr. before close.*

midtown east

⊠ NEW YORK PUBLIC LIBRARY   ♿ LIBRARY
42nd St. and 5th Ave.   ☎212-768-4242 🖳www.nypl.org

You may recognize the lions (named "Patience" and "Fortitude") that valiantly guard the entrance to this marble temple of learning: *Ghostbusters, The Day After Tomorrow,* and *Sex and the City* all filmed scenes at the NYPL. The **Rose Main Reading Room** measures over 23,000 square feet and has astounding, mural-covered ceilings 52 ft. from the floor. For a century, people from all walks of life have used it as a study and research space. The NYPL is also home to several priceless treasures, including a ⊠**Gutenburg Bible** and copy of **The Declaration of Independence.** Throughout the year, the library hosts scores of free film screenings, lectures, classes, and exhibitions. Check the website or information desk for schedule information.

✦ Ⓢ *B, D, F, M to 42nd St./Ave. of the Americas (6th Ave.); 7 to 5th Ave./42nd St.* ☼ *General research hours Sept-May M 10am-6pm, Tu-W 10am-9pm, Th-Sa 10am-6pm, Su 1-5pm. 1hr. tours leave from the information desk at Astor Hall M-Sa 11am-2pm and Su 2pm.*

⊠ JAPAN SOCIETY   ♥♿ CULTURAL CENTER
333 E. 47th St., at 1st Ave.   ☎212-715-1270 🖳www.japansociety.org

The **Japan Society** must hold some kind of record for the non-profit with the most offerings and events throughout the year. The society of best known for their cutting-edge and historical artistic exhibitions, but that's just the tip of the Mochi ball. They have language classes, calligraphy classes, business lectures, family events, film series featuring the most avant-garde in Japanese cinema, lectures by Martha Stewart (we kid you not!), and dance performances just to name a few highlights. And you didn't hear it from us, but celebrities of the alternative world such as **Bjork** and **Matthew Barney** have been known to hang around the Society building.

✦ Ⓢ *4, 5, 6, 7, S to Grand Central; 6 to 51st St./Lexington Ave.; E, M to Lexington Ave./53rd St.* Ⓢ *Prices vary by attraction and exhibition.* ☼ *Open M-F 11am-6pm (Gallery Exhibitions closed M), Sa-Su 11am-5pm.*

⊠ THE UNITED NATIONS   ♥♿ SIGHT
1st Ave., between 42nd and 48th St.   ☎212-963-4479 🖳www.un.org

After passing through an extremely thorough security check, you will enter the **General Assembly Building** lobby, which is filled with permanent pieces of international art as well as temporary exhibitions promoting environmentalism, peace, cultural understanding, and other warm and fuzzy political values. To your right as you enter is a stained glass window designed by Belarusian artist **Marc Chagall.** A **Norman Rockwell** mosaic, **Japanese Peace Bell,** and Chinese ivory carving are also exhibited throughout the building. The only way to see the General Assembly is to take a **guided tour,** available in 15 different languages and led by guides from around 20 countries. The tours also provide the opportunity to see the **Universal**

Declaration of Human Rights as well as objects such as a guitar made out of an AK47 and artifacts from Nagasaki. Other interesting UN destinations include the **Conference Building,** the 39-floor **Secretariat Building,** the **Evgeniy Vuchetich** statue called *Let Us Beat Swords into Plowshares* and the **Dag Hammarskjöld Library,** a 1961 gift from the Ford Family.

✦ Ⓢ *4, 5, 6, 7, S to 42nd St./Grand Central.* ⓘ *Tours are cash only.* Ⓢ *$16, students and seniors $11, children $9.* Ⓩ *Audio and guided tours M-F 9:30am-4:45pm; audio tours only Sa-Su 10:30am-4:15pm.*

BRYANT PARK   ⚁ PARK

6th Ave., between 40th and 42nd St.   ☎212-768-4242 💻www.bryantpark.org

Bryant Park has always has always been able to bring New Yorkers together. Once a burial ground for the city's poor, it's now a popular lunch spot. On a pleasant day, the lawn is covered with city-folk munching on their takeout Caesar salads. Late June through late August, HBO and Time Warner Cable show free films on Mondays at sundown as part of the **Bryant Park Film Festival** (p.166), and in early July through mid-August, 106.7 Lite FM hosts **Broadway in the Park** on Thursdays at 12:30pm. The popular carousel *($2 per ride)* runs from 11am-8pm June through October *(until 9pm on Halloween).*

✦ Ⓢ *B, D, F, M to 42nd St./Ave. of the Americas (6th Ave.); 7 to 5th Ave./42nd St. Behind the New York Public Library.* Ⓢ *Film Festival and Broadway in the Park free.* Ⓩ *Open daily 7am-9pm, in summer until 11pm.*

GRAND CENTRAL TERMINAL   ⚁✉ TRAIN STATION

E. 42nd St. between Madison and Lexington Ave., where Park Ave. should be   ☎212-340-2583 💻www.grandcentralterminal.com

Although Grand Central Station serves the **Metro-North Railroad, New York City Subway,** and **MTA New York City Bus,** you don't have to be catching a train to make a trip to the beautiful, Beaux-Arts Grand Central Terminal. The station is a shopping destination in its own right, with 50 stores and a surfeit of restaurants, food stands, and cocktail lounges. The **Grand Central Market** on the main level presents a dizzying array of chocolates, cheeses, breads, meats, and pastries (with samples galore if you're in need of a snack). You can also get your daily dose of transportation history at the **New York Transit Museum's Gallery Annex and Store** (Ⓩ *Open M-F 8am-8pm, Sa-Su 10am-6pm* ☎212-878-0106). Tours leave from the information desk in the main concourse Wednesdays at 12:30pm and from the Sculpture Garden of the Whitney Museum (see information below) Fridays at 12:30pm.

✦ Ⓢ *4, 5, 6, 7, S to 42nd St./Grand Central.* Ⓢ *Admission free. Municipal Arts Society tours suggested donation $10, Grand Central Partnership tour free.* Ⓩ *Terminal open daily 5:30am-2am. Tours sponsored by the Municipal Arts Society W 12:30pm; meet at information desk on the main concourse. Tours sponsored by the Grand Central Partnership F 12:30pm; meet in the Sculpture Court of the Whitney Museum at Altria on East 42nd St. across from Grand Central Station.*

ST. PATRICK'S CATHEDRAL   ⚁ CATHEDRAL

Southeast corner of 5th Ave. and 51st St.   ☎212-753-2261 💻www.stpatrickscathedral.org

Everyone wanted a Gothic Revival church in the 1850s when **James Renwick** designed **St. Patrick's Cathedral** in 1858. Unfortunately, the **American Civil War** rudely interfered with construction until 1865, and the Cathedral did not open until 1879. Today, St. Patrick's is invariably filled with penitent tourists, passing from one of the many Saints' altars to the next to light votive candles. Favorites include **St. Jude, St. Brigid,** Patroness of the Americas **Our Lady of Guadalupe,** and the first American-born Saint, **Elizabeth Ann Seton.** For a more peaceful experience, try a visit to the smaller **Lady Chapel** by the South Transept.

✦ Ⓢ *E,M to 5th Ave./53rd St.* Ⓢ *Free.* Ⓩ *Mass M-F 7, 7:30, 8am, noon, 12:30, 1, 5:30pm. Confession after every morning mass and noon-1:20pm; Sa 8am, noon, 5:30pm; Su 7, 8, 9, 10:15am, confession noon-12:45pm and 3:30-5:30pm.*

THE WALDORF-ASTORIA HOTEL   ♿✉ HOTEL

301 Park Ave., between 49th and 50th St.   ☎212-355-3000 ▣www.waldorfastoria.com

The Waldorf-Astoria Hotel is an American landmark, and proud of it. The **Cocktail Terrace** contains American songwriter **Cole Porter's** flower-covered, brown Steinway. Visitors entering the lobby pass an exhibition with objects from the history of the hotel, including an event book from 1915 and antique place settings. (The 1945 film *Weekend at the Waldorf* also plays on loop in this exhibition. Apparently it never gets old.) In the center of the lobby, the two-ton **Waldorf-Astoria Clock** (1893) contains the busts of Cleveland, Harrison, Washington, Grant, Lincoln, Franklin, Jackson, and odd-Brit-out Queen Victoria. At the Waldorf-Astoria, more than anything else, they love food. Different editions of the **Waldorf-Astoria Cookbook** can be found sprinkled throughout the hotel. The tour even goes through the kitchen and includes lunch. For $95 you too can enjoy a historic brunch at this historic hotel.

✞ Ⓗ *6 to 51st St.; E, M to Lexington Ave./53rd St.* Ⓢ *Tours $50, include lunch at Peacock Alley or Oscar's; Su brunch $95.* ⏱ *Tours Th and Sa at 11:30am. Brunch in winter Su 11:30am-2:30pm.*

ROCKEFELLER CENTER   ✉♿ SIGHT

Between 48th and 51st St., 5th and 6th Ave.   ☎212-332-6868 ▣www.rockefellercenter.com

Developed by **John D. Rockefeller Jr.** beginning in 1930, **Rockefeller Center** is a microcosm of Midtown Manhattan, complete with food, shopping, entertainment, and art. One of the most notable sights is the Lee Lawrie and Rene Chambellan statue of **Atlas** on 5th Ave. between 50th and 51st Streets. The statue was originally treated with hostility because of its purported resemblance to Italian dictator Benito Mussolini. Another nod to the boys of Greek mythology is Paul Manship's Gold-leaf **Prometheus** Statue in the **Tower Plaza**, a sunken space between 49th and 50th Streets. The plaza leads the double life of a Christmas Tree embellished skating rink in the winter and an overpriced cafe in the spring and summer. The main entrance to Rockefeller Center is on 5th Ave., between 49th and 50th St. The foliage-rich **Channel Gardens** (separating the **Maison Francaise** on the left and the **British Empire Building** on the right) contain many more pieces of art and six glistening pools of water. Behind Tower Plaza is the **General Electric** building (a.k.a. **30 Rockefeller Center,** made immortal by Tina Fey), offers daily tours of the Center. Toward 49th Street the **NBC Studio Tour** allows guests to go behind the scenes of **Saturday Night Live, Late Night with Jimmy Fallon,** and **30 Rock.** Toward 51st St. you'll find the **Radio City Music Hall**, home to the high-kicking, wide-grinning Rockettes. You can meet one of them on a tour of the theater, every day from 11am-3pm.

✞ Ⓗ *B, D, F, M to 47th-50th St.* Ⓢ *$21, ages 6-12 $14, seniors $19; guided tours $15; art + observation deck combo $30. NBC Studio Tour $19.25, ages 6-12 and seniors $16.25. Radio City Tours $18.50, ages 12 and under $10, ages 62 and over $15.* ⏱ *Observation Deck between 50th and 51st St., enter on 50th St. Observation Deck open daily 8am-midnight; Rockefeller Center tours leave from GE building every hour 10am-7pm, except at 6pm; NBC Tours leave from 2nd level of NBC Store M-W 8:30am-5:30pm, Th 8:30am-6pm (M-Th every 30min.), F-Sa 6:30am-6:30pm, Su 9:15am-4:30pm (F-Su every 15min.); Radio City Tours daily 11am-3pm.*

SONY WONDER TECHNOLOGY LAB   ♿ MUSEUM

550 Madison Ave., at 55th St.   ☎212-833-8100 ▣www.sonywondertechlab.com

This is a budding science nerd's paradise. Upon entering, guests take photographs of themselves and create a "digital watermark" that is downloaded to an ID card. They then use that card to participate in the many hands-on exhibitions, from creating an animated character to programming a robot. The whole thing is very **Star Trek** and tons of fun.

✞ Ⓗ *N, R, Q to 5th Ave./59th St.* Ⓢ *Free.* ⏱ *Open Tu-Sa 10am-5pm, Su noon-5pm. Last entry 30min. before close.*

CHRYSLER BUILDING ♿ SIGHT

405 Lexington Ave., at E. 42nd St.

In 1930, Chrysler Corporation founder Walter Chrysler wanted his monument to the car to be the tallest building in the world. Unfortunately for Chrysler, George Ohrstrom of the Bank of Manhattan and John Jakob Raskob of General Motors also wanted their buildings to be the tallest in the world. Thus, the **Great Skyscraper Race,** a competition fraught with secrets and trickery, began. The Chrysler building, designed by architect William Van Alen was briefly the world's tallest until the Empire State Building opened in 1931. Measuring 1046 ft. and 4¾ in., the spire is meant to evoke a 1930 Chrysler car's radiator grille. The gargoyles of chromium and nickel outside the 59th floor are styled after hood ornaments, and the lightning bolts on the facade symbolize the energy of the new machine. The Art Deco lobby, laden with African marble, onyx, and amber, contains beautiful elevators of Japanese Ash. An Edward Trumbull painting originally executed on canvas and subsequently cemented to the ceiling depicts the Chrysler assembly line. Although the building is a New York icon, it ruined Van Alen's career. An unsatisfied Chrysler accused the architect of embezzlement and refused to pay him.

[S] 4, 5, 6, 7, S to 42nd St./Grand Central. $ Free. ⏰ Open daily 8am-6pm.

roosevelt island

Once known as "Welfare Island," this land was long used to contain New York's unwanted and forgotten—an asylum, a smallpox hospital, and a prison all shared the very limited space here throughout the 19th and early 20th centuries. Famous inhabitants **Mae West** and **Billie Holliday** both served very brief time on the island for various misdemeanors. The **Goldwater Hospital** to the south and the **Coler Hospital** to the north are living reminders of the island's legacy. In the 1970s, a planned community was established and modern rentals and condos built, lending the island its somewhat artificial look. Divided into **Southtown** and **Northtown,** Roosevelt Island houses some 12,000 residents.

SOUTHPOINT PARK AREA NEIGHBORHOOD

At the island's southern tip, **Southpoint Park** *(open daily 8am-dusk)* provides amazing vistas of Manhattan. A promenade runs along it's western edge, offering benches and more views across the East River. The **Blackwell House** is the revolutionary-era farmhouse of the Blackwell family, who owned the island from 1676 to the early 19th century. Just north, the **Chapel of the Good Shepherd,** built in the 1880s and frequented by the island's sick during its welfare days, now houses both Protestant and Catholic congregations. Toward the northern tip of the island, you'll find the remarkable **Octagon,** once an asylum whose conditions shocked Charles Dickens, and later part of the City Hospital. Today, it's the lobby of a huge apartment building. At the northern edge, **Lighthouse Park** provides views of Manhattan and Queens that center on the 1872 **lighthouse,** which once assisted boats navigating treacherous sections of the East River.

Take Tramway from 59th St. and 2nd Ave. to Roosevelt Island. $ Southpoint Park open 8am-dusk.

TRAMWAY TRANSPORTATION

The island is accessible via the F Subway line, but a more exciting option is the Tramway system. The 4½min. crossing from the Manhattan terminal on 59th St. and Second Ave. takes you 250 ft. above the East River and deposits you right in the middle of the island. The bright red trams have become landmarks—you may remember them from the first *Spider-Man*, in which a tramload of passengers is saved from the Green Goblin's murderous clutches by our web-slinging hero. The tram system was under repair and scheduled to re-open in early 2011. ✈ Ⓢ *4, 5, 6, N, R, W to 59th St. and Lexington Ave.* ℹ *Once on the island, you can travel up and down Main St. on the cheap minibus.* Ⓢ *One-way pass $2. MetroCards accepted.* ⏰ *Trams leave every 15min. M-Th 6am-2am, F-Sa 6am-3:30am, Su 6am-2am.*

upper east side

▨ METROPOLITAN MUSEUM OF ART ✈♿❄ MUSEUM
1000 5th Ave., at 82nd St. ☎212-879-5500 🖳www.metmuseum.org

The Met is not only a world-class museum—it's essentially several world-class museums rolled into one. The medieval galleries in the western section of the ground floor are chock-full of capitals and altarpieces. The Chinese galleries on the northern end of the second floor are brimming with priceless treasures from the Ming Dynasty. The Egyptian galleries on the Northern end of the ground floor house an entire reconstructed temple (the **Temple of Dendur**). Then there are the European paintings and sculptures, the Greek, Roman, and Byzantine art, the weapons, and the musical instruments. The Met is like that ideal family vacation where the grandparents play golf, kids play in the pool, and the parents drink by the pool: there is truly something for everyone. ✈ Ⓢ *4, 5, 6 to 80th St./Lexington Ave.* Ⓢ *Suggested donations from adults $20, students $10, seniors $15. Children 12 and under free. Audio tours $7.* ⏰ *Open Tu-Th 9:30am-5:30pm, F-Sa 9:30am-9pm, Su 9:30am-5:30pm.*

▨ GUGGENHEIM MUSEUM ✈♿❄ MUSEUM
1071 5th Ave., at 89th St. ☎212-423-3500 🖳www.guggenheim.org

Unlike many of its counterparts, the Guggenheim is not a survey museum. This means that much like South Park's Eric Cartman, the curators at the Guggenheim "do what they want." The show in the rotunda, the larger spiral in Frank Lloyd Wright's innovative architectural creation, changes every three to four months and features different works from within and without the Guggenheim's permanent collection. The Guggenheim is famous for displaying a wide variety of media, including conceptual art, video art, and performance art. The works in the Thannhauser Gallery in the annex stay more or less constant throughout the year. The pieces in this collection were given to the Solomon R. Guggenheim Foundation by Justin K. Thannhauser, a German art dealer who fled the Nazi regime's attack on "degenerate art." The collection includes many works by **Wassily Kandinsky** and **Pablo Picasso,** the most famous of which may be a painting depicting his young mistress (*Girl With Yellow Hair*). Other early Modernist rock stars repped in this collection include Gauguin, Degas, Monet, van Gogh, and Cezanne. ✈ Ⓢ *4, 5, 6 to 86th St. Walk North on Lexington Ave. Turn left on 88th St. and walk 3 blocks to 5th Ave. The Guggenheim is between 88th and 89th St.* ℹ *Call* ☎212-423-3539 *about wheelchair accessibility. F 5:45-7:45pm "pay what you wish."* Ⓢ *$18, students and seniors $15, children under 12 free.* ⏰ *Open Su-W and F 10am-5:45pm, F 10am-5:45pm, Sa 10am-7:45pm.*

▨ LEO CASTELLI GALLERY Ⓖ GALLERY
18 E. 77th St., between Madison and 5th Ave. ☎212-249-4470 🖳www.castelligallery.com

The Leo Castelli Gallery is a landmark of postwar American art. These guys showed **Andy Warhol** before he was cool. Exhibitions range from your standard Roy Lichtenstein and Robert Morris to contemporary, younger artists. ✈ Ⓢ *6 to 77th St. Press the buzzer for 3A, then enter the building and take the stairs on your right to the 3rd floor.* Ⓢ *Free.* ⏰ *Open Sept-May 10am-6pm, June-July 10am-5pm.*

FRICK COLLECTION

♿ MUSEUM

1 E. 70th St., at 5th Ave. ☎212-288-0700 🖥www.frick.org

Once the collection of industrialist big wig Henry Clay Frick, the Frick Collection is now open to the public. Frick's collection represents a grab-bag of artists ranging from Filippo Lippi to Thomas Gainsborough to Monet. Pieces are separated into rooms sometimes based on period, sometimes based on nationality of the artist, and sometimes based on a loose, general theme, which may cause surprise for viewers unused to seeing a Velazquez on the same wall as a Turner. Don't miss the three paintings by **Vermeer** in the collection (only around 40 survive worldwide).

🚇 [S] 6 to 68th St. Walk North on Lexington and turn left onto 70th St. $ $18, students $5, seniors $12. Su 11am-1pm "pay what you wish." i Children under 10 not admitted. Free audio tour. Library free and open to the public. ⏰ Open Tu-Sa 10am-6pm, Su 11am-5pm. Library open M-F 10am-5pm, Sa 9:30am-1pm.

MUSEUM OF THE CITY OF NEW YORK (MCNY)

♿ MUSEUM

1229 5th Ave., at 103rd St. ☎212-534-1672 🖥www.mcny.org

Although the museum's permanent collection includes over 1.5 million objects, the really fun part of the MCNY is its schedule of temporary informational and artistic shows focused on New York culture. Shows may be anything from a recreation of the opulent interiors of New York homes to a retrospective of Charles Addams (of Addams Family fame) cartoons. Exhibitions for 2011 include *Ain't Nothing Like the Real Thing: The Apollo Theater and American Entertainment* *(Jan 31-Apr 25)*, and *The American Style* *(late Mar or early Apr-late July)*, a show about the American Colonial Revival. Come on Wednesday nights during July and early August for "Speakeasy" '20s-themed cocktail parties *(6-9pm)*.

🚇 [S] 6 to 103rd St. $ Suggested donation $10, students/seniors $6, under 12 free, family $20. Free audio and guided tours available at information desk. ⏰ Open Tu-Su 10am-5pm. Closed New Year's Day, Thanksgiving, and Christmas.

WHITNEY MUSEUM OF AMERICAN ART

♿ MUSEUM

495 Madison Ave., at 75th St. ☎212-570-3676 🖥www.whitney.org

The Whitney is world-renowned for its collection of works by heavyweights of American art such as Rothko, Warhol, and Martin. These gems can be found on the fifth floor. The lower galleries are dedicated to newer, oftentimes more experimental (read: kookier) pieces. For treats like Matthew Barney video art about a distracted satyr's attempt to draw with the horn of a different satyr, check out these lower galleries.

🚇 [S] 6 to 77th St. $ $18, students $12, ages 19-25 or over 61 $12, 18 and under free. F 6-9pm "pay what you wish." ⏰ Open W-Th 11am-6pm, F 1-9pm, Sa-Su 11am-6pm.

CHURCH OF SAINT JEAN BAPTISTE

♿ CHURCH

Corner of Lexington Ave. and 76th St. ☎212-472-2853 🖥www.sjbrcc.net

Aesthetically unassuming on the outside, this church is drop-dead gorgeous on the inside. Green marble pillars; highly detailed wall and ceiling paintings bordered by gold trim; and windows depicting the life of Christ, events from the lives of various saints, and scenes from the Old Testament line the interior walls of the church. A shrine to St. Anne with gold stars lining the wall behind it is situated at the northern wall of the church. A visit is worthwhile, but check the mass schedule to avoid awkwardly interrupting church services.

🚇 [S] 6 to 77th St. Walk South on Lexington. The church will be on the right. ⏰ Su masses 9, 10:30am, noon, 5:30, 7:30pm; weekday masses 7:30am, 12:15, 5:30pm, Sa masses 9am, 12:15, 5:30pm, Holy Hour every 3rd Sunday 4pm. Rosary M-Sa noon. Confession M-F 11:45am-12:10pm, Sa 11:45am-12:10pm, 4:30-5:30pm, Su 7-7:30pm.

TEMPLE EMANU-EL

 ♿ SYNAGOGUE

1 E. 65th St., at 5th Ave.   ☎212-744-1400 🖳www.emanuelnyc.org

Built in 1927, Temple Emanu-El is the largest Reform temple in the world. The sanctuary seats 2500 and 3000 families belong to the congregation (imagine the bar mitzvah schedule). The scale, significance, and beauty of the temple make it definitely worth a visit.

✴ Ⓢ *N, R, or W to 5th Ave.* ◷ *Worship services M-Th 5:30pm, F 5:15pm (organ recital at 5pm), Sa 10:30am (organ recital at 10:15am), Su 5:30pm. Torah study Sa 9:15am.*

central park

CENTRAL PARK

 ♿ PARK

59th to 110th St., 5th Ave. to Central Park W.   ☎212-310-6600 🖳www.centralparknyc.org

The **Central Park Conservancy**, which runs the park and offers public programs, has five visitor centers offering brochures, calendars of events, and free park maps, at Belvedere Castle. The **Charles A. Dana Discovery Center** *(☎212-860-1370)*, at 110th St. between 5th St. and Lenox (6th Ave.) features educational programs for all ages and rents fishing poles to be used at nearby Harlem Meer, while the **North Meadow Recreation Center** *(☎212-348-4867)*, mid-park at 97th St., features indoor and outdoor climbing walls, basketball, and handball courts. **Carriage tours** *(From Central Park S. ☎212-487-4398* Ⓢ *$35 for 1st 20min., $10 for each additional 15min.)* and **bicycle tours** *(Central Park Bike Tours from 203 W. St. ☎ 212-541-8759 🖳www.centralparkbiketour.com* Ⓢ *$49 per 2hr., children $40 per 2hr.* ◷ *Tours M-F 10am, 1, 4pm, Sa-Su 9, 11am, 1, 4pm.)* are available in the park. Additionally, **NYSKATEOUT** offers **in-line skate tours** *(From 72nd St. and Central Park W. ☎212-486-1919* 🖳www.nyskate.com Ⓢ *$40 per hr.* ◷ *Tours May-Sept Tu-Th and Sa-Su 9am, 1pm, 5pm.)* Finally, the Central Park Conservancy sponsors free **walking tours.** Call or check online for schedule and location *(☎212-772-0210* 🖳*www.centralparknyc.org/walkingtours).*

    The **Children's District** area of Central Park offers plenty of activities to amuse any child or child-at-heart. In the 19th century, the **Dairy** provided fresh milk to the city's children and their families. Now the house serves as a visitors' center and gift shop. *(65th St. ☎212-794-6564* ◷ *Open Tu-Su 10am-5pm.)* The **Chess and Checkers House** visitors' center offers maps and information as well as chess

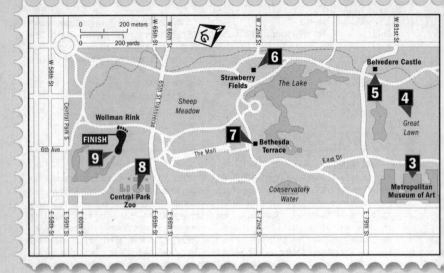

central park

Yesterday you climbed to the top of the Statue of Liberty; your days have been filled with sidewalk-shopping, and your nights with bar-hopping. In short, you're pooped, and craving a slightly more low-key endeavor. What better place to find it than the pastoral paradise smack-dab in the middle of the city—Central Park? This is, of course, not to say that Central Park will offer you respite from touristy hoopla. Still, the greenery and chirping birds is a welcome change from smog and cursing cabbies. Below we've organized some of the must-see sights for your walk in the park.

1. CONSERVATORY GARDEN. To enter the park, take the Subway to the 110th St. stop at Central Park N. Station. Use the park entrance at Malcolm X Dr., and take a left onto East Dr., following it to the Conservatory Garden way in the northeastern region of the park. With the Fountain of the Three Maidens in its center, this garden is an international smorgasbord of botanical splendor, with separate sections maintained in the English, French, and Italian styles.

2. THE RESERVOIR. From there, take a stroll south to the Jacqueline Kennedy Onassis Reservoir; you'll have to cross 97th St. Transverse Rd. This marvel contains more than one billion gallons of water and used to be the source of the city's water supply. A birdwatcher's wet-dream, the reservoir is a wildlife haven, boasting exotic species of both the botanical and aviary varieties.

3. METROPOLITAN MUSEUM OF ART. Continuing south across 86th St. Transverse Rd., you'll soon come to the Metropolitan Museum of Art—or, as we like to call her, the Met. Housing over 2 million works of art, she's not to be missed, even if museums aren't usually your thing. The art at the Met spans 5,000 years of history, so you're bound to find something that catches your eye.

4. THE GREAT LAWN. Your brain will probably need a breather after all that museum time. When you exit the Met, cross over East Dr. and take a load off on the Great Lawn, situated between 79th and 86th Transverse Rd. Open from mid-April to mid-November, the lawn is one of the most ideal picnic spots in the country.

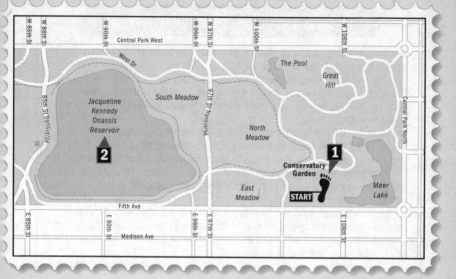

5. BELVEDERE CASTLE. Located on the southern part of the Great Lawn (just before you hit 79th St. Transverse Rd.) is Belvedere Castle, a small Victorian building that now serves as the National Weather Service's base in New York City.

6. STRAWBERRY FIELDS. Next on your journey, walk south through the Ramble, past the boast house and the lake, to Strawberry Fields, where you can pay homage to the Beatles's frontman in this peaceful area of the park, designated as a quiet space. Named for the quartet's hit "Strawberry Fields Forever," this section of Central Park is an ode to the world peace about which Lenon dreamed.

7. BETHESDA TERRACE. The central and perhaps most iconic section of Central Park. Bethesda Terrace consists of an upper and lower terrace joined by two imposing staircases. The upper terrace overlooks Bethesda Fountain, which is surrounded by droves of tourists, vendors, and street performers in any given season. The terrace connects to the northern part of the Mall, the main, elm-flanked promenade of the park. To get to Bethesda Terrace from Strawberry Fields, simply walk along 72nd St. Transverse Rd.

8. CENTRAL PARK ZOO. If you thought you couldn't see polar bears and sloths in the middle of the Big Apple, you were wrong. From Strawberry Fields, follow West Dr. south, and take a left onto 65th St. Transverse Rd. The zoo will be along the edge of the park on your right, you animal you.

9. WOLLMAN RINK: Finish off your Central Park adventure at Wollman Rink, a world-famous ice-skating venue and one of Hollywood's favorite backdrops, located south of 65th St. Transverse Rd. To exit the park from the rink, follow East Dr. to the southeastern corner of the park. The 5th Ave. Subway station will be nearby.

WALKING TOUR

Let's Go
www.letsgo.com

top dog in central park

Just after entering Central Park at 5th Ave. and 65th St, visitors are faced with a printed sign with a plea for donations from the Central Park Conservancy Foundation. The sign features some cheesy pun about statue upkeep costing "an arm and a leg." Whatever the cost of upkeep for the over 50 statues in Central Park, this, from my perspective, is extreme over-spending. Visitors to Central Park only care about one statue: Balto.

I first felt childish when I immediately (and loudly) exclaimed "Balto!" upon encountering the statue of that famous sled dog memorialized by Disney. Balto, who bravely led his team of sled dogs to Nome, transporting diphtheria antitoxins to the afflicted. My embarrassment turned to fascination when I noticed that tourist after tourist was climbing to the top of Balto's little pedestal to take a picture with the courageous canine.

Like I said, there are over 50 statues in Central Park. I saw many of them today over the course of the several hours I spent there. I saw no tourists excitedly taking pictures with any of the other statues. No other statue I encountered elicited the same delight and devotion as Balto.

Davida Fernandez-Barkan

and checkers equipment. *(Mid-park at 64th St. ☎212-794-4064 ⏰ Open Apr-Oct Tu-Su 10am-5pm, Nov-May W-Su 10am-5pm.)* In the winter months, visitors can ice skate at **Wollman Rink.** *(East side between 62nd and 63rd St. ☎212-439-6900 $ M-F $9.50, Sa-Su $12, over 59 M-F $4.75, Sa-Su $8.25, children M-F $4.75, Sa-Su $5. Skate rentals $5. $ Open late Oct-early Apr M-Tu 10am-2:30pm, W-Th 10am-10pm, F-Sa 10am-11pm, Su 10am-9pm.)* In the summer, the rink doubles as **Victorian Gardens Amusement Park.** *(☎212-982-2229 $ M-F $6.50, Sa-Su $7.50. $2-3 per ride or unlimited ride wristband M-F $12, Sa-Su $14. ⏰ Open M-Th 11am-7pm, F 11am-8pm, Sa 10am-9pm, Su 10am-8pm.)* For more amusement, ride the **Carousel** *(Mid-park at 64th St. ☎ 212-879-0244 $ $2 per ride. ⏰ Open Apr-Nov M-F 10am-6pm, Sa-Su 10am-4:30pm.)* The famous **Central Park Wildlife Center (the Zoo)** and **Tisch Children's Zoo** are located on the east side between 63rd and 66th, off of 5th Ave. *(☎212-439-6500 ⏰ Open Apr–Oct M–F 10am–5pm, Sa-Su 10am–5:30pm, Nov–Mar M-Su 10am–4:30pm.)* The statue of **Balto,** the sled dog immortalized by Disney, stands regally on the East side at 67th St.

Sheep Meadow *(Western side of the park, 66th-69th St.)* is designated as a "quiet area," where park visitors can sit on blankets and read, picnic, and nap. For a relaxing walk, amble along the elm and statue-lined paths of **The Mall** *(Mid-park between 66th and 72nd St.)* to **Bethesda Terrace and Fountain** *(at the end of the Mall, at 72nd St.)*. East of Sheep Meadow, free concerts and performances by **Summerstage** play throughout the warmer months at the **Naumberg Bandshell** and **Rumsey Playfield.** Schedules and show times are available online *(🖥www.summerstage.org)*.

Head to the lake and **Strawberry Fields** to explore your sentimental side. Try renting your very own rowboat at **Loeb Boathouse.** *(Mid-park at 76th St. $ 1st hr. $12, every additional 15 min. $3. Refundable $20 deposit required. ⏰ Open daily 10am-6pm.)* The **Loeb Boathouse** offers a tranquil atmosphere for lakeside dining. *($ Lunch entrees $19-27, dinner $20-40, brunch $16-25. ⏰ Open Apr-Nov noon-4pm and 5:30-9:30pm. Sa-Su brunch 9:30am-4pm, dinner 6-9pm.)* Next check out **Strawberry Fields** *(West side between 71st and 72nd St.)* a memorial to 🖼**John Lennon** across from **The Dakota,** the apartment building at which he was shot. Yoko Ono battled for this space against City Council members who would have preferred a Bing Crosby memorial. Although the Central Park Conservancy designates the fields as a "quiet area," musicians playing Beatles music thankfully ignore this label. On any given day, park visitors may sit around the **"Imagine" mosaic** and listen to the strummed chords of "Yesterday." On the eastern edge of **The Lake** *(71st through 78th St.)*, adults and children alike steer remote-controlled boats on the **Conservatory Water** *(East side from 72nd to 75th St.)*. North of The Lake, birdwatchers, nature enthusiasts, and people just looking for some respite from the day can wander through the winding trails of **The Ramble.** Stick to the pathways and avoid rambling after dark.

Next, head to the Great Lawn, where you'll find that **Belvedere Castle** *(Just off 79th St. ☎212-772-0210 $ Free. ⏰ Open Tu-Su 10am-5pm.)*, the home of the New York Meteorological Observancy, provides a stunning view of **Turtle Pond** *(Mid-park between 79th and 80th St.)*. Hundreds of eager Shakespeare enthusiasts arrive at 7am to wait in line (or "on line" as New Yorkers say) for free tickets to **Shakespeare in the Park** at the **Delacorte Theatre** *(Mid-park at 80th St. ☎ 212-539-8650 💻www.publictheater.org)*. The **Shakespeare Garden**, said to contain every plant, flower, and herb in the Bard's works lies near the **Swedish Cottage Marionette Theater.** Imported from Sweden in 1879, the cottage now houses year-round marionette performances. *(☎212-988-9093 💻www.CityParksFoundation.org $ $8, ages under 12 $5. Reservations required. For schedules and showtimes call.)*

The **Reservoir's Conservatory Garden** features landscaping in the French, Italian, and English styles. *(Reservoir 85th-96th St., Reservoir Conservatory Garden, East side from 104th-106th St., enter at 5th Ave. and 105th St. or gate inside park at 106th St. ☎212-360-2766 ⏰ Open spring-fall 8am-dusk.)* Within the garden stands the **Burnett Fountain**, a memorial to beloved author of *The Secret Garden*, Frances Hodgson Burnett. Kids of all ages enjoy swimming and skating at **Lasker Rink and Pool** *(Mid-park between 106th and 110th St. Rink: ☎212-534-7639. Pool: ☎212-534-7639. $ Rink $6.25, children $3.50, seniors $2.25. Skate rentals $5.50. Pool free. ⏰ Rink open daily in winter. Pool open July-Aug daily 11am-2:45pm and 4-6:45pm.)* The **Charles A. Dana Discovery Center** and **Harlem Meer** occupy the very top eastern portion of the Park *(106th to 110th St. ☎212-860-1370. $ Free. ⏰ Open Apr-Oct Tu-Su 10am-5pm, Nov-Mar Tu-Su 10am-4pm.)* The **Harlem Meer Performance Festival** is staged at the Discovery Center, offering free concerts during June, July, and August *(☎212-860-1370 for performance schedule)*.

upper west side

LINCOLN CENTER — PERFORMING ARTS

Columbus Ave., between 62nd and 66th St. ☎212-721-6500 💻www.lincolncenter.org

Welcome to the Mecca of performing arts. Start your pilgrimage at Lincoln Center's revamped **David Rubenstein Atrium** on Broadway between 62nd and 63rd Streets. The visitor's center offers free performances, day-of discounted tickets, and Wi-Fi, as well as information about Lincoln Center's two different opera companies, two ballet companies, several classical music ensembles, and the famous **Jazz at Lincoln Center.** With your back to Columbus Ave. and facing the **Josie Robertson Plaza,** you can see the famous **Metropolitan Opera House**, designed by Wallace K. Harrison, also responsible for the United Nations building. The opera house is home to the **Metropolitan Opera,** the world's largest classical music organization. To the right of The Met (as its friends call it) is the **New York Public Library for the Performing Arts,** which is open to the public and provides a large collection of reference materials on dance, music, and theater *(⏰ M noon-8pm, Tu-W 11am-6pm, Th noon-8pm, F 11am-6pm, Sa 10am-6pm)*. To the left of the opera house is the **New York State Theater,** where the **New York City Ballet** and the **New York City**

Opera show their stuff. The **Big Apple Circus** *(☎212-268-2500 💻www.bigapplecircus.org)* occasionally sets up tent in the **Guggenheim Bandshell** within **Damrosch Park** (the nondescript concrete square behind the New York Theater).

The **New York Philharmonic** resides at **Avery Fisher Hall,** to the right of the plaza. To the right of the Opera house are the **Vivian Beaumont Theater** and the **Mitzi E. Newhouse Theater,** which host musicals and plays. Both are situated within an Eero Saarinen-designed glass box.

Across 65th St. is the **Juilliard School,** notable for both its prestige and its prevalence in pop culture. No other performing arts school can boast such distinguished real and imaginary alumni, from **Robin Williams** to **Laura Linney,** Julia Stiles in **Save the Last Dance** to the kids of **High School Musical 3.** The newly designed, space-agey-yet-intimate **Alice Tully Hall** features Juilliard performances and serves as home to the ever innovative **Chamber Music Society of Lincoln Center.** Behind Juilliard is the Samuel B. and David Rose Building, where the **Walter E. Reade Theater** screens foreign movies and artsy film festivals.

*✣ [S] 1 to 66th St. **i** Info booth in Rubenstein Atrium. $ $15, students and seniors $12, under 12 $8. ⏰ Times for tours of theaters and galleries posted every M. Tours are approximately 1¼ hr. and leave from the Rubenstein Atrium. Juilliard Tours are free and leave from the admissions office (on the second floor) M-Th at 11:45am. Call ☎212-799-5000 to make a reservation.*

AMERICAN MUSEUM OF NATURAL HISTORY 👍♿ MUSEUM

Central Park W., between 77th and 81st St. ☎212-769-5200 💻www.amnh.org

Both science fanatics and the rest of us will find something to astonish and excite the nerdy child within among the enormous dinosaur skeletons, priceless jewels, and artifacts from cultures around the world that fill this treasure trove of curiosities. It wouldn't be a visit to the Museum of Natural History without a trip to the 📷**dinosaur halls** to see the T. Rex, triceratops, and brontosaurus (the world's largest free-standing dinosaur!) skeletons. Everything you see in this hall is a real fossil, not a plaster imitation. The Halls of Vertebrate Origins display the largest, most diverse display of vertebrate fossils in the world, including a huge "family tree" of vertebrates dating from up to 500 million years ago. The lower levels contain the halls of African mammals, reptiles and amphibians, and primates, as well as halls dedicated to various world cultures. Among the Polynesian statues and costumes in the Margaret Mead Hall of Pacific People are the red cape and "thumbstick" that the eccentric Mead herself was famous for using. Before you leave, be sure to check out the 87 ft. **Hayden Planetarium, Cosmic Collisions Space Show** and the **Morgan Memorial Hall of Gems,** home of the famous **Star of India.**

✣ [S] B, C to 81st St. $ Suggested donation $16, students and seniors $12, children $9; admission with IMAX film, space show, or special exhibition $24, students and seniors $18, children $14; all-inclusive admission $32, students and seniors $24.50, children $20. ⏰ Open daily 10am-5:45pm, closed Thanksgiving and Christmas. Free tours with admission at 10:15, 11:15am, 12:15, 1:15, 2:15, and 3:15pm; meet at entrance to Akeley Hall of African Mammals. Free audio tours at the Rose Center on the lower level.

NEW YORK HISTORICAL SOCIETY 👍♿ MUSEUM

170 Central Park West at 77th St. ☎212-873-3400 💻www.nyhistory.org

At the **New York Historical Society,** history isn't just Civil War mementos and Tiffany lampshades. In addition to the permanent collection housed on the fourth floor, the society hosts a number of non-traditional, slightly off-beat exhibitions (the 2010 season included an entire show dedicated to the **Grateful Dead**). The society also offers a series of "Distinguished Speaker" lectures, featuring the likes of Stephen Breyer and E. L. Doctorow.

✣ [S] 1, B, C to 81st St. $ $9; seniors, educators, military $9; children under 12 free. Distinguished speaker series, $20 per event. ⏰ Tu-F noon-8pm, Sa 10am-6pm, Su 11am-5:45pm.

TRUMP INTERNATIONAL HOTEL AND TIME WARNER CENTER   ♿ SIGHT
59th St., Columbus Circle

If you're reading this guide, you probably can't afford a room at the Trump International Hotel and Tower. They range from a mere $950 per night to a heftier $3,200. You can still admire the imposing 52-story building from below before heading across the street to the **Time Warner Center,** the home of a power-pack of business offices, condos, restaurants, and shops, as well as a hotel, **Jazz at Lincoln Center** venue, and the Time Warner World Headquarters. A **Whole Foods Market** inhabits the basement, should the mood to do some grocery shopping strike you.

⌗ Ⓢ *1, 9, A, B, C, D to 59th St./Columbus Circle.* ⓘ *Trump Hotel:* ☎*888-448-7867* ▣*www. trumpintl.com; Time Warner Center:* ☎*212-823-6300* ▣*www.shopsatcolumbuscircle.com.* ⌕ *Time Warner Center shops open M-Sa 10am-9pm, Su 11am-7pm.*

morningside heights

▦ CATHEDRAL OF SAINT JOHN THE DIVINE   ♿ CHURCH
1047 Amsterdam Ave., between 110th and 113th St.   ☎212-316-7540 ▣www.stjohndivine.org

The largest cathedral in the world, the **Cathedral of Saint John the Divine** is not your average Gothic church. Take a closer look at the beautiful stained-glass windows in the nave: one depicts a human skeleton and another shows an antique television. You can look as closely as you want at these windows by taking a **Vertical Tour,** which allows you to climb to the top of the cathedral's 124 ft. spiral staircase and even stand on a buttress (it's not a dirty word). *(Call* ☎*866-811-4111 for more information.)* The cathedral provides a venue for hundreds of concerts, most of them free or with a suggested donation. *(Call the box office at* ☎*212/932-7347 for schedule information.)* Outside of the cathedral, the **Children's Sculpture Garden** features works by artists in kindergarten through high school. Since 1985, 12 works are chosen annually to be cast in bronze and included in the garden.

⌗ Ⓢ *1 to Cathedral Parkway.* Ⓢ *Suggested donation $3.* ⌕ *Open daily 7am-6pm. Services M-Sa 8, 8:30am, 12:15, 5pm, Su 8, 9, 11am, 4pm.*

COLUMBIA UNIVERSITY   ♿ UNIVERSITY
Morningside Dr. and Broadway, from 114th and 120th   ☎212-854-4900 ▣www.columbia.edu

Originally chartered as King's College in 1754, the university changed its name during the American Revolution. President Seth Low moved the campus from 49th and Madison to its current location in 1807, feeling that the then-farmland would be a less distracting, "healthier" environment for students and professors. The majestic **Low Library** is named after Old Seth. **Pupin Hall,** just behind the library, is the site where the first atom was split, the first x-ray photo in the United States was taken, FM radio was developed, and of course, the "maser," the awkwardly named precursor to the laser was invented.

⌗ Ⓢ *1 to 116th St./Columbia University.* ⓘ *Groups of 12 or more should call* ☎*212-854-4900 or email kc2173@columbia.edu to make reservations.* ⌕ *Visitor's Center at Low Library open M-F 9am-5pm. Tours 11am and 3pm, information sessions for prospective students 1hr. before.*

GRANT NATIONAL MEMORIAL   MEMORIAL
Near the intersection of Riverside Dr. and 122nd St.   ☎212-666-1640 ▣www.nps.gov/gegr

Ulysses S. Grant led the Union troops to Civil War victory, served as Commander-in-Chief of this fine nation from 1869-1877, and once received a $20 speeding ticket for riding his horse too quickly down a Washington street. Well, this is where he chills now, in his own personal granite casket, next to his wife Julia, who also has her own personal granite casket. The upper level contains a miniature museum with Grant artifacts and memorabilia, including the commemorative spoon that was distributed during the cornerstone laying ceremony in 1892.

⚡ Ⓢ *1 to 125th St./Broadway.* Ⓢ *Free.* 🕐 *Open daily 9am-5pm. Tours at 10, 11am, 2, 3pm.*

RIVERSIDE CHURCH
                             ♿ CHURCH
490 Riverside Dr., at 120th St.   ☎212-870-6700 🖳www.theriversidechurchny.com

If there's one thing they love in Morningside Heights, it's Gothic architecture. The architects who designed Riverside Church were particularly influenced by churches in Chartres, Barcelona, and Gerona. A photograph of Dr. Martin Luther King Jr., who gave his legendary speech condemning the Vietnam War here in 1967, can be found in the Dr. Martin Luther King Junior Wing. The Laura Spelman Rockefeller Memorial Carillon, containing 74 bronze bells and filling five floors, was given to the church by John D. Rockefeller in memory of his mother. Visitors can hear the bells on Sundays at 10:30am and 3pm. Another gift from John, Heinrich Hoffman's famous **Christ in Gethsemane** of 1890, hangs in the **Gethsemane Chapel.**

⚡ Ⓢ *1 to 116th St.* *i* *Meet in the 1 balcony.* Ⓢ *Free.* 🕐 *Open M-Sa 9am-5pm, Su 1-5pm. Services Su 10:45am. Tours after Su services.*

harlem

🏛 APOLLO THEATER
                         ✈♿❄ THEATER ❺
253 W. 125th St.   ☎212-531-5300 🖳www.apollotheater.org

The Apollo has been synonymous with black entertainment for decades; a list of the ultra-famous performers who graced its stage would far exceed our space limitations. Suffice it to say that Ella Fitzgerald got her start and James Brown recorded his most famous album here. Today, the Apollo still features A-list performers—check its website for details—but the most famous and attractive draw is Amateur Night every W, when the young and talented try to hit it big in front of an infamously tough and vocal crowd. Come to boo, hiss, or cheer when appropriate.

⚡ Ⓢ *A, B, C, D to 125th St.* *i* *Tickets also available through Ticketmaster.* Ⓢ *Amateur night tickets $14-25; other prices vary, so check website for details.* 🕐 *Amateur night W 7:30pm.*

CITY COLLEGE
                                  ♿ CAMPUS
Offices at 138th St. and Convent Ave.   ☎212-650-7000 🖳www.ccny.cuny.edu

City College was founded in 1847 to cater to the children of immigrants and the working poor. Its hilltop Harlem campus—where it moved from a downtown location in 1909—has been the undergraduate home to such varied luminaries as Woody Allen and Colin Powell. In the 1920s and 30s it spawned most of the so-called "New York Intellectuals," children of Jewish immigrants who went on to have a significant impact on American literary and political life. Sleek, modern buildings mingle with Gothic structures built using rusty schist in an effort to establish the college as a "workingman's school."

⚡ Ⓢ *1 to 37th St. Campus stretches from 130th to 140th St. Enter at 138th St.* *i* *Call admissions for campus tour info.*

ABYSSINIAN BAPTIST CHURCH
                                 ♿ CHURCH
132 W. 138th St./Odell Clark Pl.   ☎212-862-7474 🖳www.abyssinian.org

In a neighborhood where seemingly every block has its own small church, the Abyssinian Baptist Church stands out with striking Gothic architecture and a rich history. Founded in 1808 by free Ethiopians forced to sit in a segregated section of New York's First Baptist Church, the Abyssinian, named after Ethiopia's archaic name, moved to its present location in 1923. Adam Clayton Powells Sr. and Jr. were pastors here; the latter represented Harlem as the first African-

sights

American in the House of Representatives. Nat King Cole was married in the church, and the prominent black composer W.C. Handy had his funeral here. The church remains at the center of the neighborhood's spiritual life under Reverend Calvin Butts, and a renowned gospel choir delivers the standards weekly. Sunday morning crowds are bounteous, so get here early and don't forget to wear your Sunday best.

🚶 Ⓢ 2, 3 to 135th St. *i* *Proper attire required.* 🕑 *Services W 6pm, Su 9 and 11am.*

MARCUS GARVEY PARK
ⓓ PARK

120th-124th St. between 5th and Madison Ave.　　🖥nycgovparks.org/parks/marcusgarveypark

Exploring Harlem can get exhausting quick, and Marcus Garvey Park is an ideal resting spot near the neighborhood's southern edge. Named after the prominent leader of the early 20th century "Back to Africa" movement, the park is full of locals playing, picnicking, and lounging beneath its shady trees. Best of all are the groups of old men who congregate along 124th St. listening to soul from boom boxes or open cars. After the catch-all, city-wide feel of Central Park, Marcus Garvey provides a reassuring dose of neighborhood intimacy.

🚶 Ⓢ 2, 3 to 116th St. or 125th St.

ISLAMIC CULTURAL CENTER OF NEW YORK
ⓓ RELIGIOUS SITE

1711 3rd Ave.　　☎212-722-5234

This mammoth structure in East Harlem was New York's first building designed as a mosque. Completed in 1991 after decades of wrangling and delays, it now welcomes about 4000 worshipers weekly. Visiting hours vary greatly, and it may be difficult to get in during certain hours; check the entrance on E. 97th St.

🚶 Ⓢ 6 to 96th St. 🕑 *Prayers F 1pm in summer, 12:30pm in winter.*

SCHOMBERG CENTER FOR RESEARCH IN BLACK CULTURE
ⓓ LIBRARY, MUSEUM

515 Malcolm X Avenue　　☎212-491-2200 🖥nypl.org/locations/schomburg

The popular and hugely valuable Schomburg Center is a true goldmine of documents and exhibits on African and African-American culture. A steady rotating cycle of exhibits from art shows to one-man plays keeps things fresh, but it's the enormous archival collection—its earliest sections were donated by black scholar Arturo Schomburg to the New York Public Library's Harlem branch in 1926—that truly impresses. Over five million documents are stored here, including those of Malcom X, Nat King Cole, and Marcus Garvey (original recordings of his celebrated speeches are on hand), as well as centuries-old oral histories and artworks.

🚶 Ⓢ 2, 3 to 135th St. *i* *See website for events schedule.* Ⓢ *Free admission to exhibits, but donations welcome.* 🕑 *Open M-W noon-8pm, Th-F 11am-6pm, Sa 10am-5pm.*

brooklyn

WILLIAMSBURG AND GREENPOINT

🖾 BROOKLYN BREWERY
ⓓ 🍺 BREWERY

79 North 11th St.　　☎718-486-7422 🖥www.brooklynbrewery.com

Founded in 1987 by a reporter and a banker, Brooklyn Brewery continues to brew the ubiquitous Brooklyn Lager and Brooklyn Brown Ale. One of the few factories in Williamsburg still operating, the Brewery is generous enough to open its doors to the public on weekends. Get some beer straight from the source—and give your evening a jump-start—at Friday night happy hours. The very curious can get their kicks with the free tours Saturday and Sunday, complete with a free beer at the end.

⚡ Ⓢ *L to Bedford Ave.* Ⓢ *Happy hour beer $4 each or 6 for $20.* ⏰ *Happy hour F 6-11pm; brewery open Sa noon-8pm, Su noon-6pm; tours Sa hourly 1-5pm, Su hourly 1-4pm.*

williamsburg galleries

Williamsburg's thriving art scene has garnered much attention over the past decade, but even as the cutting edge makes its way inland, the neighborhood's numerous small galleries are still featuring challenging, varied works from both rising and established names. Check ◼ **www.freewilliamsburg.com** for a complete listing of galleries.

RUSSIAN ORTHODOX CATHEDRAL OF THE TRANSFORMATION OF OUR LORD
CHURCH

228 North 12th St.   ◼ www.roct.org

Northwestern Brooklyn's history as a center for Eastern European immigration lives on in the Polish neighborhood of Greenpoint to Williamsburg's north, but this towering cathedral by McCaffern Park still thrives after almost a century. Built between 1916 and 1922, the cathedral's Greek-cross plan is housed in a distinctive yellow brick wall exterior and topped by towering domes, a striking contrast to the stark urban setting around it.

⚡ Ⓢ *L to Bedford Ave.* ⏰ *Vespers Sa 6pm; divine liturgy Su 9am.*

PIEROGI   ♿ GALLERY

177 N. 9th Street   ☎718-599-2144 ◼ www.pierogi2000.com

Pierogi has become one of Williamsburg's most acclaimed galleries thanks to eclectic shows—two per month simultaneously shown—by artists like Lawrence Wiener, Gene Oldfield, Ken Weathersby, and Sarah Walker. Appropriately, pierogis and even vodka enliven the openings each month. The gallery provides "flatfiles," or bundled collections of each artist's work, for browsing; they're also online in a searchable database on the gallery's website.

⚡ Ⓢ *L to Bedford Ave.* ⏰ *Open Tu-Su 11am-6pm.*

CAUSEY CONTEMPORARY AND WILLIAMSBURG   ♿ GALLERY

92 Wythe Ave.   ☎718-218-8939 ◼ www.causeycontemporary.com

A large, factory-like space is divided in two to feature roughly two artists each month (10 per year). The result feels wonderfully uncluttered and direct. The focus is on painting, sculpture, and photography.

⚡ Ⓢ *L to Bedford Ave.* ⏰ *Open M 9am-5pm, W-Sa 11am-7pm, Su noon-6pm.*

PARKER'S BOX   ♿ GALLERY

193 Grand St.   ☎718-388-2882 ◼ www.parkersbox.com

One of the neighborhood's most cosmopolitan galleries, Parker's Box features a variety of exhibitions, from performance art to mixed media to painting, sculpture, and photography.

⚡ Ⓢ *L to Bedford Ave. or J, M, Z to Marcy Ave.* ⏰ *Open Th-Su 1-7pm.*

FULTON LANDING AND DUMBO

ST. ANN'S WAREHOUSE   ♿❄ THEATER

38 Water St.   ☎718-254-8779 ◼ www.stannswarehouse.org

Just steps from the river, St. Ann's attracts some of the most challenging and adventurous performance programming in the city. Prices are usually steep, but the shows are worth it. Events are occasionally musical, but experimental theater is the focus, whether it's a puppet theater festival or an acclaimed drama. It has become a DUMBO favorite ever since moving here from St. Ann's and the Holy Trinity Episcopal Church in 2000.

[S] F to York St. $ Tickets $20-30. ⏰ Showtimes vary; check website for show details.

GALAPAGOS ART SPACE ♿ ❄ THEATER

16 Main St. ☎718-222-8500 💻www.galapagosartspace.com

Galapagos, which arrived here in the early 2000s from Williamsburg, prides itself on its bizarre, sometimes indescribable shows. There's a weekly floating cabaret show, for one. Other performances are devoted to dance, theater, film, music, and the visual arts, ranging from circus acts to contemporary opera productions to indie rock concerts. The building recently became totally green and features several levels. The first floor is a bar and lounge area, while above, the performance space and a 1600 sq. ft. indoor lake await. And, of course, the river is just down the block.

[S] F to York St. or A, C to High St. Walk to Main St. between Plymouth and Water St. $ Tickets free-$20. Check website for individual performance details. ⏰ Performance times vary; most begin 8-10pm.

BROOKLYN BRIDGE PARK PARK

1 Main St. ☎718-802-0603 💻www.brooklynbridgepark.org

Brooklyn Bridge Park is still a work in progress. By project's end, planners hope to have reclaimed about 4 mi. of coast for the park. What exists today isn't bad, though it is segmented. The Cove, in between Manhattan and Brooklyn Bridges at the end of Main St., is a rocky outpost by the river with grassy areas, benches, and a small strip of beach. Pier 1, just south of the Brooklyn Bridge, is a brand-new addition that offers stunning views of the bridge and the skyline beyond. Check out the outdoor Movies With a View series to see films projected in front of the (no doubt distracting) urban vista.

[S] F to York St. or A, C to High St.

VINEGAR HILL NEIGHBORHOOD

Between the East River, Front St., the Brooklyn Navy Yard, and Bridge St.

If you thought DUMBO was a tiny neighborhood, check out diminutive Vinegar Hill to the north by the Brooklyn Navy Yard. Just a few blocks in size, this quiet corner of Brooklyn features some beautifully preserved 19th-century Federal-style buildings along cobblestone streets. There are plenty of warehouses and other industrial accoutrements nearby, so the quaintness shouldn't get to you. The neighborhood was named after a battle during the Irish Rebellion of 1798 to attract Irish laborers working at the neighboring Navy Yard.

[S] F to York St.

BROOKLYN HEIGHTS AND DOWNTOWN BROOKLYN

BROOKLYN HEIGHTS PROMENADE WALKS

Between Remsen and Orange St. by the East River

The best views of the Manhattan skyline can be had from this elevated riverside walkway. Sweeping views of the borough, along with the impressive expanse of the Brooklyn Bridge and the Manhattan Bridge behind it, draw crowds of tourists and locals when the weather is right. The **Statue of Liberty** is easily visible across the way. To best enjoy this collection of dozens of postcards rolled into one, try the many benches along the way. Come on July 4 for amazing, front-row seats to the East River fireworks display.

[S] 2, 3 to Clark St.

BROOKLYN HISTORICAL SOCIETY

⊷❉ MUSEUM

128 Pierrepoint St. (at Clinton St.) ☎718-222-4111 ⬛www.brooklynhistory.org

Brooklyn's fascinating history is encapsulated on the three floors of the Society's beautiful red-brick building, completed in 1881 and full of ornate facade flourishes. Most of the exhibits are present on a rotating basis. Some recent ones included photographic exhibits on the Tivoli Towers in Crown Heights and several collection of Dodgers memorabilia. You'll probably run into a great deal of Dodgers nostalgia, but it's the whole diverse sweep of Brooklyn history that's really on hand.

❀ Ⓢ 2, 3 to Clark St. or M, R to Court St.-Borough Hall. Ⓢ $6, students $4. ⏱ Open W-F noon-5pm, Sa 10am-5pm, Su noon-5pm.

PLYMOUTH CHURCH HOUSE OF THE PILGRIMS

❀❉ CHURCH

75 Hicks St. (at Orange St.) ☎718-624-4743 ⬛www.plymouthchurch.org

There's a lot of history in this large but unassuming structure in quiet Brooklyn Heights. The church was founded in 1847, and Henry Ward Beecher, brother of *Uncle Tom's Cabin* author Harriet Beecher Stowe, served as its first pastor. Beecher's fervent, dramatic sermons against slavery—he would even imitate a slave auctioneer to encourage audience members to purchase the freedom of actual slaves—drew huge crowds and an even larger reputation as a center for abolitionism. The church backed its words up with action, and it soon became known as the Grand Central Depot on the Underground Railroad. Abraham Lincoln attended a service after delivering his famous speech at Cooper Union in 1860. His pew is marked with a silver plaque. Hours are restricted and snagging a tour requires advance effort, but the rich history of the church warrants it.

❀ Ⓢ 2, 3 to Clark St. ⏱ Church offices open M-F 9am-5pm. Services Su 11am. Call ahead for tours, available M-F 10am-4pm, Su noon-4pm.

NEW YORK TRANSIT MUSEUM (MTA)

⊷❉ MUSEUM

Boerum Pl. and Schermerhorn St. ☎718-694-1600 ⬛www.mta.info/mta/museum

The entrance to the MTA's own museum is a discontinued Subway entrance; the rest of the underground museum may not be as ingenious, but it is fascinating in its revealing look at the everyday work of the city's public transport system. You can check out the different fares charged throughout the decades (5 cents?!) and check out an artificial street intersection, complete with historical examples of traffic lights, buses, and trolleys. A collection of photos, videos, and text pays tribute to the builders of the Subway system.

❀ Ⓢ 2, 3, 4, 5 to Borough Hall; A, C, F to Jay St.-Borough Hall; 2, 3, to Hoyt St.; A, C, G to Hoyt-Schermerhorn St. Ⓢ Admission $5. ⏱ Open Tu-F 10am-4pm, Sa-Su noon-5pm.

ST. ANN AND THE HOLY TRINITY EPISCOPAL CHURCH

 CHURCH

157 Montague and Clinton St. ☎718-875-6960 ⬛www.stannandtheholytrinity.org

Built between 1844 and 1848, this majestic church is one of the finest examples of Gothic Revival architecture in the country. The highlight is the 55 stained glass windows, the earliest examples of their kind in the United States (and still widely considered the best of their time). The truncated tower is a distinctive landmark. Back when there was a spire, it was used as a navigation mark by sailors. The church was unused and fell into disrepair during the 1960s, but St. Ann's Parish transferred in 1970 and refurbished the building. Previous occupants included a St. Ann's School and a St. Ann's Warehouse, the experimental theater company that the church housed before the company relocated to their DUMBO warehouse in 2000.

❀ Ⓢ M, R to Court St.-Borough Hall; 2, 3, 4, 5 to Borough Hall. ⏱ Open M-F noon-2pm. Su services 11am.

WILLOW STREET NOS. 155-159

ARCHITECTURE

Willow St. between Clark and Pierrepont St.

This preserved set of row houses, dating from the early 1830s, are aesthetic highlights in a neighborhood full of stiff competition. They are some of the oldest examples of Federal-style architecture in the city.

⚏ Ⓢ *2, 3 to Clark St.*

BOROUGH HALL

&. ❄ ARCHITECTURE

209 Joralemon St. (at Fulton St. Mall)   ☎718-802-3700 🖰www.brooklyn-usa.org

Once the stately city hall of sovereign Brooklyn in the 19th century, this 1849 structure is now merely Borough Hall. That doesn't change the fact that magnificent seating can be had on its steps, perfect for wolfing down that halal food. Brooklyn diehards can check out the tourist center outside for maps, memorabilia, and mementos.

⚏ Ⓢ *2, 3, 4, 5 to Borough Hall or M, R to Court St.-Borough Hall or A, C, F to Jay St.-Borough Hall.*
⌚ *Open M-F 9am-5pm.*

PARK SLOPE AND PROSPECT PARK

▨ PROSPECT PARK

PARK

W. Flatbush Ave., Ocean Ave., Parkside Ave.   ☎718-965-8951 🖰www.prospectpark.org

Designed by Frederick Law Olmsted and Calvert Vaux soon after their completion of Central Park, 585 acre Prospect Park is a true oasis of green space in the heart of Brooklyn. Central Park may be better known and more frequently visited, but Olmsted and Vaux considered this their crowning achievement. Unlike Manhattan's offering, Prospect Park lets you easily forget the city while walking through its forests, meadows, and lakes.

To the North, at Grand Army Plaza designed by Olmsted and Vaux as the park's main entrance, the Soldiers' and Sailors' Memorial Arch leads visitors to the Long Meadow, a 1 mi. stretch of unbroken field filled with sunbathers, Frisbee throwers, and their extended families. To the south is the Ravine, where Brooklyn's only forest grows around a steep gorge. The **Lefferts Historic House,** built in the 1700s by a Dutch family, includes items and relics of Brooklyn's history since pre-Colonial days among its preserved rooms. The imposing turrets of the **Litchfield Villa,** built in the mid-1800s and now a headquarters for the Parks and Recreation department, rise above the west edge of the park at 95 Prospect Park W. near 5th St. The Prospect Park Bandshell is the site of the Celebrate Brooklyn Festival, a series of free, first-come, first-served shows held throughout June, July, and August. The festival's focus is musical, but the Bandshell also boasts an enormous movie screen just in case. The large Prospect Park Lake yawns across the park's southern half. The **Audubon Center** and the park's Visitor Center are located in a large, historic boathouse along its "Lullwater." North of the boathouse, the **Prospect Park Zoo** includes 400 animals of 80 species, including wallabies, a red panda, a tamarin, and assorted other birds, amphibians, mammals, and reptiles. At the park's center is the **Nethermead,** a wide meadow that is more isolated and thus less crowded than the Long Meadow. The **Kensington Stables** provide horses for rental from 10am to sunset. The Wollman Rink is available for pedal boating in summer and ice skating in winter. The **Prospect Park Tennis Center,** in the Parade Ground at the park's southern edge, provides indoor and outdoor courts.

⚏ Ⓢ *2, 3 to Grand Army Plaza; F to 15th St./Prospect Park; B, Q, S to Prospect Park.* Ⓢ *Lefferts Historic House, Litchfield Villa, and the Audubon Center free. Zoo admission Jan-June $7, July-Dec $8. Group lessons at Kensington Stables $47 per hr., private lessons $57 per hr. Rides $25 per hr. Pedal boating on Wollman Rink $15, ice skating $5, skate rentals $6.50. Tennis Center*

Imagine you're in a big city and you're looking to party. In a typical urban metropolis, you might use public transportation to get to that party. You could board the train or bus decked out in your festive attire and get off at the stop closest to your social gathering. But New York is not your typical big city. In New York, public transportation is the party.

According to Wikipedia, the tradition of the Subway party dates back to the opening of the New York Subway system in 1904, at which citizens wore tuxedoes and top hats and drank champagne to celebrate the occasion. In the 1980s and 90s, the nightclub-hopping, ecstasy-popping Club Kids often used Subway cars as a venue for their general merrymaking. Today, Subway party culture is going strong, with websites such as yelp, Facebook, and MySpace making it easier than ever to spread the word about parties.

Subway parties come in all shapes and sizes, from themed costume parties to crazy ragers with loud music and dancing. Traditionally, they occur on the last car, with party attendees meeting at a designated stop and riding through the line together.

court rates: $7 per person per hr., 7-11am $40 per hr. ⏰ Lefferts Historic House open June Th-Su noon-5pm, July-Aug Th-Su noon-6pm, Sept Th-Su noon-5pm, Oct-Nov Sa-Su noon-5pm. Litchfield Villa open M-F 9am-5pm. Audubon Center open June-Aug Th-Su noon-5pm, Sep-Nov Sa-Su noon-4pm. Prospect Park Zoo open Mar 27-Oct M-F 10am-5pm, Sa-Su 10am-5:30pm, Nov-Apr 1 daily 10am-4:30pm. Kensington Stables open daily 10am-sunset. Pedal boating on Wollman Rink open June Th-Su noon-5pm, July-Aug Th-Su noon-6pm, Sept Th-Su noon-5pm, first half of Oct Th-Su noon-5pm. Ice skating on Wollmann Rink open Nov-Mar, hours vary. Tennis Center open daily 7am-11pm.

sights

🏛 BROOKLYN BOTANIC GARDENS
PARK, BOTANIC GARDENS

Main entrance 1000 Washington St. ☎718-623-7200 🌐bbg.org

Founded in 1910 on a reclaimed waste dump, the Brooklyn Botanic Gardens stretch over 52 acres and feature 10,000 taxa of plants. Far smaller than the New York Botanic Garden in the Bronx, the BBG still manage to pack in the sights. The **Cranford Rose Garden** includes 1400 species of rose. The beautiful **Cherry Esplanade** and the nearby **Cherry Walk** are filled with cherry trees donated to the park by the Japanese government. The Japanese Hill-and-Pond Garden is a beautiful collection of different landscapes in the Japanese tradition, with Japanese architectural touches for extra authenticity. In spring, these three areas hold the **Sakura Matsuri Festival** to celebrate the blossoming of the cherry trees. The Shakespeare Garden includes 80 species of plant mentioned in the playwright's works (with appropriate quotes). The **Bluebell Wood,** south of the **Cherry Esplanade,** blooms into azure glory around May. The Steinhardt Conservatory presents climate-controlled exhibits on Earth's different ecosystems. Just outside, the **Lily Pool Terrace** displays almost 100 species of water lily and other aquatic plants. A small Herb Garden specializes in all plants edible.

⚐ Ⓢ S to Botanic Garden; B, Q, S to Prospect Park; 2, 3, to Eastern Parkway/Brooklyn Museum. Ⓢ $8, students $4. ⏰ Tu-F 8am-6pm, Sa-Su 10am-6pm.

🏛 BROOKLYN MUSEUM
⚐♿❄♨🔊 MUSEUM

200 Eastern Pkwy. ☎718-638-5000 🌐www.brooklynmuseum.org

New York's second-largest art museum, after you-know-what, is still one of the largest in the country. Its collections span the millennia from ancient Egyptian works to the newest and boldest contemporary art. Opened in 1897, the museum structure is an imposing steel frame building on the northern edge of Prospect Park.

The large **Rubin Pavilion** and **Lobby**—recently outfitted with an open-air space above—gives way to exhibits of African art, the first of their kind in the US when they appeared in 1923. The second floor features East Asian, Southeast Asian, and Islamic Art. The third floor is focused on ancient Egyptian exhibits, probably the museum's main claim to fame; only the British Museum in London and the Egyptian Museum in Cairo have more extensive collections. Next door, European paintings are fittingly organized around the large Beaux Arts Court, a striking concert and private event space with a glass-brick floor, arches, and chandeliers. The fourth floor focuses on contemporary art; the Elizabeth A. Sackler Center for Feminist Art includes Judy Chicago's landmark *Dinner Table*, now on permanent display. The Luce Center for American Art claims most of the space on the fifth floor. The museum's **Target First Saturdays** open up the museum on Saturday nights. On these nights, you can tour the exhibits for free, watch performances in the Rubin Lobby, or listen and dance to DJs spinning in the Beaux Arts Court. It's a unique experience, but the massive crowds obviously distract from the art. If the art's your focus, plan on a daytime visit.

⚏ Ⓢ *2, 3 to Eastern Parkway-Brooklyn Museum.* Ⓢ *$10, students $6. 1st Sa of each month free 5-11pm.* Ⓩ *Open W-F 10am-5pm, Sa-Su 11am-6pm. 1st Sa of each month 11am-11pm.*

BROOKLYN PUBLIC LIBRARY   ♿ ❄(ᵖ)   LIBRARY

10 Grand Army Plaza   ☎718-230-2100 █www.brooklynpubliclibrary.org

The main branch of the Brooklyn Public Library presides over Grand Army Plaza. The building itself is a mammoth gray structure with a curved facade—very Art Deco (it opened in its present form in 1941). Inside are over one million items, from books to magazines to anything else. The highlight is the Brooklyn Collection, which gathers together memorabilia from throughout the borough's history. The S. Stevan Dweck Center for Contemporary Culture is a new auditorium that holds lectures, readings, and other events throughout the year.

⚏ Ⓢ *2, 3 to Grand Army Plaza. Walk to the corner of Flatbush Ave. and Eastern Pkwy.* Ⓩ *Open M 9am-6pm, Tu-Th 9am-9pm, F 9am-6pm, Sa 10am-6pm, Su 1-5pm.*

SUNSET PARK AND GREEN-WOOD CEMETERY

GREEN-WOOD CEMETERY   ✈⚰ CEMETERY

Main entrance at 5th Ave. and 25th St.   ☎718-768-7300 █www.green-wood.com

This enormous, 478 acre cemetery just southwest of Prospect Park is a quiet green space that rivals its massive neighbor for sheer isolation from the urban environment nearby. Immaculately designed (it was modeled after the landmark Mt. Auburn Cemetery in Cambridge, MA) and spacious enough to warrant a few visits, Green-Wood was established in 1838 and still celebrates a pastoral American romanticism in its lush landscapes and peaceful paths. In the second half of the 1800s it was *the* burial place of choice for New York's upper crust and even became one of the country's top tourist attractions. Famous residents among the 600,000 internees include **Leonard Bernstein, FAO Schwartz, Boss Tweed,** and **Charles Ebbets** (owner of the ⬡**Brooklyn Dodgers**).

⚏ Ⓢ *M,R to 25th St.* Ⓢ *Free.* Ⓩ *Labor Day to Memorial Day weekend open daily 8am-5pm; Memorial Day weekend to Labor Day open daily 7am-7pm.*

CONEY ISLAND AND BRIGHTON BEACH

👍 CONEY ISLAND — THEME PARK, BEACH

Most attractions along Surf Ave. and Riegelmann Boardwalk 🖥www.coneyisland.com

America's most famous playground is not nearly as grand or popular as in its *fin de siècle* heyday, but it retains a scruffy, nostalgic charm. Its storied past lives on most memorably in two ancient rides: the **Wonder Wheel,** *(W 12th St. and Boardwalk ☎718-372-2592 🖥www.wonderwheel.com),* a 150ft. tall Ferris wheel built in 1920 and distinguished by two separate rings of passengers cars (it's now the centerpiece of Deno's Wonder Wheel Park), and the world-famous **Cyclone** *(W. 10th St. and Boardwalk or Surf Ave. ☎718-372-7099 🖥www.coneyislandcyclone.com),* a wooden roller coaster built in 1927. Those looking for more modern thrills can check out the brand-new **Luna Park** *(1000 Surf Ave. at W. 10th St. ☎718-373-5862 🖥www.lunaparknyc.com),* a small but richly packed theme park with intense rides like the **Electro Wheel,** which spins you around while inclining and declining a curved rail, and the dizzying **Air Race,** which spins you around in about three simultaneous ways (only the most interesting paths of projectile vomit for the Coney Island devotees).

Those interested in the park's history should check out the upstairs **Coney Island Museum** *(1208 Surf Ave. at W. 12th St. ☎718-372-5159 🖥www.coneyisland.com/museum.shtml),* a small, ultra-cheap, and endearingly shabby top-floor collection of memorabilia from eras past. Old posters, photos, postcards, bumper cars, and other recovered items clutter the museum, and a fascinating documentary on the area's history is worth watching in its entirety. In the same building, **Sideshows by the Seashore** *(1208 Surf Ave. at W. 12th St. ☎718-372-5159 🖥www.coneyisland.com/museum.shtml)* continues another iconic Coney Island tradition, presenting bearded ladies, contortionists, mermaids, sword swallowers, and others in the noble "freak" tradition. Catch burlesque at the beach shows there Thursday and Friday nights in the summer. Inquire at the desk or go online for info on "Sideshow School" classes.

The Coney Island Beach has drawn huge summer crowds for well over a century. Stoll along the **Riegelmann Boardwalk,** which stretches along the coast for 2½ mi. from W. 37th St. to Corbin Pl. in Brighton Beach, to experience the neighborhood's bustling main street, lined with food stands, restaurants, bars, and the occasional "shoot the freak" contest.

If you can, visit during Coney Island holidays. The **Mermaid Parade** in June includes antique cars, raunchy floats, animals, and many costumes. *The Village Voice's* **Siren Music Festival,** held in July, draws huge crowds to free indie and experimental rock concerts.

⇄ [S] D, F, N, Q to Coney Island-Stillwell Ave. Ⓢ Wonder Wheel $6 per ride. Cyclone $8 per ride. Luna Park: individual rides $3-5, 4hr. unlimited-ride pass $26. Coney Island Museum $1. Sideshows by the Seashore $7.50. Burlesque shows Th $10, F $15. ⏰ Deno's Wonder Wheel Park open Memorial Day-Labor Day daily 11am-midnight; Sept-Oct and Apr-May Sa-Su noon-9pm. Cyclone open May 14-Labor Day daily noon-11pm; April 7-mid-May and Labor Day-Sept weekends noon-11pm. Luna Park open June-Sept M-F noon-midnight, Sa-Su 11am-midnight. Coney Island Museum open early June-early Sept Th-Su noon-5pm; Sept-May Sa-Su noon-5pm. Sideshows by the Seashore open M-F 1-8pm, Sa-Su 1-9pm. Burlesque shows May-Sept Th 9pm, F 10pm.

NEW YORK AQUARIUM — 🎟♿❄ AQUARIUM

602 Surf Ave. ☎718-265-3474 🖥www.nyaquarium.com

A key Coney Island attraction since 1957, New York's 🗺**Aquarium** is one of the best in the country. Over 8000 extraordinarily diverse animals live here, from the usual suspects (seals, whales, sharks) to bizarre species of fish and turtles. The spacious facilities also include an Aquatheater showcasing the stunts of California sea lions. A new Planet Earth 4D theater just outside the entrance offers all-encompassing visual and audio presentations of aquatic life.

⚓ Ⓢ F, Q to W 8th St.-NY Aquarium. Ⓢ $13, 4-D theater entrance $6, full package $17. ⏱ Memorial Day-Labor Day open M-F 10am-6pm, Sa-Su 10am-7pm; Labor Day-Halloween open M-F 10am-5pm, Sa-Su 10am-5:30pm; Nov-Apr open daily 10am-4:30pm.

MCU PARK
⚓♿♺♻ BASEBALL STADIUM

1904 Surf Ave. (at W. 17th St.) ☎718-507-8499 ▣www.brooklyncyclones.com

The Dodgers are long gone, but the minor-league ⓆBrooklyn Cyclones, affiliated with the NY Mets, have been attracting locals since their debut in 2001. The 7500-seat stadium itself, until recently known as Keyspan Park, provides views of Coney Island's attractions and does its best to fit in with the neon lights and bold colors.

⚓ Ⓢ D, F, N, Q to Coney Island-Stillwell Ave. ⓘ Mets tickets also available at the ticket office. Ⓢ Seats $8-17. ⏱ Season runs from mid-June to early Sept; game times vary. Ticket office open M-F 9am-5pm, Sa-Su 11am-4pm.

queens

Queens in its enormity is home to a variety of exciting sights for people with all types of interests. Jazz enthusiasts will be pleased to find out that many jazz greats, from Billie Holiday to Louis Armstrong have lived in Queens. Queens College runs the Louis Armstrong House Museum in Corona (Queens Jazz Trail Map: ▣www.ephemerapress.com/queens.html). The lobby of Flushing Town Hall is filled with autographed photos of jazz stars who have also performed there.

For those who love art, Astoria and Long Island City are must-sees. The ▨Museum of the Moving Image and P.S.1 Contemporary Art Center are not to be missed. Finally, sports fans will be completely in their element at Flushing Meadows Corona Park, home to Citi Field where the Mets Play and the USTA National Tennis Center, the sight of the US Open. No matter your proverbial bag, there's something in Queens for you.

ASTORIA AND LONG ISLAND CITY

▨ P.S.1 CONTEMPORARY ART CENTER
⚓♿ MUSEUM

22-25 Jackson Ave., at 46th Ave. ☎718-784-2084 ▣www.ps1.org

Located within what was once a school building, P.S.1 is now an exhibition for the newest, hottest, and weirdest in contemporary art. Installation pieces on the stairwells and top floor, including works by William Kentridge and James Turrell, form the center's only "permanent collection." The exhibitions throughout the rest of the gallery, featuring everything from video to installation art to performance art, change roughly every four months. Note: hanging out at P.S. 1 is a sure-fire way to increase your hipster street cred.

⚓ Ⓢ 7 to 45th Rd./Courthouse Sq.; E, V to 23rd St.-Ely Ave.; G to 21st St./Jackson Ave. Ⓢ Suggested contribution adults $10, students and seniors $5. ⏱ Open M, Th-Su noon-6pm.

▨ AMERICAN MUSEUM OF THE MOVING IMAGE
⚓♿ MUSEUM

35th Ave., at 36th St., Astoria ☎718-784-0077 ▣www.movingimage.us

An entire museum dedicated to the material culture of moving images. That means they have the fur coat Renée Zellweger wore in Chicago and the Gumby costume Eddie Murphy wore on Saturday Night Live. They have old cameras and kinetoscopes and functioning theaters that mimic the movie palaces of the 1920s. They even have an assortment of classic video game machines that you can play (4 tokens for $1). In early 2011, the museum will finish an expansion project designed by architect Thomas Leeser that will double its previous size. New features will include a 264-seat theater, a 68-seat screening room, more gallery space for interactive art, and classrooms.

⚓ Ⓢ G, R, V to Steinway St. Walk 1 block down Steinway St., turn right on 35th Ave. Ⓢ $7. ⏱ Open Tu-F 10am-3pm.

SOCRATES SCULPTURE PARK

♿ PARK

At the end of Broadway, across the Vernon Blvd. Intersection. ☎718-956-1819 🖥www.socratessculpturepark.org

A public park and installation space which also hosts a series of educational events to inform the public on useful themes such as how to make paper and how to properly decorate your bicycle. The **Summer Solstice Celebration** *(June 21)* is popular, as is the **Outdoor Cinema** series *(W at 7pm)*. A complete listing of events, festivals, and markets can be found on the website. All events are free.

[S] N, W to Broadway. $ Free. ⏰ Open daily 10am-dusk.

ELMHURST AND CORONA

LOUIS ARMSTRONG'S HOUSE

HISTORICAL SIGHT

34-56 107th St. ☎718-478-8274 🖥www.satchmo.net

From 1943 to 1971, jazz hero Louis Armstrong could have lived anywhere in the world, but he chose to spend the last 28 years of his life in Corona, Queens with his fourth wife, Lucille. Whether it's because of the luxurious bathroom where Armstrong posed for a 1971 Time Magazine article, the study where he indexed all his music, or the kitchen where he cooked his favorite dish, red beans and rice, is unclear, but visitors inevitably come out of the 40min. tour feeling like they have a new friend. Recordings of Armstrong's scratchy voice that fill the rooms on the tour make him seem omnipresent. They also convey his affinity for Brussels sprouts and surprising appreciation of the Beatles ("If they'd only get a haircut...").

[S] 7 to 103rd St. $ $8; students, seniors, and ages under 12 $6; under 4 free. ⏰ Tours every hr. Tu-F 10am-4pm, Sa noon-4pm. Garden and visitors' center open until 5pm.

FLUSHING

QUEENS MUSEUM OF ART

♿ MUSEUM

Flushing Meadows/Corona Park ☎718-592-9700 🖥www.queensmuseum.org

The Queens Museum of Art presents an unlikely marriage of exhibitions by contemporary artists and memorabilia from the 1939-40 and 1964-65 World's Fair. The star attraction is a 1:1200 (1 in.=100 mi.) scale model of New York City created for the 1964-65 World's Fair by Robert Moses and Raymond Lester. Viewers originally enjoyed the panorama from a simulated "helicopter ride" within an enclosed balcony above the model. Binoculars are available at the gift shop so that you can find your favorite street or building.

[S] 7 to Willets Point/Shea Stadium or 111th St. $ Suggested donation $5, students and seniors $2.50, ages under 5 free. ⏰ Open W-Su noon-6pm, tours Su 2, 3 and 4pm.

FLUSHING TOWN HALL

♿ CULTURAL CENTER

137-35 Northern Blvd. ☎718-463-7700 🖥www.flushingtownhall.org

Since it was built in 1862, the Flushing Town Hall has changed hands several times. Now run by the **Flushing Council on Culture and the Arts,** the center is one part concert venue and gallery, one part educational facility, and one part support system for the local artists, who are allowed to use the hall's Steinway pianos and sell their wares in the gift shop. The hall hosts a wide range of performances, many of them free or at budget prices. The entrance and stairwell are filled with autographed pictures of just about every jazz artist you could name, all of whom performed here.

[S] 7 to Flushing/Main St. $ Suggested donation $5. Tickets for concerts and events $5-$50. Student tickets available. ⏰ Box office open M-F 10am-5pm, Sa-Su 2hr before performances. Building open to public Sa-Su noon-5pm.

QUEENS BOTANICAL GARDEN

♿ NATURE PRESERVE

43-50 Main St. ☎718-886-3800 🖥www.queensbotanical.org

Located in the heart of Flushing, the Queens Botanical Garden is a colorful palette of floral goodness. Highlights include a **Rose Garden,** an **Ornamental Grass Garden**, and a **Bee Garden** where honey is made before your very eyes! Treat your nose to a **Kaltman Family Fragrance Walk,** which is lined with particularly fragrant plants. Information about guided tours and events can be found in the visitors' center (on your right when you use the Main St. entrance).

⚡ Ⓢ 7 to Main Street/Flushing. ⑤ $4, seniors $3, students and ages 3-12 $2. Free W 3-6pm, Su 4-6pm. 🕐 Open Apr 1-Oct 31 Tu-Su 8am-6pm; Nov 1-Mar 31 Tu-Su 8am-4:30pm.

UNISPHERE
♿ MONUMENT
In Flushing Meadows/Corona Park ☎718-760-6565 💻www.nycparks.org

This 140 ft., 700,000 lb. model of the Earth was erected in honor of the **New York World's Fair** in 1964, when space travel was the hot new thing. Rising 12 stories high, **Unisphere** is the largest world model ever created. Gilbert D. Clarke may not have anticipated the development, but it has also become Queens' signature monument.

⚡ Ⓢ 7 to Willets Point/Shea Stadium or 111th St. ⑤ Free. 🕐 Open daily.

CITI FIELD
♿ ⚾ BASEBALL STADIUM
Roosevelt Ave. ☎718-507-8499 💻newyork.mets.mlb.com

The Mets' fans mean business. You can see it on the adulatory bricks of the fan-walk as you approach the entrance to Citi Field, which has been the team's home since 2009. Although on the streets the Mets are often called the "Amazin' Mets," or the "Miracle Mets" they were not always such. The team holds the record for most losses, a distinction they earned in 1962 during their first season. Since then, they have played in four World Series and have won two. You can see the Amazin' Mets play a home game at Citi Field, which is also home to the famous **Home Run Apple** from the old **Shea Stadium,** the **Mets Hall of Fame,** and an enormous, neon-blue

queens . flushing

cool off without slowing down

Summer in The City. Anyone who has been to NYC in July or August knows that means stifling heat, palpable humidity, and desperate trips to Mr. Softee (it tastes good even if it doesn't really make you feel any less like you are in a steam room).

According to the *New York Times*, Tuesday, July 6, 2010, high 103, was New York's hottest day since August 9, 2001. The last time it was almost this hot and blown feeder lines at a power utility in Long Island City left area residents pioneer-style for several days.

Now I don't know how to prevent power outages. But I do know the best place to go to escape the infernal heat of a New York City summer. And it isn't the swimming pool. Or the library. Or an ice cream parlor. No, the answer to summer woes is right under the feet of millions of New Yorkers: that wonderful, amazing invention, the Subway.

The air conditioning on Subway cars is by far the most powerful I have encountered. Sometimes I leave the station feeling downright chilly. So when it gets too hot to set foot outside, why not just stay underground? Choose a line, ride to the end, and reverse. Or even choose a new one. The options are endless.

The Subway is a frosty escape conveniently located anywhere in the city you happen to be. And the best part is, it only costs $2.25. There is quite literally no faster way to beat the heat than on a train.

Davida Fernandez-Barkan

"42" at the entrance to the park, which is a tribute to Jackie Robinson.

✈ Ⓢ 7 to Willets Point/Shea Stadium or 111th St. Ⓢ Tickets $11-460. ☎ Box office open M-F 9am-5pm, Sa-Su 9am-6pm; tickets also available 2½hr. prior to games.

THE ROCKAWAYS

◪ JAMAICA BAY WILDLIFE REFUGE   NATURE PRESERVE
On Broad Channel, Jamaica Bay   ☎718-335-1000 ▣www.nps.gov

The 9155 acres of the Jamaica Bay Wildlife Refuge can provide a welcome change of pace from the hustle and bustle of New York City. The preserve's main trail stretches for about 2 mi. around **West Pond,** which was created in 1952 at the request of Parks Commissioner **Robert Moses.** The wildlife refuge is one of the prime birding locations, as some very enthusiastic park rangers will inform you. Over 325 species have been sighted here, and birders from far and wide makes pilgrimages to the park every year to spot a **Solitary Sandpiper** or a **Yellow-bellied Sap.**

✈ Ⓢ A or S to Broad Channel, or Q53 Bus from Roosevelt Ave./Jackson Park $2.25. Ⓢ Free. ☎ Visitors' center open daily 9am-5pm except Thanksgiving, Christmas, and New Year's. Park open sunrise-dusk.

JACOB RIIS PARK   PARK, BEACH
Just west of Rockaway Beach   ☎718-318-4300 ▣www.nps.gov

Founded in 1936 by **Robert Moses** as a public beach for those who lacked the time and the money for the ritzier **Jones Beach,** this park is a favorite spot for biking, swimming, playing sports, and summer merrymaking in general. An enormous castle of a bathhouse serves as an exhibition and lecture space.

✈ Ⓢ A or S to Rockaway Beach/116th St., then take Q22 bus westward. Ⓢ Free. ☎ Open 6am-midnight. Lifeguard on duty 9am-6pm M-F, 9am-7pm Sa-Su. Swimming permitted only when lifeguard is on duty.

ROCKAWAY BEACH   BEACH
Beach 3rd St. to Beach 149th   ☎718-318-4000 ▣www.nycgovparks.org

The **NYC Department of Parks and Recreation** takes its beaches seriously. Rockaway Beach, for instance, takes up about 170 acres along **Jamaica Bay.** They don't skimp on the lifeguards either; those *Baywatch* wannabes are stationed practically every 10 ft., even when only a couple of people can be seen practicing their doggy paddle. In nice weather, on the other hand, the heavy lifeguard action is justified. On these days, New Yorkers from all over the boroughs flock to Rockaway Beach for swimming, surfing, sunbathing, and snoozing in the sun.

✈ Ⓢ A marked "Far Rockaway" to all stops between Beach 36th St. and Beach 67th St., or A marked "Rockaways" or A, S to all stops between Beach 90th St. and Rockaway Park/Beach 116th St. Ⓢ Free. ☎ Lifeguard on duty 10am-6pm Memorial Day through Labor Day. Swimming permitted only when lifeguard is on duty. Promenade open 6am-10pm.

the bronx

Despite the Bronx's reputation as an unforgiving concrete jungle, it's large enough to contain several enormous parks and green spaces where you can forget the whole urban blight problem. Yankee Stadium, the Bronx Zoo, and the New York Botanical Garden are top draws, while the far-flung Van Cortlandt and Pelham Bay Parks offer semblances of natural refuge for the truly dedicated.

◪ BRONX ZOO   ✦◊ ZOO
Entrances on Bronx Park South, Southern Blvd., East Fordham Rd., and the Bronx River Pkwy.
☎718-220-5100 ▣bronxzoo.com

The Bronx Zoo, founded in 1899, is no spring chicken. The grounds swarm at all working hours of the day with countless school groups, especially in the spring. There is more than enough here to fill an entire day, an entire planet's wealth of organisms sampled and condensed, 4000 animals all told, into 265 acres. Closest to the main south entrance south are the African Plains, where **peacocks, lions,** and **gazelles** somehow coexist in peace, with the help of some judicious barriers. Nearby is a baboon reserve and grounds for bears—spot the ever-elusive polar bear. Work your way through the **Himalayan Highlands** to **Tiger Mountain,** then up to a **Monkey House** and a building devoted to the unique wildlife of Madagascar. Several aviaries in the zoo's northwestern corner teem with species both exotic and familiar. The **World of Reptiles** building is fascinating; hardest to forget are the enormous pythons, usually averse to humans. The **Mouse House** is surprisingly entertaining, featuring enormous species from Latin America. There are several special exhibits within the zoo that carry their own prices (see below); best among them is a trip on the **Wild Asia Monorail,** which should be your first destination if time is limited. Asian Wildlife—including red pandas, hippos, elephants, tigers, wild horses, and more peacocks—sport around spacious grounds for your viewing pleasure.

✦ Ⓢ *2, 5 to West Farms Sq./East Tremont Ave. Walk along Boston Rd. 3 blocks north; 2, 5 to East 180th St. and follow signs to zoo; 2, 5 to Pelham Parkway and follow signs to zoo. Buses: The BXM 11 express runs along Madison Ave. and stops at 26th, 32nd, 39th, 47th, 54th, 63rd, 70th, 84th, and 99th St. before heading directly to the zoo's Pelham Parkway entrance ($5.50 one way, MetroCards accepted; buses leave M-Sa every 30min., Su every hr.). i Free maps available at the entrance.* Ⓢ *$15. Children's Zoo, Congo Gorilla Forest, Butterfly Garden $3 each. Wild Asian Monorail $4. Camel rides and 4D Theater $5 each. Total Experience tickets (full admission) $27 (does not include camel rides).* ◷ *Open M-F 10am-5pm, Sa-Su 10am-5:30pm.*

▨ NEW YORK BOTANICAL GARDEN

✦🕭 GARDENS

Moshulu Gate entrance on Dr. Theodore Kazimiroff Blvd.　　☎718-817-8700 ▣www.nybg.org

Just north of the Bronx Zoo, this enormous 250 acre garden, plant museum, and research laboratory makes for a considerably less frenetic visit. Leisurely strolls are more in vogue here, the right pace for a visit to the 50 acre forest that preserves the natural look of the borough pre-urbanity. The Rock Garden, with its much-photographed waterfall, is a must-visit. The Rockefeller Rose Garden features 3500 variants of the flower, while the Twin Lakes support aquatic plant life and waterfowl. The Enid A. Haupt Conservatory, built in 1902 and graced with a now-famous glass-domed greenhouse, is home to the permanent exhibit A World of Plants, where you can experience Earth's full range of plant species. Tram rides *($2 for 30min.)* give you a quick greatest-hits version of the garden. Get maps, brochures, and pick-me-ups at the Visitors Center Cafe.

✦ Ⓢ *B, D, 4 to Bedford Park Blvd./Lehman College; walk downhill to Kazimiroff Blvd., turn left, and walk one block to Mosholu Gate entrance. The Bx26 bus also runs from the Subway station to the gate. Trains: The Metro North-Harlem line from Grand Central Terminal has a Botanical Garden stop right by the gate.* Ⓢ *$6, students $3. Admission free W and Sa 10am-noon.* ◷ *Open Tu-Su 10am-6pm.*

YANKEE STADIUM

✦🕭♟ STADIUM

East 161st St. and River Ave.　　☎718-293-4300; ▣www.yankees.com

The new Yankee Stadium opened its doors in spring 2009 amid much controversy. Beyond the complaints over taxpayer dollars lay a deeper concern: a New York landmark had been demolished. The old stadium, built in 1923, was home to one of the most successful and storied teams in sports history. Today, its remains lie across the street from the Bronx Bombers' current home. What's done is done, though—and for what it's worth, the new stadium is an impressive achievement. More or less mimicking its predecessor in limestone exterior and interior touches, the stadium provides 63% more space. Over 130 concession stands cater to game crowds. The Yankee Museum at Gate 6 is packed with valuable memorabilia

the bronx

worth millions and the "Ball Wall" features countless balls signed by past legends and present stars alike. Guided tours of the stadium visit the Yankee Museum, Monument Park (a memorial located by the center-field fences that commemorates famous Yankees), a dugout, and the clubhouse/batting cages.

⚡ Ⓢ *4, B, D to 141st St.-Yankee Stadium.* Ⓢ *Game ticket prices vary greatly, from bleachers (around $15) to terrace seats ($50-80) to main sections ($55-120) to field seating ($125-300); available online at yankees.com and other vendors. Classic tours $20 per person. Game schedule varies; check online for details.* ⓩ *Classic tours M-F every 20min. noon-1:40pm. Buy tickets online at yankees.com.*

VAN CORTLANDT PARK
👤 PARK

Northwest Bronx, east of Broadway. ☎718-601-1553 🖳www.vancortlandt.org/vcpark.org

This large park spreads across the northeastern section of the Bronx, bordering the very upscale Riverside neighborhood and ending at the border with Westchester county. Though the park isn't the most beautiful in the city—it pales in comparison to Manhattan's Central and Brooklyn's Prospect Parks—the space is ideal for athletes who come for the golf course, football, soccer, and baseball fields, tennis courses, tracks, and numerous forest running paths. Rock outcroppings to the northwest draw hikers and amateur mountaineers. Take care in some of the park's less developed areas; some trails are not extensively developed and could easily get you lost.

⚡ Ⓢ *1 to 242nd St.-Van Cortlandt Park or 4 to Woodlawn.*

VAN CORTLANDT HOUSE
✦ HOUSE, MUSEUM

Van Cortlandt Park, just north of 242nd St. ☎718-543-3344 🖳www.vancortlandthouse.org

The Bronx's oldest house rests in the southeastern corner of the park that share its name. Built in 1748, the stone house was briefly held by George Washington in his days as a general, became a museum in 1897 and has since preserved its colonial and 18th-century styles. History buffs will love the preserved rooms, from the dining room to the bedchambers to the nursery, complete with dollhouse. A 20th-century herb garden waits outside.

⚡ Ⓢ *1 to 242nd St.-Van Cortlandt Park.* Ⓢ *$5, students $3.* ⓩ *Open Tu-F 10am-3pm, Sa-Su 11am-4pm.*

EDGAR ALLAN POE COTTAGE HOUSE

E Kingsbridge Rd. and Grand Concourse ☎718-881-8900 🖳www.bronxhistoricalsociety.org

Everyone's favorite tormented 19th-century American author lived in this humble dwelling, which was once a rural cottage with views over the Bronx hills to Long Island, from 1846 to 1849. His wife, Virginia, died of tuberculosis here (you can see her deathbed), the residence where Poe wrote some of his most famous poems, including "Annabel Lee" and "The Bells." The small house displays some Poe manuscripts and preserves much of the original furniture. It will be closed 2010-2011 for renovations.

⚡ Ⓢ *4, B, D to Kingsbridge Rd.* Ⓢ *$5, students $3.* ⓩ *Open Sa 10am-4pm, Su 1-5pm; guided group tours on weekdays by appointment only.*

WAVE HILL
✦👤 HOUSE, PARK

West 249th St. and Independence Ave. ☎718-549-3200 🖳www.wavehill.org

This 28 acre estate perched in Riverside on the slopes by the Hudson River is a beautiful find for those willing to brave the transportation difficulties to get here. The mansion was first built in 1843, housed such luminaries as Theodore Roosevelt's family and Mark Twain, and was rebuilt extensively after a fire in the 1920s, after which conductor Arturo Toscanini briefly called it home. The estate is covered in a wide variety of gardens, some formal and some deliberately wild. There's also an Alpine House displaying high-altitude plants, an aquatic garden, and 10 additional acres of woodland.

⌗ Ⓢ *1 to 242nd St.; a free shuttle leaves from the Burger King on Broadway every hr. at 10min. past the hr. 9:10am-3:10pm. A return shuttle leaves Wave Hill every hr. noon-5pm. Or: A to West 207th St., then Bx7 or Bx20 northbound bus to 252nd St., then 5min. walk down 252nd St. to Wave Hill entrance on Independence Ave.* Ⓢ *$8, students $4.* ⓒ *Open Apr 15-Oct 14 Tu-Su 9am-5:30pm; Oct 15-Apr 14 Tu-Su 9am-4:30pm. Free garden and conservatory tours leave from the Perkins Visitor Center at 2pm.*

WOODLAWN CEMETERY
               ♿ CEMETERY
Main entrance at Webster Ave. and East 233rd St.   ☎718-920-0500◼www. thewoodlawncemetery.org

One of the most extensive cemeteries in the entire US is full of dead celebrities. Over 300,000 people are laid to rest in its 400 acres. Jazz fans take note: here you can find Miles Davis, Duke Ellington, Lionel Hampton, King Oliver, and Max Roach. Oscar Hammerstein, Joseph Pulitzer, Robert Moses, Herman Melville, and other famous names also lie here. The grounds are hilly but quiet, a nice break from the Bronx bustle.

⌗ Ⓢ *4 to Woodlawn.* ⓒ *Open daily 8:30am-5pm.*

PELHAM BAY PARK
               ♿ PARK
Northeastern Bronx   ☎718-430-1890 ◼www.nycgovparks.org

Pelham Bay Park sits on storied land. Colonial religious dissident Anne Hutchinson tried to start a colony here and was killed by natives. Later, the Americans and British duked it out here at the Battle of Pell's Point in 1776. New York's largest park (a whopping 2700 acres) is also its least reachable. Tucked in the far northeastern corner of the Bronx, it's large enough for a week's worth of activities: the requisite fields, tennis and basketball courts, and hiking and running trails are here to make all that sport possible. The park is distinguished by its coastline; 600 acres are tidal, and Orchard Beach (the Bronx's only public beach) stretches for over a mile along the bay. The Bartow-Pell Mansion, built between 1836 and 1842, is surrounded by serene formal gardens that were added later in the period between 1914 and 1917. The Bronx Victory Column, which memorializes servicemen and women from the Bronx, and the Bronx Equestrian Center, which offers horseback tours of the park, both find their home in this urban oasis.

⌗ Ⓢ *6 to Pelham Bay Park.* Ⓢ *Bronx Equestrian Center horse back riding lessons: $40 for 30min., $65 per hr. Mansion entry $5, students $3.* ⓒ *Park open dawn to dusk. Stables open 9am-dusk. Mansion open W and Sa-Su noon-4pm.*

staten island

▨ STATEN ISLAND FERRY
         ♿♺❡ FERRY, TRANSPORTATION
South Ferry in Manhattan and St. George Ferry in Staten Island   ☎718-876-8441

Over 80,000 passengers ride this famous ferry every day. The vast majority are Staten Islanders commuting to work, but a handful are tourists eager to catch the stunning (and, of course, free) views of the Statue of Liberty, Ellis Island, and the Manhattan skyline. It's become a classic part of any New York visit, so succumb to the temptation—and, while you're there, check out some of Staten Island's own sights.

⌗ Ⓢ *1, N, R, W to South Ferry in Manhattan.* Ⓢ *Free.* ⓒ *Runs 24hr., every 30min. during the day, every hr. at night.*

▨ SNUG HARBOR
         ♿ PARK, GARDEN, MUSEUM
Entrance at 1000 Richmond Terr.   ☎718-815-7684 ◼www.snug-harbor.org

These beautiful grounds once housed up to 1000 retired sailors as a maritime home and hospital in the 19th and 20th centuries. In 1975, the City of New York purchased it and turned it into a catch-all garden and cultural space, extending over 83 acres and holding 28 historic buildings. It's enough to simply walk through the gardens and manicured landscape, but the several museums and performance spaces are also worth their own visits.

The Main Hall facing you as you enter is the site's oldest and most majestic building. Built in 1833, it now houses the **Eleanor Proske Visitors Center,** where you can pick up maps and other info, and is connected to the galleries of the Newhouse Center for Contemporary Art. Check out the nautical themes of the interior, from constellations and Neptune on the ceiling to compass points on the floor. The **New York Chinese Scholar's Garden** is modeled on gardens of the Ming Dynasty in China; the landscaping and buildings are beautiful, and there's plenty of shade for muggy days. **Connie Gretz's Secret Garden** nearby is modeled on the eponymous European-style formal garden of Frances Hogson Burnett's classic. Nearby, the **Healing Garden** is an expansive natural memorial to the 267 residents of Staten Island who died on September 11. The **Tuscan Garden** includes an Italian neo-Renaissance villa that once served as dorms for nurses; a vineyard is currently being developed on the site. Annual summer concerts take place on the **South Meadow Stage** (check the website for details), while crowds of kids loudly enjoy the exhibits at the **Staten Island Children's Museum,** housed in a former barn.

⇟ From the ferry terminal, take the S40 bus or S96 bus to the Snug Harbor entrance stop on Richmond Terr. $ Entrance to grounds free. Entrance to Newhouse Center $3, students $2. Entrance to Chinese Scholar's Garden $5, students $4. Entrance to Children's Museum $5. ⏰ Grounds open daily dawn-dusk. Newhouse Center open Tu-Su 10am-5pm. Chinese Scholar's Garden open Apr-Oct Tu-Su 10am-5pm; Nov-Mar W-Su 10am-4pm. Children's Museum open July-Labor Day Tu-Su 10am-8pm; Labor Day-June Tu-F noon-5pm.

HISTORIC RICHMOND TOWN ♿ HISTORIC SITE, MUSEUM

441 Clarke Ave. ☎718-351-1611 💻www.historicrichmondtown.org

Anybody who grew up near the East Coast probably remembers some school trip to a preserved colonial town with staff dressed in period wear and refusing to answer your annoying questions about TV. Here's your chance for nostalgia: Richmond Town stretches over 100 acres and preserves many buildings from the colonial era to the 19th century. A museum at the heart of the complex includes documents and exhibits on Staten Island's history from earliest to present times. Old-fangled festivals and events also take place here, from Independence Day celebrations to square dancing to county fairs. The "town" is very small, and the subject is clearly of narrow interest, but history diehards will love this stuff.

⇟ Bus S74 to Richmond Rd. and St. Patrick's Place. $ $5, students $3.50. ⏰ Open W-Su July-Aug 11am-5pm; Sept-June 1-5pm. Guided tours Sept-June W-F 2:30pm, Sa-Su 2, 3:30pm.

RICHMOND COUNTY BANK BALLPARK 👟♿🍸🍴 SPORTS VENUE, STADIUM

75 Richmond Terr. ☎718-720-9265 💻www.siyanks.com

If Yankee Stadium is too much for you, head south to the home of their farm league: the proud **Staten Island Yankees.** If you get the right seats, you may be able to see the Manhattan skyline rising above the game. The season runs from June to September; check the website for schedule details. Fridays are the best days—you may get 🎆**fireworks** over the stadium after the game.

⇟ Turn right from the ferry station and follow signs to the park entrance (5min.). $ Tickets $6-18. ⏰ Box office open during games and M-F 9am-5pm.

JACQUES MARCHAIS MUSEUM OF TIBETAN ART ♿❄ MUSEUM

338 Lighthouse Ave. ☎718-987-3500 💻www.tibetanmuseum.org

This beautifully located hilltop museum is a great bit of randomness in Staten Island. Almost 65 years old, the museum holds the private collection of artist and Himalayan enthusiast Jacques Marchais. The placement on a hill—and the two-building design—are meant to replicate the experience of a Buddhist monastery. Exhibits on all things Tibet can be found inside: photos, old paintings, sculpture, musical instruments, and books. A Buddhist altar is sometimes used by actual Tibetan Buddhist monks, consecrated by the **Dalai Lama** himself. The terraced gardens outside are designed for meditation and provide views of the Lower Bay. Inquire at the desk about special events and educational opportunities, including guided meditation. A two-day festival in October centers on craft-making and mask-designing.

🚌 *Bus S74 to Richmond Rd. and Lighthouse Ave. Walk uphill along Lighthouse Ave. to the museum.* ⓢ *$5, students $3.* ⏰ *Open W-Su 1-5pm.*

ALICE ADAMS HOUSE MUSEUM
🏃‍♂️♿ HOUSE/MUSEUM

2 Hylan Blvd.   ☎718-816-4506 🖥www.aliceausten.org

Alice Austen was one of the earliest photographers of note. Her work, much of it depicting upper-class individuals and street scenes of *fin de siècle* New York, reflected her upbringing. This museum uses her own cottage, nicknamed "Clear Comfort" and dating from the 1700s, to present some samples of her work alongside more modern photography exhibits. The grounds by the water are perfect for strolling and view-catching.

🚌 *Bus S51 to Hylan Blvd.* ⓢ *Suggested donation $2.* ⏰ *Museum open Mar-Dec Th-Su noon-5pm. Grounds open daily dawn-dusk.*

staten island

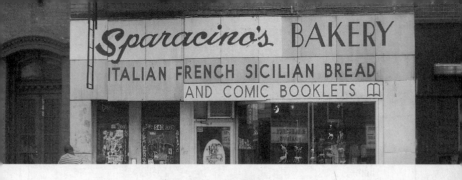

FOOD

There's plenty to eat in New York City besides ⬚big apples. In fact, there's everything to eat. From fine dining to street treats, the city has something for any palate and any budget. New York's immigrant past means the city is a literal melting pot for all cuisines, so you can eat dim sum in Chinatown, cannoli in Little Italy, and souvlaki in Astoria...all in an afternoon (we won't judge). Sure, the premier restaurants are a bit more expensive, but cheap eating is never tastier than in New York City. After all, you're in the home of the **bagel,** the **Magnolia cupcake,** and **Nathan's first hot dog.** But just because you're trying to tighten your belt doesn't mean you should eat any less. If you're really craving a meal in one of Manhattan's finer restaurants without going broke, schedule your visit around **Restaurant Week** in either winter *(Jan-Feb)* or summer *(June-July),* when Manhattan's finest restaurants offer three-course meals at standardized (and affordable) fixed prices (☎*212-484-1200* 💻*www.nycvisit.com).* Dig in.

greatest hits

- **EAST MEETS EAST.** Spend all night at Veselka (p.113), the East Village's finest 24hr. Eastern European deli.
- **HOT AND COLD.** Experience the spicy wasabi flavor and many more at the Chinatown Ice Cream Factory (p.103).
- **MYSTERY MEAT** is nowhere on the menu at Cafeteria (p.116), a trendy and delicious American restaurant in Chelsea.
- **GET "LUDACRIS"** or the "President Barack Obama" at Amy Ruth's (p.128), home to the best fried chicken platters in Harlem.

student life

Put down the Easy Mac—you have no excuse for microwaving when you're in New York. The city has delicious food at every hour, but here are some places that students especially hunger for.

- **LINE UP** for the best slices in the city at **Bleecker Street Pizza.** Believe us, it's worth the wait.
- **BIG NICK'S PIZZA AND BURGER JOINT** is a 24hr. restaurant serving the largest portions of every drunk food you've ever craved. Go big or go home.
- **AFTER SOME LATE NIGHT PARTYING DOWNTOWN,** head to **Mamoun's Falafel** in St. Mark's Place, open daily until 5am.
- **STUDENTS LOOKING TO ENJOY COFFEE** among a more intellectual crowd should stroll to the **Hungarian Pastry Shop** near Columbia University.

lower manhattan

SMORGAS CHEF SCANDINAVIAN [2]

53 Stone St. ☎212-422-3500 🖥www.smorgaschef.com

Enjoy your Swedish meatballs and lingonberries *($17)* on a rustic wooden table on the cobblestoned Stone St. or inside positioned near the real tree in the middle of the restaurant. A popular brunch spot, they offer a *prix-fixe* brunch *($17)* Saturdays and Sundays 11am-5pm, complete with an entree, coffee, and brunch cocktail. You can even add unlimited champagne for $10. The Scandinavian vanilla waffles *($10)* are a win.

[S] 4, 5 to Bowling Green; or 1 to South Ferry. $ Appetizers $6-9. Burgers and sandwiches $11-15. Entrees $17-26. Brunch $10-22. Desserts $6-7. Beer $6-8. Cocktails $8-10. 🕒 Open daily 11am-10pm.

ADRIENNE'S PIZZA BAR PIZZA [2]

43 Stone St. ☎212-248-3838 🖥www.adriennespizzabar.com

At lunchtime, this pizza joint is packed with folks chowing down on cookie-sheet size pies *($17.50)*. Choose a marinara, white, or an old fashioned base, then add toppings *($3-4)* to your heart's content. The sandwiches—try the caprese *($8)*—are also ample and delicious. In the summer, guests often flock to the outdoor seating on historic Stone St.

[S] 4, 5 to Bowling Green; or 1 to South Ferry. $ Pizza $17.50. Toppings $3-4. Sandwiches $8. Salads $6-$11.50. Pasta $8-9. Beer $6. Wine $9-10. 🕒 Open M-Sa 11:30am-midnight, Su 11:30am-10pm.

MADE FRESH DAILY CAFE [1]

226 Front St. ☎212-285-2253 🖥www.madefreshdailybakeshop.com

This is a bright and cheery bakeshop and cafe with a knack for jazzing up old favorites. Cases in point: the deviled egg salad *($7.75)* and spicy grilled cheese *($7.75) sandwiches.* Ingredients are natural, organic, unrefined, and farm fresh, and the delectable bakery items are baked either on-site or by local establishments such as the **Doughnut Plant.** The Cupcake of the Day *(mini $1.50, full-sized $2.75)* alone is worth the trip.

[S] 2, 3, J, M, Z to Fulton St.; or A, C to Broadway-Nassau. Between Beekman St. and Peck Slip. $ Breakfast $7.50-9.50. Salads $9-12. Sandwiches $8-10. Bakery $2-6. Drinks $2-5.50. Ice cream $4 per scoop. 🕒 Open daily 8am-4:30pm.

soho and tribeca

RUBEN'S EMPANADAS
🍴⊗🍸 LATIN AMERICAN ❶

505 Broome St. ☎212-334-3351

These doughy delights come with tons of different meat, poultry, seafood, and vegetarian fillings. For dessert, try an apple empanada or a guava and cheese empanada ($2.25). Don't miss happy hour, when you can get an the empanada of your choice and wine or beer ($7).

🚇 Ⓢ C, E to Spring St. Ⓢ Empanadas $4-4.50. Dessert empanadas $2.25. Coffee drinks $1.50-3.50. Wine and beer $5. ⌚ Open M-F 9am-10:30pm, Sa 9am-10pm, Su 10am-7pm.

BUBBY'S
🍴⊗🍸 AMERICAN ❷

120 Hudson St. ☎212-219-0666 🖥www.bubbys.com

Everything you love about the classic American diner: the late hours, the comfort food, etc., except at Bubby's you know that ice cream in your milkshake is homemade using local, fresh ingredients, and the beef for your burger was raised ethically just across the river at Brooklyn's Heritage Foods. Bubby's advice to "save room for pie" (apple, cherry, peanut butter, key lime, and others) should most definitely be heeded.

🚇 Ⓢ 1 to Franklin St. Walk to Hudson St., at Moore St. Ⓢ Appetizers $9-12. Entree salads $17-24. Burgers and sandwiches $15-17. Entrees $17-23. Wine $9-10. Beer $5-8. Mixed drinks $10-13. Desserts $2.50-7. ⌚ Open M 8am-midnight, Tu-Su 24hr.

COLUMBINE
🍴 AMERICAN ❶

229 W. Broadway ☎212-965-0909 🖥www.columbine229.com

For tasty treats in Tribeca, step into this charming little sandwich- and coffee-shop. Columbine's Jerk Chicken Sandwich ($8) with mango-cilantro relish will add some spice to your day, and the LA COLOMBE espresso will wake you up in no time. The enormous, freshly baked cookies in a variety of flavors will make the perfect dessert or snack.

🚇 Ⓢ A, C, E, N, R to Canal St. Walk to Broadway and White St. Ⓢ Bakery $2-3.50. Coffee drinks $2-4.50. Soup $5-6.75. Salads and sandwiches $4.50-9.50. ⌚ Open M-F 8am-6pm.

ANTIQUE GARAGE
🍴&🍸 MEDITERRANEAN ❸

41 Mercer St. ☎212-219-1019 🖥www.antiquegaragesoho.com

True to its name, the Antique Garage is located in a former garage filled with, you guessed it, antiques! A red sofa here, a maritime painting there, a smattering of incongruous lighting fixtures scattered around the general premises. The food happens to be of the Mediterranean variety; if you find yourself unable to choose an appetizer, go for the mixed *mezze* platter ($24-28), which includes humus, tzatziki, circassian chicken, eggplant salad, shepherd salad, and borek. The grilled halloumi cheese salad ($16-18) is beyond delicious. At the end of your meal, the check will be delivered to you in a special antique tin.

🚇 Ⓢ J, M, N, Q, R, Z, 6 to Canal St. Ⓢ Appetizers $8-28. Salads $12-20. Entrees $18-28. Sandwiches $10-20. Wine $10-12. Beer $8. ⌚ Open M-Th noon-11pm, F noon-midnight, Sa 11am-midnight, Su 11am-11pm.

CUBANA CAFE
⊗⊗ CUBAN, BRAZILIAN ❶

110 Thompson St. ☎212-966-5366 🖥www.cubanacafeelchulo.com

The walls of this Cuban/Brazilian eatery are painted in the pink, blue, and yellow hues you think of when you visualize Havana. They also hold messages such as "No Cerveza, No Trabajar" and display pictures of children crowded around antique Buicks. Try the *palomilla (pounded sirloin marinated in orange, lime, and rosemary, served with onions, rice and beans, $15)* or the *ensalada de aguacate (avocado, shrimp, mango, and mixed greens, $9)*. A mango martini ($8) will complement either. Who really needs an excuse for a mango martini?

✦ Ⓢ C, E to Spring St.; R to Prince St. Ⓢ *Quesadillas $8-9.50. Sandwiches $4-9.50. Salads $6.50-9. Soup $4.50-7. Entrees $11-16.50. Breakfast $6.50-9. Wine and beer $6.50. Mixed drinks $7-11.* ☼ *Open daily 11:30am-11:30pm.*

KELLEY AND PING ASIAN GROCERY AND NOODLE SHOP   ⊛⊗✇ ASIAN ❶

127 Greene St.   ☎212-228-1212 ▧www.kelleyandping.com

Meticulous pyramids of cans of curry paste, jars of exotic loose teas, and rows of terra cotta warriors surround you when you nibble your pan-Asian noodles at the wooden tables of Kelley and Ping. With dishes such as Pad Thai *($8.50-$11),* Korean "twice fried" chicken *($14),* and Malaysian curried noodles *($10.50-$13),* your meal can be a culinary journey through the Asian continent. Load up on cookies and candies *($0.25)* for dessert or a snack later.

✦ Ⓢ R to Prince St. Walk to Greene St., between W. Houston and Prince St. Ⓢ *Appetizers $4-14. Lunch boxes $8.50. Soups $8-13. Noodles $11-14. Entrees $13-18. Beer $6. Wine $7.* ☼ *Open daily 11:30am-5pm and 5:30-11pm.*

JEAN CLAUDE   ⊛&✇ FRENCH ❷

137 Sullivan St.   ☎212-475-9232 ▧www.jeanclauderestaurant.com

The chefs at this charming French restaurant devote equal energy on aesthetic and gastronomic aspects of their creations. The menu includes roasted codfish *($18)* with roasted potato puree, tomato and caper salpicon, and ginger aromatic sauce and sauteed skate *($17)* with couscous, Portobello mushroom, Italian capers, and balsamic vinaigrette. It may be advisable to avoid the vegetarian platter *($15);* the portions are meager, though it is very pretty.

✦ Ⓢ C, E to Prince St. Ⓢ *Appetizers $7-15. Entrees $15-23. Wine $7-10. Prix-fixe (M-Th 6pm-7:30pm) $25.* ☼ *Open M-Th 5:30pm-11pm, F-Su 5:30pm-11:30pm.*

LUPE'S EAST LA KITCHEN   ⊛⊗✇ MEXICAN ❷

110 6th Ave.   ☎212-966-1326 ▧www.lupeskitchen.com

Lupe's offers a Mexican menu that makes an exceptional effort at accommodating vegetarians: they even make tamales with red chili filling *($10.25)* and spinach and cheese enchiladas *($10.25).* But do not despair, meat eaters; you can have your tamales filled with chicken *($11)* and your enchiladas made with beef *($10).* Weekend brunch is an exciting time at Lupes, with some offerings that are more "East LA" such as the banana pancakes *($6.50),* and others that are south-of-the-border-style such as the chile relleno burrito *($9).*

✦ Ⓢ 1 to Canal St.; or A, C, E to Canal St./Ave. of the Americas; or C, E to Spring St./Ave. of the Americas. Walk to 6th Ave. and Watts St. Ⓢ *Appetizers $1.50-5. Entrees $9-14. Salads $3.25-8.25. Lunch entrees $7-11. Desserts $1.75-3. Margaritas $6. Mojitos $7. Beer $5.* ☼ *Open M-Tu 11:30am-11pm, W-Sa 11:30am-midnight, Su 11:30am-11pm.*

SALUGGI'S   ⦿⊗✇ PIZZA ❷

325 Church St.   ☎212-226-7900

An old-fashioned New York pizza joint, complete with checkered tablecloths and indoor street lamps. The fruit of their brick oven can be either menu-prescripted, as in the Blue *(gorgonzola, walnuts, mozzarella, and caramelized onions; $14-21)* or customized using a list of ingredients that includes all of the usual suspects as well as such innovative toppings as almonds and capicola *($2-3 per topping).* Even vegans can enjoy their delicious daiya cheese pizza. A comprehensive assortment of subs, pasta, and other entrees is also available.

✦ Ⓢ 1, A, C, E, N, Q, R to Canal St. Find Church St. between Lispenard and Canal St. Ⓢ *Appetizers $4-13. Entrees $14-18. Pizza $12-25. Subs $7-12. Beer $5-6. Wine $6-7.* ☼ *Open M-Sa 11am-10pm, Su 11am-7pm.*

chinatown

Every possible variety of East and Southeast Asian cuisine can be found in Chinatown's tangle of streets. The old Cantonese standbys compete with newer arrivals from other regions of China—Shanghai chief among them, though Szechuan, Malaysian, Thai, and Vietnamese are also readily available. The restaurants can be bewilderingly repetitive—the same spare decor, the same dishes, even the same garish menus—but those willing to explore and experiment will quickly discover the neighborhood's remarkable diversity. Best of all, a lot can still be had for very little, a modern-day Manhattan miracle.

▧ CHINATOWN ICE CREAM FACTORY ⊜も ICE CREAM ❶
65 Bayard St. ☎212-608-4170 ▣chinatownicecreamfactory.com

This 30-year-old and ever popular Chinatown institution is a welcome reprieve from the glut of repetitive restaurants that surround it. "Exotic flavors" like lychee (Chinese fruit), wasabi, and black sesame are served up alongside "regular flavors," sorbets, sundaes, and milkshakes. Get here early in the day to avoid lines.

‡ Ⓢ 6, J, M, N, Q, R, W, Z to Canal St. ⑤ 1 scoop $3.75, 2 $5.75, 3 $7. ⍚ Open daily 10am-10pm.

▧ JOE'S SHANGHAI ⊜も CHINESE ❷
9 Pell St. ☎212-233-8888 ▣joeshanghairestaurants.com

Though Joe's got its start in Flushing in 1995, the Chinatown branch has become legendary in its own right, attracting massive crowds—a line is essentially a permanent part of its storefront. Crowds come for a 150-item menu filled with noodle soups, meat dishes, and seafood. Mostly, though, people come for the famous *xiao long bao*, or soup dumplings. You'll be asked if you want some when first seated; say yes. Nibble a hole in the dumpling, suck the soup out, eat the rest, and ascend into heaven.

‡ Ⓢ 6, J, M, N, Q, R, W, Z to Canal St. ⑤ 1 order of dumplings $6; entrees $11-20. ⍚ Open daily 11am-11:15pm.

▧ PHO NHA TRANG ✎も VIETNAMESE ❷
87 Baxter St. ☎212-223-5948

Chinatown is no stranger to Vietnamese restaurants, which have staked their claim in the neighborhood over the past 20 years. Pho Nha Trang is one of the most highly regarded, serving up genuine pho (rice noodle soup, Vietnam's national soup), fried frog legs, and barbeque pork paste for dirt-cheap prices. The decor isn't much (those wall-to-wall mirrors get distracting)–but who was asking for much anyway? There's another branch at 148 Centre St.

‡ Ⓢ 6, J, M, N, Q, R, W, Z to Canal St. ⑤ Dishes $5-14. ⍚ Open daily 10am-11pm.

EXCELLENT DUMPLING HOUSE ⊜も CHINESE ❶
111 Lafayette St. ☎212-219-0212

Hilarious name aside, this small, plain eatery on Chinatown's eastern edge is a great find for modest helpings—from the dumplings to the dim sum to the noodle soup. A celebration of the small, the very cheap, and the unique, right down to a hand-painted sign proudly announcing that amazing name. It's fun just to recommend this place.

‡ Ⓢ 6, J, M, N, Q, R, W, Z to Canal St. ⑤ 6 dumplings $5, dim sum $2-5, noodle soup $4.75-6. ⍚ Open daily 11am-9pm.

CHANOODLE EXPRESS ✎も CHINESE ❷
79 Mulberry St., between Canal and Bayard St. ☎212-349-1495

Just south of Little Italy on Mulberry St., popular Chanoodle celebrates a different kind of pasta. Its noodle dishes *($6-9)* are extensive and cheap, and you can also try the crispy quail legs *($5)* on the side. Despite the exotic dishes, though, Chanoodle does what it can to attract Little Italy's tourists—forks and knives are more common than chopsticks, and the decor is a bit more elaborate than its plainer neighbors to the south.

🚉 [S] 6, J, M, Z to Canal St. $Entrees $5-12. 🕐 Open M-Th 11am-10pm, F-Sa 11am-11pm, Su 11am-10pm.

PHO VIET HUONG 💳♿ VIETNAMESE ❷

73 Mulberry St. ☎(212) 233-8988

The huge menu at this Vietnamese restaurant is a marvel—over 200 items, including vegetarian options like black mushrooms and sauteed watercress. Tons of cheap rice dishes are also up for grabs. Added bonus: the bamboo hut roofs and plastic palm trees adorning the back and side walls doing their best to make you forget you're downtown.

🚉 [S] 6, J, M, Z to Canal St. $ Entrees $5.50-17.50. 🕐 Open daily 10:30am-10:30pm.

FRIED DUMPLING 💵♿ CHINESE, TAKEOUT ❶

106 Mosco St., between Mott and Mulberry St. ☎212-941-9975

Oh, yes. Presenting the cheapest of the cheap: a small, absolutely no-fuss hole-in-the-wall just a few steps from Columbus Park and the Federal Plaza. You'll probably see officials in suits and jury duty members on breaks mingling with the locals here, all of them giving hurried orders to the frenetic two-person staff behind the counter. The dumplings are nothing to drool over, but they're tasty enough and so beautifully cheap.

🚉 [S] 6, J, M, Z to Canal St. $ 5 dumplings $1, 5 pork fried buns $1, 30 frozen dumplings $5. 🕐 Open daily 10am-10pm.

XO KITCHEN 💵♿ CHINESE ❶

148 Hester St. ☎212-965-8645

An enormously varied menu raise XO's two locations (the XO Cafe and Grill is located on 96 Walker St.) above the crowded pack. Hong-Kong style lo mein can easily complement a start with Japanese appetizers or dim sum treats. Throw in some commonly ambitious decorations and you have delicious cosmopolitanism, Chinatown-style.

🚉 [S] B, D to Grand St. or 6, J, M, N, Q, R, W, Z to Canal St. $ Entrees $5-13. 🕐 Open M-Th 8am-11pm, F-Sa 8am-11:30pm, Su 8am-11pm.

BUDDHA BODAI 💳♿ CHINESE, KOSHER ❷

5 Mott St. ☎212-566-8388 💻buddhabodai.net

No, we didn't stutter. Buddha Bodai is a certified kosher, vegetarian Chinese restaurant that attracts tourists and locals alike and is particularly popular among the Jewish community. The cheap lunch special draws a crowd, while more expensive entrees like Chinese water spinach or tofu in ceder sauce keep things interesting. As if they weren't already interesting enough.

🚉 [S] 6, J, M, Z to Canal St. $ Lunch special M-F 11am-4pm $7, entrees $7-18. 🕐 Open daily 10am-10pm.

NICE GREEN BO RESTAURANT 💳♿ CHINESE (SHANGHAI) ❷

66 Bayard St. ☎212-625-2359

Joe's Shanghai gets the attention, but Nice Green Bo (until recently New Green Bo) is another recognized favorite among Shanghai-style restaurants in the area. Its following can be chalked up to its soup dumplings and to a varied menu that encompass seafood, Shanghai lo mein, and casserole dishes, without breaking a sweat.

🚉 [S] 6, J, M, N, Q, R, W, Z to Canal St. $ Dumplings $5-7. Entrees $7.25-17. 🕐 Open daily 11am-11pm.

GRAND SICHUAN

&♿ CHINESE (SZECHUAN) ❷

125 Canal St., by Manhattan Bridge ☎212-625-9212

Szechuan food from China's inland Sichuan province is not readily found in Chinatown; tiny Grand Sichuan by the Manhattan Bridge is an ideal, simple corrective. They threw the frills out of here years ago, but kept the traditional spiciness, and let luxurious regional standards like kung pao chicken and double-cooked pork. Or go with the Chairman and order one of Mao's 22 favorite dishes on offer here.

✦ Ⓢ B, D to Grand St. or 6, J, M, N, Q, R, W, Z to Canal St. Ⓢ Lunch special M-F 11:30am-4pm $5. Entrees $8-20. ♨ Open daily 11:30am-11pm.

JAYA

✦♿♨ MALAYSIAN ❷

90 Baxter St. ☎212-219-3331

There are a few Malaysian restaurants scattered throughout the neighborhood, but Jaya's menu is one of the largest. It's dizzyingly varied, too; Malay dishes share space with Indian, Thai, and Indian offerings. Start with the Indian pancakes, move on to the Chinese drunken chicken, and end with Malaysian curry chicken. Or you can, you know, make the trip several times, one for each regional cuisine on display.

✦ Ⓢ 6, J, M, N, Q, R, W, Z to Canal St. Ⓢ Entrees $10-15. ♨ Open M 11am-10:30pm, Tu-Th 11am-11pm, F-Sa 11am-midnight, Su 11am-11pm.

PING'S SEAFOOD

✦⊗♟ CHINESE, SEAFOOD ❸

22 Mott St. ☎212-602-9988

Ping is a very well known Hong Kong chef who made his start here, spent a few years developing his craft in Flushing, and has triumphantly returned with this multi-storied and elaborate restaurant. It's one of the fanciest—and most popular—restaurants around, but if you're too much of a timid cheapskate to dish out the $75 shark fin soup you may find some consolation in the always-reliable dim sum menu.

✦ Ⓢ 6, J, M, Z to Canal St. Ⓢ Dim sum $4-5. Entrees $12-75. ♨ Open daily 10:30am-midnight.

JING FONG RESTAURANT

✦⊗ CHINESE, DIM SUM ❷

20 Elizabeth St. ☎212-904-5256

Jing Fong's huge banquet hall, known by the huge Chinese characters on its exterior, is the site of massive crowds all scrambling to signal a waiter over for a tray. Jing Fong will confuse and overwhelm—but practiced dim sum lovers will be in paradise.

✦ Ⓢ 6, J, M, N, Q, R, W, Z to Canal St. Ⓢ Dim sum $6-20. ♨ Open daily 9:30am-10pm.

PHO BANG

&♿ VIETNAMESE ❶

157 Mott St. ☎212-966-3797

Another Vietnamese establishment named after the national soup, Pho Bang prides itself on its authenticity. No faux pho here; and if you're not in a soup mood (though one bowl is enough for a meal), cheap rice dishes offer a reprieve.

✦ Ⓢ J, M to Bowery, B,D to Grand St., or 6, J, M, N, Q, R, W, Z to Canal St. Ⓢ Entrees $4.50-19.50. ♨ Open daily 10am-10pm.

LUNCH BOX BUFFET

&♿ CHINESE, BUFFET ❶

195 Center St. at Hester St. ☎212-941-1273

Lunch Box Buffet is as simple and unimaginative as its name. Come in, line up, be directed through a cafeteria-style line of offerings (the staff will help you out and, unfortunately, regulate your portions), and pay at the end. A simple stop for those unwilling or unable to wait; the so-so quality is redeemed by the added convenience.

✦ Ⓢ 6, J, M, N, Q, R, W, Z to Canal St. Ⓢ 4 choices with soup and rice or 5 choices with soup $4.50. ♨ Open daily 10am-9pm.

chinatown

little italy

Despite (or because of) Little Italy's transformation into a self-conscious theme park, its few blocks remain a go-to destination for seekers of delicious Italian cuisine. Pizza, pasta, freshly imported slabs of mozzarella, cannoli, gelato—they can all be had at your will (or the will of the waiters urging you inside). Some establishments proudly announce their late-19th or early-20th century origins. So swallow your in-search-of-the-genuine pride—and grab some pastries at Ferrara while you're at it.

FERRARA 💳♿❄ ITALIAN, BAKERY, ICE CREAM ❶
195 Grand St. ☎212-226-6150 💻ferraracafe.com
Five generations of the same family have run this famous Little Italy institution since 1892, so don't even think about skipping it while in the area. Known primarily as a bakery serving small, delicious pastries, Ferraro also has a gelato stand out front that is almost always crowded in hot weather. If you don't want the *stracciatella* gelato outside, try some *sfogliatelle* inside. Capiche?
🚏 [S] 6 to Spring St.; 6, J, M, N, Q, R, W, Z to Canal St.; or B, D to Grand St. $ Gelato $3.50-6.25. Pastries $1.50-4. ⏰ Open M-F 8am-midnight, Sa 8am-1am, Su 8am-midnight.

LOMBARDI'S PIZZA 💳♿🍸❄☁ ITALIAN, PIZZERIA ❸
32 Spring St. ☎212-941-7994 💻firstpizza.com
Lombardi's is the nation's oldest pizzeria (founded 1905). Luckily, they never rest on their laurels, and they stick to the founding fathers' basics: a coal oven, brick walls, checkered tablecloths, and plenty of tomato and mozzarella. Crowds flock to this institution, so try to avoid standard lunch and dinner hours.
🚏 [S] 6 to Spring St. or J, M to Bowery. $ Small (6 slices) $15.50. Large (8 slices) $19.50. Toppings $3. Calzones $12. ⏰ Open M-Th 11:30am-11pm, F-Sa 11:30am-midnight, Su 11:30am-11pm.

LA MELA RESTAURANT 💳♿🍸❄☁ ITALIAN, PIZZERIA ❸
167 Mulberry St. ☎212-431-9493 💻www.lamelarestaurant.com
At merely 25 years old, La Mela isn't as ancient as some of its neighbors. It may outdo them all in cultivating a neighborhood feel, though. Shirking the fancy for the friendly, La Mela has lined its walls with photographs and lets its tables spill out onto the sidewalk. The menu is full of old standards like fettuccine alfredo and shrimp marinara—but you don't go to a place like La Mela, or Little Italy, for originality.
🚏 [S] 6 to Spring St., 6, J, M, N, Q, R, W, Z to Canal St., or B, D to Grand St. $ Entrees $7-24. ⏰ Open M-Th 11am-2am, F-Sa 11am-3am, Su 11am-2am.

CAFFE PALERMO 💳♿❄☁ ITALIAN, BAKERY, CAFE ❷
148 Mulberry St. ☎212-431-4205 💻www.caffepalermo.com
Palermo has been perfecting its pastries for over 35 years, no mean feat in a place where you can't adjust a camera without hitting some cannoli. Palermo rests most of its pride on that pastry, the mainstay of an extensive menu of small baked goods and larger cakes. Ferrara has the age and the reputation, but Palermo has become almost as famous; you better make visits to both.
🚏 [S] 6 to Spring St., 6, J, M, N, Q, R, W, Z to Canal St., or B, D to Grand St. $ Pastries $4.50-5.50, cakes $6.50/slice. ⏰ Open daily 10:30am-11pm.

nolita

Calm Nolita's offerings aren't as interesting as Little Italy's delicious kitsch or Chinatown's mouth-watering sprawl, but the cafes and coffeeshops here make a great afternoon stop. The clientele is young and fashionable without being pushy about it.

we want liquor!

New York City. Modern. Progressive. Without the slightest vestige of prudery or stuffiness—or so the man sitting across the restaurant from me last weekend during Sunday brunch thought. I was quietly enjoying my French vanilla brioche toast when I heard a voice incredulously ask, "I can't order a mimosa?"

The source of this man's frustration was the New York state law prohibiting the sale of alcohol before noon on Sundays. Sundays mornings are for church, you alcoholic.

The man was sitting with his friend and both of their wives. He began to playfully argue with the waitress. Or rather, he sounded playful, but he definitely wanted that mimosa. The manager, taking pity on the unfortunate waitress eventually walked over to appease the man:

"It's 11:45. You only have 15 minutes to go!"

"Yes, but I've wanted 3 by now."

Next, the manager had an idea:

"I agree. It's a ridiculous law. I mean, I would understand liquor stores not being able to sell alcohol, but it seems alright for people to enjoy a drink with their meal."

"Exactly. Well, as long as you bring it at 12, and not at 12:03 or 12:05."

"Sir, I will bring it at 11:59." And away he walked, making the man feel a sense of victory simply by conceding that the rule was obnoxious, but preventing the rule intact.

Davida Fernandez-Barkan

CAFE HABANA
🍴⛧❄☕ CAFE, LATIN AMERICAN ❷
17 Prince St. (at Elizabeth St.)　　　　　☎212-625-2001 🖳www.cafehabana.com

This corner cafe epitomizes Nolita's effortless cool without being frustratingly upscale. Mexican and Cuban favorites like huevos rancheros and Cuban sandwiches attract crowds of 20-somethings eating lunch and dinner. Try their famous corn dishes. You can either sit down in the corner restaurant or take out from their stand one door away on Elizabeth St.

🍴 Ⓢ 6 to Spring St.; B, D, F, V to Broadway-Lafayette St. Ⓢ Entrees $6.50-12. ☼ Open daily 9am-midnight.

CAFE GITANE
🍴⛧♒☕ CAFE ❷
242 Mott St. (at Prince St.)　　　　　　　　　☎212-334-9552

Another one of Nolita's foreign-influenced cafes, Gitane draws on Moroccan influences to create an edgy but comfortable vibe in its spare corner space. Youngish crowds gather for Moroccan couscous, *hachi parmentier*, and generous salad options. Pastel walls add just enough flavor to the place, creating a Mediterranean feel. There's also outdoor seating.

🍴 Ⓢ 6 to Spring St.; B, D, F, V to Broadway-Lafayette St. Ⓢ Entrees $8-13. ☼ Open M-Th 8am-midnight, F-Sa 9am-12:30pm, Su 8am-midnight.

CIAO BELLA GELATO
🍴⛧ ICE CREAM ❶
285 Mott St.　　　　　　　☎212-431-3591 🖳www.ciaobellagelato.com

There's plenty of gelato to be had a few blocks south in Little Italy, but the clean, small, and untrammeled Ciao Bella is a delicious and quieter alternative. Get in, order a gelato (unique and irresistible flavors like maple ginger snap and Turkish pistachio abound), sundae, or float, and make your exit. Try for the shaded

nolita

benches just outside. Perfect for nomads on hot days.

✚ Ⓢ *6 to Spring St.; B, D, F, V to Broadway-Lafayette St.* Ⓢ *1 scoop $3.25, 2 $4.75, 3 $6.* Ⓩ *Open M-Sa 11-9, Su 11-7.*

GIMME! COFFEE ✆♿ CAFE ❶
225 Mott St. ☎877-446-6325 🖳www.gimmecoffee.com

This small takeout coffee outpost, one of several around the city and even the state, has a growing reputation among caffeine lovers. A unique crowd congregates in its red, claustrophobic interior rich with the scents of well made espresso and cappuccino. There's no seating, so grab something for the road or find a nearby bench.

✚ Ⓢ *6 to Spring St.; B, D, F, V to Broadway-Lafayette St.* Ⓢ *Espresso $2.25, cappuccino $3.50, latte $3.75-4.50.* Ⓩ *Open M-F 7am-9pm.*

NOLITA HOUSE ✆⊗❄✿ AMERICAN, STANDARD ❸
47 East Houston St. ☎212-625-1712 🖳www.nolitahouse.com

Nolita House's aesthetic is unique enough: its logo is a red schoolhouse, and its walls are appropriately lined with chalkboards and old black-and-white school photos. A varied menu offering cheap tacos ($4) alongside more expensive American entrees like pizzas and burgers keeps the dust away. You can also come for their weekend bluegrass brunches and well-stocked bar.

✚ Ⓢ *B, D, F, V to Broadway-Lafayette St.* Ⓢ *Entrees $8-22.* Ⓩ *Open M-W 11:30am-3:30pm and 5-11pm; Th-Sa 11:30am-3:30pm and 5pm-2am; Su 11:30am-3:30pm and 5-11pm.*

lower east side

🔳 YONAH SCHIMMEL KNISHERY ✆⊗ SHOP ❶
137 E. Houston St. ☎212-477-2858 🖳www.yonahschimmel.com

As a sign in this famous knishery says, "You don't have to be Jewish to eat a knish." Very true. And for 100 years, Yonah Schimmel's people have offered their fluffy, delectable knishes to Jews and gentiles alike. They come in all flavors: classics include potato, mushroom, and vegetable, while some cheese knish options are apple, blueberry, chocolate, or apple strudel. They also sell generous portions of homemade kugel ($5) and homemade yogurt, borscht, and soup ($6). So try a knish. And per the directions on a different sign, maybe "Send knishes to your mother in Florida."

✚ Ⓢ *F, M to Lower East Side/2nd Ave. Knishery between Forsych and Eldridge St.* Ⓢ *Knishes $3.50, cheese knishes $4. Homemade yogurt, borscht, soup $6. Latkes $2. Kugel $5. Coffee and tea $1.25.* Ⓩ *Open M-Th 9am-7pm, F-Sa 9am-8pm, Su 9am-7pm.*

🔳 DOUGHNUT PLANT ✆♿ SHOP ❶
379 Grand St., at Norfolk St. ☎212-505-3700 🖳www.doughnutplant.com

The Doughnut Plant: delivering circular happiness to New York's Lower East Side for a century. They offer both smaller, dense cake doughnuts ($2.25-3) and larger fluffy yeast doughnuts ($2-2.50). With a taste for adventure, these creative bakers move beyond the bounds of your everyday flavors, developing treats such as the lavender flower doughnut and *tres leches*. A cup of organic coffee ($1-1.50) or milk from the milk bar ($2-2.50) completes this delicious snack!

✚ Ⓢ *F, J, M, Z to Delancey St./Essex St.* Ⓢ *Tea $1.50-3.* Ⓩ *Open Tu-Su 6:30am-7pm (until doughnuts are sold out).*

🔳 SCHILLER'S LIQUOR BAR ✆♿(((•)))✿ AMERICAN ❷
131 Rivington St., at Norfolk St. ☎212-260-4555 🖳www.schillersny.com

Remember the song about 99 bottles of beer on a wall? At Schiller's, they have literally hundreds of numbered bottles of...well, maybe it's not beer, but it's certainly alcoholic. The wine on the menu is conveniently classified as "Cheap" *($6 glass, $15 carafe)*, "Decent" *($7 glass, $19 carafe)*, and "Good" *($8 glass, $21 carafe)*, so you know exactly what you're getting yourself into. Cocktails are very site-specific, with options such as the **Delancey, New York Sour**, and **Jerry Thomas Manhattan** *($12)*. The food items are similarly New-York-minded *(New York Strip $29)*. And you don't have to be engaging in heavy drinking or eating to hang out here; the free Wi-Fi encourages many a laptop user to linger awhile.

⚓ Ⓢ *F, J, M, Z to Delancey St./Essex St.* Ⓢ *Appetizers $8-12. Salads and sandwiches $11-17. Entrees $14.50-29. Desserts $7. Beer $4-6. Wine $6-15. Carafe of mixed drinks $12.* ✪ *Open M-W 11am-1am, Th 11am-2am, F 11am-3am, Sa 10am-3am, Su 10am-midnight.*

🔖 PINK PONY   ◐占 FRENCH CAFE ❷

176 Ludlow St., between Houston and Stanton St.   ☎212-253-1922 📧www.pinkponynyc.com

When you sit at your little, pink rose-embellished table, be prepared to be whisked away on a culinary journey to Paris. Executed in the style of an endearingly-cluttered French cafe, the Pink Pony is filled with books, oversized wine bottles, and photographs of celebrities past and present. Franco-favorites on the menu include *steak au poivre ($22)* and *crème brûlée ($8)*. If your visit is brunch-oriented, ask about the pancakes *du jour ($8)*.

⚓ Ⓢ *F, J, M, Z to Delancey St./Essex St.* Ⓢ *Entrees $8.75-22. Salads $6-9. Appetizers $6-12. Sandwiches $8-11. Brunch $1.75-10. Beer $6. Wine $8-$11.* ✪ *Open daily 10am-1am.*

SUGAR SWEET SUNSHINE   ◐占 SHOP ❶

126 Rivington St., at Essex St.   ☎212-995-1960 📧www.sugarsweetsunshine.com

Sugar Sweet Sunshine is a bakery's bakery, and their cupcakes are the most formidable of their achievements. Other bakeries would be content with merely chocolate, vanilla, and maybe a few different colors of frostings. Not so here. The cupcake flavors are perfectly paired with icings for an explosively tasty indulgence. Pumpkin cake with cream cheese ice cream. Coconut cake with meringue. Red velvet cake with almond buttercream. It's just too exquisite to be true.

⚓ Ⓢ *F, J, M, Z to Delancey St./Essex St.* Ⓢ *Cupcakes $1.50, 1 dozen $18. Mini cupcake $1. Layer cakes $25-200. Cheesecake slice $5, whole cake $45. Mini Cheesecake $1.50-2. Cookies $0.50-$0.75 each. Muffins $2. Brownies $2.50. Pudding from $4. Coffee and tea $1-$4.50.* ✪ *Open M-Th 8am-10pm, F 8am-11pm, Sa 10am-11pm, Su 10am-7pm.*

FREEMAN'S   ◐占♉ AMERICAN ❷

Freeman Alley, off Rivington St.   ☎212-420-0012 📧www.freemansrestaurant.com

Walk down this graffiti alley and you will suddenly feel as though you have entered somebody's 19th-century cottage on the Hudson. The walls have lots of taxidermy: we're talking deer, birds, a wild boar of some variety, and lots of antlers. The menu has a wild-game flavor, with an emphasis on trout. At lunch, you can order both the smoked trout with hard boiled egg, horseradish cream, and toast *($11)* and the Grilled Eden Brook trout with thyme, garlic, and lemon *($16)*. The soup of the day is generally a unique and tasty starting option.

⚓ Ⓢ *F, M to 2nd Ave. At the end of Freeman Alley, off Rivington St., between Bowery and Chrystie St.* Ⓢ *Appetizers $6-15. Lunch entrees $9-16, dinner entrees $13-26. Brunch $10-14. Desserts $7-9. Wine $9-20. Beer $6-12.* ✪ *Open M-F 11am-4pm and 6pm-11:30pm, Sa-Su 10am-4pm and 6-11:30pm.*

KOSSAR'S BIALYS   ◐占 SHOP ❶

367 Grand St., between Essex and Norfolk St.   ☎212-473-4810

Bialys are legit New York, and these bialys, baked under the kosher supervision of Rabbi Shmuel Fishelis, are about as legitimate as they come. Kossar's also happens to be New York's oldest bialy bakery, and true bagel and bialy connoisseurs know that this is their best option for fresh, fluffy bialys. The bakery closes on Friday nights but opens after Shabbat for an all-night bialy-selling extravaganza that doesn't end until 8pm on Sunday.

🧭 [S] J, M, Z to Delancey St. $ Bialys $0.90. Bagels $1. Small bulka $1, large bulka $2. Sesame stick $1. Mini onion disk $1. Mini bagel $0.90, low-carb bagel $1.75. ⏰ Open M-Th 6am-8pm, F 6am-3pm, Sa sundown-Su 8pm.

CLINTON ST. BAKING COMPANY ♿⊛ AMERICAN [2]

4 Clinton St., by E. Houston St. ☎646-602-6263 💻www.clintonstreetbaking.com

The delicious fare here is all American in one sense or another: Southern Breakfast *($14)*, Po' Boy Catch of the Day *($15)*, Huevos Rancheros *($14)*, etc. The decadent bakery and dessert items *(blueberry cheesecake, chocolate-banana cream pie, $7, $10 a la mode)* are perhaps the best part (these desserts definitely would not be found in a Lower East Side tenement!).

🧭 [S] F, J, M, Z to Delancey St./Essex St. $ Breakfast $9-15. Lunch $10-16. Appetizers $8-12. Entrees $13-23. Desserts $3-9. Beer $6-15. Wine $8-13. ⏰ Open M-F 8am-4pm and 6-11pm, Sa 9am-4pm and 6-11pm, Su 9am-6pm.

THE PICKLE GUYS 💳♿ SHOP [1]

39 Essex St., between Grand and Hester ☎212-656-9739 💻www.nycpickleguys.con

Prepare to have your mind blown by a pickle! These guys have barrels and barrels of them just waiting for you to take away and enjoy. Prefer other types of pickled produce? No problem. Choose from a long list of specialties: pickled carrots, pickled turnips, pickled celery, sour kraut, there is probably nothing in the world they can't pickle.

🧭 [S] F, J, M, Z to Delancey St./Essex St. $ 1 pickle $0.75, 3 pickles $2, 1 quart $6.25, 1 pint plum tomatoes $4, 1 pint pickled string beans $7. Platters $23-37. ⏰ Open M-Th 9am-6pm, F 9am-4pm, Su 9am-6pm.

TEANY 💳🚭 VEGETARIAN, VEGAN [2]

90 Rivington St., between Orchard and Ludlow St. ☎212-475-9190 💻www.teanyny.com

When your name is Teany, being adorable is pretty much part of the description. Every detail, from the matching yellow flowers in miniature vases to the coordinated mint green walls and microsuede couch in the petite interior to the Lilliputian bottles of water, is properly precious. The menu focuses heavily on vegan and vegetarian-friendly items *(vegan BLT $6.50)*, though it also lists plenty of healthy options for meat-consumers *(mango chutney chicken sandwich $10)*. Creative drink possibilities include various flavors of Italian sodas *($3.50)* and French sodas *(Italian soda with half and half or soymilk $4)*.

🧭 [S] F, M to Lower East Side/2nd Ave.; or F, J, M, Z to Delancey St./Essex St. $ Breakfast $3.50-9.50, salads $9-12. Sandwiches and pressed baguettes $6.50-10. Appetizers $5-10. Entrees $10-14. Beverages $2.50-4. Beer $7. Wine $8-10. ⏰ Open M-Th 10am-midnight, F 10am-1am, Sa 9am-1am, Su 9am-midnight.

TIENGARDEN 💳♿ VEGAN [1]

170 Allen St., between Stanton and Rivington St. ☎212-388-1364 💻www.tiengardener.com

A health-oriented establishment where they have replaced all animal products with nutritious, plant-based foods. You can't go wrong with the noodle dishes *($9)*, which come in a variety of types: sesame noodles, buckwheat noodles, udon noodles, and rice noodles are available. If you really want to take control of your meal, try the i-Dish *($10)*, which allows you to pick up to 4 veggies or proteins and a sauce. The vegan floats, smoothies, and sundaes *($4.50-6.50)* should not be overlooked for a glorious vegan finale!

🧭 [S] F, M to 2nd Ave./Lower East Side. $ Sandwiches and wraps $6-8. Appetizers $6. Entrees $9-13. Vegan ice cream $3.50-6.50. Smoothies $4.50. ⏰ Open daily noon-10pm. Weekend brunch noon-4pm.

FALAI 🎫♿🍸☁ ITALIAN ❸

68 Clinton St., between Stanton and Rivington ☎212-253-1960 💻www.falainyc.com

If you get tired of New York pizza and bagels, though it's hard to imagine that you could, try the daring culinary skills of the chefs at Falai. It's safe to say that you will never have tasted some of the ingredients on the menu—at least not in these combinations! The Spaghetti Chitarra *($19)* contains "laughing bird shrimp, parsley pesto, fried parsley, cannellini beans" and "sea urchins." Not even the dessert menu is predictable. For a particularly dramatic finish, try the Elementi *(Banana Raviolo, lychee and coconut caviar, almond financier, pineapple frozen air, $11).*

➔ [S] F, J, M, Z to Essex/Delancey. $ Appetizers $13-16. Pastas $16-22. Fish $25-26. Meat $28-30. Wine bottles $12-16. Desserts $4-20. ⏰ Open M-Th 6-10:30pm, Sa-Su 6-11pm, Su 5:30-10:30pm.

greenwich village

CAFFE DANTE 🎫♿🍸❄☁ ITALIAN, CAFE ❷

79 MacDougal St. ☎212-982-5275 💻www.caffe-dante.com

Caffe Dante's Italian ambience has been attracting the Village's artists, intellectuals, and other passersby since 1915. After almost a century, national pride is evident in the Italian-themed murals lining the walls and the old Italian photographs mounted next to them. And of course, there's the food: the entree menu includes a wide range of panini; the dessert selection mixes Italian pastries with always-popular gelato; and the bar is well-stocked with *vino*. Come to soak up the sunshine in outdoor seating during good weather, to warm up during winter, or to unwind at night.

➔ [S] A, B, C, D, E, F, V to West 4th St. $ Entrees $7-12. Desserts $3-7. Gelato $7.75. Hot drinks $1.50-5. ⏰ Open daily 10am-2am.

CREPERIE 🥡♿ FRENCH, TAKEOUT ❷

112 MacDougall St. ☎212-253-6705 💻www.creperienyc.com

It's easy to miss Creperie—a small hole in the wall with bright yellow-red walls and just two small counters along the side—but that's no excuse. One of Greenwich Village's best takeout options has a huge menu that belies its tiny size. Every crepe you've ever imagined is available here, from veggie options, with fillings like sautéed mushrooms, to sweet and fruity ones of sugar and lemon, baked apple, blueberry and banana, to the heavy-hitting savory classics of smoked turkey, or sautéed chicken. Cap it off with a chocolate dessert filling or just knock yourself out and ascend to heaven with a chocolate brownie, chocolate fudge, ice cream, banana, and whipped cream treat. Yes, that's one crepe.

➔ [S] A, B, C, D, E, F, V to West 4th St. $ Veggie crepes $7-9, sweet and fruity crepes $4-8, savory crepes $7-11, chocolate crepes $7-11. ⏰ Open M-Sa 9am-3am, Su 9am-2am.

MAMOUN'S FALAFEL 🥡♿ MIDDLE EASTERN, TAKEOUT ❶

119 MacDougall St. ☎212-674-8685 💻www.mamouns.com

Mamoun's has been supplying Village crowds with delicious Middle Eastern for four decades—all with barely enough room to fit a few tables and the lines constantly arriving for some of the city's most renowned falafel and shawarma dishes. Sandwiches and platters stuffed with *baba ghanoush*, tabbouleh, and kebab go for relatively cheap prices. You can add some flavor with some of Mamoun's own hot sauce *($3.50 per bottle).*

➔ [S] A, B, C, D, E, F, V to W. 4th St. $ Sandwiches $2.50-5. Platters $5-10. ⏰ Open daily 11am-5pm.

FRENCH ROAST

♥ ♿ ☕ 🔊 ☕ CAFE ❷

78 W. 11th St. at 6th Ave.   ☎212-533-2233 📧 www.frenchroastny.com/downtown

A vision of Paris in downtown Manhattan, the French Roast Cafe mimics the look and feel of a French cafe right down to the circular outdoor tables. Gallic memorabilia lines the walls, and the menu follows suit with dishes like rata-touille, croques monsieur, and sautéed spinach. In a trans-European spirit, a wide range of pastas and gelato are also available. And best of all, the cafe never sleeps: its 24/7 schedule makes the cafe both a nightspot and an ideal, caffeine-laden hangover center.

✈ Ⓢ F, L, V to 6th Ave.-14th St.; A, B, C, D, E, F, V to West 4th St. Ⓢ Coffees $2-5. Entrees $11-20. Ⓩ Open 24hr.

BLEECKER STREET PIZZA

♥ ⊗♿ PIZZERIA ❷

69 7th Ave. (at Bleecker St.)   ☎212-924-4466 📧 www.bleeckerstreetpizza.com

Jimmy Kimmel, Regis Philbin, and the Food Network have all sung the praises of this celebrated Village eatery. But the hurried servers, long lines, and plain tables mark it as a regular no-frills pizzeria peddling a simply excellent product. Crowds of returning addicts testify to its power—just watch for the small red building on the corner of Seventh Ave. and Bleecker, enter, and never forget it again.

✈ Ⓢ 1 to Christopher St. Ⓢ Slices $2.50-3.25. Whole pizza $17.50-22. Toppings $0.75 each. Heroes $7-8. Sandwiches $5-6. Ⓩ Open M-F 10am-2am, Sa 10am-5am, Su 10am-2:30am.

FAELA CUBANA

♥♿ ☕❄♿ CUBAN, BRAZILIAN ❸

543 LaGuardia Pl.   ☎212-272-6500 📧 www.faelacubana.com

Faela Cubana is worth entering just for its look alone: exuberant murals depict-ing Havana street scenes line the walls, while an etching of Pele by the door lies just below a signed Pele jersey. It's a good introduction to the menu itself, which boasts an eclectic mix of Brazilian and Cuban items. Entrees include *picadillo habana* (ground turkey), "Castro's lechour," (pulled pork), and *frango i parema* (Brazilian-style half-chicken). For breakfast, you can try the *favela* eggs or go Caribbean with simple Cuban eggs. Wash it down with a healthy sampling from the large Sangria jug on the counter.

✈ Ⓢ A, B, C, D, E, F, V to West 4th St. Ⓢ Sandwiches $8-12. Entrees $11-20. Ⓩ Open daily 9am-11:30pm.

BAMBOLEO

♥♿ ☕ MEXICAN ❷

170 Bleecker St. (at Sullivan St.)   ☎212-253-8226

This exuberant *cantina* is boldly decorated and has a menu to justify it. Dozens of chimichangas, enchiladas, burritos, and tacos can be had for affordable prices, making this one of Greenwich Village's main destinations for genuine Mexican deliciousness. And nothing goes with enchiladas (or constant *futbol* on TV) like sangria, mojitos, margaritas, and tequilas, all of them cheaper here than at many other eateries of its kind.

✈ Ⓢ A, B, C, D, E, F, V to West 4th St. Ⓢ Tacos $2.50-4. Soups $4-5. Entrees $8.50-11. Lunch special $8. Drinks $6-10. Ⓩ Open M-Th noon-midnight, F-Sa noon-1am, Su noon-11pm. Lunch special M-F noon-3pm. Happy hour daily 3-7pm.

MESKEREM

♥⊗☕❄ ETHIOPIAN ❷

124 MacDougall St.   ☎212-777-8111

The steep staircase leading down to this low-lying restaurant looks treacherous, but it's more than worth it. Forget utensils: like any genuine Ethiopian restaurant worth its *alech*, Meskerem provides you with more than enough *imbeche* (a spongy type of bread) to scoop up bite-size portions of its delicious entrees. Though meat is the star here—try the *shro wat*, ground chicken in barbeque sauce, or the *goven beswegu*, prime beef with garlic—Meskerem offers a range of veggie options for herbivores (like lentils in garlic and olive oil).

⚡ Ⓢ A, B, C, D, E, F, V to West 4th St. Ⓢ Entrees $8-14. 🕐 Open daily 11:30am-11:30pm. Lunch special M-F 11:30am-3:30pm.

QUANTUM LEAP
⊛⊗🍸❉ VEGETARIAN, HEALTH ❷
226 Thompson St.   ☎212-677-8050 💻http://quantumleaprestaurant.com

Quantum Leap has been feeding the vegetarian hordes of Greenwich Village and NYU since 1974, and it's not showing any signs of slowing. This is your first stop for barbecue vegan chicken, Zen platters, quinoa bowls, and, of course, the mandated veggie burgers. There's also an enticing selection of homemade desserts. Get semi-meaty with their salmon and dangerous with their ales and wines.

⚡ Ⓢ A, B, C, D, E, F, V to West 4th St. Ⓢ Entrees $8-11. 🕐 Open M-F 11:30am-11pm, Sa 11am-11pm, Su 11am-10pm.

MAGNOLIA BAKERY
⊛⊛⊗❉ BAKERY, PASTRY SHOP ❶
W 11th St. and Bleecker St.   ☎212-462-2572 💻magnoliabakery.com

Immortalized in **"Lazy Sunday"** and *Sex and the City*, the Magnolia has been drawing massive crowds into its tiny space for years, making it a West Village landmark. A teeming variety of freshly made cupcakes are the main highlights, with flavors ranging from ginger to pecan to peach, but a slew of other near-orgasmic pastry options make this a must-visit if you're in the neighborhood.

⚡ Ⓢ 1, 2, 3 to 14th St. Ⓢ Cupcakes $2.50-4. Other pastries $3-7. 🕐 Open M-Th 9am-11:30pm, F-Sa 9am-12:30am, Su 9am-11:30pm.

east village

▨ VESELKA
⊛⚅⊿🍸 UKRAINIAN ❶
144 2nd Ave., at E. 9th St.   ☎212-228-9682 💻www.veselka.com

What began in 1954 as a candy shop in the middle of the East Village's Ukrainian community is now a bustling Eastern European delicatessen that somehow escapes dive-delidom (although the prices are more than reasonable). Signs in capital letters behind the counter loudly advertise specialties: cold borscht *($3.50-$4.75)* and seasonal pierogies *($7-$11.50).* The menu contains classic American food, but US-style lunch and dinner entrees *(marinated chicken breast $13),* but you might have more fun by focusing on Ukrainian ones such as **Ola's Famous Veal Goulash** *($15).*

⚡ Ⓢ 6 to Astor Place. Ⓢ Entrees $7-15. Soup $3.50-4.75. Sides $3.50. Pastries $0.75-4.75. Breakfast $4-12. Beer $3-6.25. Wine $7-8. 🕐 Open 24hr.

▨ ZUM SCHNEIDER
⊛⚅🍸⊿ GERMAN ❷
107 Ave. C, at 7th St.   ☎212-598-1098 💻www.zumschneider.com

Authentic Germans serving authentic German food and authentic German beers either outside on blue-and-white checkered tablecloths or inside under a brick arch and model trees. The Wiener Schnitzel *($18)* is always a good choice, and vegetarians palates will be delighted by the Käsespätzle *(homemade spaetzle with cheese and caramelized onion, sans bacon, $15).* A good solid Bavarian beer choice is the Hacker Pschorr *($4/$5/$10).* Prost!

⚡ Ⓢ 6 to Astor Pl; N, R, W to 8th St. Ⓢ Salads $6-8. Appetizers $3-11. Entrees $14-98. Brunch $8-11. Beer $3-$8. Wine $6-$10. 🕐 Open M-Th 5pm-2am, F 4pm-4am, Sa 1pm-4am; Su 1pm-2am.

▨ ORGANIC GRILL
⊛🍸⦅ᵖⁱ⦆ VEGAN, VEGETARIAN ❷
123 1st Ave.   ☎212-477-7177 💻www.theorganicgrill.com

If you are not already a vegan or vegetarian, this restaurant may convert you. It's not all soy burgers and salads either, though both are delicious here.

Entrees such as the vegan pierogies served in a creamy, cashew sour cream sauce prove that vegans really do have more fun. The party doesn't stop with the entrees either. House-made vegan and raw organic post-meal treats include apple-berry crisps, chocolate cheesecake, and peanut-butter cream pie *($6)*.

[S] 6 to Astor Pl. Walk to 1st Ave. between 7th St. and St. Mark's Place. $ Appetizers $7-10. Entrees $10.25-17. Salads $7-12. Sandwiches $9-10. Brunch $4-11.50. Smoothies $6-7.50. Desserts $3-8. Coffee drinks $3-6. Beer $6-8. Wine $7-8. ⏰ Open M-Th noon-10pm, F noon-11pm, Sa 10am-11pm, Su 10am-10pm.

THE BEAN CAFE [1]

49½ 1st Ave., on 3rd St. ☎212-353-1477 www.thebeancoffeeandtea.com

A colorful coffee shop with a slew of creative sandwich options *($6-7)*. The brie and apple on pecan raisin bread is one of the most deliciously unique. You may decide to skip straight to dessert, however, when you see the mammoth cupcakes *($4)* in such tempting flavors as Snickers, Oreo, and peanut butter cup. The shop takes care of vegan customers with vegan cupcakes *($3.50)* and loaves *($3)* as well.

[S] 6 to Astor Pl. $ Baked goods $3-7. Hot drinks $1.50-4.35. Frozen drinks $2-4.50. ⏰ Open daily 7am-2am.

VENIERO'S BAKERY [1]

342 E. 11th St., between 1st and 2nd Ave. ☎212-674-7070 www.venierospastry.com

If you care about cannoli, if you treasure a tart, if you itch for Italian ice and gelato, please, please, *please* make a stop at Veniero's. Hundreds of irresistible pastries line up before your eyes, and handmade Italian ice and gelato in the back of the store. Have no doubt that this will be some of the best pastry you have ever lusted after—the Veniero family has had about 116 years of practice making it.

[S] 6 to Astor Pl. $ Pastries $2.25-4.75. Cakes $13-40. Cookies $13-$16 per lb. Coffee and tea $1.50-4.50. Gelato and Italian ice from $2.50. ⏰ Open M-Th 8am-midnight, F-Sa 8am-1am, Su 8am-midnight.

MUDSPOT CAFE [1]

307 E. 9th St., between 1st and 2nd Ave. ☎212-228-9074 www.mudtruck.com

A cool indie atmosphere and all-purpose menu with everything from fancy coffee and tea drinks *($1.50-5)* to pastries *($2-5)* to full sandwiches *($8)* and salads *($8-12)* make this a popular hangout at all hours of the day and night. The guacamole and chips *($8)* is just one of several options to satisfy those late-night munchies.

[S] 6 to Astor Pl. $ Coffee and tea drinks $1.50-5. Pastries $2-5. Breakfast $4.50-10. Sandwiches $8. Salads $8-13. Desserts $7-8. Beer $5. Wine $6-8. ⏰ Open M-F 8:30am-midnight, Sa-Su 8am-midnight.

SPICE COVE INDIAN [1]

326 E. 6th St., between 1st and 2nd Ave. ☎212-674-8884

Some of the hottest Vindaloo curry in the East Village comes out of this Indian treasure. You can try the famous fiery curry with vegetables, chicken, lamb or beef. If spicy is not your cup of lassi, try the coconut-flavored Malai curry instead. You may be skeptical of an Indian restaurant without a lunch buffet, but the lunch special, which includes soup, an appetizer, an entree, and naan *($6-$7, Tu-Su 12:30-4:30pm)* is a steal of a feast. Dinner specials are also available *($14-18)*.

[S] 6 to Astor Pl. $ Appetizers $5-8. Salads $5-9. Entrees $9-18. Dessert $3. Beer $3.50-6. Wine $5-6. ⏰ Open M 4:30-11pm, Tu-Th 12:30-11pm, F-Sa 12:30-11:30pm, Su 12:30-11pm; Lunch special 12:30-4:30pm.

YAFFA CAFE

●⊗Ⓨ♨ ECLECTIC ❷

97 St. Mark's Place.

☎212-677-9001 ■www.yaffacafe.com

The decorator of this fine establishment may have been having an identity crisis. At least five different styles of wallpaper cover the walls, several strings of colored lights, and an entire plastic produce section hang from the ceilings, and Colonial, Southeast Asian, and Roman centurion figurines fill up space not taken up by the leopard-spotted booths and sparkly tables. The food is vegetarian and health food-centric, with several chicken, turkey, and seafood options mixed in. Start with a Middle Eastern Platter *(hummus, tahini, baba ganoush, $9)*, then progress to a stir fry *(vegetable $10, shrimp $14, chicken $12)* or a pasta dish *($10-14)*.

✦ Ⓢ *6 to Astor Pl. Walk East to St. Mark's Pl., between 1st Ave. and Ave. A.* ⓢ *Salads $9-12. Sandwiches, wraps, and burgers $5-10. Appetizers $5-10. Entrees $10-15. Desserts $5.25. Wine $8.* ⌚ *Open 24hr.*

POMMES FRITES

●♨& FRENCH FRIES ❶

123 2nd Ave.

☎212-674-1234 ■www.pommesfrites.ws

A little Belgian cottage peddling that most European of all snacks, French fries and mayo! And not just plain mayo either. Oh no, they have honey mustard mayo, pesto mayo, roasted garlic mayo, wasabi mayo, Vietnamese pineapple mayo... they ought to call this place the Mayo Clinic. Other condiments include cheese sauce, ketchup, and mustard if you are boring.

✦ Ⓢ *6 to Astor Pl. Walk to 2nd Ave. between E. 7th St. and St. Mark's Pl.* ⓢ *Regular $4.50. Large $6.25. Double $7.75. Sauces $1 each. Combo of 3 sauces $2.50. Ketchup, especial, frite sauce, vinegar, Tabasco, yellow mustard, chopped raw onion free.* ⌚ *Open M-Th 11:30am-1am, F-Sa 11:30am-3:30am, Su 11:30am-1am.*

MOISHE'S BAKE SHOP

●& BAKERY ❶

115 2nd Ave., between E. 6th and 7th St.

☎212-505-8555

You'll find warm pastries sold by even warmer people at this 40-year-old kosher bake shop. If you're lucky, you may even get to meet the jolly Moishe himself. At $0.75, the bagels and bialys have to be some of the cheapest in Manhattan, and Moishe cuts a special deal on a cinnamon or cheese danish with coffee *($2)*. Try one of four flavors of Hamentashen—they're not just for Purim! *($1-2.50)*. If you really want to indulge, the matzah-style thin, crispy sugar kichel is superb *(2 for $5)*.

✦ Ⓢ *6 to Astor Pl.* ⓢ *Coffee $0.50. Bagels and bialys $0.75. Rugelach $13 per lb. Hamentaschen $1-2.50. Babkas and sugar kichel 2 for $5.* ⌚ *Open M-Th 7am-9pm, F 7am-1hr. before sundown, Su 7am-9pm.*

WESTVILLE EAST

●⊗♨ AMERICAN ❷

173 Ave. A, at E 11th St.

☎212-677-2033 ■www.westvillenyc.com

A little piece of the Wild West in the middle of the East Village. You can get a 12 oz. char-grilled Newport steak *($17)* if you're feeling very West Texas, or stick with the baked challah bread French toast *($9)* if you're feeling more New York. Yes, it's a rare establishment that offers both the Hebrew National Hot Dog *($2.50-8)* and grilled pork chop *($13)*. Whichever you choose, a piece of blueberry or apple pie *($5, a la mode no extra charge)* will be the perfect way to end your meal.

✦ Ⓢ *6 to Astor Pl.* ⓢ *Appetizers $5-10. Salads $6-10.50. Entrees $12-18. Burgers $7.50-11. Hot dogs, and sausages $2.50-10. Desserts $3-6. Brunch $2.50-10. Wine $7-$8.50.* ⌚ *Open M-F 11:30am-11pm; Sa-Su 10am-11pm.*

FRANK

●Ⓨ♨ ITALIAN ❷

88 2nd Ave.

☎212-420-0202 ■www.frankrestaurant.com

At Frank, you can dine on spaghetti *($10)* and bruschetta *($3 per piece)* amid a hodgepodge of china and black and white pictures of other people's family. Almost every recipe has been contributed by some mysterious family member

("Uncle Tony's Gnocchi," "Grandma Carmella's tomato and meat gravy," etc.) They may not be *your* Uncle Tony or Grandma Carmella, but they have come up with some delicious recipes, whoever they are.

⚑ Ⓢ 6 to Astor Pl. Ⓢ Pasta $10-13. Appetizers $3-13. Entrees $15-18. Sandwiches $10-14. Breakfast $7-11. Desserts $9. Beer $6-16. ☼ Open M-Th 10:30am-1am, F-Sa 10:30am-2am, Su 10:30am-midnight.

CAFECITO
●●Ⓧℐ CUBAN ❷

185 Ave. C, between 11th and 12th St.   ☎212-253-9966 ▧www.cafecitonyc.com

Feasting on *Playa Varadero (boniato hash, bollos, avocado, mixed greens, black beans and white rice, $12)*, sipping a *café con leche ($2.75)*, and listening to smooth salsa beats amid yellow walls and festive cushions, you may think that you stepped into a little Cuban cafe. If you really want to party Havana-style, stop in anytime Monday or Tuesday night when drinks are $5 each and appetizers are half off. The crispy empanadas *($7.25)* border on addictive.

⚑ Ⓢ 6 to Astor Pl.; N, Q, R to 8th St. Ⓢ Appetizers $4.50-$11. Sandwiches $9-11. Entrees $12-15. Soups and salads $4-14. ☼ Open M-W 11am-11pm, Th 11am-noon, F-Sa 11am-2am, Su 11am-11pm.

PINISI CAFE AND BAKERY
●Ⓧ BAKERY ❶

128 E. 4th St., between 1st and 2nd Ave.   ☎212-614-9079 ▧www.pinisibakerynyc.com

Lovers of sweets flock to this tiny neighborhood bakery for a slice of its delicious cakes *($5)* or a gourmet cupcake. The most popular is the Red Velvet, followed closesly by the Lavender. Individually, these little pieces of frosted perfection are $3 each, but you should probably just buy a dozen, when they drop by 50¢. You can never have too many cupcakes, right?

⚑ Ⓢ 6 to Astor Pl. Ⓢ Cupcakes $3. Cake slices $5. Cookies $0.50. Rugelach $2.50. Coffee and tea $1.50-3. ☼ Open daily 7am-11pm.

CUCINA DE PESCE
Ⓧℐ ITALIAN ❷

87 E. 4th St., between 2nd and 3rd Ave.   ☎212-260-8600 ▧www.cucinadepesce.com

Pasta or fish? Pasta or fish? Should I have the pumpkin ravioli *($11)* or the monk fish in lobster sauce *($14)?* Such will be your struggle when you dine at this Italian eatery. If you can't make up your mind, you can have pasta and fish—just order the seafood lasagna *($14)* or the linguini with shrimp and calamari *($15)*. Problem solved!

⚑ Ⓢ 6 to Astor Pl. *i* Only American Express accepted. Ⓢ Appetizers $7-10. Pasta $10-15. Meat $12-19. Fish $14-19. ☼ Open M-Th 3:30-11pm, F-Sa 3:30pm-midnight, Su 3:30-11pm.

chelsea

▧ CAFETERIA
●&ℐ AMERICAN ❷

119 7th Ave.   ☎212-414-1717 ▧www.cafeteriagroup.com

The meatloaf comes with garlic mashed potatoes, green beans, and roasted to-mato relish *($15)*. The blueberry pancakes are made with ricotta and come with lemon zest and cream *($11)*. The inspiration is Aunt Jemima, the execution is Wolfgang Puck. Also featuring a spirited list of cocktails *($11-13)* and mocktails *($5-6)*.

⚑ Ⓢ 1 to 18th St. Ⓢ Breakfast $6-12. Appetizers $6-13. Salads $8-15. Entrees $14-20. Beer $6-8. Mixed drinks $11-13. ☼ Open daily 24hr.

▧ WESTSIDE MARKET
●& GROCERY STORE ❷

77 Seventh Ave., at 15th St.   ☎212-807-7771 ▧www.wmarketnyc.com

You may never have been shocked and awed by a grocery store before, but there is a first time for everything. Cheeses, artisan beers, sandwiches, hot entrees, sushi, salads, sides, homemade spreads, meats, granolas, candies, coffees, teas, juices...they have everything, and they have a lot of it. Whether you're gourmet-only or a shopper on a budget, this store has enough options to keep staring wide-eyed at food for longer than is generally socially acceptable.

✠ Ⓢ 1 to 18th St. Ⓢ Cheese $5-27 per lb. Artisan beer 6-pack $12-20. Homemade spreads from $3 per lb. Sushi $6.15-9.75. Wraps and sandwiches $6-7. Meat $3-9 per lb. Hot entrees $5-16 per lb. Produce $0.89-4 per lb. Ⓞ Open daily 7am-midnight.

▨ THE CITY BAKERY   ◆& BUFFET ❷
3 W. 18th St., between 5th and 6th Ave.   ☎212-366-1414 ▣www.thecitybakery.com
Restaurateurs in Chelsea sometimes give their establishments misleading names. This "bakery," for instance, is actually a buffet-style restaurant. Gourmet pastas, including the best macaroni and cheese in the neighborhood, salads, homemade soups, fresh baked goods; grab a plate and load up! Just like your high school cafeteria, but with edible food.

✠ Ⓢ L, N, Q, R, M to Union Sq.; or 4,5,6 14th St./Union Square. Ⓢ Salads and hot entrees $14 per lb. Yogurt and fruit $7.50 per lb. Bakery $0.75-$6. Pizzas and sandwiches $3.50-$9. Soup $5-7. Ⓞ Open M-F 7:30am-7pm, Sa 8am-7pm, Su 10am-6pm.

ROSA MEXICANO   ◆&Ⴤ MEXICAN ❷
9 E. 18th St., between Broadway and 5th Ave.   ☎212-533-7159 ▣www.rosamexicano.com
In the Chelsea restaurant business, presentation is everything, and this Mexican-inspired restaurant just about takes the *torta*. Every dish, from the chicken tacos ($13.50-18.50) to the **Enchiladas de Pulpo** ($14), a world apart from the ones your *abuela* made, is a work of art. You almost don't want to eat it. But don't stare too long, the food is even more delicious than it looks.

✠ Ⓢ R, W, F, M to 23rd St., or L, N, Q, R, W, 4, 5, 6 to 14th St./Union Square. Ⓢ Appetizers $8-14. Quesadillas and tortas $11.50-13.50. Tacos $13.50-19. Enchiladas $11.75-24. Tacos $14-20. Tequila $11-19. Margaritas $11-18. Wine $8-10. Ⓞ M-Th 11:30am-10:30pm, F-Sa 11:30am-11:30pm.

PARADISE CAFE   ◆& COFFEESHOP ❶
141 8th Ave, at 17th St..   ☎212-647-0066
Hipsters and businessmen alike gather at this brightly colored cafe papered with original art to sip their fair-trade certified coffee and use free Wi-Fi. The menu contains an overwhelming number of sandwiches, wraps, salads, and bakery items for both meat eaters and vegetarians. On summer days, the large windows are opened to let in the breeze. Paradisiacal indeed.

✠ Ⓢ A, C, E, L to 8th Ave./14th St.; or 1 to 18th St. Ⓢ Salads $7.50-9.50. Sandwiches $4-8.25. Breakfast $1.50-$8.25. Smoothies $4.50-$5.50. Bakery $1.90-$4. Coffee and tea $1.30-4. Ⓞ Open daily 7am-7pm.

BETTER BURGER   ◆& BURGERS ❶
178 8th Ave., between 19th and 20th St.   ☎212-989-6688 ▣www.betterburgernyc.com
You know the American burger has developed an attitude when the condiment bar includes "Karma Ketchup" (ketchup with curry, cumin, coriander, and cardamom). Yes, the burger has gone in for a makeover and come back tastier, healthier, and more creative. It now comes in chicken, turkey, and soy form ($5-7.45). Fries, too, have their noses in the air; they insist on being AIR-BAKED instead of deep-fried. Instead of ordering a milkshake, you can wash it all down with milk- or fruit-based smoothies in eight different flavors.

✠ Ⓢ C,E to 23rd St./8th Ave. Ⓢ Burgers $5-8. Sides $2.25. Salads $3.45-9. Soups $3-4. Smoothies $4.25-5.25. Ⓞ Open M-Th 11am-11:30pm, F-Sa 11am-midnight, Su 11am-11:30pm.

RUB   ◆&Ⴤ BARBECUE ❷
208 W. 23rd St.   ☎212-524-4300 ▣www.rubbbq.com
They call him the "Baron of Barbeque." That's because Paul Kirk, head chef of

RUB (Righteous Urban Barbeque), has won 425 cooking awards and holds a coveted position in the **Barbecue Hall of Fame.** You can feast on the Baron's spicy, tangy barbecue greatness on pork-, fish-, chicken-, duck-, or even, if you are of the vegetarian persuasion, Portobello mushroom-form. An order of deep-fried Oreos *($5)* or bacon chocolate-chip cookies *($6)* will help you close your feast in true Kansas City-barbecue style.

✦ Ⓢ *1 to 23rd St.* Ⓢ *Appetizers $7-9. Sandwiches $9.25-12. BBQ by the lb. $17-18. Platters $15.50-24. Chicken $4.75-19. Ribs $12.50-24. Specialties $15.50-289. Beer $6. Mixed drinks $7-12.* Ⓩ *Open daily 11:30am-11:30pm.*

ELMO
♥♿⚲♈ NEW AMERICAN ❸

156 7th Ave., at 19th St. ☎212-337-8000 🖵www.elmorestaurant.com

Don't be misled into thinking the name has anything to do with Sesame Street; this place is for grown-ups. You can tell from the modern art hanging from the ceiling, the creative cocktails like the Blood Orange Cosmo *($11)*, and the fact that the French fries are truffle-filled *($9)*. The waiters, clad in black shorts and matching shirts, will treat you like family. Or at least call you "Love."

✦ Ⓢ *1 to 23rd St.* Ⓢ *Appetizers $7-10. Salads $7-17. Mixed drinks $11. Wine $8-10.* Ⓩ *Open daily M-F 11am-midnight, Sa 11am-1am, Su 10am-11pm.*

VYNL
♥♿⚲♈ THAI DINER ❷

102 8th Ave., at 15th St. ☎212-400-2118 🖵www.vynl-nyc.com

With a ceiling that looks like a giant disco ball sky dotted by record-shaped raindrops, colorful mosaic tables, and little shrines to music on the walls, complete with Michael Jackson and "Yellow Submarine" dolls, you can't possibly sit in this restaurant and not be having fun. The interactive menu, with items such as "Your" Grilled Cheese Sandwich, is similarly fun. Choose from six different breads, seven different cheeses, and optional add-ons such as bacon and avocado *($7)*.

✦ Ⓢ *1, 2, 3, A, C, E, L to 14th St./8th Ave.* Ⓢ *Appetizers $6-12. Soups and salads $7-13. Burgers $10-11. Sandwiches $7-10. Entrees $11-17.* Ⓩ *M-Th 11am-11pm, F 11am-midnight, Sa-Su 9:30am-midnight.*

LE ZIE 2000
♥♿⚲♈ VENETIAN ❸

172 7th Ave., between 20th and 21st St. ☎212-206-8686 🖵www.lezie.com

Because Italian restaurants are generic and cliché, Le Zie 2000 specializes in *Venetian* food. Which means that they serve lasagna, ravioli, fettuccine, gnocchi, and spaghetti *($12-16)*. The linguini with clams, garlic, and olive oil *($14)* is delicious.

✦ Ⓢ *1 to 18th St. or 23rd St.* Ⓢ *Appetizers $6-17. Pasta $12-16. Entrees $15-17. Wine $8.* Ⓩ *Open M-F noon-11pm, Sa-Su 11am-11pm.*

POP BURGER
♥♿♈ DINER ❷

58-60 9th Ave., between 14th and 15th St. ☎212-414-8686 🖵www.popburger.com

The innovative **Pop Burger** is a 3 oz. patty, usually served with a clone or two. You can eat it in the counter area, which resembles a cross between a modern art gallery and beach-style food stand, or in the swanky lounge area, paired with a cocktail *($12-15)*. But choose wisely: at the counter, twin pop burgers cost a reasonable $6.75, while in the lounge the price skyrockets to $15 for a trio.

✦ Ⓢ *A, C, E, L to 14th St.* Ⓢ *Burgers and sandwiches $7-9. Salads $6-10. Sides $3.50-5. Soda and shakes $2-6. Dinner $12-25. Beer $5-11, mixed drinks $12-15, wine $11/44-$16/60.* Ⓩ *Open M-Th 11am-2am, F-Sa 11am-5am, Su 11am-2am. Lounge opens at 5pm.*

union sq., flatiron district, murray hill

Restaurants are the highlights of these neighborhoods: the old commingles with the brand new, the affordable with the ultra-chic, and a diverse array of cuisines are represented in a cultural no-man's-land. Many of the heftier, better-quality restaurants are predictably expensive, but the cafes and sandwich shops offer good-sized meals in more inviting settings. **Curry Hill,** a large group of South Asian restaurants and grocery shops, lies along the upper 20's and lower 30's around **Lexington** and **Third Avenues.**

👍 EISENBERG SANDWICH SHOP 💳♿❄ DELI, TAKEOUT ❷

174 5th Ave. (near W. 22nd St.) ☎212-675-5096

This legendary (and legendarily cramped) sandwich shop has been dishing out the goods since 1929. The sheer range of options is huge: from reuben to grilled cheese to tuna and on to countless others, familiar and otherwise. Small breakfast options and burgers help round out the selection. Lines are long, but not even the massive crowds have taken away the family feel of this neighborhood favorite.

🚇 [S] F, V, N, R to 23rd St. $ Sandwiches $3.50-9. Burgers $6.50-9.50. 🕐 Open M-Th 6:30am-8pm, Sa 8am-6pm, Su 8am-4pm.

CAFE PRAGUE 💳🚭❄📶 CAFE, PASTRY SHOP ❷

2 W. 19th St. (near 5th Ave.) ☎212-929-2602

Everybody's favorite Eastern European city is the theme of this new, high-ceilings Flatiron eatery. Affordable entrees like creamed spinach and beef-stuffed peppers are complemented by breads, slushies, and smoothies. And there are plenty of sandwiches along the deli bar. If that doesn't suit you, try the cheap, all-day Czech breakfast.

🚇 [S] F, V, N, R to 23rd St. $ Breakfast $3.25-8. Lunch $8.50-9.50. Sandwiches $5-8. Pastries $3-6. 🕐 Open M-W 7am-8pm, Th-F 7am-9pm, Sa 8am-9pm, Su 9am-9pm.

SHAKE SHACK 💳♿🍸🌳 OUTDOOR, TAKEOUT ❷

11 Madison Ave. ☎212-889-6600 💻www.shakeshack.com

It's just outgrown its toddler years, but the Shake Shack has already become one of the most famous food stops in a wide radius. There may not be anything unusual in the selection itself—standards like burgers, dogs, hand-spun shakes, and sundaes—but the quality is enough to constantly draw long lines stretching out toward the Madison Square Park entrance. Rotating frozen custards (a different flavor each day) is just another reason to keep coming back and waiting in line. There's plenty of outdoor seating next door, but even that fills up. Luckily, you have plenty of park space at your hands.

🚇 [S] N, R to 23rd St. Southeastern corner of Madison Square Park. $ Burgers and dogs $4-9. Shakes $5.25-7. Beer and wine $5-6.50. 🕐 Open daily 11am-9pm.

SPOON 💳♿❄ CAFE, DELI ❷

17 W. 20th St. ☎646-230-3000 💻www.spoonnyc.com

There's a turn-of-the-century feel to this isolated Flatiron cafe. Old-school lights illuminate finely etched walls and ceilings, and the space extends all the way to the back (you'll find some seating there). But the clientele and staff are mostly youthful, attracted by sandwiches, salads, and other deli standards. Their *prix-fixe* brunch menu draws rave reviews. Of course, you can always settle for a simple item from the espresso bar.

🚇 [S] F, V, N, R to 23rd St. $ Sandwiches $7.50-9. Salads $9-10. 🕐 Open M-F 7:30am-5:30pm, Sa-Su 10am-4pm.

CAFE MEDINA

♨⊗❄ MOROCCAN, DELI ❷

9 E. 17th St. ☎212-242-2777 🖳www.cafemedina.com

They've got quite the entrance: come in and you're immediately faced with ▮**jugs** of delicious juice and a counter full of salad ingredients. Go on a bit further and you'll hit some of the most acclaimed soups in New York. With flavors like chicken coconut, salmon clam chowder, and chilled avocado (and that's just for starters), Medina has been pulling in soup fanatics for years. Juices, smoothies, and yogurts might go down well with them, too.

⌖ Ⓢ F, V, N, R to 23rd St. Ⓢ Soups $4-6. Salads $7-10.50. Sandwiches $7-8.50. Pastries $1.75-2.50. ⌚ Open M-W 7am-8pm, Th 7am-7pm, F-Sa 8am-5pm.

PONGAL

♨♿♈❄ INDIAN, KOSHER ❷

110 Lexington Ave. (near 27th St.) ☎212-696-9458 🖳www.pongalnyc.com

Finally, an Indian kosher vegetarian restaurant for the rest of us. Approved *subji* (veggie) and *utthappan* (a kind of pizza with the ingredients baked right into the "crust") dishes are the perfect lead-in to the dessert items: Indian ice creams and cheese balls in syrup. All for affordable prices and in a thin but sumptuously decorated space. It's a crowded market in Curry Hill, but Pongal impresses with unique dishes and friendly atmosphere.

⌖ Ⓢ 6 to 28th St. Ⓢ Entrees $7-12. ⌚ Open M-Th noon-10:30pm, F-Sa noon-11:30pm, Su noon-10:30pm.

midtown west

🏵 EMPANADA MAMA

♨♈♿ PAN LATIN ❶

763 9th Ave., between 51st and 52nd St. ☎212-698-9008 🖳www.empmamanyc.com

The menu at this watermelon-color-schemed empanada restaurant pays tribute to many different countries, from the predictable empanada with ground beef, olives, sauteed onions, and potatoes (Brazil) to the seemingly incongruous sausage sauteed with sauerkraut (Poland). You really can't go wrong with these little bundles of flavor ($2-3) no matter from where they hail, or with the ample tropical cocktail options. Try a passion fruit margarita ($8).

⌖ Ⓢ C, E to 50th St. Ⓢ Empanadas $2-3. Salads and soups $5-10. Entrees $12-15. Tapas $5-8. Desserts $2.50-4.50. Fruit shakes $4.45. Juice $2.50. Wine $5-7. Mixed drinks $5-9. Tequila shots $5-10. Beer $6. ⌚ Open daily 24hr. Happy hour M-Th 3-6pm, 1-4am.

🏵 THE COFFEE POT

♨♿(ᵖ) CAFE ❶

350 W. 49th St., at 9th Ave. ☎212-265-3566

Whether you are in need of sustenance, caffeine, rest, free Wi-Fi, or for some reason, do not carry your computer with you at all times (gasp!) and need internet access, this coffee house will help you get exactly what you need. The coffee, tea, and smoothie bar is fully stocked, and the food options include fresh bakery treats and a variety of healthy sandwiches and wraps, like the 190-calorie Grilled Vegetable Burrito ($6.45). Stop in for a sip, bite, or (web)surf, and continue your day full-force!

⌖ Ⓢ A, C, E, 1, 2, 3 to Penn Station. *i* Internet access $8 per 1hr. Ⓢ Hot drinks $1.55-4. Chilled drinks $2.25-4.75. Smoothies $4.20-4.25. Breakfast $1.25-5.25. Muffins and scones $2.25. Cupcakes $2-2.50. Sandwiches and wraps $6.45. ⌚ Open 7am-11:30pm.

YUM YUM TOO

♨♈♿ THAI❷

662 9th Ave., at 46th St. ☎212-247-2228 🖳www.yumtoo.com

A trendy, Thai orchid of a restaurant with a peerless lunch special. You get an entree and the choice of two side options (soup, salad, appetizer, or drink). Although the menu does offer the standard Pad Thai and different variations on

food

fried rice, more exciting options include Pad See-ew Black Noodle ($9-10) and Jungle Curry ($11-$19).

✱ Ⓢ A, C, E to 50th St. Ⓢ *Appetizers $4-8. Salads $4-8. Entrees $9-19. Lunch Specials $7-14. Beer $5. Wine $6.22-8.25. Mixed drinks $6-9.* ☼ *Open M-Th and Su noon-11:30pm, F-Sa noon-1-am. Happy hour daily noon-6:30pm, 10pm-midnight.*

AMY'S BREAD
●⊗ BAKERY, CAFE ❶

672 9th Ave., between 46th and 47th St.   ☎212-977-2670 🖥www.amysbsread.com

Organic rustic Italian, whole wheat oat pecan with golden raisins, cheese biscuit, freshly baked pizza, chocolate pecan chubbie cookie, butterscotch cashew bar, cupcakes, homemade pudding...are you getting hungry yet? Enjoy any of these, or choose from a lengthy list of salads and sandwiches with a cup of coffee or tea in the adorably old-fashioned dining area. You can also take it with you for sustenance during your day of sightseeing.

✱ Ⓢ A, C, E, to 42nd St.; N, R to 49th St.; or C, E, 1 to 50th St. Ⓢ *Sweets $1.35-$4.65. Savories $2.75-5.25. Sandwiches $4.50-7.50. Salads $7.25. Beverages $1-4.25.* ☼ *Open M-F 7:30am-11pm, Sa 8am-11pm, Su 9am-6pm.*

BURGERS AND CUPCAKES
●⛶ AMERICAN ❶

458 9th Ave., between 35th and 36th St.   ☎212-643-1200

A once-in-a-lifetime (sort of) opportunity to be a burger architect and build your own ideal sandwich of messy goodness. First, choose your patty *(hamburger, salmon, turkey, veggie, lemon grilled chicken breast, crispy chicken breast, portobello mush-room, $6.50),* then select any and all toppings that will enhance the quality of your creation. They have all the classic options, with some particularly creative ones, like goat cheese and turkey bacon *(toppings $1 each).* Complete the perfection with a delicious cupcake or Häagen-Dazs milkshake.

✱ Ⓢ A, C, E, 1, 2, 3 to Penn Station. Ⓢ *Burgers $6.50. Cupcakes $2.50-3.50. Salads $4-6. Sides $2.50-4.50. Pizzas $8-17. Brunch (Sa-Su only) $5-9.* ☼ *Open M-F 8am-10pm, Sa-Su 11am-10pm.*

BOMBAY MASALA
●Ⓨ⊗ INDIAN ❸

148 W. 49th St., between 6th and 7th Ave.   ☎212-302-8150

Bombay Masala has been kneading its naan in the US longer than any other Indian restaurant. Climb the red-carpeted stairs to the second floor for the lunch buffet *($13, M-F 11:30am-3:30pm).* The Saag Paneer has a unique, creamy quality, and the curry has an intriguing bite. A big Taj Mahal beer *($8)* will wash it all down nicely.

✱ Ⓢ B, D, F, M to 47th/50th St./Rockefeller Ctr. Ⓢ *Entrees $12-23. Lunch buffet $13. Wine $7 per glass. Beer $5-8.* ☼ *Open M-Th 11:30am-10:30pm, F 11:30am-11pm, Sa noon-11pm, Su 4-10:30pm.*

midtown east

🏢 MOONSTRUCK DINER
●⛶Ⓨ AMERICAN DINER ❶

250 E. 58th St., between 2nd and 3rd Ave.   ☎212-752-1711 🖥www.moonstrucknyc.com

A glistening, gemstone-studded world where the food is so cheap and delicious that it must be magic! Breakfast *($1.30-12)* is an especially enchanting deal. Specials start at $6 and include coffee or tea and juice. All portions, from those of the eggs *($.65-$10),* to the salads *($7.50-$12)* to the long list of pasta favorites *($12.50)* are enormous, and the menu itself is similarly gigantic. You are sure to find something that makes your moonstones skip!

✱ Ⓢ 4, 5, 6, N, Q, R to Lexington Ave./59th St. *i $10 min. for credit cards.* Ⓢ *Burgers and sand-wiches $6.25-12. Appetizers $5.25-9.75; entrees $13.75-22.25. Coffee and tea $1.20-2. Wine $5. Beer $5-6.* ☼ *Open M-Th 7am-midnight, F-Sa 24hr., Su 7am-midnight.*

TANAKA
    ◆✲ JAPANESE ❷

222 E. 51st St.   ☎212-308-6976

The walls are a combination of clean wood and soft greens, and guitar music plays softly in the background. Though the guitar music may not be strictly Japanese (The Beatles' "Yesterday" has been heard, as has a version of "Guantanamera"), the ambience is perfect for you to enjoy tasty sushi, teriyaki, and tempura. You can get your sake *($4-6)* hot or cold and finish it off with some mochi or tempura ice cream *($3.50).*

✦ Ⓢ *1, C, E to 50th St.; or B, D, E to 7th Ave.* Ⓢ *Sushi $3-14. Lunch box $9. Appetizers $1.50-7. Entrees $10-20. Beer $4. Sake $4-6.* ☒ *Open M-F 11:30am-11pm, Sa 12:30pm-11pm, Su 3:30-11pm.*

MANGIA
    ◆✦☋ ITALIAN, AMERICAN ❷

16 E. 49th St., between Madison and 5th Ave.   ☎212-754-7600 🖳www.mangiatogo.com

Mangia is two fantastic restaurants rolled into one. For a relaxing, waiter-served meal, head upstairs. For a quick, delicious, custom-created eating experience, stay downstairs. Food is served buffet-style, so you get no more and no less than what you want. Exquisite entrees include grilled Norwegian salmon *($13),* chicken milanese *($12),* and filet mignon *($14).* You can also make a meal out of the side station, with dozens of mouth-watering sides and salads of all kinds *($4.50 per lb.).* Another of Mangia's gems is the fresh juice bar, where the juice man (or woman) will make a fresh-squeezed beverage before your very eyes!

✦ Ⓢ *E, M, 6 to 53rd St.* Ⓢ *Sandwiches and panini $2.50-12. Salads $8-11. Sides $4.50 per lb. Small-plate meals $6 per lb. Custom salads $4.50 +$0.75-2 per topping. Breakfast $2-6.25. Fresh juices $4.50-5.50. Entrees $9.50-14. Pizza $7.50. Sweets $0.75-$5.* ☒ *Open M-F 6:30am-5:30pm.*

upper east side

MON PETIT CAFE
    ◆✲☋ CAFE ❷

801 Lexington Ave., at 62nd St.   ☎212-355-2233 🖳www.monpetitcafe.com

Visiting Mon Petit Cafe is a little like stepping into the movie *Amélie*. Recordings of French men singing soulfully play in the background, the walls are a cheery blend of sponged yellow and gold, and French-speaking waitresses write words like "Steak Marchand de Vin" on a blackboard in the middle of the restaurant. Some prices are slightly steep, but hey, it is the Upper East Side. Try the lobster ravioli in a cream tomato sauce *($19)* or, for breakfast, one of a variety of omelets *($12).* If this is slightly out of your price range, you can still much the classic croissant *($3).*

✦ Ⓢ *N, R, W, 4, 5, 6 to 59th St., F to Lexington Ave. Walk north on Lexington Ave. The cafe will be on the right at 62nd St.* Ⓢ *Appetizers $8-16, entrees $19-30, breakfast $3-16, wine $7.50-13, beer $6.* ☒ *Open daily 8am-10pm.*

EJ'S LUNCHEONETTE
    ◉✲ DINER ❶

1271 3rd Ave., at 73rd. St.   ☎ 212-472-0600

A classic '50s-style diner with a 21st-century twist. You'll find all of the beloved health abominations of traditional American cuisine, such as double cheeseburgers *($12.50),* chili cheese fries *($7.50),* and milkshakes *($5.25),* but you'll also encounter options less detrimental to your waistline and cholesterol level. The Health Kick Omelette *($9.45),* featuring egg whites, mushrooms, tomatoes, and basil, or the Veggie Burger topped with sprouts and guacamole will keep both your heart and your taste buds happy. Oh, and your wallet will also be smiling. This is some of the cheapest and most appetizing food on the Upper East Side.

food

♯ Ⓢ 6 to 68th St. Ⓢ Breakfast $4.25-11. Sandwiches and burgers $6.45-$12.50. Salads $9.50-$14.50. Beer $5-$5.50. ☼ Open M-Tu 7:30am-10pm, W-Th 7:30am-10:30pm, F-S 7:30-11pm, Su 7:30-10pm. Brunch Sa-Su 7:30am-3pm.

LE PAIN QUOTIDIEN ⚘ ORGANIC FOOD ❶
1134 Madison Ave., between 84th and 85th St. ☎212-327-4900 ▣ www.lepainquotidien.com
Satisfy your craving for croissants at this French-style *boulangerie* and restaurant chain, with locations throughout Manhattan. You can sit at the large, wooden, communal table in the middle of the restaurant, or at your own table if you prefer your meals to be private affairs. The menu is largely organic, including a wide selection of homemade breads. The quiches ($12-13) are particularly noteworthy.
♯ Ⓢ 6 to 86th St. *i* Other locations throughout New York City. Ⓢ Breakfast $3.30-8.50, lunch $10-15. ☼ Open M-F 7am-7:30pm, Sa-Su 8am-7:30pm.

BARKING DOG LUNCHEONETTE ⊛ ⍩ ⌂ AMERICAN ❶
1678 3rd Ave., at 94th St. ☎212-831-1800 ▣
American classics like chicken pot pie ($13) and steaks ($22) served at breakneck speeds will leave you wagging your tail. The **Country Breakfast Special** (*two eggs, hash browns, choice of ham, bacon, or sausage, and a biscuit, $6*), available until 4pm, might be the best deal on the Upper East Side.
♯ Ⓢ 6 to 94th St. Ⓢ Breakfast $3-13. Lunch $5-14. Appetizers $5-10. Dinner entrees $12-22. Beer $4.50-5.50. Wine $6.50-7.50. ☼ Open daily 8am-11pm.

IL VAGABONDO ⚘ ITALIAN ❸
351 E. 62nd St., between 1st and 2nd Ave. ☎212-832-9221 ▣ www.ilvagabondo.com
Despite a name that suggests the rough-and-ready, Il Vagabondo is a lovely, quiet place to dine. Start with an appetizer like the tomato and mozzarella with basil ($8.25), then move on to the chicken marsala ($21.50) or one of several other Italian-American favorites. Finish with an espresso ($3.10) in true Italian fashion.
♯ Ⓢ N, R, W, 4, 5, 6 to 59th St. Ⓢ Appetizers $8-10. Pasta $14.50-17.50. Entrees $19.50-32.50. Wine $8. ☼ Open M-F noon-3pm and 5:30-11:30pm, Sa 5:30-11:30pm, Su 5:30-11pm.

CANDLE CAFE ⚘⍩ VEGETARIAN ❷
1307 3rd Ave. ☎(212) 472-0970 ▣ www.candlecafe.com
Featuring sleek, black furniture, an impressive selection of wines, and a vegan and vegetarian menu of food made with exclusively organic ingredients, Candle Cafe provides a tantalizing blend of yuppie and hippie. These people breath tofu and can do almost anything imaginable with seitan. Try the Cajun seitan sandwich ($14), followed by a slice of vanilla cheesecake with chocolate crust ($8).
♯ Ⓢ 6 to 77th St. Walk up 77th St. to 3rd Ave. The cafe will be on the right. Ⓢ Appetizers $4-12. Entrees $13-20. Wine $8-$11. Beer $7-9. Mixed drinks $4-7. ☼ Open M-Sa 11:30am-10:30pm, Su 11:30am-9:30pm.

SERENDIPITY 3 ⚘ DESSERTS ❷
225 E. 60th St., between 2nd and 3rd Ave. ☎212-838-3531 ▣ www.serendipity3.com
If fun and random were restaurants, they would be Serendipity 3. Sparkly chandeliers, a pink gastronomic room, and a "general store" selling toys and candy make for a wildly entertaining dining atmosphere. The menu is eclectic, not to say confused, listing items as diverse as dim sum ($7.50) and crepes ($13.50-18.50), in addition to American favorites, like foot-long hot dogs ($8.50). However, the real reason you shouldn't miss this restaurant is the mouth-watering array of sundaes ($9.50-22) with names like Can't Say No (*humble pie ice cream, banana, hot fudge, and whipped cream; $15*). Seriously, how can you say no to that?
♯ Ⓢ N, R, W, 4, 5, 6 to 59th St. Ⓢ Appetizers $4-12.50. Entrees $13.50-$23. Desserts $7-22.50. ☼ Open M-Th 11:30am-midnght, F 11:30am-1am, Sa 11:30am-2am, Su 11:30am-midnght.

upper east side

BROTHER JIMMY'S BBQ

☛ BARBEQUE ❷

1485 2nd Ave.   ☎212-288-0999 🖳www.brotherjimmys.com

Brother Jimmy's BBQ is a pork-lover's paradise. Southern Style Ribs ($21),
Carolina Pulled Pork ($17), barbeque pork sandwiches ($10.50). You name it,
they have it, in addition to chicken, fish, and hamburgers. Cartoons of pigs cover
the wooden walls, an alternately cute and morbid touch. This country kitchen
becomes a bumpin' bar after dark, with drinks ranging from Nattie Lite ($3.75) to
Johnny Walker Blue Label ($45).

🚇 Ⓢ 6 to 77th St. Walk east to 2nd Ave. Ⓢ Appetizers $7.25-17.50; entrees $13-19.50; sandwiches and burgers $7.25-10.75; brunch $8-9.50; wine $7-7.50 per glass, $29-31 per bottle; beer
$3.75-7. 🕐 Open daily noon-1am.

DYLAN'S CANDY BAR

☛ CANDY STORE ❶

1011 3rd Ave., at 60th St.   ☎646-735-0078 🖳www.dylanscandybar.com

Imagine a place where you can buy almost any kind of sweet treat. Where even
the furniture has candy in it. Where grown men tell you that they are "candy-
tastic" today. Yes, my friends, Candyland is a real place, and that place is known
as Dylan's Candy Bar. The main level holds hundreds of thousands of pounds of
bulk candy, the upper level houses a cafe with mouth-watering cupcakes and ice
cream, and the lower level boasts fudge, candy "apparel and accessories," and
a "nostalgia shoppe" featuring all the classic candies of yore. Whether you are
looking for a gummy bra-and-panty set, a lollipop with a real worm larvae in it,
or just a selection of obscure M and M colors, Dylan's Candy Bar is here to meet
all of your candy needs.

🚇 Ⓢ 4, 5, 6 to 59th St. Take 59th St. west to 3rd Ave. Candy shop is on the left. Ⓢ Cupcakes $4.
Ice cream $4-8. Coffee $2-3. 🕐 Open M-Th 10am-9pm, F-Sa 10am-11pm, Su 10am-9pm.

upper west side

🍴 BIG NICK'S BURGER JOINT AND PIZZA JOINT ☛♿🍷 BURGERS, PIZZA, GREEK ❶

2175 Broadway, at 77th St.   ☎212-362-9238 🖳www.bignicksnyc.com

Big Nick's is kind of a big deal. The menu, listing over 30 kinds of pizza ($11-29)
and over 35 kinds of burgers ($6-12.50), would take weeks to read and some of
the food is cheaper than the Subway ride you took to get here. Vegetarians, Big
Nick loves you, too! He offers a wide variety of veggie options, including veggie
chili ($4-5.50), hotdogs, ($6), burgers ($6.50-$9), and even vegetarian meatballs
so that you too can enjoy a meatball hero sub ($10). To top it all off, Big Nick's
is open 24hr. daily!

🚇 Ⓢ 1 to 79th St. 𝒊 $10 min. for credit cards. Ⓢ Appetizers $1.30-10. Burgers $6-$12.50. Pizza
$11-29. Entrees $9-27.50. Beer $3.50-8. Wine $6. 🕐 Open 24hr.

🍴 BARNEY GREENGRASS STURGEON KING

♿ JEWISH ❶

541 Amsterdam Ave. and 86th St.   ☎212-724-4707 🖳wwww.barneygreengrass.com

You could come to Barney Greengrass Sturgeon King for a corned beef sandwich
($9.50). You could come for an order of cheese blintzes ($12). You could come for
the best bagel and lox sandwich on the Upper West Side ($12.75). But for over
100 years, King Barney has wanted you to order one thing: sturgeon. You can
get it any way you want it; sturgeon sandwich ($17.75), sturgeon platter ($35.50),
eggs with a side of sturgeon ($17.75). If a dish could have sturgeon in it, they've
added it. If you've got some extra cash to blow, consider trying one of the caviar
platters ($14-399).

🚇 Ⓢ 1 to 86th St. Ⓢ Appetizers $7-18; sandwiches $2.50-20.50, smoked fish platters $25-85,
salads $13-22.50. 🕐 Open Tu-F 8:30am-4pm, Sa-Su 8:30am-5pm. Store open Tu-Su 8am-6pm.

ALICE'S TEA CUP

♥☒ TEA SHOP ❷

102 W. 73rd St.

☎212-799-3006 🖳www.alicesteacup.com

Come celebrate your Un-birthday with Alice, the Mad Hatter, and the March Hare in this whimsical, English-style tea shop. Alice's signature tea is a blend of Indian black and Japanese green, with hints of vanilla and rose petals. The menu lists a full assortment of teas and edibles, including a series of tea services with tea, sandwiches, and scones *("The Nibble" $23; "The Jabberwocky" $38)*. Guests may purchase souvenirs, scones *($3)*, and tea in bulk on the way out of the shop.

♯ Ⓢ *1, 2, 3 to 72nd St.* Ⓢ *Tea $6 for a 3-cup pot., $8 for a 6-cup pot. Breakfast $6-17. Sandwiches $8-13. Sweets $6-10. Tea service $23-38.* Ⓩ *Open daily 8am-8pm.*

GOOD ENOUGH TO EAT

♥♈ AMERICAN ❷

483 Amsterdam Ave. and 83rd St.

☎212-496-0163 🖳www.goodenoughtoeat.com

New Yorkers sometimes like to pretend that they're in the country, rather than a giant city. That's why you, too, can sit and dine indoors behind a real white picket fence, among ceramic likenesses of cows and chickens. Particularly famous for their four-grain pancakes *($10.50-11.50)*, Good Enough to Eat specializes in country favorites.

♯ Ⓢ *1 to 86th St.* Ⓢ *Breakfast $6-11.75. Sandwiches $10.50-13.50. Salads $11-16. Entrees $14.50-21.50. Desserts $3-7.* Ⓩ *Open M-F 8am-10:30pm, Sa 9am-11pm, Su 9am-10pm.*

BEARD PAPA SWEETS CAFE

♥♿ DESSERTS ❶

2167 Broadway, between 76th and 77th

☎212-799-3770 🖳www.beardpapas.com

For a quick treat, head over to Beard Papa Sweets Cafe. Try one of their famous cream puffs *($1.75)*, or a "Paris Brest," shaped like a bicycle wheel in honor of the *Paris Brest et Tour* Bicycle Race *($2.25)*. Because Japanese ice cream is the obvious complement to French pastry, the shop also sells Mochi ice cream *($1.25)*.

♯ Ⓢ *1, 2, 3 to 72nd St.* Ⓢ *Pastries $1.75-$2.10. Hot and cold drinks $1.25-$3.25.* Ⓩ *Open M-Th 10am-9pm, F-Sa 10am-10pm, Su 10am-9pm.*

MAMA MEXICO

♥♿♈ MEXICAN ❷

2672 Broadway, at 102nd St.

☎212-864-2323 🖳www.mamamexico.com

Mama Mexico is definitely where the fiesta's at. They have your burritos *($14-16)* and fajitas *($17-25)*, as well as an epic selection of seafood options such as the Fuente de Mariscos (calamari, mussels, crab meat, and shrimp with tomato, garlic, white wine, and veggies over white rice). Live mariachi every night from 7-11pm. Tall Margaritas *($9-10)* are so strong they'll knock you on your *nalgas* will have you singing all through dinner.

♯ Ⓢ *1 to 103rd St.* Ⓢ *Appetizers $7-17. Margaritas and other mixed drinks $9-10. Beer $5.* Ⓩ *Open M-Th noon-midnight, F-Sa 11am-2am, Su noon-midnight.*

JOSIE'S RESTAURANT AND JUICE BAR

♥♿ RESTAURANT ❸

300 Amsterdam Ave.

☎212-769-1212 🖳www.josiesnyc.com

This place serves foods you've never even heard of. In fact, you may find yourself ordering something just to find out what it is. Take, for example, the steamed organic edamame *($6.25)*. A glossary in the margins of the menu provides assistance to the clueless majority. If you're feeling less adventurous, Josie's also offers a selection of less mystifying options such as stir fries *($13-20)*. Fresh-squeezed juices *($3.25-8)* go well with the standard and obscure menu choice alike.

♯ Ⓢ *1, 2, 3 to 72nd St.* Ⓢ *Appetizers $5-15. Entrees $11-20. Beer $5.75-6.50. Wine $8. Mixed drinks $9.75-$12. Juices $3.25-$8.* Ⓩ *Open M-F 11:30am-10:30pm, Sa-Su 4-10:30pm.*

CAFE LALO

●☒♈ CAFE ❷

201 W. 83rd St.

☎212-496-6031 🖳www. cafelalo.com

Covered with old French posters and filled with people socializing over a sea of different kinds of cakes, Cafe Lalo is also the coffee shop where Meg Ryan and Tom Hanks arrange their first meeting in the 1998 film **You've Got Mail.** Possibly the most exciting part of the menu is the "International Brunch" section (served every day until 4pm), with selections modeled after various world cuisines. The Parisian Breakfast *($6)* consists of a croissant and *cafe au lait*, the Caribbean Breakfast *($8.25)* is tropical fruit salad and a pastry, and, of course, the New York Breakfast *($15)* is a bagel and lox with coffee.

⚑ Ⓢ *1 to 79th St. Walk uptown and make left onto 83rd St. toward Amsterdam Ave.* Ⓢ *Brunch $6-15. Sandwiches $11-13; pastries $2-4.50. Cheesecake $7.50. Ice cream $7. Cheese plates $13-25. Wine $8. Beer $5-6. Coffee drinks $2-9.* Ⓩ *Open M-Th 8am-2am, F 8am-4am, Sa 9am-4am, Su 9am-2am.*

ALOUETTE
☀♥ RESTAURANT ❸

2588 Broadway and 98th St. ☎212-222-6808 🖳www.alouettenyc.com

A relaxing retreat from the bustling streets of the Upper West Side. Featuring innovative and exciting, if geographically confused, entrees such as Salmon with Isreali Couscous and Baby Bok Choi in Herbal Broth *($19)*. Brunch is served Sundays from 11am-4pm, and offers the most delicious French Vanilla Brioche Toast *($12)* you will ever consume in your life. An extensive list of both French and international wines is also available.

⚑ Ⓢ *1, 2, 3 to 96th St.* Ⓢ *Appetizers $8-11. Entrees $18-26. Brunch $12-25. Wine $7.50.* Ⓩ *Open M-Sa 5-11pm, Su 11am-4pm and 5-10pm.*

morningside heights

🍴 THE HUNGARIAN PASTRY SHOP
((•))☕🍴 BAKERY, CAFE ❶

1030 Amsterdam Ave., at 111th St. ☎212-866-4230

This place is a favorite among Columbia and Barnard students, who convene here to socialize and work. Students and tourists alike gladly wait in line for enormous croissants with butter and jelly or *rigo jancsi* (cube-shaped pastries with chocolate sponge cake and chocolate cream). Careful—they're pretty addictive.

⚑ Ⓢ *1 to 110th St..* Ⓢ *Pastries $2-3.75. Coffee and tea $2.* Ⓩ *Open M-F 7:30am-11:30pm, Sa 8:30am-11:30pm, Su 8:30am-11:30pm.*

🍴 TOM'S RESTAURANT
🍴 DINER ❶

2880 Broadway, at 112th St. ☎212-864-6137 🖳www.toms-diner.com

Tom's Restaurant is the subject of Suzanne Vega's hit a cappella song "Tom's Diner." It is the old haunt of Jerry, Elaine, George, Kramer. And at Tom's Restaurant, they don't let you forget it. The walls are papered with pictures of Seinfeld characters. Lest we forget which '90s sitcom featured the establishment on our way out the door, an autographed photograph of the Seinfeld cast is situated next to the cash register. Probably the only restaurant in Morningside Heights to offer a souvenir menu.

⚑ Ⓢ *1 to 110th St..* Ⓢ *Appetizers $5-15. Sandwiches and burgers $3.75-10.50. Entrees $6.50-21. Desserts $1.75-5.45. Breakfast $1.25-16.* Ⓩ *Open M-Th 6am-1:30am, F-Sa 24hr., Su 6am-1:30am.*

🍴 APPLE TREE SUPERMARKET
☀⛄🍴 GROCERY STORE ❶

1225 Amsterdam Ave. ☎212-865-8840 🖳http://theappletreemarket.com

Everything you could ever want is in this supermarket: cheeses, fruits, veggies, beer, sandwiches, a salad bar, an oatmeal bar, drugstore items, granola bars, lasagna, samosas... Seriously, anything you could ever want. Think of something. We bet they have it.

⚑ Ⓢ *1 to 116th St. Between 120th and 121st St.* Ⓢ *Cheeses $5-13 per lb. Sugar and fat-free muffins $1.65. Beer $1.25-5. Sandwiches $4-6.25. Salad bar $2.75 with add-ins $0.50-$2. Sushi $4.50-$5.50.* ⌚ *Open 24hr.*

SYMPOSIUM
●●Ⴘ GREEK ❷

544 W. 113th St. ☎212-865-1011 ▣www.symposiumnyc.com

Although the word "symposium" may conjure up images of stuffy professors and boring lectures, it actually comes from the Greek word *simpinein*, which literally means "drink together." The Greeks have always known how to have a good time, and the folks at Symposium are no exception. You and your friends can merrily drink and eat together in this colorful, fun atmosphere. Start out with an order of stuffed grape leaves *($6)*, then try the *exohiko (lamb pie with vegetables and "secret ingredients," $15)*.

⚑ Ⓢ *1 to 110th. Between Broadway and Amsterdam.* Ⓢ *Appetizers $5.75-$13. Entrees $8-22. Desserts $5. Wine $7-42. Beer $4.50. Spirits $7-8.* ⌚ *Open daily noon-10pm.*

AMIR'S FALAFEL
●Ⴅ MIDDLE EASTERN ❶

2911-A Broadway ☎212-749-7500

You know you're near a college campus when you can get falafel and pizza, not only in the same restaurant, but in the same dish. And for under $5. At Amir's Falafel, they seem to have put a Middle Eastern twist on many of the college staples. For the purists among you, they also offer unadulterated falafel *($3.50-5)*, shawarma *($5.75-7)*, and hummus bowls *($5.75-8)*.

⚑ Ⓢ *1 to 110th St.* Ⓢ *Food $2.25-10. Desserts $1.25-2.15. Drinks $1.25-3.50.* ⌚ *Open M-Sa 11am-11pm, Su 11am-10pm*

MASSAWA
●Ⴅ␛ ETHIOPIAN ❷

1239 Amsterdam Ave., at 121st St. ☎212-663-0505 ▣www.massawanyc.com

Roll up your sleeves: it's time to enjoy traditional Ethiopian and Eritrean food such as *shiro (pureed chickpeas with ginger and spices; $13)* and simmered monkfish *($16)*. You might want to wash your hands first too, as food from this region is traditionally eaten without silverware, using flat, African bread, *injera*. Enjoy a glass of mango juice with your meal, but the optional fresh ginger is so strong and spicy, it might make your eyes water!

⚑ Ⓢ *1 to 116th St.* Ⓢ *Appetizers $6-8. Entrees $9-18. Drinks $4-11.* ⌚ *Open daily noon-11pm.*

TOAST
●Ⴅ␛ AMERICAN ❷

3157 Broadway, between Tieman Pl. and La Salle St., near 125th St. ☎ 212-662-1144 ▣www.toastnyc.com

Celebrate your visits to American landmarks the Riverside Church and Grant's Tomb with a meal at Toast. You will find specials from around the United States, such as the New York Strip Steak *($18)*, and Cajun Tilapia *($13)*. The gazpacho *($5)* is not American, but it is delicious. Also featuring a full bar with a vast quantity of both domestic and imported beers.

⚑ Ⓢ *1 to 125th St.* Ⓢ *Appetizers $4-14. Sandwiches and burgers $8-10. Entrees $11-18. Beer $6. Wine $5-32. Mixed drinks $7-10.* ⌚ *Open M-W 11am-11pm, Th-F 11am-midnight, Sa 10am-midnight, Su 10am-11pm. Bar open later.*

NUSSBAUM AND WU
●Ⴅ DELI ❶

2897 Broadway, at 113th ☎212-280-5344 ▣www.nussbaumwu.com

The perfect place to duck in for a cup of coffee *($1.50-$2.45)*, a sandwich *($4-8)*, or one of a number of mouth-watering bakery items *($2.50-$5)* after touring the Columbia campus. Featuring gluten-free pizza from the oh-so-cleverly-named Mozzarelli's and a salad bar with unlimited toppings for $8.

⚑ Ⓢ *1 to 110th and 116th St.* Ⓢ *Bakery Items $2.50-5. Bagels $1-4.50. Pizza $2.25-5. Smoothies $4.50-5.50. Sandwiches $4-8.* ⌚ *Open M-Sa 6am-11:30pm, Su 6am-11pm.*

morningside heights

harlem

The now-distant southern roots of Harlem's African-American community live on through the soul food brought from below the Mason-Dixon line. If it's not waffles, biscuits, and collard greens you're craving, head east to check out Spanish Harlem's endless rows of Mexican and Puerto Rican eateries. Or go foreign in Harlem proper: new African and Caribbean restaurants testify to the neighborhood's proud diversity.

🏛 AMY RUTH'S ●👶 SOUL FOOD, SOUTHERN ❸

113 West 116th St. ☎212-280-8779 🖳www.amyruthsharlem.com

In a neighborhood full of southern cuisine, Amy Ruth's still manages to stand out as a true exemplar of Harlem's proud soul food tradition. It's even named after the owner's grandmother, whose cooking in the turn-of-the-century south continues to inspire today's plentiful, affordable menu. Entrees are named after black celebrities and prominent figures, so you can finally enjoy some Ludacris (fried chicken wings) without the guilt afterwards. A new addition: The President Barack Obama (fried, smothered, baked, or fried BBQ chicken).

✠ Ⓢ B, C to 116th St. or 2, 3 to 116th St. Ⓢ Breakfast $6-9. Entrees $8-16. ☾ Open M 11:30am-11pm, Tu-Th 8:30am-11pm, F 8:30am-5:30pm, Sa 8:30am-7:30pm, Su 7:30am-11pm.

🏛 LES AMBASSADES ●👶 SENEGALESE ❷

2200 Frederick Douglass Blvd. ☎212-666-0078 🖳www.patissereidesambassades.com

Les Ambassades is one of the highlights of Harlem's so-called "Little Senegal," centered on the intersection of 116th St. and Frederick Douglass Blvd. The Senegalese cuisine here is impossible to resist, from the *merguez*, lamb sausage on a baguette, to the lamb shank to the croque monsieur, a French staple. Come to the weekend brunches for delicious omelettes filled with things like mussels and red peppers. And, since this is a patisserie, there's a healthy selection of specialty breads and sandwiches.

✠ Ⓢ B, C to 116th St. Ⓢ Salads and sandwiches $7-10. Dinner $11.50-13.50. ☾ Open M-Th 7am-2am, F 7am-3am, Sa-Su 8am-3am. Brunch Sa-Su 11am-5pm.

AFRICAN KINE ●👶♟❄ SENEGALESE ❷

256 W. 116th St. ☎212-666-9400 🖳www.africakine.com

Another Senegalese restaurant, this one boasting two stories and a hugely varied menu. Everything's an adventure: for lunch, try *souhoukhou*, fish and vegetables, or *foufou*, lamb and fish; for dinner, order *dibi*, grilled lamb, cow foot soup, or any other of the dozens of items on hand. The cheap desserts are an added bonus—sample the couscous with sour cream and vanilla extract.

✠ Ⓢ B, C to 116th St. 𝒊 Many entrees are only served on certain days, so ask your waiter. Ⓢ Lunch entrees $10. Dinner entrees $11-15. Desserts $3-4. ☾ Open daily 12:30pm-2am.

EL PASO ●👶 MEXICAN ❸

1643 Lexington Ave. ☎212-831-9831 🖳www.elpasony.com

Lexington and 3rd Ave. are filled to the brim with Mexican restaurants boasting similar menus and looks. This central branch of El Paso goes the extra mile with a striking facade and extensive Mexican-themed decor. The result may be a little cheesy, but the food is genuine. The entree menu is extensive, going beyond staples to include *camarones poblanos*, jumbo shrimp with corn, *chuletas asadas*, broiled pork chop, and the *mole poblano*, a mix of chocolate, chilies, plantains, tomatoes, nuts, raisins, and cinnamon. Ooh.

✠ Ⓢ 6 to 103rd St. 𝒊 Other branches at 237 East 116th St. and 64 East 97th St. Ⓢ Tacos $2.25-2.50. Tortas $5.50-7. Entrees $9-17. ☾ Open daily 11am-11pm.

food

DINOSAUR BBQ

⬥&♿ BARBECUE, SOUTHERN ❸

646 West 131st St.

☎212-694-1777 ◼www.dinosaurbarbque.com

This gargantuan wooden house, self-described as "a genuine rib joint," houses some gargantuan meat dishes (and, very often, gargantuan crowds). Chief among the carnivorous offerings are pork ribs decked out with the restaurant's own BBQ sauce. You can also try the "Big Ass Pork Plate" *($13.75),* a testament to the testosterone-fueled atmosphere here. A package deal *($47)* will get you food for four to five, including chicken, ribs, three sides, cornbread, and, of course, one bottle of Dinosaur BBQ Sauce.

✤ Ⓢ 1 to 125th St. *i* Live blues, jazz, rock, and funk Th-Sa nights. Ⓢ Lunch specials from $6. 3 ribs $10. Other entrees $15-22. Ⓠ Open M-Th 11:30am-11pm, F-Sa 11:30am-midnight, Su noon-10pm.

MANNA'S SOUL FOOD AND SALAD BAR

⬥& SOUL FOOD, SOUTHERN ❷

2331 8th Ave./Frederick Douglass Blvd.

☎212-749-9084

No waiting here! The various branches of Manna's, a hugely popular Harlem chain, are simple cafeteria-style affairs where you can go at your own pace. The offerings are standard soul food fare—fried chicken (fried everything), collard greens, and other down homey staples. If the image of closing veins gets to you, the salad bar is similarly extensive. Seating upstairs.

✤ Ⓢ A, B, C, D to 125th St. *i* Other branches at 70 West 125th St., 54 East 125th St., and 786 Malcolm X Blvd. Ⓢ Cold salad bar $5.49 per lb., hot food $5.49 per lb., meat only $6.49 per lb. Ⓠ Open M-Sa 10am-9pm, Su 10am-8pm.

ITZOCAN BISTRO

⬥& MEXICAN, FRENCH ❸

1575 Lexington Ave.

☎212-423-0255 ◼www.itzocanbistro.com

Spanish Harlem is filled to the brim with crowds of Mexican restaurants, but chef Anselmo Bello at Itzocan Bistro has gone the extra mile, using French techniques to prepare his homeland's cuisine. The result is a constant surprise; wild mushroom *huitlacoche* crepes and adobo-marinated duck breast keep you guessing. It's on the expensive side, but well worth the uptown splurge.

✤ Ⓢ 6 to 103rd St. Ⓢ Entrees $17-22. Ⓠ Open daily 5-11pm.

brooklyn

WILLIAMSBURG

Williamsburg has its share of self-aware genre restaurants and vegan cafes, but interspersed among the expected is a remarkably diverse array of Middle Eastern, Mexican, Polish, and Greek food. With prices still at Brooklyn lows, it's worth the quick Subway ride from Manhattan just for a speedy lunch or dinner trip followed by a hasty exit if you're allergic to quirkiness.

DINER

⬥⊗♿ AMERICAN NOUVEAU ❷

85 Broadway

☎718-486-3077 ◼www.dinernyc.com

The broken-down wooden exterior of this converted 1920s diner still proudly shows its age, but the young regulars and constantly changing menu help keep the cobwebs away. You can't predict the specials on any given day, so just expect variety: lunch items may include boudin sausage and fried chicken sandwich, dinner may feature beef tongue rillette and coq au vin, dessert could possibly be lemon sabayan tart. Or maybe not. There's only one way to find out. Check out the Diner Journal *(◼www.dinerjournal.com),* available next door, for a generous selection of sample recipes.

✤ Ⓢ J, M, Z to Marcy Ave. *i* Many menu items change daily; check website for current specials. Ⓢ Entrees $8-14. Ⓠ Open Th 11am-midnight, F-Sa 11am-1am, Su 11am-midnight.

OASIS

🍴♿ MIDDLE EASTERN ❷

161 N. 7th St. ☎718-218-7607

Chances are this ever-crowded, no-frills Middle Eastern eatery will be the first thing you see when leaving the Bedford Ave. station. Follow the line to the cheap falafel, shawarma, and shish kebab sandwiches and plates on offer. Or go for the cheap homemade pies. Omnivores can enjoy a large veggie menu featuring the likes of stuffed grape leaves and tabbouleh.

🍴 Ⓢ *L to Bedford Ave.* Ⓢ *Sandwiches $3-5. Plates $6-15. Veggie dishes $3-10. Pies $2.50-4.* ⌚ *Open daily 11am-2am.*

LA SUPERIOR

🍴♿ MEXICAN ❷

295 Berry St. ☎718-388-5988 🖥www.lasuperiornyc.com

The neighborhood's best Mexican restaurant is tucked away in a mostly residential corner; seek it out for food that hasn't made any north-of-the-border concessions. On offer are *huaraches* (masa base with toppings), *alambre de res* (grilled skirt steak), *panuchos de cochinita* (pork in banana leaves), *torta ahogada* (a sandwich "drowned" in chili sauce), and more. For snacks, you'll find cheap tacos, traditional Mexican soups, and Mexican sodas. It seems that the name is actually merited.

🍴 Ⓢ *J, M, Z to Marcy Ave. or L to Bedford Ave.* Ⓢ *Tacos $2.50. Brunch $5-12. Entrees $5-14.* ⌚ *Open M-Th 12:30pm-midnight, F-Sa noon-2am, Su 12:30pm-midnight.*

PIES N' THIGHS

🍴♿ SOUTHERN ❷

166 S 4th St. ☎347-529-6090 🖥www.piesandthighs.com

Some simple Southern comfort in north Brooklyn. Pies n' Thighs lives up to its magnificent name with a range of decadent fried dishes (fried chicken or catfish "boxes") and regional favorites like pulled pork. For breakfast, you can try their acclaimed doughnuts or get an early start on dessert with an ample selection of homemade pies. Health inspectors are wary—but it was recently featured on the *Today Show*, and where fried food and Matt Lauer meet, resistance is futile.

🍴 Ⓢ *J, M, Z to Marcy Ave.* Ⓢ *Pies $4.50-6. Breakfast $2.50-7. Entrees $6-12.* ⌚ *Open M-F 8am-midnight, Sa-Su 10am-midnight; brunch Sa-Su 10am-4pm.*

FABIANE'S CAFE AND PASTRY

🍴♿☕🍴 CAFE, PASTRY SHOP ❶

142 N. 5th St. ☎718-218-9632 🖥www.fabianescafeandpastry.com

Fabiane's Brazilian namesake and owner received most of her training in French cuisine, and the resulting fusion—mixed with an organic sensibility—shows in a varied menu encompassing smoked duck sandwiches, chicken quesadillas, and organic acai made with Brazilian berries. Come in good weather, when the cafe is exposed to and overflowing with the shaggy crowds of Bedford Ave.

🍴 Ⓢ *L to Bedford Ave.* Ⓢ *Breakfast $3.50-8. Salads and sandwiches $7-10.25. Entrees $5-10. Desserts $5.* ⌚ *Open M-Sa 7:30am-11pm, Su 7:30am-10pm.*

GOODS

🍴♿ AMERICAN ❶

Corner of Metropolitan Ave. and Lorimer St. 🖥www.goodsfood.com

This new takeout stand housed in a converted silver RV camper is already attracting attention and crowds—all deserved, since the breakfast biscuits are cheap, the burgers heaped with toppings, and the Sunday brunches centered on fried chicken. The menu is small and fledgling, so expect developments over the coming months. Seating is available in the new garden in the back.

🍴 Ⓢ *L to Lorimer St.-Metropolitan Ave.* Ⓢ *Breakfast $2-3. Lunch/dinner $4.75-8.25.* ⌚ *Open M-Th 7am-10:30pm, F 7am-midnight, Sa 9am-midnight, Su 9am-10pm.*

PAPA LIMA SANDWICH

🍴Ⓧ🔊 DELI ❷

362 Bedford Ave. ☎718-215-7720 🖥www.papalimasandwich.com

It's hard to resist sandwiches with names like Wilbur (grilled ham, cheddar, and pear on wheat), Evil Reuben (turkey, coleslaw, dressing, and provolone on rye), and Charlie Brown (pulled roast chicken, bacon, tomato, arugula, and basil mayo

on wheat). All sides and toppings are bought locally and prepared fresh. Weirdly geometrical picnic tables, green walls, and free Wi-Fi make you feel at home.
➜ [S] J, M, Z to Marcy Ave., L to Bedford Ave. $ Breakfast $5-8. Sandwiches $6-12. ⏰ Open M-F 9am-7pm, Sa-Su 10am-8pm.

PARK SLOPE

👍 CAFE STEINHOF
💳🚭🍸❄ AUSTRIAN [2]

422 7th Ave. (at 14th St.) ☎718-369-7776 💻www.cafesteinhof.com

Yes, yet another Austrian restaurant/music venue/makeshift film theater in Park Slope. But Steinhof attains its Alpine peak above the crowd with an appropriately delicious menu (beef *gulasch* and *sauerbraten* and *jaegerschnitzel*, oh my) and crazy modernist interior decorating—complete with Expressionist-style paintings on the wall and an indescribable ceiling scheme. It's a refreshing bit of irreverence amid the family-friendly neighborhood fun.
➜ [S] F to 7th Ave. $ Sandwiches $6-9. Lunch entrees $6-11. Dinner entrees $10-14. Desserts $5. ⏰ Open M 5-11pm, Tu-Su 11am-4pm and 5-11pm. W concerts begin 10:30pm, Su film screening times vary (check website for details).

👍 OZZIE'S CAFE AND TEA
💳🚭📶 CAFE [2]

249 5th Ave. or 57 7th Ave. ☎888-699-4371 💻www.ozziescoffee.com

Other cafes of Ozzie's ilk wish they had the space and comfort on offer at its two locations. With a cosmopolitan selection of roasts hailing from Ecuador to Ethiopia to Mexico to France to the United States, there's always something for the next visit—and the complimentary Wi-Fi for those laying down $5 or more pretty much mandates an extended stay.
➜ For 249 5th Ave. location: [S] M, R to Union St.. Walk to Garfield St. and 5th Ave. For 57 7th Ave. location: [S] B, Q to 7th Ave. or 2,3 to Grand Army Plaza. Walk to 7th Ave. at Lincoln Pl. $ Coffee and tea $1.75-3.75. Sandwiches $6.50. Pastries $2-5. ⏰ Open daily 7am-10pm.

STONE PARK CAFE
💳♿🍸 AMERICAN, CAFE [3]

324 5th Ave. (at 3rd St.) ☎718-369-0082 💻www.stoneparkcafe.com

The American standards at this brightly lit, parkside restaurant—hangtown fry for breakfast, colorado lamb loin for lunch or dinner, cappuccino cheesecake for dessert—have made it a Park Slope favorite. This cafe is a perfect distillation of the neighborhood itself: clean, green, pleasant, satisfying, and a bit expensive. Hang out at the corner cafe if the entrees are too much of a budget stretch.
➜ [S] M, R to Union St. or 9th St.-4th Ave.; F to 9th St.-4th Ave. $ Entrees $10-25. ⏰ Open Tu-F 11:30am-2:30pm and 5:30-10pm, Sa 11:30am-2:30pm and 5:30pm-midnight, Su 11:30am-2:30pm and 5:30-9pm.

CONVIVIUM OSTERIA
💵🚭🍸☀ MEDITERRANEAN [4]

68 5th Ave. (at St. Mark's Pl.) ☎718-857-1833 💻www.convivium-osteria.com

This quaint spot banks heavily on your desire for all things pastoral, southern European, and seaside. The decor is rustic with lots of stone walls and arched doorways, and a green outdoor space in back—and the food is drawn mostly from Italy, Spain, and Portugal, satisfyingly varied, from braised rabbit to Spanish tapas. All this refinement basically insists that you recite some memorized poetry to your date. Or something.
➜ [S] D, M, N, R to Pacific St.; B, Q, 2, 3, 4, 5 to Atlantic Ave.; 2, 3 to Bergen St. $ Appetizers $6-27. Entrees $15-28. ⏰ Open M-Th 6-11pm, F-Sa 5:30-11:30pm, Su 5-10pm.

CHIP SHOP
💵🚭🍸 BRITISH [2]

383 5th Ave. (at 6th St.) ☎718-832-7701 💻www.chipshopnyc.com

The Chip Shop throws itself into the world of earthy British pub grub with admirable to-hell-with-it pride. British memorabilia, from Bowie posters to Tube signs to the ubiquitous Union Jack, stare down from yellow walls at the small but communal dining area. Fish and chips, of course, dominate. The dozen-plus varieties on offer should teach you a lesson in the ethics of cuisine stereotyping. There's a takeout stand around the corner on 6th St.

🚶 Ⓢ *F, M, R to 9th St.-4th Ave.* Ⓢ *Entrees $6.50-12.* Ⓠ *Open M-Th and Su 10am-9pm, F-Sa 10am-11pm.*

LOBO ⬤⊗🍸 TEX-MEX ❸

188 5th Ave. (at Sackett St.) ☎718-636-8886 🖥www.lobonyc.com

If Park Slope is feeling a bit too...twee, Lobo's Texas swagger will set you right. We can start with the cowhide on the booths and continue onto the meaty offerings, like chicken fried steak (making all the single-genre meats look bad) and drunken chicken *(pollo baracho).* Enchiladas, tacos, chalupas, and fajitas round up this delicious mix.

🚶 Ⓢ *M, R to Union St.* Ⓢ *Breakfast $6.50-10. Entrees $10-21.* Ⓠ *Open M-W and Su 11am-10pm, Th 11am-midnight, F-Sa 11am-1am.*

BROOKLYN HEIGHTS

SIGGY'S GOOD FOOD ⬤⊗🍸♿ ORGANIC/HEALTH FOOD ❷

76 Henry St. ☎718-237-3199 🖥www.siggysgoodfood.com

Siggy's proudly organic ingredients will appeal to that granola crunch inside you. Face it: you probably need to eat healthier, anyway. Even the wine and beer is organic, and the salad menu impresses with quinoa, avocado, and tofu galore. But meat isn't totally out; Siggy's generous sandwich and burger menu includes organic steak along with the likes of "Cheese Lover Heaven."

🚶 Ⓢ *2, 3 to Clark St.* Ⓢ *Entrees $9-17.* Ⓠ *Open Tu-F 11:30am-10pm, Sa-Su 10am-10pm.*

TUTT CAFE ⬤⬤⊗♿ MIDDLE EASTERN ❷

47 Hicks St. (at Middagh St.) ☎718-722-7777 🖥www.tuttcafe.com

Though Atlantic Ave. along the Heights' southern edge has been totally colonized by Middle Eastern eateries, Tutt comes as a surprise amidst the quiet residential streets to the north. It's a treat: all the favorites like falafel and *merguez* sandwiches and plates, along with *lambajin* pizza and baklava for dessert. There's also an impressive salad menu, featuring tabbouleh and hummus.

🚶 Ⓢ *2, 3 to Clark St. or A,C to High St.* Ⓢ *Sandwiches $4-8. Salads $4-6. Plates $6-11. Pizza $7-9.* Ⓠ *Open daily 11am-11:30pm.*

WATERFALLS CAFE ⬤♿ MIDDLE EASTERN ❷

144 Atlantic Ave. (at Clinton St.) ☎718-488-8886

The western edge of Atlantic Ave. is a gold mine for lovers of Middle Eastern cuisine: Yemeni restaurants rub shoulders with Lebanese and Egyptian choices. Waterfalls is one of the less prepossessing ones, a simple eatery with a large menu covering all your Mid East needs. The salad and maza selection is especially impressive with items like *baba ghanoush*, stuffed grape leaves, and *mohamara* (walnuts, red pepper, garlic, and spices).

🚶 Ⓢ *4, 5 to Borough Hall.* Ⓢ *Salads and sandwiches $4-10. Platters and specials $7-15. Pizza $7-9.50.* Ⓠ *Open daily 11am-11pm.*

SAHADI IMPORTING COMPANY ⬤♿❄ MIDDLE EASTERN, MEDITERRANEAN

187 Atlantic Ave. ☎718-624-4550 🖥www.sahadis.com

This grocery teems with imported Mediterranean items, from instant falafel to no-nonsense rice pilaf. There's also a room filled with fresh salad items, sweets, and dried fruits and vegetables. Crowds of locals can make navigation difficult.

🚶 Ⓢ *4, 5 to Borough Hall.* Ⓠ *Open M-Sa 9am-7pm.*

HEIGHTS CAFE ⬤♿♿ AMERICAN ❸

84 Montage St. (at Hicks St.) ☎718-625-5555 🖥www.heightscafeny.com

This sleek and somewhat upscale option along busy Montague St. attracts an older clientele. But the outdoor seating (great people-watching opportunity) and plentiful sandwiches, wraps, pizzas, and salads on the menu may be enough to gentrify you.

✢ Ⓢ *M, R to Court St.-Borough Hall or 4, 5 to Borough Hall.* Ⓢ *Sandwiches, wraps, and salads $9-14. Entrees $17-24.* ⌚ *Open daily noon-11pm.*

DUMBO

DUMBO GENERAL STORE
⊛♿♪ AMERICAN ❷

111 Front St. (at Washington St.)   ☎718-855-5288 ▣www.dumbogeneralstore.com

The DGS, barely attempting to conceal the high ceilings and exposed walls that mark it as a former industrial space, is a perfect fit in this post-warehouse neighborhood. Classic American style food is spiced up by a panini menu, and the huge tables establish a refreshingly open, communal vibe.

✢ Ⓢ *F to York St. or A, C to High St.* *i Night closing times vary.* Ⓢ *Breakfast $6.25-12. Panini $8-12. Entrees $8-14.* ⌚ *Open M-Th 7:30am-10pm, Sa 8am-10pm, Su 9am-10pm.*

GRIMALDI'S PIZZERIA
⊛♿♪❋ PIZZERIA ❷

19 Old Fulton St.   ☎718-858-4300 ▣www.grimaldis.com

The hugely popular Grimaldi's has quickly turned into a DUMBO favorite; expect to wait, most likely outside, on weekends. You'll be mingling with locals and skyline-seeking tourists alike; the coal-oven pizzeria is just down the block from the waterfront and ferry landing.

✢ Ⓢ *F to York St. or A, C to High St.* Ⓢ *Pizzas $12-14. Calzones $14-16.* ⌚ *Open M-Th 11:30am-11pm, F 11:30am-11:45pm, Sa noon-11:45pm, Su noon-11pm.*

BROOKLYN ICE CREAM FACTORY
⊛♿❧ ICE CREAM ❶

1 Water St. (at Old Fulton St.)   ☎718-246-3963 ▣www.brooklynicecreamfactory.com

The factory is perhaps best known for its distinctive location—a twenties-era firehouse right on the waterfront—but brave the lines and try a scoop or two for fresh, house-made ingredients and toppings. The views from the deck in front are spectacular, especially on the hot summer days that make this a go-to stop for many borough-hopping tourists.

✢ Ⓢ *F to York St. or A, C to High St.* Ⓢ *1 scoop $3.50, 2 $5.50, 3 $6.50. Sundaes and milk shakes $6.50-7.50.* ⌚ *Open M-Th and Su noon-10pm, F-Sa noon-11pm.*

PEDRO'S MEXICAN BAR AND RESTAURANT
⊛⊗♪❧ MEXICAN ❷

73 Jay St. (at Front St.)   ☎718-797-2851

Watch your head in Pedro's hot, semi-subterranean depths; the ceiling is low, perfect for trapping the delicious scents from the exposed kitchen. The stark menu is packed with Mexican and Spanish standards. Along with the vibrantly colored building, it's a nice departure from the industrial surroundings.

✢ Ⓢ *F to York St. or A, C to High St.* Ⓢ *Appetizers and entrees $3-12.* ⌚ *Open M-Th and Su 11am-midnight, F-Sa 11am-2am.*

COBBLE HILL, BOERUM HILL, CARROLL GARDENS, RED HOOK

▨ ROBIN DES BOIS
⊛♿♪❧ FRENCH ❸

195 Smith St. (between Warren and Baltic St.)   ☎718-596-1609 ▣www.sherwoodcafe.com

That's "Robin Hood" for those of you who aren't Francophones, who should swallow your pride and check out this amazingly designed French restaurant. A huge, slanting chandelier welcomes you to a dream-like interior complete with stone chimney, many random wall assortments, a projection screen, many Robin des Bois movie posters, and a beautifully quiet outdoor space shrouded in leaves. The menu is equally beguiling, filled with Gallic standards like mustard-crusted salmon and lamb merguez sandwiches.

✢ Ⓢ *F, G to Bergen St.* Ⓢ *Salads $6.50-8.50. Entrees $9-20.* ⌚ *Open M-Th and Su 11am-midnight, F-Sa noon-1am.*

ETON

⊛⊗ ASIAN, TAKE-OUT ❶

559 Sackett St. (at Smith St.) ☎718-222-2999

Eton elevates takeout to art-form level. Here, you'll get your delicious dumplings, but you'll also have the options to cover them in homemade shaved ice or a selection of handmade sauces including plum and ginger vinegar flavors. It's easy to miss off busy Smith St., but if you're on the go—or just want to relax in nearby Carroll Park—a quick, cheap stop here is essential.

⌗ Ⓢ F, G to Bergen St. or Carroll St. Ⓢ 5 dumplings for $3.75. Bubble tea $4. Ⓞ Open M-Th and Su noon-10pm, F-Sa noon-11pm.

CUBANA CAFE

⊛⚬♿♈⌂ CUBAN, LATIN AMERICAN ❷

272 Smith St. (between Degraw and Sackett St.) ☎718-858-3980

Cubana makes its distinctive claim on an already vibrant street: its small space, mostly outdoors, is adorned with slick wall paintings and designs, attracting a young clientele who dine on pulled pork and dream of revolution. Other offerings from the Caribbean and Latin America abound, from palomilla to oven-roasted red snapper.

⌗ Ⓢ F, G to Bergen St. or Carroll St. Ⓢ Sandwiches $4.50-9. Entrees $9.50-11.50. Ⓞ Open M-F 11am-11pm, Sa-Su 10am-11pm.

PROVENCE EN BOITE

➥♿(((•)))♈⌂ FRENCH ❸

263 Smith St. (at Degraw St.) ☎718-797-0707 ▧www.provenceenboite.com

It's another French restaurant on Smith St.! Unlike the tricked-out grandeur of Robin des Bois, Provence en Boite goes for a simpler, lighter design, with French memorabilia on the walls and a delicious selection of breads and pastries egging you in at the entrance. On fair-weather, open-window days, you may get a hint of the relaxed Provence vibe they're going for. The menu is, as necessary, filled with all kinds of delicious: *steak frites*, *coq au vin*, *lapin aux olives* (that's roasted rabbit), and sautéed scallops.

⌗ Ⓢ F, G to Bergen St. or Carroll St. Ⓢ Salads and sandwiches $4-7. Entrees $11-16. Ⓞ Open daily 7:30am-11pm.

CONEY ISLAND AND BRIGHTON BEACH

You can get your carnival and beach food—cotton candy, ice cream, burgers, hot dogs, and all things fried—along the crowded Riegelmann Boardwalk. But for the real goods, explore **"Little Odessa,"** the Russian-Ukrainian community in Brighton Beach, where much Eastern European scrumptiousness awaits.

🔣 CAFE GLECHIK

⊛⊗❋ UKRAINIAN-RUSSIAN, CAFE ❷

3189 Coney Island Ave. ☎718-611-0494 ▧www.glechik.com

It's easy to miss, but this small Russian-Ukrainian cafe delivers the goods for cheap. In a plain interior, filled with locals who know what they're eating, heaps of delicious Ukrainian *vareniki* and Russian *pelmeni*, two delicious variants in the proud Eastern European dumpling tradition, are served for only a few dollars. You can also go with meat dishes including kebab and seafood, or try some rabbit or chicken-gizzard stew.

⌗ Ⓢ B, Q to Brighton Beach. Ⓢ Dumplings (25 per order) $5-8. Meat dishes $9.50-15. Stews $11.50-19.50. Ⓞ Open daily 9am-10pm.

PRIMORSKI

➥♿(((•)))♈❋ RUSSIAN, GEORGIAN, NIGHTCLUB ❸

282 Brighton Beach Ave. ☎718-891-3111 ▧www.primorski.net

Your one-stop source for all foods Russian and Georgian: reliable *pilmeni* and *blini*, a kind of Russian crepe, *borscht*, racks of lamb, shish kebab, and chicken schnitzel. The dark interior dotted with Christmas lights, is classier than most of the plain establishments along Brighton Beach Ave., but the food is affordable—especially if you're here for the cheap lunch specials, which include salad, soup, a lunch entree, and a side order. At night the restaurant turns into one of the main nightlife spots in the neighborhood, with live entertainment and a huge dance floor.

✚ Ⓢ *B, Q to Brighton Beach.* Ⓢ *Appetizers $3-10. Entrees $9-19. Lunch entrees $6.* ⓣ *Open M-Th 11am-midnight, F 11am-2am, Sa 11am-3am, Su 11am-1am. Live entertainment starts M-Th 8pm, F-Su 9pm.*

NATHAN'S FAMOUS
●🖐♿♨ AMERICAN ❶

1310 Surf Ave. (at Stillwell Ave.)   ☎718-946-2202 ▪www.nathansfamous.com

Nathan Handwerker made his local fame by charging five cents per hotdog when competitors were charging 10. Nearly a century later, Nathan's hot dogs have become landmarks of American cuisine. Since the food stand's beginnings in 1916, many branches have opened throughout the country. But the Coney Island original still draws the crowds, many of them tourists who make Nathan's their first stop upon arrival. The ESPN-broadcast and quite disgusting hot dog eating contest has taken place here since 1916. If you've had enough of hot dogs, you can also try their burgers and seafood items.

✚ Ⓢ *F, D, N, Q to Coney Island-Stillwell Ave.* Ⓢ *Hot dogs $3-4. Burger meals $5-11. Seafood $4-15.* ⓣ *Open daily 8am-1am.*

queens

🖋 TAI PAN BAKERY
●♿ BAKERY ❶

37-25 Main St., between 37th and 38th St.   ☎718-461-8668

If you think you can't get anything worthwhile for a dollar, you need to visit Flushing's finest, the Tai Pan Bakery. You'll find stacks and stacks of pastries and small sandwiches, most of them for only a buck. A small coffee *($1)* or a large coffee *($1.50)* may be worth the splurge. Pastries come in all shapes and sizes, from the familiar danishes and sweet rolls, to the more exotic Roasted Pork Pineapple Bun. The bestseller is the egg custard tart.

✚ Ⓢ *7 to Main St.* Ⓢ *Pastries $1-3. Coffee $1-1.50. Cakes $12-22. Hot food $2.50-4.50.* ⓣ *Open daily 7:30am-8:30pm.*

🖋 THE LEMON ICE KING OF CORONA
●♿ SHAVED ICE ❶

52-02 108th St.   ☎718-669-5133

For 65 years, the people of Queens have lined up year-round for a taste (or a large helping) of the Lemon Ice King's famous shaved ice. If lemon is not your thing, the king has plenty of other options to choose from including banana, chocolate, coffee, pistachio, rainbow. There are around 40 flavors total! Smaller sizes are traditionally eaten straight out of a paper cup, without the interference of a spoon.

✚ Ⓢ *7 to 111th St.* Ⓢ *Shaved ice $1.50-3.* ⓣ *Open daily 10am-midnight.*

🖋 RINCON SALVADOREÑO
♿♨ SALVADORIAN ❷

92-15 149th St., at Jamaica Ave.   ☎718-526-3220

Just like eating in the rainforests of El Salvador...if rainforests were made of plastic. Even if the flowers and plants aren't real, you'll still be so struck by the vibrant colors of this restaurant that you'll find yourself reaching for your camera. The food matches the decor in its vibrant authenticity; savor tamales, plantains, enchiladas, and tortillas, and for those who have trouble deciding on one, they offer a variety of mixed plates *($8-11.50).*

✚ Ⓢ *E, J, Z to Jamaica Center/Parsons/Archer Ave.* ℹ *$20 min. for credit cards.* Ⓢ *Small plates $0.50-3, larger plates $2.50-23. Beer $4-7. Wine $4.* ⓣ *Open M-F 6am-11pm, Sa-Su 9am-11:30pm.*

UNITED BROS FRUIT MARKET

✦♿ GROCERY STORE ❶

32-24 30th Ave.

☎718-932-9879

As you walk down 30th Ave. in Astoria, you will be confronted by mounds of beautiful fruits and vegetables, just waiting to be plucked from the stands. Exotic fruits like mangoes *(2 for $1)* and papayas *($2 per lb.)*, more run-of-the-mill produce such as broccoli *($2 per head)* and apples *($1.49 each)*, it's all here and it's all ripe for the picking. The market is open 24hr., so whether you're just starting out or stumbling home from the bars, you can have delicious fruit whenever you want it.

✦ Ⓢ *N, W to 30th Ave.* Ⓢ *Bananas $0.79 per lb., apples $1.49 per lb, papaya $2 per lb., mangoes 2 for $1, quinces $3.49 per lb., sweet corn 5 for $2, broccoli $2 per head, potatoes $0.59 per lb., herbs $1-3 per bunch.* ⌚ *Open 24 hr.*

HING LONG SUPERMARKET

✦♿ SUPERMARKET ❶

41-22 Main St.

☎718-358-8889

If somebody blindfolded you and dropped you in the middle of this supermarket, you probably would have no idea you were still in the United States. Most of the signs are in Chinese, as is the majority of the conversation. This is the perfect place to get all of your favorite Asian treats—like mochi, pocky, and exotic produce—for low prices!

✦ Ⓢ *7 to Main St.* Ⓢ *Shrimp $4.29-6.69 per lb. Noodles $1-2 for 10-15oz. Produce $1.29-1.79 per lb. Mochi $1.59 for 7.4oz. Pocky $4 for 4.47oz.* ⌚ *Open daily 7:30am-11pm.*

JOE'S SHANGHAI

☺♿ CHINESE ❷

136-21 37th Ave.

☎718-539-3838 🖳www.joesshanghai.com

"Joe's Shanghai." The name indicates the perfect marriage of "American Chinese Food (Chinese Food Lite)" and "Chinese Chinese Food (the real deal)." Sure, you can get your beef with broccoli *($12.35)* or your Kung Pao Chicken *($11.15)*, but you might also choose to order the sliced kidneys with mixed vegetables *($5.35)*, the steamed buffalo carp fish belly *($16)*, or the braised buffalo carp fish belly *($16)*. Who knows when you'll get the chance again?

✦ Ⓢ *7 to Flushing/Main St.* Ⓢ *Appetizers $1.65-7. Entrees $7-31. Beer $4-4.50. Sake $6.50. Rice wine $26. Desserts $3-5.* ⌚ *Open M-Th 11am-11pm, F-Sa 11am-midnight, Su 11am-11pm.*

KUM GANG SAN

✦♿♿ KOREAN ❷

138-28 Northern Blvd.

☎718-461-0909 🖳www.kumgangsan.net

Any hour of the day or night, you can find people at Kum Gang San enjoying their sushi *(a la carte $2.50-$10, maki $9-$21)*, barbecues *($18-$50)*, or Gook *(Korean soup, $11-12)*. The fun doesn't stop after you finish your meal either. Before they go, all guests receive a small dish of ice cream and a miniature piece of buttered corn on the cob.

✦ Ⓢ *7 to Flushing/Main St.* Ⓢ *Appetizers $8-18. Entrees $11-50. Sushi maki $9-21. Wine $8-9. Mixed drinks $7-8.* ⌚ *Open 24hr.*

JUJU'S HOT SPOT

✦♿ CARIBBEAN ❶

135-14 Jamaica Ave.

☎718-523-0804

Stopping into JuJu's Hot Spot is like taking a quick Caribbean vacation. You can almost taste the beaches and sun in the curry shrimp *($10)* and jerk chicken *($6-8)*. A favorite among regulars is the oxtail, served with rice and beans *($10)*. Try a homemade lemonade or ginger beer *($1.50-$2)* with your tropical feast and end with some pineapple cake before heading back to the States.

✦ Ⓢ *E Jamaica-Van Wyck.* Ⓢ *Breakfast $3-6. Entrees $6-12. Lunch special $3-5. Sides $.75-3. Juices $1.50-3.50.* ⌚ *Open M-Sa 8:30am-10pm, Su 8:30am-7pm. Lunch special M-F 11:30am-2:30pm.*

food

JACKSON DINER

≉✧ INDIAN ❷

37-47 74th St., between 37th and 38th Ave.

☎718-672-1232

Not so much a diner as it is an Indian restaurant, this Jackson Heights restaurant specializes in Northern Indian cuisine such as Tandoori Chicken *($12)* and Seekh Kabab *($15)*. The one exception to the Northern Indian spread, is the dosa *(from $5)*, a rice flour pancake that hails from Southern India. At the lunch buffet *($10)*, you can watch the creation of these giant pancakes before your very eyes! "Indian Cocktails" such as the Mango Martini *($7.50)* add a kick to any meal at the "diner."

⚡ Ⓢ *7 to 74th St./Broadway E, F, G, R, V to Jackson Heights/Roosevelt Ave.* Ⓢ *Lunch buffet $10. Appetizers $4-10. Entrees $10-24. Desserts $4.50. Cocktails $6.50-8.50. Beer $5-8.* Ⓩ *Open M-Th 11:30am-10pm, F-Sa 11:30am-10:30pm, Su 11:30am-10pm.*

UNCLE GEORGE'S GREEK TAVERNA

≉✧ GREEK ❷

33-19 Astoria Blvd., at 34th St.

☎718-626-0593 ▇www.unclegeorges.us

It is said that Uncle George himself proclaimed the need to, "Give them lots of good food for a low price!" As far as Greek restaurants in Astoria go, Uncle George definitely does give you a decent bang for your buck. Hits include the Gyro Platter *($8)* and stuffed grape leaves.

⚡ Ⓢ *N, W to Broadway; G, R, V to Steinway St.* Ⓢ *Appetizers $4-12. Entrees $8-$17.75. Wine carafe $3, half kilo $6, kilo $12. Beer $3.50-4.50.* Ⓩ *Open daily 24 hr.*

ELIAS CORNER

≉✧✧ SEAFOOD ❸

24-02 31st St.

☎718-932-1510

At Elias Corner, there are no menus: only a reputation for fresh, delectable seafood. As an appetizer, try an order of octopus or shrimp. Their most popular fish are the St. Peter's and Bronzini, followed closely by the Red Snapper. Eating on the patio, you can almost imagine that you are by the seaside enjoying the morning's catch.

⚡ Ⓢ *N, W to Astoria Ditmars Blvd.* Ⓢ *Salads $3-9. Appetizers $11-18. Seafood $17-29. Sides $4-6. Wine $5.* Ⓩ *Open dailly after 4pm-midnight.*

ZORBA'S SOUVLAKI PLUS

≉✧✧ GREEK ❶

29-05 23rd Ave.

☎718-956-7266 ▇www.zorbasnyc.com

They have souvlaki *($2.50-$5.50)*, tzatziki *($3)*, biftekia *($8.75)*, and the rest of your Greek favorites, and they have them cheap. But they also have hamburgers, wraps, panini, salads, soups, pizza, desserts, and breakfast, served all day. Let's give Zorba's a round of applause.

⚡ Ⓢ *N, W to Astoria Ditmars Blvd.* Ⓢ *Sandwiches, wraps, burgers $3.25-$8.75. Souvlaki $2.50-$5.50. Greek plates $8.75-$11.50. Breakfast $1-7. Salads $4-$8.50. Desserts $2-3.* Ⓩ *Open daily 11am-7pm.*

TOURNESOL

✧ FRENCH ❸

50-12 Vernon Blvd.

☎718-472-4355 ▇www.tournesolnyc.com

Not your typical French restaurant. Every dish served at this charming bistro, from the Grilled Calamares with Cucumber and Avocado Salad *($8.50)* to the Duck Leg Confit with Plum Salad *($16)*, is a work of culinary art. The wine list is intimidating, to say the least, with an extensive array of wines from France and around the world. Monday through Wednesday, they offer a tempting prix-fixe menu featuring an appetizer, an entree, and a dessert.

⚡ Ⓢ *7 to Vernon Blvd.-Jackson Ave., G to 21st St.* Ⓢ *Appetizers $7.50-$12. Entrees $14-18. Daily specials $20-25. Brunch $7-15. Wine $7-15.* Ⓩ *Open M 5:30pm-11pm; Tu-Th 11:30am-3pm and 5:30pm-11pm; F 11:30am-3pm and 5:30pm-11:30pm; Sa 11am-3:30pm and 5:30pm-11:30pm; Su 11am-3:30pm and 5pm-10pm.*

queens

the bronx

Those adventurous enough to explore the Bronx's food offerings really can't miss the borough's Little Italy in Belmont along Arthur Ave. Here is all the taste of Manhattan's Little Italy with little of the annoying aplomb. The neighborhood pastry shops have been around for decades, while the popular pizzerias are still filled with those who don't come with cameras and souvenirs attached. Don't miss the **Arthur Avenue Retail Market,** founded in 1940 *(2344 Arthur Ave., ☎718-295-5033 💻www.arthuravenue.com ⏰ Open M-Sa 7am-6pm),* a central shopping space where you can find a butcher shop, a deli, fruit stands, a grocer, and a florist.

👍 GIOVANNI'S
💳♿🍸 ITALIAN, PIZZERIA [3]

2343 Arthur Ave. ☎718-933-4141 💻www.giovannisrestaurant.net

From the front, Giovanni's looks like your standard neighborhood pizzeria: small, narrow, and crowded. Head to the back, though, and you'll find ample seating and a bar for kicks. With plentiful meat and pasta specials for (relatively) affordable prices, Giovanni's stands out in a crowded field. Bonus: a dinner special gets you a free glass of wine.

 # [S] B, D to Fordham Rd. $ Pizza $11-19. Entrees $8-22. Lunch specials from $10. Dinner specials from $13. ⏰ Open M-Sa 11am-10pm; Su noon-9pm.

👍 GINO'S PASTRY SHOP
💵♿ PASTRY SHOP, BAKERY [1]

580 East 187th St. ☎718-584-3558

Gino's has been around since 1960 but seems to have resisted the impulses to change or self-mythologize; the interior is still small, plain, and simple. All the fuss, thankfully, is focused on the bevy of pastries and breads behind the counter—which is stuffed by owners and loyal staff members who have become institutions themselves. This is cheap, delicious, time-tested sustenance for your neighborhood walk.

 # [S] B, D to Fordham Rd. $ Breads $1-5. Pastries $1-6. ⏰ Open M 9am-5pm, Tu-Su 9am-7pm.

ANN AND TONY'S RESTAURANT
💳🍸 ITALIAN [3]

2407 Arthur Ave. ☎718-933-1469 💻annandtonysonline.com

The same family has been running the same restaurant in the same location since 1927. It's hard to argue with the Napolitano clan's long-standing recipes, even if the prices are on the high side. Your typical pasta *(farfalle napoli)* and the house-recipe veal are here alongside "Chef Anthony's Italian Classics" (tripe, eggplant parmigiana, and the wallet-busting giambotta).

 # [S] B,D to Fordham Rd. $ Entrees $17-35. ⏰ Open Tu-Th noon-1pm, F-Sa noon-11pm, Su 1-9pm.

MADONIA BAKERY
💵♿ PASTRY SHOP, BAKERY [1]

2348 Arthur Ave. ☎718-295-5573

No, this isn't the neighborhood's newest addition; with its bare walls and simple interior, Madonna just hides it's age well. The place has actually been serving a generous selection of specialty breads (olive, prosciutto, jalapeno, and more) and pastries since 1918. The bakery's also said to fill its dessert case with the best cannoli on Arthur Ave.

 # [S] B,D to Fordham Rd. $ Breads $1-5. Pastries $0.50-4. ⏰ Open M-Sa 6am-7pm, Su 6:30am-6pm.

NIGHTLIFE

Pigeons in New York are far outnumbered by **night owls.** From Brooklyn dive bars to A-list Meatpacking District lounges, the city has nightlife to satisfy every kind of partier. While you can get a drink at almost any hour, most clubs don't get going until after midnight, and a good night in New York usually lasts until 4am. Fortunately, the Subway runs 24hr., so you can get back to your hostel without dropping any extra cash. Considering how pricey the New York scene can be, you may want to save up by doing some pre-party drinking before you hit any clubs. New Yorkers pride themselves on style, so leave your sneakers at home and put on something nice. These days, indoor public spaces are all non-smoking. If you want to light up you'll be among the many New York smokers hanging outside the doorway of every city nightspot. Chelsea and Greenwich Village are Manhattan's GLBT nightlife centers, while the Lower East Side, the East Village, and Williamsburg offer the best of the rest. To keep up on the latest openings and parties, keep your eye on publications like *The Village Voice*, *Time Out New York*, and *New York Magazine*.

greatest hits

- **SNAPSHOTS AND TEQUILA SHOTS** are both options at Niagara (p.150), a bar with its own photo booth. You'll never forget how much fun you had.

- **BUDS AND BUDDIES.** Become best friends with New York's coolest bartenders at 200 Orchard St. (p.144) on the Lower East Side.

- **MATERIAL BOYS** dance to Madonna at Xes Lounge (p.152), one of the hottest gay bars in Chelsea.

- **SECRET GARDEN.** Hop on the Subway to drink outside with friends at the Beer Garden at Bohemian Hall (p.161) in Astoria.

lower manhattan

▩ VINTRY WINE AND WHISKEY
⛳♿♻♻♻ BAR

57 Stone St.,   ☎212-480-9800 ▨www.vintrynyc.com

Considered to be the premier wine and whiskey bar in New York City, Vintry Wine and Whiskey has 100 wines available by the glass and 200 whiskeys. This does *not*, however, mean that you have to be a Wall Street investment banker to drink here; you can get a shot of whiskey for just $4. Enjoy a plate of cheeses ($16) while you sip your wine from a stool with legs custom-made by a motorcycle mechanic. Not sure what to order? The bartenders know their stuff and will be happy to help you out.

‡ Ⓢ 2, 3 to Wall St. or R, W to Whitehall-South Ferry Ⓢ Small plates $3.50-$6. Cured meats $5-8. Desserts $7-9. Drinks from $4. ◱ Open M-W 11:30am-2am, Th-F 11:30am-4am, Sa 4pm-4am, Su 4pm-1am.

▩ KILARNEY ROSE
⛳Ⓒ♻ BAR, RESTAURANT

127 Pearl St., betwen Hanover and Wall St.   ☎212-422-1486 ▨www.killarneyrose.com

A two-for-one bar experience: the top floor is a lounge with trendy furniture and flat-screen TVs, while the bottom is a traditional Irish-style pub. Essential Gaelic wisdom is distributed overhead at the latter (e.g. "There are no strangers here, just friends who have yet to meet" and "There is nothing like a pint of stout"). The unbelievably cheap booze starts at just $4 and all pints (both domestic imported) are $4 on Saturdays and Sundays.

‡ Ⓢ 2, 3 to Wall St. or R, W to Whitehall-South Ferry. Ⓢ Wine from $5. Beer from $4.50. Other alcoholic drinks from $4. Bar menu $5-17. Full menu appetizers $4-10. Sandwiches $10-11. Salads $12-13. Entrees $10-15. ◱ Open daily 11am-4pm. Kitchen open until midnight.

▩ FISH MARKET
⛳♿♻ BAR, RESTAURANT

111 South St., between Beekman St. and Peck Slip ☎212-227-4468 ▨www.fishmarketnyc.com

Alcohol and fish: a match made in...bars near large bodies of water, most frequently. Fish Market offers top-notch deals for both. Sundays and Mondays you can get $5 draughts and $1 oysters. When the weekend rolls around, it is time for "Sexy Saturday" ($5 Absolut Shots, bucket of 5 beers $18-20). The fish tank on the wall reminds us of whom we have to thank for making establishments like this possible.

‡ Ⓢ 2, 3, J, M, Z to Fulton St. Ⓢ Beer $4.50-$6. Wine $7-8. Cocktails $9-11. Appetizers $9-22. Entrees $9-24. Sandwiches $9-13. Salads $4-12. ◱ Open daily 11:30am-4am. Happy hour M-Th 5-9pm.

HEARTLAND BREWERY

♣ 👶 🎵 ❦ BAR, RESTAURANT

93 South Seaport ☎646-572-2337 🔳www.heartlandbrewery.com

The unique and uniquely named beers at this American brewpub are concocted at the Heartland Brewery in Clinton Hill, Brooklyn, which brews 20,000 kegs yearly. The Indian River Light (a light pale ale with a dash of orange blossoms and coriander) is among the most popular, although the Grateful Red Lager, Smiling Pumpkin Ale, and Not Tonight Honey Lager have undoubtedly more ingenious names (availability varies by season).

✦ Ⓢ F to East Broadway. Ⓢ Half-pint beer $5; pint $7; 23oz $10. Appetizers $8-11. Entrees $13-24. Sandwiches $11-13. Desserts $5-6. ⌚ Open M-Th 11:30am-11pm, F-Sa 11:30am-midnight, Su noon-10pm.

ULYSSES FOLK HOUSE

♣ 👶 🎵 ❦ BAR, RESTAURANT

95 Pearl St. ☎212-482-0400 🔳www.ulyssesfolkhouse.com

Ulysses is a deluge of decoration choices: Irish folk songs on the wall ("I'll Tell Me Ma" and "Paddy Doyle's Ass" are among the best), Classical illustrations of Ulysses, Pre-Raphaelite pictures of Ulysses, an entire gallery of James Joyce pictures, etc. The drinks and food are no less overwhelming. Almost every day of the week is a different special: Monday starting at 4pm, you can get any lobster for $19. Tuesday nights 5-7pm you can get free samples of international beers. Wednesdays all night long, you can get six oysters and a pint of Guinness for $12. Saturday evening there's live music; Sunday morning they have brunch...it just doesn't stop!

✦ Ⓢ 2, 3 to Wall St. or R, W to Whitehall-South Ferry. Ⓢ Beer $6. Wine $8. Mixed drinks $6.50. Appetizers $7-14. Sandwiches and wraps $9-15. Entrees $14-24. Brunch $20. ⌚ Open daily 11am-4pm.

STONE STREET TAVERN

♣ ⊗ 🎵 ❦ BAR, RESTAURANT

85 Pearl St. ☎212-785-5658 🔳www.stonestreettavernnyc.com

Stone Street Tavern, with its ornate chandeliers and modern-art covered walls, brings an ultra-cool blend of old and new to historic 17th-century Stone St. Ladies, be sure to stop in on Wednesday nights ($5 Cosmos and Appletinis). The tavern is also a prime location for the Stone Street Festival in May and the Stone Street Oyster Festival in September.

✦ Ⓢ 2, 3 to Wall St. or R, W to Whitehall-South Ferry. Ⓢ Beer $6-9. Wine $8-9. Mixed drinks $10-13. Appetizers $10-12. Sandwiches $12-17. Entrees $15-22. ⌚ Open M 11:30am-1am, Tu-Th 11:30am-2am, Sa noon-2am, Su noon-1am.

FRESH SALT

♣ ⊗ ❦ BAR, RESTAURANT

146 Beekman St., between Front St. and FDR Dr. ☎212-962-0053

Equipped with wooden tables and stools and old maritime implements, Fresh Salt has the charm of an old Dutch ship. They even keep a Battleship board game, in case the mood strikes. The galley is open until 4am and serves foods much more interesting than your typical mozzarella sticks. Try the pita melt with pesto sauce, mild pecorino, fresh mozzarella, and asiago cheese ($6).

✦ Ⓢ 2, 3, J, M, Z to Fulton St. Ⓢ Beer $6. Wine $7-8. Liquor $6-10. Sandwich $9. Pita melts $6-10.50. Plates $8-9. Brunch $10. ⌚ Open daily 10am-4am. Happy hour daily 4-8pm.

JEREMY'S ALE HOUSE

♣ ⊗ ❦ BAR

228 Front St. ☎212-964-3537 🔳www.jeremysalehouse.com

Autographed bras of all sizes hang festively from the ceiling and pieces of police and fire department T-shirts cover the walls. You may not have expected to find a dive bar in the South St. Seaport area, but Jeremy runs with the best of them. While other bars worry about elegant dishes and ambience, here it's all about the pints ($5) and hot dogs ($2). They even have 🔳Donkey Kong.

✦ Ⓢ 2, 3, J, M, Z to Fulton St; or A, C to Broadway-Nassau. Between Beekman St. and Peck Slip. Ⓢ Beer $4.75-5.50 per pint. Mixed drinks $6. Appetizers $3-12. Grill items $1.50-8. Seafood $6-11. ⌚ M-F 8am-midnight, Sa 10am-midnight, Su noon-midnight.

lower manhattan

OPEN DOOR GASTROPUB

✎⊗♀ BAR, RESTAURANT

110 John St., between Pearl St. and Cliff St. ☎212-608-0200 ▣www.opendoornyc.com

This "gastropub" offers the exciting opportunity to drink and eat in a gallery of the many varieties of Victorian doors in Dublin. Not just pictures: actual, life-size, vibrantly-colored doors. The bartenders serve between 50 and 60 beers from behind a curving, dark wood bar, as well as a slew of different whiskeys. Enjoy your beer with an inventively gourmet menu, such as the pretzel fried bird *(Cornish hen, $18)*.

⌘ Ⓢ *2, 3, J, M, Z to Fulton St.* Ⓢ *Beer $6.50-$14. Wine and mixed drinks $8-12. Appetizers $7-14. Sandwiches $14. Entrees $16-20. Brunch $11-17. Brunch with unlimited mimosas $25.* ☾ *Open M-W 11am-2am, Th-Sa 11am-4am, Su 11am-1am.*

MORAN'S

✎⟐♀ BAR, RESTAURANT

103 Washington St., between Washington and Greenwich St. ☎212-732-2020 ▣www.moransnyc.com

When you first see the neo-Gothic facade, stained-glass windows, and likeness of St. George above the entrance door, you will probably think you are about to step into a church. And a church this was until 1979. Now it is an emerald-interior bar and restaurant where tourists and Financial District big shots alike consume large quantities of alcohol and "comfort food." The shepherd's pie *($16)* goes perfectly with a pint of Guinness.

⌘ Ⓢ *1, R, W to Rector St..* Ⓢ *Beer $5-6. Mixed drinks $8-10. Wine $8. Appetizers $6.50-22. Sandwiches $11-16. Entrees $15-26.* ☾ *Open daily 10am-10pm. Kitchen open until 9pm.*

the young and the id-less

Plenty of college underclassmen who come to New York City complain about the city's strict attitude toward clubbing for minors and those under 21. New York and its bouncers seem pretty friendly—until you try to get in. For the little ones still not old enough to party without penalty, here's some advice.

- **MIDDLE EASTERN-STYLE PUBS NEAR ST. MARK'S PLACE.** Although most places cater hookah to the 18+ crowd, minors are still allowed. Most restaurants serve smoldering baklava and other eastern desserts dripping with chocolate and delicious cholesterol.

- **NEW AGE FRO-YO SHOPS IN MANHATTAN.** An onslaught of Pinkberry and Red Mango franchises have proliferated up and down the island in recent years, and the trend is only growing as the 18-25 demographic eats up the modern décor and "mood" lighting. Despite the overbearing interior design, the menus at these frozen yogurt chains do provide a satisfying alternative to cocktails at the Ritz. OK, maybe not, but the walnut and mochi toppings will still make anyone happy.

- **AMC EMPIRE 25 ON 42ND STREET.** As the largest movie megaplex in Manhattan, this Times Square cinema offers 25 screens hosting the latest releases, with leg room that makes first-class flights look like a gyp. Thanks to stadium seating, moviegoers can enjoy a flick from the front row without needing a trip to the chiropractor.

nightlife

soho

▨ LUCKY STRIKE

⊗✎ BAR

59 Grand St. ☎212-941-0772 ▣www.luckystrikeny.com

Poussez to enter this French-style bar, where the drinks are written in faded letters on glass above the bar. You can feast on a *croque monsieur ($14)* or *steak frites ($25)* as you gaze at a *L'Eclipse* movie poster.

✈ Ⓢ *1 to Canal St./Varick St.; or A, C, E to Canal St./Ave. of the Americas.* Ⓢ *Beer $7. Wine $8-10. Well drinks $8. Appetizers $8.50-13.50. Sandwiches $11.50-14.* ⌚ *Open M-W noon-1am, Th noon-2am, F-Sa noon-2:30am, Su noon-1am. Happy Hour 4-7pm.*

▨ THE EAR INN ✈⛓ BAR
326 Spring St. ☎212-431-9750 ▦www.earinn.com

Don't miss your chance to party in one of New York's most experienced drinking establishments. Originally built at the end of the 1700s for **James Brown,** George Washington's African-American aide, the house became the site of a brewery in the 1800s, then a speakeasy in the 1920s, then an unnamed bar referred to simply as "The Green Door" by sailors after Prohibition. The current name was the result of an attempt to eschew the Landmark Commission's arduous process for obtaining new signage (the right half of the B in the neon "BAR" sign was painted black).

✈ Ⓢ *C, E to Spring St.* Ⓢ *Beer $4-6.50. Wine $7.50-9. Appetizers $6-7. Burgers and sandwiches $6-9. Entrees $10-13.* ⌚ *Open daily noon-4am. Kitchen open until 1am.*

▨ GRAND BAR AND LOUNGE ✈⛓ LOUNGE
310 W. Broadway ☎212-963-3588 ▦www.sohogrand.com

On the second floor of a luxurious hotel with industrial accents is a lounge with stylish chairs and sofas where you can enjoy a Dirty SoHo *(Stolichnaya Gold vodka, olive brine, assorted olive skewer, $15)* into the wee hours of the morning. If you get there before midnight, you can also order serious entrees such as the New York strip steak *($28).*

✈ Ⓢ *1, A, C, E to Canal St.* Ⓢ *Mixed drinks $13-18. Beer $8-28. Wine $11-23. Liquor $12-55, Champagne $14. Appetizers $12-16. Entrees $15-28. Desserts $9-10.* ⌚ *Open daily 6am-3pm. Kitchen open until midnight.*

MILADY'S ⛓ BAR
160 Prince St. ☎212-226-9069

If you want to skip the swank and posturing of some SoHo bars and just want cheap drinks and good food served by congenial people, head to this little treasure, tucked away on the corner of Prince and Thompson. Instead of wondering whether people are judging your wardrobe choices, you can do the things normal people do in bars: play pool, watch sports, and fiddle with the jukebox while you throw back Drunken Palmers and Pink Miladys.

✈ Ⓢ *C, E, to Spring St./Avenue of the Americas.* Ⓢ *Beer $5-6. Wine $6. Appetizers $5-9. Sandwiches $8-10. Entrees $11.* ⌚ *Open daily 11am-4pm. Kitchen closes M-Th midnight, F-Sa 1am, Su 11pm.*

MERC BAR ✈⛓ BAR
151 Mercer St ☎212-966-2727 ▦www.mercbar.com

Merc Bar seems to have taken its inspiration from Native American interior design; tall wooden walls, long boats hanging from the ceilings, and a decorative assortment of antlers. Comfy, holstein-clad cube chairs cover the floor. Merc Bar's motto is "just a bar," so don't come asking for food other than the free bowls of pretzels situated generously around the establishment.

✈ Ⓢ *N, Q, R to Prince St.* Ⓢ *Beer $6-9. House mixed drinks $13-14. Wine from $10.* ⌚ *Open M-Th 5pm-2am, F 5pm-4am, Sa 4pm-4am, Su 4pm-2am.*

THE CITY WINERY ✈⛓ WINERY, LIVE MUSIC
155 Varick St., at Vandam St. ☎212-608-0555 ▦www.citywinery.com

A real-life winery in a renovated, 19th-century building in downtown New York City. Try a glass of the City Winery Rosé of Pinot Noir or take home a bottle of the Downtown White or Van Dam Zin. If you're hungry, you can munch on pretzels *($5)* or flatbread pizzas *($13-17)* made with lees from the wine barrels. The winery hosts frequent musical performances. Sundays

soho

(11am-2am) feature klezmer brunches, with lox and bagels and the soulful sounds of the ▓**klezmer clarinet.**

✈ Ⓢ *C, E to Spring St.* ℹ *Sometimes the winery is only open to performance ticket holders; call to confirm that it is open to the general public.* Ⓢ *Wines $9-164. Beer $7-16. Food $6-24. Winery tours free.* ⓩ *Open daily 11:30am-3pm and 5-11pm. Winery tours M-F 12:30-6pm.*

THE ROOM
✦⛶ BAR

144 Sullivan St., between Prince St. and W. Houston St.   ☎212-477-2102 ▣www.theotheroom.com

Beer and wine from all over the world is served in this tiny but extremely hip bar, where the furniture takes up most of the floor space, works by local artists appear on the walls, and alternative music plays in the background. Satisfy your craving for fine alcohol with one of 30 different wines and 60 different beers.

✈ Ⓢ *C, E to Spring St. Walk to Sullivan St., between Prince St. and W. Houston St.* Ⓢ *Beer $6-20. Wine $8-15.* ⓩ *Open daily 5pm-4am.*

RAOUL'S
✦ BAR

180 Prince St.   ☎212-966-3518 ▣www.raouls.com

An authentic French bistro where you can pair your drink with gourmet appetizers and entrees such as the chèvre cannelloni with grilled eggplant, baby zucchini, and green tomatoes *($21)* or the *pâté maison* with baby spinach and walnuts *($10)*. Take in the evening air in the garden room in the back, or simply enjoy the charmingly eclectic assortment of paintings on the wall.

✈ Ⓢ *N, Q, R to Prince St. Follow Prince to bar between Thompson and Sullivan St.* Ⓢ *Wine averages $12-13. Beer $6. Mixed drinks $12-16. Appetizers $10-19. Entrees $21-39.* ⓩ *Open daily 5pm-2am. Kitchen open M-Th 5:30-midnight, F-Sa 5:30pm-1am, Su 5:30pm-midnight.*

BAR 89
✦⛶ BAR

89 Mercer St.   ☎212-274-0989 ▣www.bar89.com

This martini-oriented bar is a sea of black leather, sharp angles, and irises. A popular drink choice is the St. Germain, made with Absolut Pear, St.-Germain elderflower liqueur and champagne. The watermelon martini uses a puree made from scratch. Other hits include the coconut and Starburst-flavored martinis.

✈ Ⓢ *N, Q, R to Prince St. Walk to Mercer St. between Spring and Broome St.* Ⓢ *Beer $7-12. Martinis $14-17. Appetizers $9-36. Sandwiches $9.50-16.50. Salads $7-16. Desserts $6-11.* ⓩ *Open M-Th noon-1am, F-Sa noon-2am, Su noon-1am.*

THE EMERALD PUB
✦⛶ BAR

308 Spring St.   ☎212-226-8512

The Emerald Pub is caught between a dive bar and an upscale lounge, with serial microsuede cube chairs on one side and typical bar accoutrements on the other: a model human skull, miscellaneous trophies, and even a bear pelt. The back wall holds a mosaic, constructed in part with parts of Jagermeister bottles. Happy hour *(5-8pm)* is especially happy on Thursdays and Fridays, when the bar holds a free barbecue for customers.

✈ Ⓢ *C, E to Spring St. Follow Spring St. to bar between Hudson St. and Greenwich St.* Ⓢ *Beer $4-6. Well drinks $6.* ⓩ *Open daily 11:30am-4am. Half-price happy hour 5-8pm.*

lower east side

▧ **200 ORCHARD ST.**
✦⛶✠ BAR

200 Orchard St., at E. Houston St.   ☎212-253-2235 ▣www.200orchard.com

Focused on being an inclusive, neighborhood establishment, the bartenders here are hands-down the nicest, friendliest people you will ever meet in a bar. The drinks, already reasonably priced, are borderline-absurdly cheap during the late happy hour from 6 to 10pm *(Beer/well drinks $3-5; sandwiches made especially to* *order at the barside kitchenette, $6).* One 200 Orchard St. bartender wishes it to be known that he is on a search for **the last Diners Club card** and will award a free drink to the person who brings it to the bar.

🚉 [S] F, M to 2nd Ave./Lower East Side. $ Wine and beer $6-7. ⏰ Open daily 6pm-4am. Happy Hour 6-10pm.

👍 BARRAMUNDI — 🚬♿🍸 BAR

67 Clinton St., between Stanton and Rivington ☎212-529-6999 🖥www.barramundiny.com

A festive bar with a sense of humor (see mounted deer's head on wall wearing blond wig and framed by plastic knives) and a delicious array of drinks and bar food. Favorite libations include infused vodkas and sangria. The bar menu goes beyond humdrum French fries and chicken wings. You can enjoy a chopped salad *($10)* with your cocktail or even a half rack of ribs *($19).*

🚉 [S] F, J, M, Z to Essex St./Delancey. ℹ Sangria 2 for 1 during daily happy hour, 6-9pm. $ Beer $4-7. Wine $7-10. Cocktails $8. Bar Food $7-19. ⏰ Open daily 6pm-4am. Happy Hour daily 6-9pm. Kitchen open until 10pm.

👍 LOLITA — 🚭🍸🚬 BAR, LOUNGE

266 Broome St., at Allen St. ☎212-966-7223 🖥www.lolitabar.net

The perfect alternative-artsy-cute-edgy-quirky blend. Contemporary art on the wall changes around once every two months, and sometimes, when you're lucky, they rock an old-school record player.

🚉 [S] F, J, M, Z to Essex St./Delancey St. ℹ Only American Express accepted. $ Beer $4-8. Mixed drinks $7-12. Wine $8-9. ⏰ Open daily 5pm-2am, usually 4am on weekends. Happy hour 5-8pm.

SUNITA — 🚬🚭🍸 BAR/LOUNGE

106 Norfolk St., between Delancey and Rivington ☎212-253-8860 🖥www.sunitabar.com

This inviting bar is famous for fresh, hand-crafted cocktails with freshly pureed ingredients. The Jalapeño Passion Fruit Martini, a fabulous combo of fruit and zing, is a crowd favorite and also happens to be a 👍**Bond Girl** cocktail.

🚉 [S] F, J, M, Z to Delancey St./Essex St. $ Beer $6-7. Wine $8. Mixed drinks $10-14. ⏰ Open Tu-Sa 6pm-4am.

THE MAGICIAN — 🎵♿🍸 BAR

118 Rivington St. ☎212-673-7881

The tiled floors and round tables make The Magician look like an establishment that might sell home-cooked meals. Don't be fooled: the only things they cook up at this place are cheap drinks and fun crowds. The jukebox and flatscreen TV make this a great place to party.

🚉 [S] F, J, M, Z to Essex St./Delancey St. $ Mixed drinks $5-$9.50. ⏰ Open daily 5pm-4am.

ST. JEROMES — 🚬♿🍸 BAR

155 Rivington St., between Clinton and Suffolk ☎212-533-1810

At the door to this rock n' roll dive bar, you're greeted by a praying saint, the bar's mascot, which should put you in a pious mood for the night. Live DJs spin beats every night, and Buds are $2 until midnight. At any time, you can order a "Happy Meal," which consists of a Bud and a Jameson shot. Should bring you right back to your childhood.

🚉 [S] F, J, M, Z to Essex St./Delancey St. $ Drinks $2-10. ⏰ Open daily 6pm-4am.

THE DELANCEY — 🚬♿🍸 BAR

168 Delancey St., between Clinton and Attorney St. ☎212-25-9920 🖥www.thedelancey.com

The Delancey's smooth, cool bar with a red glow and an old-fashioned charm. For an open-air drinking experience, head to the palm-laden rooftop deck. The basement lounge is a venue for many a delightful show, including a popular Burlesque night on Tuesdays around 9pm.

🚉 [S] F, J, M, Z to Delancey St./Essex St. $ Mixed drinks $6-12. ⏰ Open M-W 5pm-2am, Th-Sa 5pm-4am, Su 5pm-2am.

NURSE BETTIE
● ᱚ ❦ BAR

106 Norfolk St., between Delancey and Rivington St. ☎212-477-7515 ▦www.nursebettieles.com
A small but hoppin' bar and lounge, with old-fashioned wallpaper and suggestive
(borderline scandalous!) likenesses of ladies on the wall. They're old, though, so
it's classy. These ladies come to life (sort of) during free, live burlesque shows on
Wednesday and Thursday nights.
❦ Ⓢ F, J, M, Z to Essex St./Delancey St. Ⓢ Drinks $6-9. Happy Hour draft beer and well drinks
$4. ⏱ Open M-W 6pm-2am, Th-Sa 6pm-4am, Su 6pm-2am. Happy hour M-Th 6-10pm, F-Sa
6-9pm, Su 6-10pm.

---

hypochondriac's rx

Looking for a toothbrush is easy in a city where a Duane Reade sits on practically
every other city block, but those seeking quick medical advice on that mystery
mole might find what they're looking for just as easily. The omnipresent drugstore
that monopolizes most of Manhattan recently opened its fifth walk-in medical
center near the Port Authority Bus Terminal. Marketed to people looking for quick
opinions on non-emergency issues, the almost makeshift set-up hires actual MDs
to diagnose problems and refers them back to their primary physician to continue
treatment if needed. Oh, and they take insurance. (1627 Broadway, New York, NY,
located between 7th and 8th Ave. at West 50th St.)

---

greenwich village

Village nightlife is a many-splendored thing. Most of the neighborhood's fame began
in its nightspots—in the theaters, speakeasies, and music clubs that lay at the edge
of the avant-garde. Many of those storied establishments exist, albeit in diluted
form. But there's way more where that came from: the **Washington Square Park** area
is crowded with dive bars and clubs catering to a young, energetic crowd; the **West
Village** has its share of mellower taverns with older patrons; **Christopher Street** lies at
the center of some of the city's best ☑**GLBT nightlife**; and the **Meatpacking District** to
the northwest is a true orgy of hyper-gentrification, limos, beautiful people, plastic
people, celebrities, exclusive clubs, solemn bouncers, and endless lines.

◪ FAT BLACK PUSSYCAT
● ᱚ ❋ ❦ DIVE BAR

130 W. 3rd St.　　　　　　　　　　　☎212-533-4790 ▦www.fatblackpussycat.com
The mellow Fat Black Pussycat draws the young in with an extensive and
relatively cheap beer selection. Grab a seat in the wooden booths in back and
etch your name into the table alongside countless others. A connected room
to the left offers more of a lounge feel, with mood lighting, sofas, and plush
velvet seats. The Village Underground performance space (see **Arts and Culture**)
is connected to the bar.
❦ Ⓢ A, B, C, D, E, F, V to West 4th St. Ⓢ Beer $3-8. Mixed drinks $6-12. Pitchers $10 and shots
$3 on M-Th and Su. ⏱ Open daily 1pm-4am.

◪ THE BACK FENCE
● ❋❋ ❦ DIVE BAR, LIVE MUSIC

155 Bleecker St.　　　　　　　　　　☎212-475-9221 ▦www.thebackfenceonline.com
Tiny but vital, the Back Fence has been holding steady onto its prime corner
location since 1945. The space is small and the crowds might induce claustro-
phobia, but a constant lineup of live performers—two to three each night—will
keep your attention. Despite its long history, the bar retains its rugged feel—right

down to the sawdust on the floor. An oldie but a goodie.

♿ Ⓢ *A, B, C, D, E, F, V to West 4th St.* Ⓢ *Cover F-Sa $5. Beer $3-8. Mixed drinks $7-12.* ☾ *Open M-Th 3:30pm-4am, F 2pm-4am, Sa 1pm-4am.*

CORNER BISTRO
●&❄ NEIGHBORHOOD BAR

331 W. 4th St. (at Jane St.)　　　　　☎212-242-9502 🖳www.cornerbistrony.com

The Corner Bistro is a perfect distillation of the West Village: old, stately, friendly, and still mildly bohemian. The burgers, often rated the best in New York, are the main draw. The Bistro Burger is especially popular, with beef, onions, bacon, and cheese. But the experience of simply drinking in the Bistro seems nostalgic in itself. Its dark wood floors and walls, aging but lively bartenders, and comfortably local clientele seem to resurrect the feel of more storied decades past.

♿ Ⓢ *A, C, E, L to 8th Ave.-14th St.* Ⓢ *Beer $5-9. Burgers $6-7.* ☾ *Open M-Sa 11:30am-4am, Su noon-4am.*

HENRIETTA HUDSON
●&❄⛾▼ GAY AND LESBIAN

438 Hudson St.　　　　　　　　　　☎212-924-3347 🖳www.henriettahudson.com

While Christopher St. nightlife caters mostly to gay men, Henrietta Hudson is a well-regarded option for the ladies. This "bar and girl" is one of New York's prime lesbian hotspots, featuring three rooms, two bars, DJs, and an occasional cage in the middle of the dance floor. The atmosphere is sweaty; on weekends the crowds can become overpowering, and many prefer the more chill (and far less expensive) weeknights. But if you're looking for something raucous, Henrietta Hudson's got it on weekends.

♿ Ⓢ *1 to Houston St.* *i* *Happy hour (2-for-1 drinks) M-F 4-7pm.* Ⓢ *Cover F-Sa $10. Beer $3-7. Mixed drinks $7-13.* ☾ *Open M-W 5pm-2am, Th-Sa 5pm-4am, Su 2am-4am.*

THE STANDARD BIERGARTEN
●&⛾⛵ OUTDOOR BEER GARDEN

848 Washington St.　　　　　　　　☎212-645-4646 🖳www.standardhotels.com

With its looming, gray, riverside mass, the Standard Hotel crowns the Meatpacking District's chic-on-steroids atmosphere. Its outdoor beer garden below is a friendly (if packed) spot for those tired of the exclusivity of nearby clubs. Sit and enjoy a hearty beer or hefty German snacks on long picnic tables. A screen set up in front ocassionally projects games and other videos. In a city where space is coveted, you'll need some outdoor nightlife for a change.

♿ Ⓢ *A, C, E, L to 14th St.-8th Ave.* Ⓢ *$8 ticket gives you 1 beer, 1 giant pretzel, or 2 sausages.* ☾ *Open M-W 4pm-midnight, Th 2pm-midnight, F 2pm-1am, Sa noon-1am, Su noon-midnight.*

FAT CAT
●⊗⛾❄ JAZZ CLUB, DIVE BAR

75 Christopher St. (at 7th Ave.)　　　☎212-675-6056 🖳www.fatcatmusic.org

The Village's cheapest jazz club will be far more appealing to young, cash-strapped fans than the pricey options down the way. But this sprawling downstairs establishment really goes the distance: besides the live jazz, there are 10 pool tables, plenty of board games for your drunk competitive pleasure, and some swanky lounging areas if the Parcheesi is getting you knackered. For a low cover, that's a lot of entertainment—and huge crowds know it.

♿ Ⓢ *A, B, C, D, E, F, V to West 4th St.; 1 to Christopher St.* Ⓢ *Cover $3. Beer $4-8. Mixed drinks $6-11. Pool tables $5.50 per hr.* ☾ *Open M-Th 2pm-5am, F-Sa noon-5am, Su 1pm-5am.*

VBAR AND CAFE
●&❄(((•))⛾ CAFE, DIVE BAR

225 Sullivan St.　　　　　　　　　　☎212-253-5740 🖳www.vbar.net

Mellow student cafe by day, mellow drinking hole by night, VBar is perfect for a relaxed evening out or a breathing spot in between wilder venues. Tiny tables rub elbows with a small bar. A book collection and plenty of wine bottles adorn the walls.

♿ Ⓢ *A, B, C, D, E, F, V to West 4th St.* Ⓢ *Beer $6-10. Wine $8-12.* ☾ *Open M-Th 8am-2am, F 8am-4am, Sa 9am-4am, Su 9am-2am.*

greenwich village

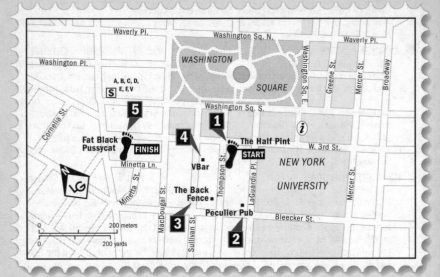

greenwich village nightlife

After spending your days in NYC perusing the halls of world-class museums and haggling with street vendors, you'll probably be looking for a banging nightlife scene. Greenwich Village offers just that—whether you're a college kid, or just a co-ed at heart. We've consolidated some of the hottest nightlife spots in the neighborhood into a single walking tour—are you up to the challenge?

1. THE HALF PINT. Begin your nocturnal adventure at the Half Pint, 76 W. 3rd St., at Thompson St. To get here, take the Subway to W. 4th St. Station; walk southeast down West 4th. St., passing through Washington Sq.; take a left onto Thompson St.; walk for one block, and you've reached the Half Pint. By then, you'll be ready to sample one of its 200 international beers.

2. PECULIER PUB. Next, hit up the iconic Peculier Pub, only a block away from the Half Pint. Simply walk down Laguardia Pl., and take a right onto Bleeker St. Peculier Pub is at 145 Bleeker St. Called a "veritable museum of beer," this Greenwich Village institution is over 30 years old.

3. THE BACK FENCE. By this point, you'll want to have a glass of water. After you've hydrated, stroll down Bleecker St. (toward 6th Ave.) for 1 block, and you'll hit the Back Fence a (155 Bleecker St.), with constant live music and tons of beer on tap. Go ahead and throw peanuts on the floor.

4. VBAR. From Bleecker, just take a right onto Sullivan St.; VBar is situated at 225 Sullivan St. A student cafe during the day, VBar offers a low-key wine and beer bar for a breather from the raging; be aware that seating is very limited.

5. FAT BLACK PUSSYCAT. Finish the night off at Fat Black Pussycat at 130 W. 3rd St. To get here from Sullivan St., take a left onto W. 3rd St. Reputedly "where friends meet," the Pussycat has a DJ and dancing every Saturday. And, luckily, it's right by the W. 4th St. Subway station.

EMPLOYEES ONLY 💳♿🍸❄⛅ SPEAKEASY

510 Hudson St. ☎212-242-3021 💻http://employeesonlynyc.com

Legendary Village speakeasies like Chumley's may be closed for the time being, but Employees Only does its best to emulate the spirit of the Jazz Age in its own bizarre way. Bartenders wear chef's outfits and handlebar mustaches as they serve you a proud selection of unique, lovingly prepared cocktails. The sleek interior design, topped off by paintings on the wall, adds to the classy, romantic feel.

⇄ [S] 1 to Christopher St. $ Beer $4-7. Mixed drinks $6-13. ⏰ Open daily 6pm-4am. Weekend brunch 11:30am-4pm.

PECULIER PUB 💵⊘🍸 DIVE BAR

145 Bleecker St. ☎212-353-1327

A Mecca for beer fans, Peculier Pub keeps over 300 brews on tap. Beer pervades the place, from the bottle-cap mosaics on the walls to the shelves of international selections. You can try those worldwide tastes, since the menu is organized geographically. But don't expect classy cosmopolitanism; the pub can get crowded and pushy on weekends. What else should beer fans expect?

⇄ [S] A, B, C, D, E, F, V $ Beer $3-7, by the liter $8-10. ⏰ Open M-Th 5pm-2am, F 3:30pm-4am, Sa 2pm-4am, Su 4pm-2am.

BOOTS AND SADDLE 💳♿🍸▼ GAY AND LESBIAN

76 Christopher St. ☎212-633-1986 💻www.bootsnsaddle.com

This popular Christopher St. bar attracts a variety of ages. It may have removed much of the Western memorabilia of previous years, but it still goes for a fun saloon vibe. Shirtless bartenders work the drinks, go-go boys show up every night at 5pm, and regular events like karaoke night *(Su and M)*, comedy night *(Tu)*, and Strip Search *(Sa)* keep things interesting.

⇄ [S] 1 to Christopher St. ℹ Happy hour ($3 beer) daily noon-10pm. $ Beer $4-10. Mixed drinks $6-11. ⏰ Open daily noon-4am.

THE HALF PINT 💳⊘🍸❄⛅ PUB

76 W. 3rd St. (at Thompson St.) ☎212-260-1088 💻www.thehalfpint.com

The title and atmosphere at this expansive restaurant and pub indicate a British bent, but the food is all about America (think many salads and burgers). The beers, though, encompass the world: you can get Australian, British, and American brews from the tap or in bottles. With a moody, dark-wood ambience lightened by crowds of students from neighboring NYU, this is the perfect place to pretend that you go to school in Greenwich Village.

⇄ [S] A, B, C, D, E, F, V to West 4th St. $ Entrees $11-15. Beer $3-6. Mixed drinks $6-11. ⏰ Open M-Th 10am-2am, F-Sa noon-4am, Su 10am-2am.

CHI CHIZ 💵♿🍸▼ GAY AND LESBIAN

135 Christopher St. ☎212-462-0027

One of the few GLBT bars in New York geared specifically toward African-Americans, Chi Chiz attracts a loyal crowd to its diminutive, plain space. There's barely enough room to fit the bar, a pool table in the back, and a DJ stand, but it makes up for its size issues with friendliness—crowds stand in the front and often spill out onto the sidewalk. A standard drink menu complements a small food menu devoted mostly to southern standards.

⇄ [S] 1 to Christopher St. $ Beer $3-6. Mixed drinks $5-10. ⏰ Open daily 6pm-4am.

STONEWALL INN 💳⊘❄🍸▼ GAY AND LESBIAN

53 Christopher St. ☎212-488-2705 💻www.thestonewallinnyc.com

The Stonewall Inn occupies a seminal position in American gay culture. It was here in June 1969 that police raids inspired protests and riots, sparking the beginning of the modern gay rights movement. Today, the Stonewall remains a national icon, though the current bar is actually a remake of the one that existed in 1969, and a reliable, if often tourist-heavy nightspot. The bottom level features a bar and pool table; dancing to pop, disco, and show tunes happens on the second floor.

🜲 Ⓢ *1 to Christopher St.* Ⓢ *Beer $3-8. Mixed drinks $6-13.* 🕓 *Open daily 2pm-4am.*

GASLIGHT
&🚻♿♀ LOUNGE

400 W. 14th St. (at 9th Ave.) ☎212-807-8444 🖵www.gaslightnyc.com

Gaslight looks like it should belong to the ritzy Meatpacking nightclub crowd: a huge space, a fancy sign, lofty ceilings and ritzy furniture. But you can relax in this lounge's spacious confines, where the classy Edwardian decor somehow doesn't make for a stuffy or exclusive crowd. It does draw crowds, though. In less busy moments, you can relax on comfortable sofas and admire the chandeliers.

🜲 Ⓢ *A, C, E, L to 8th Ave.-14th St.* Ⓢ *Beer $4-9. Mixed drinks $8-14.* 🕓 *Open daily 1pm-4am.*

HOGS AND HEIFERS SALOON
◉◉⊗♀ DIVE BAR

859 Washington St. ☎212-929-0655 🖵www.hogsandheifers.com

Fans of the 2000 masterpiece *Coyote Ugly* may have some déjà vu at Hogs and Heifers: aggressive female bartenders manning a dusty downtown joint, barking at patrons through megaphones, and, of course, dancing on the bar are all here. Though named after another downtown bar with a similar shtick, the film mimicked this bar's look, even recreating it across the street when they were refused permission to shoot inside the real thing. The place isn't for everyone—especially for those averse to being berated via megaphone—but it's lovably dirty, right down to the countless bras of former customers hanging above the bar (**Julia Roberts** is in there somewhere). The urban-redneck feel works best when the biker contingents are in full force. Cleaner types may drift in on weekend nights, though.

🜲 Ⓢ *A, C, E, L to 8th Ave.-14th St.* Ⓢ *Beer $2-7. Mixed drinks $6-11.* 🕓 *Open M-F 11am-4am, Sa 1pm-4am, Su 2pm-4am.*

east village

▨ NIAGARA
⊗&♀ BAR

112 Ave. A, at corner of E. 7th St. ☎212-420-9517

Old soda shop meets edgy night owl nest; for example, the walls are adorned with cartoons drawn lovingly onto plastic panels with markers. Live DJs and a dance floor make this establishment only partially about drinking and all about having a good time. Commemorate your night with a picture at the in-house photo booth!

🜲 Ⓢ *6 to Astor Pl.* Ⓢ *Beer $5. Well drinks $6. Top shelf $9-10. Mixed drinks $10.* 🕓 *Open daily 4pm-4am. Happy hour 4-8pm.*

▨ MAMA'S BAR
&⊗♀ BAR

34 Ave. B, at 3rd St. ☎212-777-5729 🖵www.mamasbarnyc.com

We are unsure of who exactly "Mama" is, but evidently she likes bright colors, well-worn, antique couches, and enormous golden frogs. Oh, and she also likes to serve cheap drinks. You can and probably should hang out with Mama, whoever she is, any night of the week.

🜲 Ⓢ *F, J, M, Z to Essex St./Delancey St.* Ⓢ *Beer from $3. Top shelf $8.* 🕓 *Open daily 5pm-4am. Happy hour 5-8pm.*

▨ ACE BAR
&🚻♀ BAR

531 E. 5th St., between Ave. A and Ave. B ☎212-979-8476 🖵www.acebar.com

Skee ball, darts, pool, video games—It's just like when you used to go to Chuck E. Cheese's, except now you have booze. Special touches such as a giant, holographic werewolf poster, a skeleton with a witch's hat, and a collection of 106 retro lunchboxes heighten an already jocular mood.

🜲 Ⓢ *6 to Astor Pl.* Ⓢ *Beer from $3. Well Drinks $5-6.* 🕓 *Open M-F 4pm-4am, Sa-Su 3pm-4am.*

MCSORLEY'S OLD ALE HOUSE

😑⊗⛛ BAR

15 E. 7th St.   ☎212-473-9148 ✉www.mcsorleysnewyork.com

McSorley's has been serving its ale to East Villagers since 1854, making it the oldest bar in New York State. They keep things simple here: you can have McSorley's Light or McSorley's Dark, and everyone gets two drafts for $5. A cheese plate means a plate of American or Aged Cheddar *($3 small, $4 large)*, and sandwiches come with ham, turkey, liverwurst, cheese, or turkey variety *($4)*. It may not be gourmet, but it's kept people filling wooden tables on the sawdust-covered floors seven nights a week for 156 years.

✚ Ⓢ *6 to Astor Pl.* Ⓢ *Ale 2 for $5. Most Sandwiches $4. Cheese and crackers $3-4.* ⓧ *Open M-Sa 11am-1am, Su 1pm-1am.*

CHERRY TAVERN

😑⊗⛛ BAR

441 E. 6th St., between Ave. A and 1st Ave.   ☎212-777-1448

At this most divey of dive bars, there are two specials: the Old Glory *(shot of whiskey and a PBR, $5)*, and the Tijuana *(shot of tequila and a Tecate beer, $5)*. Monday night is iPod night: you bring it, they play it.

✚ Ⓢ *6 to Astor Pl.* Ⓢ *Beer $6-9.* ⓧ *Open daily 6pm-4am. Happy Hour 6-9pm.*

LUNASA

⬤&⛛ BAR

126 1st Ave., between 7th St. and St. Mark's Pl.   ☎212-228-8580 ✉www.lunasabar.com

Its kind of like they took a dive bar and gave it a makeover. They kept all of the cool stuff, like board games and lots of seating, but they cleaned it and put up some interesting art. And turned the lights on. The outdoor patio in the back is a great place to partake of the extensive draft and bottled selection on warm, summer nights.

✚ Ⓢ *6 to Astor Pl.* Ⓢ *Drinks from $6.* ⓧ *Open M-F 2pm-4am, Sa-Su 11am-4am. Happy Hour M-F 4-7pm.*

CONTINENTAL

😑⊗⛛(ʸ) BAR

25 3rd Ave., between 8th and 9th St.   ☎212-529-6924

A bar that allows you to multitask: improve your knowledge of classic cinema while reaching a pleasantly buzzed state on very cheap alcohol. Illuminated old movie posters starring the likes of Humphrey Bogart and Rita Hayworth grace the walls, and a subtitled film is usually projected on the back wall. Need more activities? Surf the web using free Wi-Fi or impose your musical will on the establishment at the jukebox.

✚ Ⓢ *6 to Astor Pl.* Ⓢ *Beer $4-5, Mixed Drinks $6-9.* ⓧ *Open daily 4pm-4am. Happy hour 4pm-8pm.*

EASTER BLOC

😑⊗▼⛛ BAR

505 E. 6th St., between Ave. A and Ave. B   ☎212-777-2555 ✉www.easternblocnyc.com

Enter this red and black, barracks-style building and you will find yourself in a land of 1970s gay porn, animal heads, and likenesses of a certain Teletubby. A different DJ spins every night, and there are go-go dancers on the weekends.

✚ Ⓢ *6 to Astor Pl.* Ⓢ *Drinks from $6.* ⓧ *Open daily 7pm-4am.*

BIG BAR

&⬤⛛ BAR

73 E. 7th St., between 1st and 2nd Ave.   ☎212-777-6969

The funny thing about Big Bar is...it's actually really small. Owned by a pair of Ukrainian brothers, this tiny beaded bar with a pink glow is a favorite among locals and NYU students alike.

✚ Ⓢ *6 to Astor Pl.* Ⓢ *Beer $5-7. Cocktails $11-12.* ⓧ *Open daily 5pm-2am, F-Sa 5pm-4am, Su 5pm-2am.*

MANITOBA'S

⬤⊗⛛ BAR

99 Ave. B, between 6th and 7th St.   ☎212-982-2511 ✉www.manitobas.com

Owned by "Handsome Dick" Manitoba of the 1970s pre-punk Dictators, this bar is filled with pictures of the likes of Iggy Pop, Patty Smith, and Sid Vicious. Joey

Ramone gave one of his final concerts in the back corner.

🎵 🚇 *6 to Astor Pl.* Ⓢ *Drinks $3-8.* ⏱ *Open daily 2pm-4am. Happy hour 2-8pm.*

chelsea

📱 BARRACUDA
🚻♿📺♈ CLUB ❷

275 W. 22nd St. ☎212-645-8613

Notorious for side-splitting drag shows Sunday through Thursday nights at around 1am, this laid-back gay bar welcomes a mixed crowd. Male voices belting Whitney Houston's "I Will Always Love You" can be heard from blocks away on Tuesdays during Karaoke night.

🎵 🚇 *C, E to 23rd St./8th Ave.* Ⓢ *No cover. Drinks $6-10.* ⏱ *Open daily 4pm-4am.*

📱 XES LOUNGE
📺♈♈ BAR, LOUNGE ❶

157 W. 24th St. ☎212-604-0212 🖥www.xesnyc.com

Sophisticated yet relaxed, this lounge is a perfect destination for a night out with friends. We're not making any promises, but they have on at least one occasion gone All-Madonna-All-Night to the delight of guests dancing along with old footage of the Material Girl. The patio in the back provides a place to catch a breath of fresh air before heading back into the thumping party.

🎵 🚇 *1, F, M to 23rd St.* Ⓢ *Beer $5-7. Martinis $10-13.* ⏱ *Open M-Tu 4pm-2am, W-Su 4pm-4am.*

SPLASH BAR
📺♿♈♈ CLUB ❷

50 W. 17th St. ☎212-691-0073 🖥www.splashbar.com

An intense, smoke-filled, two-level clubbing experience where the bartenders do not cover their perfectly-chiseled torsos, and neither do the pole dancers. Divas such as Britney Spears and Christina Aguilera have performed for the 800-1200 guests who fill Splash.

🎵 🚇 *1 to 18th St./7th Ave.; F, V to 23rd St./Ave. of Americas.* Ⓢ *Cover $10. Drinks $8-14.* ⏱ *Open daily 4pm-4am.*

VIEW BAR
📺♈▼ BAR ❶

232 8th Ave., at 23rd St., between 6th and 7th Ave. ☎212-929-2243 🖥www.viewbarnyc.com

A friendly, tropical-themed bar where the goal is to get you drunk on the cheapest but most delicious drinks possible. The bar pours out $5 cosmos Wednesdays 9am-2am, $3 frozen margaritas Tuesdays 8pm-2am, and cheap Bloody Marys, mimosas and screwdrivers on weekends. And these aren't your average Margaritas. Not only are they strong and cheap, they also come in a variety of flavors, from the Pom-a-rita (pomegranate-flavored) to the Chiquita-rita (banana flavored).

🎵 🚇 *1, C, E to 23rd St.* Ⓢ *Drinks $3-9.* ⏱ *Open M-F 4pm-4am, Sa-Su 2pm-4am.*

G
📺♿♈▼ BAR ❶

223 W. 19th St., between 7th and 8th Ave. ☎212-929-1085 🖥www.glounge.com

This small gay bar with hut-style architecture and dancers in Speedo-style bottoms almost makes you feel like you're at the beach. Grab a fruity cocktail and enjoy the view.

🎵 🚇 *1 to 18th St./7th Ave.* Ⓢ *No cover. Drinks $7-10.* ⏱ *4pm-4am.*

DUSK
♈♿(•)♈ BAR, LOUNGE ❶

147 W. 24th St., between 6th and 7th Ave. ☎212-924-4490 🖥www.duskac.com

Ultra-cool but stress-free, this lounge and bar hosts a napkin drawing contest Tuesdays during happy hour 6-11:30pm. Winners of this prestigious competition receive a drink on the house and an extra hour of happiness as well as the glory and recognition of having their masterpiece displayed for the week. For entertainment on other days, order a pizza, test out the jukebox, and enjoy the free

Wi-Fi available throughout the venue.

[S] 1, C, E to 23rd St. $ Bar $5-10. Open M-Th 5:30pm-2am, F 5pm-4am, Sa 7:30pm-4am, Su 5pm-midnight.

BAR VELOCE WINE BAR ❶

176 7th Ave., between 20th and 21st St. ☎212-629-5300 www.barveloce.com

Stop in for a glass of wine and a composed plate *($6-16)*, such as the piatto Veloce (an assortment of meat and cheese for two), and enjoy a delicious, low-lit break from the generic drinks and thumping music of many other Chelsea bars. Though fine wine and gourmet food are available, you don't have to blow your life's savings on vino and cheese; get appetizers *($3)*, beer *($6)*, or wine *($8)*.

[S] 1 to 18th St. i Call ahead about wheelchair accessibility. $ Beer $6-12. Wine $8. Mixed drinks $7-13. Appetizers $3-9. Sandwiches $4-10. Composed Plates $6-16. Open daily 5pm-3am. Kitchen open until 2:15am.

WESTSIDE TAVERN BAR ❶

360 W. 23rd St., between 8th and 9th Ave. ☎212-366-3738 www.westsidetavern.com

Set in an industrial-looking, red-brick hall and covered with black and white photographs of the old neighborhood, the Westside Tavern is fiercely proud of its Chelsea heritage. It also embraces the Chelsea present as a fun, lively hangout spot. The bar is generally populated by a healthy crowd of people drinking, playing pool, and munching on food from either the kitchen *(open until 11pm)* or a local takeout establishment.

[S] 1, C, E to 23rd St. $ Beer $4-7. Well drinks $7. Top shelf $10. Open daily 11am-4am.

JAKE'S SALOON BAR ❷

206 W. 23rd St., between 7th and 8th Ave. ☎212-337-3100 www.jakessaloonnyc.com

Yes, sports bars do exist in Chelsea. For the ESPN-addicted, a good option is Jake's Saloon, where the screens and sports channel subscriptions are plentiful, and a bartender will upon request change the channel to that game you absolutely can't miss. The kitchen offers a full menu of appetizers, entrees, burgers, sandwiches, salads, and desserts *(open M-W until 1am, Th-Sa until 2am, Su until 1am)*. Booze, sports, and food: that should hold you for a while.

[S] 1, C, E to 23rd St. $ Drinks $7-10. Appetizers $6-14. Burgers and Sandwiches $12-14. Entrees $17-28. Open M-Sa 11am-3am, Su noon-3am.

RAWHIDE BAR ❶

212 8th Ave., at 21st St. ☎212-242-9332

Saddle up; it's time to take a ride to a land where bartenders sport cowboy hats, fans are made of hubcaps, and enormous model motorcycles hang from the ceiling. Regulars say they frequent the bar for the quality of the go-go boys on Friday and Saturday nights and the cheap, strong drinks every night.

[S] 1, C, E to 23rd St. $ Drinks $4-7. Open M-Sa 10am-4am, Su noon-4am.

union sq., flatiron district, murray hill

The area around Union Square fosters many after-work spots and fancier establishments catering to the jet set. Look deeper and you'll find some more affordable and livelier options. **Third Avenue** is lined with bars, leftovers of the elevated-train days or newbies geared toward recently arrived young professionals.

PETE'S TAVERN NEIGHBORHOOD BAR

129 E. 18th St. ☎212-473-7676 www.petestavern.com

Pouring brews since 1864, Pete's is the oldest continually operating bar in New York. You can appreciate the history via the place's own 1864 ale at a huge, ornate bar that looks like a remnant of the Civil War-era itself (and take a look at that ceiling). Dark wood prevails, though on sunlit days the tavern is open to the outdoors and brightened. There's much more space beyond the bar, with rows of tables in brick-walled rooms to the back where you can try some hefty American-style dishes like burgers, pastas, and chicken parmesan.

⚑ Ⓢ *4, 5, 6, L, N, Q, R to 14th St.-Union Sq.* Ⓢ *Beer $5-8. Mixed drinks $6-10. Entrees $12-24.* Ⓒ *Open M-W 11:30am-2am, Th 11:30am-3am, F-Sa 11:30am-4am.*

THE HAIRY MONK
◉♿⚥❄ IRISH PUB, SPORTS BAR

337 3rd Ave.   ☎212-532-2929 💻www.thehairymonknyc.com

Take a final, furtive look around, grab the ring handle on the wooden door, and enter enemy territory behind the purple-and-yellow exterior. The Hairy Monk is an Irish pub packed with Boston sports fans and Boston sports memorabilia—Yankees fans beware. Things can get rowdy and crowded during a Red Sox, Patriots, or Celtics game, or on weekend nights when the Irish music is at full tilt. It can all be enjoyed better with a pint of Guinness, one of the Monk's specialties, and maybe a plate of its Irish food as well.

⚑ Ⓢ *6 to 23rd St.* ⓘ *Happy hour daily 11am-7pm; $2.50 bottles, $4.20 drafts, $1 off entire bar.* Ⓢ *Beer $3-6. Entrees $12-20.* Ⓒ *Open daily 11am-4am.*

119
◉♿❄⚥ DIVE BAR

119 E. 15th St.   ☎212-777-6158 💻www.119bar.com

119 is a true dark horse in a land of lofts and landmarks: a dark, down-and-dirty dive bar that hasn't been scrubbed up for the grandparents. You enter by way of the pool room, where the table is surrounded by couches. The bar sells its cheap drinks in another room to the right. There's not much to the place, but why should there be? It's all about the basics and scruffy charm here.

⚑ Ⓢ *4, 5, 6, L, N, Q, R to Union Sq.-14th St.* Ⓢ *Beer $3-7. Mixed drinks $6-10.* Ⓒ *Open M-F 4pm-4am, Sa-Su 6pm-4am.*

MOLLY'S
◉♿⚥❄ IRISH PUB

87 3rd Ave.   ☎212-889-3361 💻www.mollysshebeen.com

Countless Irish pubs used to line Third Ave. beneath its famous elevated train, and Molly's is one of the survivors. This is as true green as it gets, right down to the distinctive wooden door opening up to a darkened interior full of locals and regulars. The floor is covered in sawdust, the white walls decorated with rusty farm equipment, and the decor capped off with a fireplace. Then there are the Irish bartenders dishing out standards like Guinness to a very appreciative crowd. It's all homey, neighborhoodly, and lovably insular.

⚑ Ⓢ *6 to 23rd St.* Ⓢ *Pints $4-7. Entrees $10-25.* Ⓒ *Open M-Sa 11:30am-4am, Su noon-4am.*

upper east side

PAT O'BRIENS
🍸 BAR ❶

1701 2nd Ave., between 88th and 89th St.   ☎212-410-2013 💻www.patobriens.com

A little piece of Boston transported to the Big Apple. TVs broadcast Beantown sports, and Boston memorabilia spans the walls. The music is loud, the drinks are cheap, and the crowd is young and fun. No kitchen, but menus are provided from local restaurants that gladly deliver to the bar.

⚑ Ⓢ *6 to 86th St.* ⓘ *$20 min. for credit cards.* Ⓢ *Mixed drinks $5-6.* Ⓒ *Open M-F 3pm-4am, Sa noon-4am, Su noon-midnight.*

STUMBLE INN
🍸⚥ BAR ❶

1454 2nd Ave., at 76th St.   ☎212-650-0561

Thought you would never find $2 pints on the Upper East Side? Think again. Cheap booze, bumpin' music, and a friendly staff keep this place crowded every

nightlife

night. Specials every night of the week, like half-priced drinks Monday through Friday until 7pm and Ladies' Night on Wednesday, make the already economical bar dirt cheap. As one patron recently said, "It's a great place, especially if you don't have a lot of money. And this is New York. Nobody has a lot of money."

✈ Ⓢ 6 to 77th St. Ⓢ Beer $5-6, mixed drinks $5-6. Appetizers $2.50-$10. Sandwiches and burgers from $7. ⓠ Kitchen and bar open daily 11:30am-4pm.

BRANDY'S PIANO BAR
235 E. 84th St., between 2nd and 3rd Ave.

⬥❣ BAR ❷
☎212-744-4949

In the mood for a melody? At Brandy's Piano Bar, the piano man (or woman, depending on the night) will sing you a song and have you feeling alright. An intimate venue covered with old-fashioned show posters, this is the perfect place to sit back, enjoy a drink, and listen to talented musicians tickle the ivories.

✈ Ⓢ 6 to 86th St. 𝒊 2 drink min. per person per set. Ⓢ Mixed drinks $6-15. ⓠ Open daily 4pm-4am, business permitting. Live music 9:30pm-last call. Happy Hour nightly 4-8:30pm.

DOC WATSON'S
1490 2nd Ave., between 88th and 89th   ☎212-988-5300 🖳www.docwatsons.com

⬥♨❣ BAR ❷

A slightly more sophisticated option among the 2nd Ave. bars—for those who like to have a good time, but like to hear themselves think in the process. Happy hour is Monday through Friday 11am-7pm, featuring domestic beers ($2.50), pints ($3), and mixed drinks ($4). Live Celtic rock on Thursday and live Irish music on Sunday complete this bar's Irish theme. The kitchen, offering a full menu (and free delivery!), is open until 2am.

✈ Ⓢ 6 to 86th St. 𝒊 Drinks $2.50-18, appetizers $6.25-10, sandwiches and burgers $7.50-11, entrees $8.50-17. ⓠ Open daily 11am-4am. Kitchen open until 2am.

MAD RIVER
1432 3rd Ave., at 82nd St.   ☎212-988-1832 🖳www.madrivergrille.com

⬥❣ BAR ❶

American college students will immediately feel at home among the televisions broadcasting sports, impromptu games of Beirut, and a live DJ who looks like he may be out past his bedtime. An example of 2nd and 3rd Avenues' famous "frat" bars, Mad River caters to a primarily young, laid-back crowd. On Thursday nights from 6-9pm, "Drink for a Cause": profits from discounted mixed drinks ($3) and Bud Light draught beers ($1) are donated to a "Charity of the Week."

✈ Ⓢ 6 to 86th St. Ⓢ Beer $5-6, mixed drinks $5-12; appetizers $7-20, sandwiches and burgers $7-12. ⓠ Open daily noon-2am or later. Kitchen open noon-10pm.

upper west side

🏷 THE DEAD POET
450 Amsterdam Ave.   ☎212-595-5670 🖳www.thedeadpoet.com

⬥⊗♨ BAR ❶

On a wall toward the back of the bar among a group of quotations from other deceased literary figures is a sign that reads, "Man, being reasonable, gets drunk. The best of life is but intoxication—Lord Byron." It seems Byron would have approved of The Dead Poet, where the beer is plentiful and you drink for free on your birthday if you share the day with a featured literary figure. Drink 100 pints, and you get a plaque on the "Guinness Wall of Fame," which carries with it special discounts and privileges. Membership is free.

✈ Ⓢ 1 to 81st St. Located between 81st and 82nd St. Ⓢ Beer $5-10. Mixed drinks $8-10. Irish whiskey up to $14. Bar menu $7-12. ⓠ Open M-F 9am-4am, Sa 10am-4am, Su noon-4am.

🏷 THE UNDERGROUND LOUNGE
955 West End Ave., at 107th St.   ☎212-531-4759 🖳www.theundergroundnyc.com

⬥ BAR ❶

Buried beneath West End Ave. is the funky, fun Underground Lounge. The small stage housed within this bar is constantly commanded by live bands, stand-up comedians, and open mic participants. A recent event featured a game of Beirut between audience members and stand-up comics. If the audience won, the show was free. The kitchen closes at 1am every night, so you can enjoy delicious appetizers ($6-9), entrees ($9-14), and pizzas ($10-12) late.

☞ Ⓢ 1 to 103rd St. Ⓢ Beer $4-6. Mixed drinks $7-12. Wine $8. Appetizers $6-9. Sandwiches $10-19. Pizzas $10-12. Entrees $9-14. ⌚ Open daily 4pm-4am. Happy hour 4pm-8pm. Kitchen open until around 1am.

BROADWAY DIVE BAR
☞♿ BAR ❶

2662 Broadway   ☎212-865-2662 🖳www.divebarnyc.com

Happy "hour" is every day from noon to 7pm at this small and friendly bar. You can get beer for $4 and wine for $5, but what makes Broadway Dive Bar's Happy Hour really happy are the free hot dogs and candy. As if that weren't enough, they have Pac Man, Big Buck Hunter, and about 15 different board games all day, every day.

☞ Ⓢ 1 to 101st St. Ⓢ Beer $5-6, mixed drinks $6-7, wine $7-8. ⌚ Open daily 11:30am-4am.

BLUE DONKEY BAR
☞♿🍽 BAR ❶

487 Amsterdam Ave.   ☎212-496-0777 🖳www.thebluedonkeybar.com

With pool and foosball tables and an assortment of video games, The Blue Donkey is a sort of playground for grown-ups. If you'd rather just chill out, couches in the front room and a patio with seating in the back make this bar a great place to relax with friends.

☞ Ⓢ 1 to 79th St. Walk east onto Amsterdam Ave. and turn left past 83rd St. Ⓢ Beer $2.50-$7. Mixed drinks $4-8. Appetizers $3.50-$8.50. ⌚ Open M-Th 2pm-4am, F-Su noon-4am. Kitchen open until around 11pm.

DIVE 75
☞ BAR ❶

101 W. 75th St.   ☎212-362-7518 🖳www.divebarnyc.com

Board games, six TVs, a jukebox, bowls of candy, and even a tank full of fish make this the perfect bar for travelers with a short attention span. Famous for a wide variety of microbrews.

☞ Ⓢ 1, 2, 3 to 72nd St. Walk uptown onto 75th St. between Amsterdam and Columbus Ave. Ⓢ Beer $4-8. Mixed drinks from $9. Wine by the 1/2 bottle $10-32. Tequila $7-15. Margaritas $8. ⌚ Open M-Th 5pm-2am, F 3pm-4am, Sa noon-4am. Happy Hour M-Th 5pm-7pm, and F 3pm-7pm.

THE ABBEY PUB
☞⊗ BAR ❷

237 W. 105th St.   ☎212-222-8713

The people at The Abbey Pub do not take their name lightly. Booth benches are modeled after church pews and several stained glass windows are in the dining area. Guests can tone their hymn-singing voices on the fourth Su of every month at Karaoke Night. Be sure to stop in after Sunday Mass for the "Sports Brunch" menu ($2.75-$9.50).

☞ Ⓢ 1 to 103rd St. Bar just east of Broadway. Ⓢ Beer $4.50-14 (Belgian Ales), mixed drinks $6.50-8. Appetizers $3.75-13. Burgers and sandwiches $8-9. Entrees $7-15.50. ⌚ Open M-Sa 4pm-4am, Su noon-4am. Kitchen open M-Th until 11:30pm, F-Sa until 1:30am, Su until 11:30pm.

AMSTERDAM 106
☞♿(((•))) BAR ❷

938 Amsterdam Ave.   ☎212-280-8070 🖳www.amsterdam196.com

With a daily happy hour (4-7pm) where you can find $3 pints and a kitchen open until 2am, this is the perfect bar to visit any time of day. Want to drink a fine craft beer while you send some emails? You're in luck, because they have free Wi-Fi here. They also offer over 24 constantly-changing beers on tap, so you'll always have new options for great beer choices.

☞ Ⓢ 1 to 103rd St. Bar between 106th and 107th St. Ⓢ Draft beer $6-7. Mixed drinks $6. Appetizers $5-12. Sandwiches and burgers $9-12. Salads $4-12. Breakfast $6-10. ⌚ Open daily noon-4am. Happy Hour daily 4-7pm.

JAKE'S DILEMMA 💵♿☀ BAR ❶

430 Amsterdam Ave., at 81st St. ☎212-580-0556 💻www.nycbestbar.com

Hang out in the front of the bar for loud music and cheap booze. Toward the middle, watch sports or nurture your inner athlete with a pick-up game of Beirut. In the back behind velvet curtains, there is a library and lounge area where friends schmooze and couples smooch.

🧭 [S] 1 to 81st St. $ Mixed drinks $5-11. Appetizers $4-$14. Salads, sandwiches, and burgers $6-11. Deep-fried Oreos $5. ⏰ Open M-Th 4pm-4am, F 3pm-4am, Sa-Su noon-4am. Kitchen open until around 2am. Happy hour M-Th 4-8pm, F 3-8pm, and Sa-Su noon-8pm.

SHALEL LOUNGE 💵 LOUNGE ❷

65 W. 70th St. ☎212-873-2300

Search far and wide; you will not find a swankier spot. Lounge with your posse in one of the many stone alcoves, sipping wine *($10-12)* and grazing a cheese plate *($15)* or an order of **vegetable cigars.** The lights are low, the candles are lit, and the exotic beats are fresh.

🧭 [S] B, C, to 72nd St.; 1, 2, 3 to 72nd St. Lounge between Central Park W. and Columbus Ave. $ Appetizers $6-12. Entrees $15-19. Dessert $4-7. Wine $10-12. Mixed drinks $10-18. ⏰ Open M-Th 5pm-1:30am, F-Sa 5pm-3am, Su 5pm-1:30am.

SUGAR BAR 💵♿ LOUNGE ❸

254 W. 72nd St., ☎212-579-0222 💻www.sugarbarnyc.com

Thanks to Sugar Bar, you can jam to Afro-Caribbean beats and sip cocktails under a straw roof without ever leaving the Upper West Side. With live R and B, jazz, Caribbean, or African music every night, a full bar, and a menu of scrumptious soul food, this lounge is a hot place to be at night. It is even hotter on open mike nights *(Tu and Th)*. Reservations recommended up to two weeks in advance.

🧭 [S] 1, 2, 3 to 72nd St. between Broadway and West End Ave. $ Bar prices $8-13. Appetizers $10-14. Entrees $18-26. Cover charge $10. ⏰ Open Tu-W 5-11pm, Th-Sa 5pm-1am. Happy hour (2-for-1 at the bar) Tu-F 5-7:30pm.

harlem

👍 **ST. NICK'S PUB** 💵♿🍸 JAZZ CLUB

773 St. Nicholas Ave. ☎212-283-9728; 💻www.stnicksjazzpub.net

It's far uptown—all the way in Harlem's once-tony Sugar Hill district—but a legend in its own right. Duke Ellington's piano player opened the shop in 1940, but the place had been going strong since the '30s. Today, it remains the oldest continually operated jazz club in Harlem—no mean feat in a neighborhood full of legendary jazz clubs. The setting is a bit disheveled, but there's something endearing about the club's display of its aging, pealing paint. Best of all, the jazz is constant, drawing steady, devoted streams of locals and visitors to this small haven.

🧭 [S] A, B, C, D to 145th St. ℹ No cover; 2 drink min. $ Beer $4-7. Mixed drinks and wine $7-10. ⏰ Open M-Th 1pm-3am, F-Sa 4pm-4am. Nightly shows M-F starting at 10pm, Sa 7:30pm-4am, Su 7-10pm.

LENOX LOUNGE 💵♿🍸 JAZZ CLUB/RESTAURANT [❹]

288 Malcom X Blvd. ☎212-427-0253 💻www.lenoxlounge.com

Lenox Lounge has been enlivening Harlem's center since 1939. Billie Holliday and Miles Davis performed here, and Langston Hughes and Malcolm X hung out here. The front end includes some pricey dining, but the Zebra Room in the back is the real draw. Live jazz is featured every weekend night. Check the website for performance details. Show prices are steep, but you can ease the pain by really savoring Lenox's signature cocktails like the Harlem Nights, the Dizzy Gillespie, and the 👍**Ella Fitzgerald.**

₩ Ⓢ 2, 3 to 125th St. Ⓢ Dinner entrees $17-24. Zebra room cover $20 per set plus $16 drink min. per set. ♨ Dinner M-Th 4pm-midnight, F-Sa 4pm-2am, Su 4pm-midnight. Zebra room shows F-Sa 9, 10pm, and 12:30am; check website for weekday shows.

SHOWMAN'S CAFE ●♿♀ JAZZ CLUB
375 West 125th St. ☎212-864-8941

Another ancient jazz club (this one's been around since 1942), nestled in the large shadow of the Apollo—but the Showman's cool-cat vibe is relaxed, from its low-key but handsome interior to the mellow jazz that sets it apart. Showman's is the laid-back cousin to bustling, crowded St. Nick's.

₩ Ⓢ A, B, C, D to 125th St. *i* 2 drink min. per person per show. Ⓢ F-Sa $5 cover. ♨ Open M noon-1am, Tu-W noon-2am, Th noon-3am, F-Sa noon-4am. Jazz shows Tu-Th 8:30pm, 10pm, 11:30pm; F-Sa 9:30, 11:30pm, 1:30am.

brooklyn

WILLIAMSBURG
Williamsburg's nightlife has been at the center of its renaissance over the past 15 years. The mostly underground music scene that took advantage of the neighborhood's abandoned industrial spaces has been tamed, but a wide roster of now-established concert spaces still encourages developing talent. And beer can still be had for cheap.

⬛ PETE'S CANDY STORE ♿♀♨ BAR, CONCERT VENUE
709 Lorimer St. ☎718-302-3770 ▣www.petescandystore.com

Williamsburg is packed with bars and nightclubs proudly announcing their humorous/bizarre/random former lives with preserved signs and names. **Pete's Candy Store** is probably the best. The former sweets and soda dispenser has been transformed into a multi-room bar and performance space (picture an empty but fancy railway car) that hosts an incredibly varied array of events on any given night. Live music is a mainstay: two to three bands play on weekdays, four on weekends, the genres shifting from indie rock to folk to country and back again. Music usually starts at 8pm or 9pm. On Sunday afternoons at 4pm you can worship at **Revolutionary Church** with the much-pierced and much-tattooed Jay Bakker, son of the immortal Tammy Faye and Jim Bakker. Open mike nights Sundays 5-8pm, quiz-offs Wednesdays 7:30pm, Nora's Court cases (Judge Judy except funnier) first Tuesday of every month, and scattered readings, spelling bees, and stand-up acts throughout the month. Check online schedule for details. Best of all: cover is minimal to nonexistent.

₩ Ⓢ L to Bedford Ave. or Lorimer St.-Metropolitan Ave. Ⓢ Beer $4-5. Mixed drinks $10. ♨ Open M-W 5pm-2am, Th 5pm-4am, F 4pm-4am, Su 3:30pm-2am.

⬛ UNION POOL ●♿♀♨ BAR, CONCERT VENUE
484 Union Ave. ☎718-609-0484 ▣www.myspace.com/unionpool

Next up in the funny conversions sweepstakes: the Union Pool, nestled in a blank, nightmare-suburbia-looking former pool supply store beneath the Brooklyn-Queens expressway. The bar and concert space retain the store's ugly walls, but paintings, mirrors, chandeliers, and an old-school photo booth liven things up. Night crowds spill into the backyard, complete with a small fountain and a "taco truck" on summer afternoons and evenings. There's live music almost every night; Monday nights are devoted to country, the rest of the week to rock and indie. Nightly DJs in the bar cater to those sick of standing or sitting. Things get crowded during the wee hours, so go early if you want that courtyard all to yourself.

₩ Ⓢ L to Lorimer St.-Metropolitan Ave. *i* Cover for performances $5-10. Ⓢ Beer $4-5. Mixed drinks $9-11. Wine $7-9. ♨ Open M-F 5pm-4am, Sa-Su 1pm-4am.

nightlife

BROOKLYN ALE HOUSE

⊛ ♿ ⚥ (♠) BAR

103 Berry St.   ☎718-302-9811 ▣www.brooklynalehouse.com

The Ale House was around long before the young newcomers drifted into town, and there's something refreshing in its simplicity. In the back, a dart board and pool table. In the front, a well-stocked bar frequented by aging townies and fresh-faced pretty young things alike. Around the edges, maybe a few dogs—this is, after all, one of NYC's most dog-friendly bars, and if you stay long enough you'll probably see the owners.

⚡ Ⓢ *L to Bedford Ave.* **i** *Dogs welcome.* Ⓢ *Beer $4-6. Wines $7-9.* ⏲ *Open M-Th and Su noon-3am, F-Sa noon-4am.*

KNITTING FACTORY

⊛ ♿ ⚥ BAR, CONCERT VENUE

361 Metropolitan Ave.   ☎347-529-6696 ▣www.bk.knittingfactory.com

Founded in the East Village in the late '80s, the Knitting Factory has since threaded its way all the way to Los Angeles. Their Brooklyn branch is a popular bar and concert space whose crowds spill out onto Metropolitan on a nightly basis. The spacious bar in front has plenty of breathing room, but your chances of survival in the back concert room, visible from the bar but muffled and separated by a glass barrier, decrease considerably. Check website for complete calendar of events.

⚡ Ⓢ *L to Bedford Ave. or Lorimer St.-Metropolitan Ave.* **i** *Performance tickets $8-15.* Ⓢ *Beer $3-6. Mixed drinks $6-9.* ⏲ *Open M-F 5pm-2am, Sa-Su noon-2am.*

PUBLIC ASSEMBLY

⊛ ♿ ⚥ CONCERT VENUE, BAR

70 North 6th St.   ☎718-384-4586 ▣www.publicassemblynyc.com

This former mayonnaise factory has been transformed into a state-of-the-art performance space whose industrial legacy lives on in its cavernous stone walls. Back and front rooms host nightly shows with larger helpings of hip-hop than usual in Williamsburg. There's also Monday Night Burlesque, which kicks off weekly at 8pm or 9pm. Check website for event details.

⚡ Ⓢ *L to Bedford Ave.* **i** *Performance cover $7-15.* Ⓢ *Beer $5-6. Mixed drinks $6-9.* ⏲ *Open M-Th and Su 7pm-2am, F-Sa 7pm-4am.*

CHARLESTON BAR AND GRILL

⊛ ♿ ⚥ BAR, CONCERT VENUE

174 Bedford Ave.   ☎718-599-9599 ▣www.thecharlestonbar.com

The Charleston has been around since 1933 and looks appropriately battered. The bar looks like it's been around since the Great Depression, the bathroom probably began collecting graffiti around the same time, and the clientele tends to be a bit older and more grizzled than the usual fresh faces. In short, it's irresistible. We haven't even mentioned the equally tantalizing offer of free pizza with every drink over $4. There's a concert space downstairs where crowds mosh to live music on weekend nights starting at around 10pm.

⚡ Ⓢ *L to Bedford Ave.* **i** *Free pizza with with every drink over $4.* Ⓢ *Beer $4-5. Mixed drinks $4-9.* ⏲ *Open daily noon-4am.*

PARK SLOPE

BUTTERMILK BAR

⊛ ♿ ⚥ DIVE BAR

577 5th Ave. (at 16th St.)   ☎718-788-6297

Small and down to earth, Buttermilk offers a refreshing dose of grit to the increasingly upscale Park Slope scene. A young crowd fills the brick-walled, wood-floor interior over inexpensive beer and the odd board game. The first Thursday of every month is the CasHank Hootenany Jamboree, an acoustic country concert named for two of the genre's legends.

⚡ Ⓢ *M, R to Prospect Ave., F, M, R to 9th Ave.-4th St., F to 7th Ave.* Ⓢ *Beer $4-6, $3 at happy hour. Mixed drinks $6-9.* ⏲ *Open daily 6pm-4am. Happy hour 6-9pm.*

LOKI LOUNGE 🚭♿🍸☀ DIVE BAR, NIGHTCLUB

304 5th Ave. (at 2nd St.) ☎718-965-9600 💻www.lokilounge.com

The long Loki Lounge seems bathed in red velvet, but the haughty decor masks an unpretentious, even low-key option. The front is a traditional crowded bar, but the back opens up to provide fancy plush seating areas and a slightly more upscale vibe. Even further and you're in a back "garden" where potted plants do their best to make you feel at home.

⇆ [S] F, M, R to 4th Ave.-9th St., M, R to Union St. $ Beer $4-8. Mixed drinks $6-11. ⏰ Open daily 3pm-4am.

COMMONWEALTH 💳🚭🍸☀ DIVE BAR

497 5th Ave. (at 12th St.) ☎718-768-2040

This no-frills dive bar is topped off by an old-school jukebox playing a predictably eclectic mix. It's a perfect backdrop to the sleek and polished but simple interior (bar to one side, tables with random chairs to the other) and the generous patio out back.

⇆ [S] F, M, R to 4th Ave.-9th St. $ Beer $3-7. Mixed drinks $6-11. ⏰ M-F 3pm-4am, Sa-Su 2pm-4am. Outdoor patio open M-Th and Su until 11pm, F-Sa until 1am. Happy hour M-F 3-7pm ($1 off everything).

BLACK HORSE PUB 💳♿🍸 PUB

568 5th Ave. (at 16th St.) ☎718-788-1975 💻www.blackhorsebrooklyn.com

Get your pints on at this spacious British-style pub with plenty of standing room. The huge bar is fully stocked, and the hardwood floors fill up quickly with crowds coming to socialize or just watch the latest soccer match.

⇆ [S] F, M, R to 4th. Ave/9th St. $ Pints from $6. Wine $7-9. ⏰ Open daily 2pm-4am.

BROOKLYN HEIGHTS

LAST EXIT 💳♿🍸☀ DIVE BAR

136 Atlantic Ave. ☎718-222-9198 💻www.lastexitbar.com

Tucked in amid the crowd of Middle Eastern restaurants on busy Atlantic Ave., Last Exit is a surprisingly vibrant nightspot on the staid border between Cobble Hill and Brooklyn Heights. Bimonthly pub quizzes, a steady stream of popular weekend DJs, and a regrettably restricted outdoor patio draw young crowds to this small space. There's even the occasional art showing.

⇆ [S] 2, 3, 4, 5, N, R to Borough Hall; F, G to Bergen St. ℹ DJs on F, Sa, and selected weekdays. $ Beer $3-6. Mixed drinks $5-10. ⏰ Open daily 4pm-4am. Outdoor patio open 4-9pm.

WATERFRONT ALE HOUSE 💳🚭🍸 RESTAURANT, BAR, MUSIC VENUE

155 Atlantic Ave. ☎718-522-3794 💻www.waterfrontalehouse.com

This unassuming neighborhood saloon draws an older, upscale crowd to its busy Atlantic Ave. location (there's another spot in Manhattan). A jukebox plays a steady stream of oldies, a plentiful beer selection accompanies a pricey dinner menu (try the crocks of chili), and everything wraps up appropriately early–so you can move across the street to Last Exit.

⇆ [S] 2, 3, 4, 5, N, R to Borough Hall; F, G to Bergen St. $ Beer $3-7. Mixed drinks $6-12. Dinner entrees $16-25. ⏰ Open M-W 11:30am-10:30pm, Th-F 11:30am-11:30pm, Sa noon-11:30pm, Su noon-11pm. Happy hour M-F 4-7pm.

DUMBO

68 JAY STREET BAR 💳🚭❄🍸 BAR, MUSIC VENUE

68 Jay St. ☎718-260-8207 💻www.68jaystreetbar.net

Just beyond the shadow of the Manhattan Bridge, 68 Jay Street fills up early with the usual DUMBO suspects: expect new arrivals swapping gallery stories. The corner location, wooden ceilings, and low-key decor help offset any alienation. The pillars and arches disguise the building's former function as the Grand Union Tea Company's warehouse.

⚡ Ⓢ F to York St.　ℹ Live music W 8pm, Sa 9pm.　Ⓢ Beer $3.　⚟ Open daily M-W 2pm-1am, Th-Sa 2pm-2am, Su 3-11pm. Happy hour M-F 4-7pm.

BOCOCA AND RED HOOK

JALOPY THEATRE AND SCHOOL OF MUSIC
⚡♿♀ MUSIC VENUE, BAR

315 Columbia St. (at Rapelye St.)　☎718-395-3214 🖳www.jalopy.biz

The name doesn't lie: Jalopy serves mainly as a concert space hosting a near-nightly lineup of country, blues, and folk acts. You can also take ukelele and banjo lessons here, or just rent the instruments and have at it yourself. The seating in the concert space consists of church-style pews to accentuate the old-timeyness. The bar in front dispenses cheap beer and is within hearing distance of the music, but most of the crowd and the action is focused on the strummers and pickers in the back.

⚡ Ⓢ F, G to Carroll St.　Ⓢ Performance cover $10-13. Beer $2.50-6.　⚟ Tu-F 2pm-2am, Sa-Su noon-2am. Most performances start at 8pm or 9pm.

MOONSHINE
⚡♿♀⚘ BAR

317 Columbia St. (at Rapelye St.)　☎718-858-8088 🖳www.brooklynmoonshine.com

If you're not feeling sufficiently down-home for the Jalopy, the Moonshine next door is an easy alternative, though both are hard to reach from the Carroll St. Subway stop. A snarling bulldog on the window is the perfect introduction to a worn saloon, which was once a watering hole for local dock workers. Bonuses include an old piano and a pool table. The beer is dirt-cheap, the local vibe palpable, and the backyard an ideal chilling spot. You can even grill your own meat there.

⚡ Ⓢ F, G to Carroll St.　Ⓢ Beer $3-7. Mixed drinks $5-9.　⚟ Open M-F 4pm-4am, Sa-Su 3pm-4am.

queens

🏛 DUTCH KILLS
⚡♿ BAR

27-24 Jackson Ave.　☎718-383-2724 🖳www.dutchkillsbars.com

Visible on the street only by means of a small neon "BAR" sign, this prohibition-style bar boasts an infinite supply of unique cocktails that vary by season. The Sunset Park is a blend of rye whiskey, dry vermouth, peach liqueur, and Angostura bitters. If that isn't original enough for you, you can also order Bartender's Choice, whereby the man behind the counter will make you a custom drink based on your preferences, mood, or even the type of day you've had. A bar so cool it should be illegal.

⚡ Ⓢ E, V, R, G to Queens Plaza, or N,W, 7 to Queensborough Plaza.　Ⓢ Beer $6-8. Mixed drinks $10. Wine $8.　⚟ Open daily 5pm-2am.

🏛 RAPTURE LOUNGE
⚡♿ BAR

34-27 28th Ave., at 34th St.　☎718-626-8044 🖳www.rapturelounge.com

Like hanging out in your living room, except with better music, booze, and food. No tables; just big comfy couches where you can lounge around, play board games, or shoot the breeze with fellow night owls. Low lights, exotic plants, and a menu of gourmet international food (empanadas $9; crepes $7-9; hummus and pita $7) give this lounge an overwhelmingly classy ambience.

⚡ Ⓢ N, W to 30th Ave.　ℹ Happy hour nightly 5-8pm.　Ⓢ Appetizers $4-12. Sandwiches $8-10. Mixed drinks $10-11. Beer $4-6. Wine $7-9.　⚟ Open daily 5pm-3:30am.

🏛 BEER GARDEN AT BOHEMIAN HALL
⚡ BAR

29-19 24th Ave., in Astoria　☎718-274-4925 🖳www.bohemianhall.com

The beer garden feels like an outdoor festival that is open every day of the week. You can order a bratwurst ($8) and any beer ($5) and sit at a table under the stars, while listening to the live music that plays from the outdoor stage regularly: Thursdays feature live jazz *(6:30-9:30pm)*, Wednesdays are Open Jam night *(10pm-2am)*, and be sure to catch "Surprise Sundays" *(4-7pm)*. They mean Bohemian as in Central European, not Bohemian as in artsy.

✈ Ⓢ *N, W to Astoria Ave.* Ⓢ *Beer $5. Mixed drinks $6-7. Fast food $6-38.* ✪ *Open daily 10am-2:30am. Kitchen open M-Th 10am-2:30am, F-Sa 10am-11pm, Su 10am-2:30am.*

in praise/awe/fear of queens

When I first realized that I would be researching Queens I thought that my apartment's location there would make the job easy—at least easier than researching Upper Manhattan had been. "This is great!" I thought. "I'll save so much travel time!" It wasn't until I was riding the 13 Subway stops from my apartment to my first research destination that I realized how woefully wrong I had been.

Queens is the size of a small country. There are literally 8 countries in the world smaller than Queens. You haven't heard of them (because they are small), but still, they are COUNTRIES and Queens is a BOROUGH within a CITY.

Needless to say, I have saved no travel time. In fact, I have spent an average of 4 hours per day on public transportation. I have also felt like I was in about 10 different countries. For a first-time explorer of Queens, riding the Subway to a new neighborhood is like Trick-or-Treating. Will it be the Pan-Asian Metropolis of Flushing? The sleepy beaches of the Rockaways? The edgy art-land of Long Island City? You never know what you're going to get.

Davida Fernandez-Barkan

SWEET AFTON
✎❧ BAR

3009 34th St. ☎718-777-2570 🖳www.sweetaftonbar.com

First you hear the funky-yet-relaxed beat that says "I'm hip and I don't even try." Then you notice the homemade-looking jar candles covering the tables, shelves, and bar. Then you catch a tantalizing whiff of bar treats made with local ingredients, such as Beer Battered Fried McClure's Brooklyn Pickles *($5)*. And you know you've found a sweet spot to spend your night.

✈ Ⓢ *N, W to 30th Ave.* Ⓢ *Beer $5-7. Mixed drinks $8-9. Wine $7-9. Food $5-12.* ✪ *Open M-F 4pm-3:30am, Sa-Su 10am-3:30am. Kitchen open until 1am. Brunch Sa-Su 11am-4pm.*

JIMBO'S
✎❧ BAR, RESTAURANT

30-05 Astoria Blvd., between 30th and 31st St. ☎718-204-2087

If you've ever wanted to drink like a Greek with other Greeks in a Greek-owned establishment, here is your chance! Blue walls and Greek music create a Mediterranean mood, and there is live Greek music every M, W, and Sa night. The kitchen is open late, so you can responsibly line your stomach with lots of delicious Greek food.

✈ Ⓢ *N, W to Astoria Blvd.* Ⓢ *Mixed drinks $7-10. Wine $8. Beer $4-5. Appetizers $6-12. Entrees $15-25.* ✪ *Open daily noon-4am.*

ARTS & CULTURE

It's never a challenge to stay entertained in a city where even street performers can blow you away. Still, New York's best culture lies within the city's many performance venues, where some of the world's most talented and innovative artists continue to thrill New York crowds. **Broadway** remains the world's theater capital, while **comedy** and **dance** venues are scattered throughout Manhattan. Music lovers might be overwhelmed, with opportunities to hear **jazz** in Harlem, **opera** on the Upper West Side, and **rock** pretty much anywhere downtown. Check out local sources such as *The Village Voice*, *New York Magazine*, and The *New York Times* for the city's best offerings.

greatest hits

- **DINNER AND A SHOW.** Enjoy both at Joe's Pub (p.170), a trendy nightclub and performance space in the East Village.
- **THINK FAST** about a fun night of improv comedy at the Upright Citizens Brigade Theatre (p.178) in Chelsea.
- **REDISCOVER CLASSIC MOVIES** on the big screen at Film Forum (p.166).
- **GET EXPERIMENTAL** in The Kitchen (p.174), serving up theater downtown.

student life

Highbrow culture doesn't have to be expensive. During the summer, there are plenty of free outdoor options for students to get their artistic fix.

- **SHAKESPEARE IN THE PARK** puts on performances of the Bard's plays for free in Central Park. The morning ticket line lasts longer than *Hamlet,* but you can meet some eccentric New Yorkers as you wait.
- **THE NEW YORK PHILHARMONIC** performs park concerts in every borough during the summer. Public parks don't have the best acoustics, but we won't complain as long as it's free.
- **MONDAY NIGHT** is movie night all summer long. Every week, the **Bryant Park Film Festival** screens free classic films for large crowds.

dance

To see great dance, you can't do better than New York City. For ballet lovers, the **American Ballet Theatre** and **New York City Ballet** are must-sees. If you're looking for something slightly more experimental, try the **Parsons Dance Company** or the **Dance Theatre Workshop.** Venues such as **City Center** and the **Joyce Theater** showcase dance companies of all styles. If you're itching to cut a rug yourself, check out **Midsummer Night Swing** at Lincoln Center.

THALIA SPANISH THEATER 🎟♿ QUEENS

41-17 Greenpoint Ave. ☎718-729-3880 💻www.thaliatheatre.org

This theater celebrates *las artes* in all forms and from all Spanish and Latin American cultures. The only bilingual theater in Queens, this is the place to see authentic folk dance, music, and drama.

🚇 [S] 7 to 40th St./Bowery St. $ General Admission $25-30, students and seniors $22-27. ⏰ Box office open 1hr. before curtain.

AMERICAN BALLET THEATRE 🎟♿ UPPER WEST SIDE

Metropolitan Opera House at Lincoln Center ☎212-362-0590 💻www.abt.org

Once headed by ballet legend **Mikhail Baryshnikov,** this company offers the chance to see some of the best dancers in the world perform beloved favorites such as *Swan Lake, Romeo and Juliet,* and *Don Quixote.* They also perform edgier works by more modern choreographers such as Twyla Tharp and George Balanchine.

🚇 [S] 1 to 66th St./Lincoln Center. $ Tickets $25-110. ⏰ Box office open M-Sa 10am-8pm, Su noon-6pm.

MARTHA GRAHAM CENTER OF CONTEMPORARY DANCE UPPER EAST SIDE

316 E. 63rd St. ☎212-838-5886 💻www.marthagrahamdance.org

Named after legendary modern dancer and choreographer, Martha Graham, the center is home to the **Martha Graham School of Contemporary Dance** as well as the **Martha Graham Dance Company,** which performs at venues all over the city.

🚇 [S] to Lexington/59th St. Walk to 63rd St. between 1st and 2nd Ave. $ Classes at a wide range of prices depending on length and type. Single classes from $16 each. Tickets to shows from $10. ⏰ Open daily 8:30am-6pm.

NEW YORK CITY BALLET 🎟♿ UPPER WEST SIDE

New York State Theater at Lincoln Center ☎212-870-5570 💻www.nycballet.com

Co-founded by one of the biggest names in 20th-century dance, George Balanchine, the New York City Ballet is the largest dance organization in the United States. The company boasts 90 dancers, and has an active repertory of over 150 works, many choreographed by Balanchine himself. Around Christmas season, crowds flood Lincoln Center to see Balanchine's renowned version of *The Nutcracker*, complete with dancing candy canes.

[S] 1 to 66th St. $ Tickets $20-125, student rush $12. ⏰ Box office open M-Sa 10am-7:30pm, Su 11:30am-7:30pm.

MIDSUMMER NIGHT SWING — UPPER WEST SIDE

Damrosch Park, Lincoln Center ☎212-721-6500 🖥www.midsummernightswing.org

Put on your dancing shoes and head over to Lincoln Center's Damrosch Park for a night of swingin' sounds and steps. For $17, you can get a group dance lesson at 6:30pm and a spot on the dance floor. The genre of music changes nightly and includes swing, disco, and tango, so check the schedule on the website to find the style that tickles your fancy.

[S] 1 to 66th St. $ Individual tickets (dance lesson and dance floor admission) $17. ⏰ Late June to mid-July. Group dance lesson 6:30-7:15pm. Music and dancing 7:30-10pm. Tickets can be purchased at the Avery Fisher Hall Box Office until 5pm the day of the event. After 5:30pm, tickets may be purchased in Damrosch Park.

DANCE THEATER WORKSHOP — ♿ CHELSEA

219 W. 19th St. ☎212-924-0077 🖥www.dancetheaterworkshop.org

The dance theater workshop is a center of cutting-edge, experimental dance and performance art, featuring around 45 artists and 110 shows every year. The governing organization also sponsors Commissioning and Residency programs that provide artists with resources to create lots more cutting edge, experimental dance and performance art.

[S] 1 to 18th St./7th Ave. Walk to 19th St. between 7th and 8th Ave. i If in need of wheelchair access, please notify box office. $ Tickets $10-15. ⏰ Box office open M-F 5-9pm, Sa-Su noon-8pm.

JOYCE THEATER — ♿ CHELSEA

219 W. 19th St., between 7th and 8th Ave. ☎212-242-0800 🖥wwww.joyce.org

Although the building that now houses the Joyce Theater is no longer a pornographic movie house, you can still come here to get your thrills. As long as you are thrilled by dance of all genres, styles, and nationalities performed by virtuosic performers from all over the world.

[S] 1 to 18th St./ 7th Ave. i Call for accessibility information. $ Tickets $19-59. ⏰ Box Office open M-Su noon-6pm.

ALVIN AILEY AMERICAN DANCE THEATER — ♿ MIDTOWN WEST

405 W. 55th St. ☎212-767-0590 🖥www.alvinailey.org

Dynamic and original, the Alvin Ailey American Dance Theater stages modern dance through an African-American cultural lens. The school also offers classes for dancers of all ages.

[S] 1, A, B, C, D to 59th St./Columbus Circle. $ Tickets $20-85. ⏰ Box office open shortly before curtain.

THE PARSONS DANCE COMPANY — MIDTOWN WEST

229 W. 42nd St ☎212-869-9275 🖥www.parsonsdance.com

A power team of 10 dancers who strive to engage the public in modern and contemporary American dance through performances, lectures, master classes, discussions, and student programs. Performing primarily at the Joyce Theater, they have also collaborated with artists from different disciplines, such as Dave Matthews and Julie Taymore.

[S] A, C, E to 42nd St./Port Authority or 1, 2, 3, N, Q, R, S to 42nd St./Times Square. $ General $25, students $18. ⏰ Joyce Theater box office open noon-6pm.

CITY CENTER   ♦⟨ MIDTOWN WEST

130 W. 55th St., between 6th and 7th Ave.   ☎212-581-1212 ▇www.nycitycenter.org

With six resident companies (the Alvin Ailey Dance Theater, Paul Taylor Dance Company, American Ballet Theatre, the New York Gilbert and Sullivan Players, and the Manhattan Theatre Club) and a slew of other shows, the New York City Center is focused on bringing performance arts to large audiences. Programming showcases the obscurely new and old alike as well as the shows the public knows and loves.

⚡ Ⓢ *N, R, Q to 57th St./7th Ave.; B, D, E to 7th Ave./53rd St or 57th St./Ave. of the Americas.* **i** *For wheelchair accessible seats call CityTix® at ☎212-581-1212.* Ⓢ *Tickets $25-110.* ⚄ *Box office open M-Sa noon-8pm, Su noon-7:30pm.*

film

▨ FILM FORUM   ♦⟨❄ SOHO AND TRIBECA

209 W. Houston St.   ☎212-727-8110 ▇www.filmforum.org

A mainstay of New York's film scene since the early 1970s, the Film Forum has been tireless in its attempts to provide a consistently unique and innovative screening schedule. Unique premieres of films that will only open in a few other theaters across the country occur in the midst of weeks-long "revivals and repertory" series organized around classic Hollywood's great directors, great foreign directors and movements, and other thematic and historical groupings. Only the best and newest prints are used, so this is the perfect place to discover (or rediscover) classics and unknown gems from decades past. The Forum also hosts talks, signings, and other events related to the revivals.

⚡ Ⓢ *1 to Houston St., A, B, C, D, E, F, V to West 4th St.* Ⓢ *Tickets $12.* ⚄ *Showtimes vary; check website for details.*

▨ BRYANT PARK FILM FESTIVAL   ⟨ MIDTOWN EAST

Bryant Park   ☎212-512-5700 ▇www.bryantpark.org

On Monday nights during the summer, HBO and Time Warner Cable show a free movie at sundown in Bryant Park. Movie selections generally include crowd-pleasing classics such as **Bonnie and Clyde** and ▨**Monty Python and the Holy Grail.** BYOP (Bring Your Own Popcorn).

⚡ Ⓢ *B, D, F, M to 42nd St./Ave. of the Americas (6th Ave.); 7 to 5th Ave./42nd St. Park stretches from 40th-42nd St. between 5th Ave.* Ⓢ *Free.* ⚄ *Movies M nights at sundown.*

WALTER READE THEATER   ♦⟨ UPPER WEST SIDE

165 W. 65th St.   ☎212-875-5600 ▇www.filminc.com

Nestled in the Samuel B. and David Rose building of Lincoln Center, the Walter Reade Theater is home to the **International Human Rights Watch Film Festival** in June and the **New York Film Festival** in September and October.

⚡ Ⓢ *1 to 65th St. at Lincoln Center.* Ⓢ *$12, students and seniors $8.* ⚄ *Box office opens M-F at 12:30pm, Sa-Su 1hr. before first screening. Closes 15min. after the start of the final show. Box office closes at 6pm if there are no evening screenings. Tickets also available online at ▇www. ticketing.filmlnc.com.*

NEW YORK FILM FESTIVAL   ♦⟨ UPPER WEST SIDE

Walter Reade Theater, 165 W. 65th St.   ☎212-875-5600 ▇www.filmlinc.nyff

For almost 50 years, the most compelling new films have been shown at this festival. The character of the lineup changes from year to year; sometimes there is a large mainstream presence, sometimes films are almost exclusively independent. For the most part, however, people expect to munch their popcorn in front of independent and foreign films (the 2009 festival included works from 17 different countries). A noted portion of the festival is **Views from the Avant-Garde**, which features non-narrative, experimental film.

⚑ Ⓢ *1 to 65th St. at Lincoln Center* Ⓢ *$12, students and seniors $8.* ⏰ *Late Sept/early Oct box office opens M-F at 12:30pm, Sa-Su 1hr. before first screening. Closes 15min. after the start of the final show. Box office closes at 6pm if there are no evening screenings. Tickets also available online at* ■*www.ticketing.filmnc.com.*

ZIEGFELD
⚐⊗ MIDTOWN WEST

141 W. 54th St.   ☎212-765-7600 ■www.clearviewcinemas.com

Named after a Broadway theater, the Ziegfeld is a 1131-seat single-screen movie palace. As the largest single-screen cinema in New York, the Ziegfeld is often used for ritzy film premiers and events.

⚑ Ⓢ *B, D, F, M to Rockefeller Center; N, Q, R, to 57th St. Walk south to 54th St. between 6th and 7th Ave.* ⏰ *Showtimes vary. Box office opens 30min. before first show of the day.*

ANGELIKA FILM CENTER
⚐⊗❄ SOHO AND TRIBECA

18 West Houston St.   ☎212-995-2000 ■www.angelikafilmcenter.com

The Angelika is one of several downtown cinema luminaries specializing in all things foreign and indie. Their unmissable corner location is matched by a grand interior lobby defined by a chandelier suspended above sofas, all of it geared toward classy discussion of the artsy Swedish horror flick you just watched. The food bar is far better than most: in addition to the usual popcorn and sweets, you can get coffee, pastries, and vegan food.

⚑ Ⓢ *B, D, F, V to Broadway-Lafayette St., 6 to Bleecker St., R, W to Prince St. Walk to Mercer St.* Ⓢ *Tickets $13.* ⏰ *Showtimes vary; check website for details.*

IFC CENTER
⚐♿ GREENWICH VILLAGE

323 6th Ave.   ☎212-924-7771 ■www.ifccenter.com

Like its nearby cousin, the Film Forum, the IFC Center showcases a unique blend of new, foreign, indie, and documentary releases along with historical retrospectives devoted to great directors or movie genres. The theater is only a few years old—it opened in the former Waverly Theater—and holds true to the IFC's quirky ethic. Short films precede every feature, cult classics show midnights on Fridays and Saturdays, and "weekend classics" show at 11pm from Fridays to Sundays. Every cinéaste should be satisfied.

⚑ Ⓢ *A, B, C, D, E, F, V to West 4th St. Walk to 3rd St. and 6th Ave.* Ⓢ *Tickets $12.50.* ⏰ *Showtimes vary; check schedule for details.*

CINEMA VILLAGE
⚐♿❄ GREENWICH VILLAGE

22 E. 12th St.   ☎212-924-3364 ■www.cinemavillage.com

Cinema Village's location is quite distinctive: housed in a small, blue building sandwiched between taller neighbors, it immediately tries to distance itself from the usual. Its selection of films is predictably eclectic. Only the most obscure indie and foreign films qualify, often making this theater the only place to catch them in the city. Check their online schedule for events and unique, short-time screenings.

⚑ Ⓢ *4, 5, 6, L, N, Q, R, W to 14th St.-Union Square.* Ⓢ *Tickets $11, students $8.* ⏰ *Showtimes vary; check website for details.*

LANDMARK'S SUNSHINE CINEMA
⚐♿ LOWER EAST SIDE

143 E. Houston St., between Forsyth and Eldridge St.   ☎212-330-8182 ■www. landmarktheatres.com, tickets www.moviefone.com

It wouldn't be the Lower East Side without vegan cookies and an espresso bar at the concessions stand. See foreign and independent films to your heart's content at this renovated vaudeville house, declared "Best Theater for Cult Films" by *Time Out New York*. The theater shows movies of the *2001: A Space Odyssey*

film

ilk Friday and Saturday nights at the witching hour.

✠ Ⓢ *F, V to Lower East Side/2nd Ave.* Ⓢ *$12.50, seniors $9, midnight screenings $10.* Ⓠ *Showtimes vary; check website for details.*

ANTHOLOGY FILM ARCHIVES ⊛& EAST VILLAGE
32 2nd Ave. ☎212-505-5181 www.anthologyfilmarchives.org

Opened in 1969 by a group of cineastes and experimental filmmakers (including Stan Brakhage), the Anthology focuses on the margins of film—from obscure foreign works to little-known indie premieres to the latest in avant-garde cinema. Their "Essential Cinema" series is a set of 330 titles that attempt to "define the art of cinema." The theater also publishes books and DVDs and engages in film preservation work.

✠ Ⓢ *F, V to Lower East Side/2nd Ave., 6 to Bleecker St. Walk to E. 2nd St.* Ⓢ *Tickets $9, essential cinema screenings $8, students $7.* Ⓠ *Box office opens 30min. before day's 1st show. Check website for showtimes.*

BAM ROSE CINEMAS ⋗& FORT GREEN, BROOKLYN
30 Lafayette Ave. ☎718-636-4100 www.bam.org

Part of the old and expansive Brooklyn Academy of Music performance center, this acclaimed theater screens everything from mainstream releases to indie films to historical retrospectives. Special events often bring in filmmakers themselves. The theaters themselves are beautifully designed, making the trip to Brooklyn worth it.

✠ Ⓢ *2, 3, 4, 5, B, Q to Atlantic Ave.; N, R, D, M to Pacific St.; C to Lafayette Ave.; G to Fulton St.* Ⓢ *Tickets $12, matinees $7.50.* Ⓠ *Check website for showtimes.*

92 Y TRIBECA ⋗&♈ TRIBECA
200 Hudson St ☎212-601-1000 www.92ytribeca.org

The downtown branch of the 92nd Street Y, this new cultural center is a younger, retooled version of the famous Jewish-focused uptown institution. In addition to a restaurant, a live music space, a dance hall, lecture halls, and art galleries, the space also hosts a tiny, 72-seat cinema. The offerings range from American indies to foreign faves, with a healthy sampling of short films.

✠ Ⓢ *1, A, C, E to Canal St.* Ⓢ *Screenings $12.* Ⓠ *Check website for showtimes.*

classical music

▨ CARNEGIE HALL ⋗& MIDTOWN WEST
881 7th Ave. ☎212-247-7800 www.carnegiehall.org

How do you get to Carnegie Hall? Practice, practice, practice...whew, that's a bad one. In all seriousness, Carnegie Hall is generally considered the be-all and end-all of performance venues. Although it is traditionally a classical venue, jazz, folk, and various cross-cultural music also resounds from the famous stage.

✠ Ⓢ *N, Q, R to 57th St.; B, D, E to 7th Ave./53rd St. Walk down 7th Ave. and take a left onto 57th St.* Ⓠ *Box office open M-Sa 11am-6pm, Su noon-6pm.*

MERKIN CONCERT HALL ⋗&❊ UPPER WEST SIDE
129 W. 67th St., between Broadway and Amsterdam ☎212-501-3330 www. merkinconcerthall.org

Merkin Concert Hall is known for being a trailblazer of classical music. Concerts showcase new achievement in both performance and composition. Their most notable events include New Sounds Live and the Tribeca New Music Festival, which features the latest in avant-garde "melodies."

✠ Ⓢ *1 to 66th St.* Ⓢ *Tickets $20-25.* Ⓠ *Box office open M-Th noon-7pm and Su noon-7pm.*

arts & culture

NEW YORK PHILHARMONIC 🎟♿ UPPER WEST SIDE

At Lincoln Center's Avery Fisher Hall ☎212-875-5656 💻www.lincolncenter.org

One of the premier orchestras in the world, the New York Philharmonic regularly hosts the elite celebrities of classical music, such as Itzhak Perlman, Joshua Bell, and Lang Lang. During the summer, the orchestra performs a special "Summertime Classics" series, presenting a series of popular classical music from all eras.

🚇 [S] 1 to 66th St. $ Tickets $31-$112, student rush tickets available ⏰ Avery Fisher Hall box office open M-Sa 10am-6pm, Su noon-6pm. Also open until 30min. after the start of any performance. Tickets may also be purchased through CenterCharge by calling ☎212-721-6500.

CHAMBER MUSIC SOCIETY 🎟♿ UPPER WEST SIDE

At Lincoln Center's Alice Tully Hall ☎212-875-5788 💻www.chambermusicsociety.org

If you know chamber musicians, you know that they don't just play chamber music. They're *crazy* about chamber music. Well, the Chamber Music Society is analogous to the most hardcore group of chamber musicians you know, but on steroids. They attract bigger audiences than any other chamber music organization in the world. The fantastic **Chamber Music 360** deal widens their reach by allowing guests ages 21-39 to enjoy three concerts for $60.

🚇 [S] 1 to 66th St. $ Tickets $32-76, student rush tickets 50% off and $10 directly before the show. ⏰ Alice Tully Hall box office open M-Sa 10am-6pm, Su noon-6pm. Also open until 30min. after the start of any performance. Tickets may also be purchased through CenterCharge by calling ☎212-721-6500.

GREAT PERFORMERS SERIES 🎟♿ UPPER WEST SIDE

Lincoln Center ☎212-875-5456 💻www.lincolncenter.org

The Great Performers Series exists for the sole purpose of showcasing the world's most impressive talent in the performance of classical music. Soloists, chamber ensembles, orchestras, you name it—if they're great, they perform in the series.

🚇 [S] 1 to 66th St. $ Tickets $35-85. ⏰ Avery Fisher Hall box office open M-Sa 10am-6pm, Sunday noon-6pm. Also open until 30min. after the start of any performance. Tickets may also be purchased through ***CenterCharge*** *by calling ☎212-721-6500.*

MOSTLY MOZART 🎟♿ UPPER WEST SIDE

Avery Fisher Hall, other venues at Lincoln Center ☎212-875-5456 💻www.lincolncenter.org

They said it couldn't be done. They said people would never go to an indoor summer music festival. That was in 1966, when the **Mostly Mozart Music Festival** began. At that time, concerts exclusively featured the works of Wolfgang Amadeus Mozart. Now, almost 50 years later, summer at Lincoln Center would be unthinkable without the many styles of dance, music, film, and lectures that make up the festival.

🚇 [S] 1 to 66th St. $ Tickets $35-85. ⏰ Avery Fisher Hall box office open M-Sa 10am-6pm, Su noon-6pm. Also open until 30min. after the start of any performance. Tickets may also be purchased through CenterCharge by calling ☎212-721-6500.

NATIONAL CHORALE 🎟♿ UPPER WEST SIDE

Avery Fisher Hall at Lincoln Center ☎212-333-5333 💻www.lincolncenter.org

The National Chorale is one of the country's most prominent classical vocal ensemble. Their most beloved event is the annual **Messiah Sing-In** in December, which allows audience members to "hallelujah" along with the performers.

🚇 [S] 1 to 66th St. $ Tickets $30-$400. ⏰ Avery Fisher Hall box office open M-Sa 10am-6pm, Su noon-6pm. Also open until 30min. after the start of any performance. Tickets may also be purchased through CenterCharge by calling ☎212-721-6500.

FRICK COLLECTION

&♿ ♿ UPPER EAST SIDE

1 E. 70th St., at 5th Ave. ☎212-288-0700 💻www.frick.org

Because the Frick is a classy place, it hosts a chamber music series in the music room on Sunday afternoons (Monday evenings in the summertime). Come experience the soft strum of a classical guitar, the delicate drumming of piano keys, or the beautiful bowing of a violin.

♯ Ⓢ 6 to 68th St. *i* Concert attendees may view galleries at no extra charge up to 1hr. in advance. Ⓢ Tickets $30. 🕐 Summer concerts M nights 9-11:30pm, Fall-Spring Su 5pm.

METROPOLITAN MUSEUM OF ART

●♿ UPPER EAST SIDE

1000 Ave., at 82nd St. ☎212-570-3949 💻www.metmuseum.org

Ever wonder what it would be like to hear a concert next to an Egyptian temple or in a cluster of medieval sculptures? Well, now you can! The Met's concert series features a performance lineup spanning classical, jazz, popular, folk, and world genres, performed throughout the museum.

♯ Ⓢ 4, 5, 6 to 80th St./Lexington Ave. Ⓢ Tickets $25-60. 🕐 Box office telephone hours M-Sa 9:30am-5pm, Su noon-5pm; walk-up hours Tu-Sa 10am-5pm, Su noon-5pm.

CONCERTS IN THE PARK

♿ UPPER WEST SIDE

Parks throughout the city ☎212-875-5709 💻www.newyorkphilharmonic.org

Call some friends, grab some wine, spread out on a blanket, and get ready to be serenaded by one of the world's premier orchestras. Throughout the summer, the New York Philharmonic plays concerts at various parks throughout the city. Be sure to arrive early for a good spot!

♯ Ⓢ B, C to 81st St./Central Park West. Ⓢ Tickets free. 🕐 All concerts at 8pm. Check website for schedule and location.

jazz

▨ JOE'S PUB

●♿ EAST VILLAGE

425 Lafayette St., between Astor Pl. and E. 4th St. ☎212-239-6200 💻www.joespub.com

Part of the Public Theater Triumvirate that also includes **Shakespeare in the Park** and the **Joseph Papp Public Theater,** Joe's Pub is a nightclub-style venue that allows you to dine on Italian dishes while being serenaded by a range of performers. Acts are predominantly solo, and of the musical and comedic variety. At the risk of being overly promotional, *The Village Voice* says that Joe's is the "Best Excuse to Let a Single Venue Dictate Your Taste."

♯ Ⓢ 6 to Astor Pl. Ⓢ Tickets $15-20, plus $12 food or 2 drink per person min.

🕐 Box office open M 1-6pm, Tu-Sa 1-7:30pm, Su 1-6pm. Tickets can be purchased over the phone 10am-9pm at ☎212-967-7555. Tickets can be purchased online 24hr. daily.

JAZZ AT LINCOLN CENTER

●♿ UPPER WEST SIDE

Frederick P. Rose Hall at Lincoln Center ☎212-258-9800 💻www.jalc.org

Directed by jazz icon Wynton Marsalis, Jazz at Lincoln Center features the coolest of the cool in jazz performance. Concerts are held in four different concert halls: The **Rose Theater,** the **Allen Room, Dizzie's Club Coca-Cola,** and the **Irene Diamond Education Center.** Jazz at Lincoln Center is also home of the **Nesuhi Ertegun Hall of Fame,** which pays tribute to the most legendary names in jazz, from Billie Holiday to Charlie Parker.

♯ Ⓢ 1 to 66th St. Ⓢ Tickets $31-73. 🕐 Box office open M-Sa 10am-6pm and until 30min. after the beginning of the last performance. Tickets may also be purchased daily 9am-9pm by calling CenterCharge at ☎212-721-6500.

BIRDLAND

●♿♈ MIDTOWN WEST

315 W. 44th St. ☎212-581-3080 💻www.birdlandjazz.com

Named after jazz legend **Charlie Parker** (a.k.a. "Bird") who performed regularly at the original club established in 1949. The new and improved Birdland continues the tradition of presenting top-of-the-heap jazz performers such as Diana Krall, Hank Jones, and James Moody in a club setting.

✚ Ⓢ 1, 2, 3, 7, N, Q, R, S to 42nd St./Times Sq. Walk to 44th St. between 8th and 9th Ave. Ⓢ Tickets $20-50. $10 food or drink minimum. ☾ Doors open at 5pm, performances at 8:30, 11pm.

SWING 46 JAZZ AND SUPPER CLUB　　　　　　🕊⊗ MIDTOWN WEST
349 W. 46th St., between 8th and 9th Ave.　　　☎212-262-9554 ▣www.swing46.com
Get ready for a night of dining, drinking, and dancing to the sounds of world-class big bands and swing orchestras. You may even get a chance to tap your feet to a Grammy Award-winning artist!

✚ Ⓢ C, E to 50th St. Ⓢ Tickets M-F $12, Sa-Su $15. ☾ Shows generally 8:30pm or 9:30pm.

THE JAZZ MINISTRY AT SAINT PETER'S LUTHERAN CHURCH　　&. MIDTOWN EAST
619 Lexington Ave., at 52nd St.　　　　　　　☎212-935-2200 ▣www.stpeters.org
At Saint Peter's Church, jazz is a spiritual matter. All are welcome to the free or inexpensive performances held at the church. **Jazz Vespers** are Sundays at 5pm and are free and open to the public. During the summer, things get especially jazzy: **Midtown Jazz** is Wednesdays at 1pm and **Jazz on the Plaza** is Thursdays at 12:30pm on Lexington and 53rd St. See website for exact details.

✚ Ⓢ E, M, 6 to 51st St./Lexington Ave. At the Citicorp Center. Ⓢ Many events free, others with suggested donations of $20, students $10. ☾ Jazz Vespers Su 5pm. Times of other events vary.

ZINC BAR　　　　　　　　　　　　　　　🕊⊗ GREENWICH VILLAGE
82 W. 3rd St., between Thompson and Sullivan　☎212-477-8337 ▣www.zincbar.com
At **Zinc Bar,** jazz means more than just "My Funny Valentine." Styles from every letter of the jazz alphabet, from Afro jazz to bebop to samba to vocal jazz perform here. Enjoy a full bar and listen to three sets of jazz stylings per night.

✚ Ⓢ A, C, E, B, D, F, M to 4th St. Ⓢ Cover $10. 2 drink min. Early sets $10, 1 drink min. Special weeknights free or reduced cover, 1 drink min. ☾ Open daily 6pm-3am.

IRIDIUM　　　　　　　　　　　　　　　　　🕊&. MIDTOWN WEST
1650 Broadway, at 51st. St.　　　　　　　　☎212-582-2121 ▣www.iridiumjazzclub.com
Feast on Cuenca Mahi-Mahi Ceviche (*$12*), sip an Iridium Royale (*$11*), and listen to the sounds of popular jazz artists. Every Monday is a **Les Paul Tribute Monday,** when the Les Paul Trio and special guests play a concert of Paul's music in honor of that great inventor and musician. Twenty percent of the proceeds from these concerts go to the **Les Paul Foundation.**

✚ Ⓢ A, C, 1 to 50th St.; N, R to 49th St. Ⓢ Tickets $20-30, student tickets half-price Tu-Th and Su. Call box office to reserve and present ID at the door.

opera

▨ METROPOLITAN OPERA COMPANY　　　　🕊&. UPPER WEST SIDE
Metropolitan Opera House at Lincoln Center　　☎212-362-6000 ▣www.metopera.org
In the opera world, things don't get any bigger than The Met. Literally. The stage is the size of a football field, the company is the largest classical music organization in America, and the season includes around 220 performances annually. Although a ticket could cost you up to $400, there are a lot of ways to enjoy this world-renowned opera on the cheap.

✚ Ⓢ 1 to 66th St. Ⓢ Orchestra seats $90-$330, balcony $25-115, family circle $25-50. student rush M-Th $25, F-Su $35, available 10am on the day of the performance pending availability. Orchestra standing room $20, family circle standing room M-F $15. Varis rush tickets $20, purchase 2hr. before curtain, pending availability. ☾ Open Sept-May M-Sa 10am-8pm, Su noon-6pm.

opera

DICAPO OPERA COMPANY
♥❖ UPPER EAST SIDE

184 E. 76th St.   ☎212-288-9438 ◼www.dicapo.com

From classics such as *Rigoletto* and *Madame Butterfly* to an unconventional jazz series, the Dicapo Opera Company showcases performances at slightly lower prices than The Met.

♯ Ⓢ 6 to 77th St. Ⓢ Tickets $20-50. ⏰ Shows usually Th 7:30pm, F-Sa 8pm, Su 4pm.

NEW YORK CITY OPERA
♥❖ UPPER WEST SIDE

New York State Theater at Lincoln Center   ☎212-870-5630 ◼www.nycopera.com.

An opera company known for being slightly edgier than its Metropolitan next-door neighbor. The New York City Opera has hosted world premiers of works of avant-garde composers such as Arnold Schoenberg and Philip Glass, and was also the first opera company to use supertitles!

♯ Ⓢ 1 to 66th St. *i* Call ☎212-496-0600 for tickets. ⏰ Box office open M-Sa 10am-7:30pm, Su 11:30am-7:30pm.

rock, pop, punk, funk

◼ MERCURY LOUNGE
♥❖ LOWER EAST SIDE

217 E. Houston St.   ☎212-260-4700 ◼www.mercuryloungenyc.com

The lounge hosts the type of acts often deemed interesting enough to be featured on NPR. American roots and folk are recurring influences for bands that play here.

♯ Ⓢ F to 2nd Ave./Lower East Side. Walk to E. Houston St., between Essex and Ludlow St. Ⓢ Tickets $10-12. ⏰ Box Office open M-Sa noon-7pm.

NASSAU COLISEUM
♥❖ LONG ISLAND

1255 Hempstead Turnpike   ☎516-794-9300 ◼www.nassaucoliseum.com

What would you do with 63 acres? When Army and Air Force Base **Mitchel Field** was closed in 1960, the citizens of Nassau County decided to build a venue, which they named the Nassau Veterans Memorial Coliseum. The arena generally hosts sporting events and popular music concerts.

♯ Exit M4 from Meadowbrook Parkway. Ⓢ Tickets $42-721. ⏰ Tickets available online 24hr., or at the box office M-F 9:30am-4:45pm and during events until intermission.

HAMMERSTEIN BALLROOM
♥❖ ✝ MIDTOWN WEST

311 W. 34th St.   ☎212-777-1224 ◼www.mcstudios.com

Opera music used to ring through the 12,000 sq. ft. of this gorgeous old hall. Now the venue is used for popular music concerts, television awards ceremonies, and a wide range of other events.

♯ Ⓢ A, B, C, D, F, 1, 2 to 34th St. Walk west to 34th St. between 8th and 9th Ave.

ROSELAND BALLROOM
♥❖ ✝ MIDTOWN WEST

239 W. 52nd St.,   ☎212-777-6800 ◼www.roselandballroom.com

Once an ice skating and roller rink, the vibrant Roseland Ballroom now doles out fun in the form of alternative rock concerts. Venue veterans include Paul McCartney, Alanis Morissette, and Weezer.

♯ Ⓢ 1 to 50th St./Broadway, C, E to 50th St./8th Ave. Walk uptown to 52nd St. between Broadway and 8th Ave. *i* Buy tickets online at ◼www.livenation.com or at Irving Plaza box office, 17 Irving Place. Ⓢ Tickets $35. ⏰ Irving Plaza box office open M-F noon-6:30pm, Sa 1-4pm.

RADIO CITY MUSIC HALL
♥❖ ✝ MIDTOWN WEST

1260 6th Ave., at 50th St.   ☎212-307-7171 ◼www.radiocity.com

Best known for those saucy **Rockettes,** the Radio City Music Hall also presents a full schedule of rock and popular music concerts all year round.

♿ Ⓢ B, D, F, M to 47th St./Rockefeller Center. Ⓢ Tickets $35-244.50 🕐 Box office open M-Sa 11:30am-6pm.

ARLENE'S GROCERY
♥ ♿ ¥ LOWER EAST SIDE

95 Stanton St., between Ludlow and Orchard St. ☎212-995-1652 ▪www.arlenesgrocery.net

Don't be confused by the name or the outer appearance of this venue. Although it used to be a Puerto Rican *bodega*, it is now a hip bar and club, presenting music mostly of the indie rock and punk variety.

♿ Ⓢ F, M to Lower East Side/2nd Ave. Ⓢ Free entry to Butcher Bar; Band Room M free, Tu-Th $8. Fi-Sa $10, Su $8. 🕐 Open M-F from 6pm, Sa-Su from noon. Karaoke M 10pm.

BOWERY BALLROOM
♿ ¥ LOWER EAST SIDE

6 Delancey St. ☎212-533-2111 ▪www.boweryballroom.com

Standing room only to see hot indie rock bands and more. Pop culture trivia: this is the club that the drunk couple in *Nick and Norah's Infinite Playlist* want to get to when they mistake Michael Cera's car for a taxi cab.

♿ Ⓢ J, M, Z to the Bowery. Walk to Delancey St., between Chrystie St. and the Bowery. *i* Box office located at 217 E. Houston. Ⓢ Tickets $13-30. 🕐 Box office open M-Sa noon-7pm.

THE LIVING ROOM
● ♿ ¥ LOWER EAST SIDE

154 Ludlow St., between Stanton and Rivington St. ☎212-533-7235 ▪www.livingroomny.com

A low-key club featuring both rock and acoustic acts and the latest stylings by singer-songwriters. **Googie's Lounge** upstairs is a smaller venue intended mostly for performers on the greener side.

♿ Ⓢ F, M to Lower East Side/2nd Ave.; F, J, M, Z to Delancey St./2nd Ave.; F, J, M, Z to Delancey St./Essex. *i* Must be 21+ to enter. Ⓢ Usually 1 drink min. per set, suggested donation of $5 for artist's tip jar. Occasional cover. 🕐 Open M-Th 6pm-2am, F-Sa 6pm-4am, Su 6pm-2am.

PIANOS
♥ ♿ ¥ LOWER EAST SIDE

158 Ludlow St., between Stanton and Rivington St. ☎212-505-3733 ▪www.pianosnyc.com

Come see all the newest bands you've been reading about on Pitchfork. The club also offers a full bar and food menu, as well as an upstairs lounge. Edibles and drinkables are especially cheap during happy hour *(4-7pm)*.

♿ Ⓢ F, M Lower East Side/2nd Ave.; F, J, M, Z to Delancey St./Essex St. *i* Wheelchair accessible downstairs, but not on the upper lounge. Ⓢ Prices vary; often free, sometimes $8-10. 🕐 Open daily 3pm-4am. Happy hour 3-7pm.

CANAL ROOM
♥ ♿ ¥ TRIBECA

285 W. Broadway, at Canal St. ☎212-941-8100 ▪www.canalroom.com

A concert venue featuring a large number of performers of the opening-act tier, but also occasionally such big names as Jay-Z and John Legend. Thursday nights are **Back to the 80s,** featuring a perennial 80s-tribute band, **Rubix Cube.**

♿ Ⓢ A, C, E to Canal St. *i* Shows 21+ unless otherwise indicated. Ⓢ Tickets from $10. 🕐 Open 10:30am-6:30pm. Showtimes vary. Purchase tickets online or by phone.

THE BITTER END
♥ ♿ ¥ GREENWICH VILLAGE

147 Bleecker St. ☎212-679-7030 ▪www.bitterend.com

The list of former performers at this legendary Village performance venue reads like a who's-who from the last 50 years of popular music. Van Morrison, Neil Young, Bette Midler, Otis Rush, and Billy Joel are just some who have graced this smallish stage. And that's not even mentioning comedians like Woody Allen, Albert Brooks, and Cheech and Chong. And the place is still going strong, hosting up-and-coming talents in three to four shows each night. Prices are lower and the music softer at the Sunday night original acoustic shows.

♿ Ⓢ A, B, C, D, E, F, V to West 4th St. Ⓢ Cover $7-10, Su night acoustic shows $5. Beer $4-8. Mixed drinks $6-13. 🕐 Open M-Th 7:30pm-2am, F-Sa 7:30pm-4am, Su 7:30pm-2am.

CAFE WHA?

GREENWICH VILLAGE

115 MacDougal St. (at Minetta Lane)   ☎212-254-3706 ▣www.cafewha.com

Bob Dylan and Jimi Hendrix helped make the Cafe Wha? famous in the early '60s, when it was a focus point of the burgeoning folk movement. The present basement club is actually a second incarnation of the original, located where you can now find the **Comedy Cellar.** The spirit is no longer quite as free, and the cover is certainly a lot higher, but there's variety here to entertain you: Brazilian nights on Monday, R and B nights on Tuesday, and a house band performing Wednesday through Saturday.

⚑ Ⓢ *A, B, C, D, E, F, V to West 4th St.* Ⓢ *Cover M-Tu $10, Th $5, F $12, Sa $15; free entry Su and W. Beer $4-8, mixed drinks $7-12.* ◷ *Open M 9pm-2:30am, Tu-Th 8:30pm-2:30am, F-Sa 8:30pm-4am, Su 8:30pm-2:30am.*

VILLAGE UNDERGROUND

GREENWICH VILLAGE

130 West 3rd St.   ☎212-777-7745 ▣www.thevillageunderground.com

Connected to the ▣**Fat Black Pussycat** dive bar (p.146), the Underground features some of the widest-ranging acts in the neighborhood. Every night has its own flavor: open mike on Sundays, world music on Tuesdays, a range of genres from the house band Wednesday through Friday, remixes on Friday, and DJing and dancing on Saturday.

⚑ Ⓢ *A, B, C, D, E, F, V to West 4th St.* Ⓢ *Cover M $5, Tu $10, W $3, Th $10, F-Sa $10, Su $15.* ◷ *Open Su-F 8:30pm-4am, Sa 10pm-4am, Su 8:30pm-4am.*

GROOVE

GREENWICH VILLAGE

125 MacDougal St. (at W. 3rd St.)   ☎212-254-9393 ▣www.clubgroovenyc.com

With walls lined with murals of great blues and soul performers and nightly performances of R and B, soul, and funk, Groove mines a rich tradition for all it's worth. The interior is plain, with small tables and a small stage, but if you know what you're looking for in music, the Groove can be a haven—and a relatively cheap one, compared to some of the prices at other Village venues.

⚑ Ⓢ *A, B, C, D, E, F, V to West 4th St.* Ⓢ *Cover F $5-10, Sa $7-10.* ◷ *Open M-Th 3pm-3am, F-Sa 3pm-4am, Su 3pm-3am.*

IRVING PLAZA

UNION SQUARE, GRAMERCY

17 Irving Pl.   ☎212-777-6800 ▣www.irvingplaza.com

This three-level, 1600-capacity space has a rich history: built in 1888, it has housed a German theater, a Yiddish theater, a burlesque company, an Italian cinema, a Polish community center (Pope John Paul II visited it), and finally a rock venue that hosted some of the most famous punk and alternative bands of the late 1970s and 1980s. It closed and was reopened in 2007 as the Fillmore New York; it only recently switched back to its earlier name. Today it hosts up-and-coming indie and alternative bands.

⚑ Ⓢ *A, B, C, D, E, F, V to 14th St.-Union Sq. Walk uptown to 15th St. and Irving Pl.* Ⓢ *Tickets $25-40.* ◷ *Box office open M-F noon-6:30pm, Sa 2-6pm.*

theater

▣ THE KITCHEN

CHELSEA

512 W. 19th St.   ☎212-255-5793 ▣www.thekitchen.org

This nonprofit venue provides space to visual artists, playwrights, composers, dancers, and other artists to cook up the most experimental new work. Founded in 1971, The Kitchen was one of the first venues to explore video and performance art. Tickets to events are a steal, especially for students, and many are even free.

arts & culture

🚏 [S] *C, E to 23rd St./8th Ave. Walk downtown to 19th St. and west to 10th and 11th Ave.* $ *Many events free, other tickets generally around $15. Student discount of 20% for tickets over $10. Call for information about ushering in order to see shows for free.* ⏰ *Box office open Tu-Sa 2-6pm and 1hr. before curtain. Gallery open M-F noon-6pm, Sa 11am-6pm.*

👍 **SHAKESPEARE IN THE PARK** CENTRAL PARK

Central Park ☎212-539-8750 💻www.shakespeareinthepark.org

One of NYC's most beloved traditions. Every summer from early June to early August, **The Public Theatre** runs two plays by William Shakespeare. Past performers have included Natalie Portman, Denzel Washington, Christopher Walken, Al Pacino, and Meryl Streep. Tickets are distributed at the theater at 1pm, but people begin lining up before sunrise to guarantee themselves tickets. If interested in picking up tickets, try to arrive by 8am at the latest. Visit the website for more information.

🚏 [S] *N, R, W, to 5th Ave.* ℹ *Two tickets per person in morning line.* $ *Free.* ⏰ *Performances at 8pm.*

👍 **RACE** 🎟 MIDTOWN WEST

Ethel Barrymore Theater, 243 W. 47th St. ☎212-239-6200 💻www.raceonbroadway.com

It's not all song and dance on Broadway. Plays at Broadway theaters are top-of-the-line, and are often easier to find tickets to. This David Mamet play is about the part crime plays in race relations.

🚏 [S] *N, R to 49th St.; or B, D, F, M to 47th-50th St./Rockefeller Center.* $ *$59.50-121.50.* ⏰ *Performances Tu 7pm, W and Sa 2pm and 8pm, Su 3pm.*

PROMISES PROMISES 🎟♿ BROADWAY

Broadway Theatre, 1681 Broadway ☎212-239-6200 💻www.promisespromisesbroadway.com

A musical comedy based on the 1960s hit movie *The Apartment.* Original cast features everyone's favorite "Glinda" from the original cast of *Wicked*, Kristin Chenoweth and *Will and Grace's* Sean Hayes...as a straight man!

🚏 [S] *A, C, E to 7th Ave.* ℹ *Tenure of Chenoweth and Hayes' performances unknown.* $ *$56.50-$136.50* ⏰ *Performances M-Sa 8pm, W and Sa 2pm.*

IN THE HEIGHTS 🎟♿ MIDTOWN WEST

Richard Rogers Theatre, 226 W. 46th St. ☎212-307-4100 💻www.intheheightsmusical.com

An exhilarating story about Manhattan's Washington Heights Latino community that will have you jamming to the Caribbean beats in your seat.

🚏 [S] *B, D, F, M to 47th-50th St./Rockefeller Center.* ℹ *Limited wheelchair seating within the theater.* $ *$40-120.* ⏰ *Performances Tu 7pm, W-F 8pm, Sa 2pm and 8pm, Su 2pm and 7pm.*

WICKED 🎟♿ MIDTOWN WEST

Gershwin Theatre 222 W. 51st St. ☎212-307-4100 💻www.wickedthemusical.com

Since it opened in 2003, *Wicked* has become a favorite on Broadway. Set to an irresistibly poppy soundtrack, it tells the story of the Wicked Witch of the West and Glinda the Good Witch before *The Wizard of Oz*.

🚏 [S] *1, C, E to 50th St.* ℹ *Show is 2hr. and 30min. long.* $ *$56.25-131.25* ⏰ *Performances Tu 7pm, W 2pm and 8pm, Th-F 8pm, Sa 2pm and 8pm, Su 3pm.*

PRIMARY STAGES 🎟 MIDTOWN WEST

354 W. 45th St., between 8th and 9th Ave. ☎212-840 9705 💻www.primarystages.com

A company that thrives on performing new works. They also help new playwrights get their sea legs through the Dorothy Strelsin New American Writers Group.

🚏 [S] *A, C, E to 42nd St./Port Authority.* $ *Tickets $45.* ⏰ *Performances Tu-W 7pm, Th-Sa 8pm, Sa 2pm, Su 3pm and 7pm.*

BEACON THEATER ♿🎟 UPPER WEST SIDE

2124 Broadway, at 74th St. ☎212-496-7070 💻www.beacontheatre.com

Thankfully, 1986 plans to convert the Beacon Theater (est. 1929) into a disco were thwarted by a a judge who wanted to preserve the building's historic architecture. The theater has hosted every kind of performance, from opera, to ballet, to the Rolling Stones, to the Dalai Lama. Recently, the lineup has frequently featured comedians and big names in music, with regulars featuring the Allman Brothers Band.

✈ Ⓢ 1, 2, 3 to 74th St./Broadway. *i* For wheelchair-accessibility information call ☎212-465-6085. Ⓢ Tickets $39.50-$124.50. Ⓩ Box office open M-Sa 11am-7pm, Sa noon-6pm.

QUEENS THEATRE IN THE PARK
✈♿ FLUSHING MEADOWS
In Flushing Meadows Corona Park ☎718-760-0686 🖳www.queenstheatre.org
In the middle of **Flushing Meadows Corona Park** is a circular pavilion, which looks as though it has flying saucers growing out of it. Built for the 1964 World's Fair, it houses a main stage, a cabaret-style theater, and a black-box theater. Comedians, dancers, actors, poets, musicians, and a slew of other performers make use of these spaces throughout the year. In the summer, a Latin Festival showcases artists performing largely in Spanish.

✈ Ⓢ 7 to Willets Point/Shea Stadium or 111th St. Ⓢ Tickets $18-42. Ⓩ Box office open Tu-Sa noon-6pm.

ABC NO RIO
LOWER EAST SIDE
156 Rivington St., between Clinton and Suffolk St. ☎212-254-3697 🖳www.abcnorio.org
Activism meets art in a series of events including gallery exhibitions, poetry readings, and punk and experimental music. A darkroom, silkscreen print shop, computer center, and Zine Library is available to the public. Check calendar on the website for hours.

✈ Ⓢ F, J, M, Z to Delancey St./Essex St. Ⓢ Tickets $3-15. Darkroom $6 per hr.

BOWERY POETRY CLUB
✈♿ LOWER EAST SIDE
308 Bowery, between Houston and Bleecker St. ☎212-496-7070 🖳www.bowerypoetry.com
A venue that books alternative and world music in addition to current literary talents reading their own works. It's not all berets and roses either—the **Literary Death Match** series is a cut-throat (and hysterical) competition for the LDM Championship. Open Mic Night is Monday at 10pm, and the **Urbana Poetry Slam** is Tuesdays at 7pm *(sign-up at 6:30)*.

✈ Ⓢ 6 to Bleecker St.; or B, D, F, M to Broadway/Lafayette St.; or F, M to 2nd Ave./Lower East Side. Ⓢ Prices vary. Some events free, others $7-10. Ⓩ Open M-F 5pm-4am, Sa-Su noon-4am.

THE PUBLIC THEATER
✈♿ EAST VILLAGE
425 Lafayette St. between E. 4th St. and Astor Pl. ☎212-539-8750🖳www.publictheater.org
Run by the same people who brought you **Shakespeare in the Park** and **Joe's Pub, The Public Theatre** strives to bring the best in new theater to the people.

✈ Ⓢ 6 to Astor Pl.; or N, R, W to 8th St./NYU. *i* Call ☎212-967-7555 for tickets. Ⓢ Ticket prices vary. Ⓩ Box office open Su-M 1-6pm, Tu-Sa 1-7:30pm; phone box office open 10am-9pm.

THEATER FOR THE NEW CITY
☻♿ EAST VILLAGE
155 1st Ave., between E. 9th and 10th St. ☎212-254-1109 🖳www.theaterforthenewcity.net
A winner of both the Pulitzer Prize and the Mayor's Stop the Violence Award, the theater produces between 30 and 40 new American plays each year. The theater also offers a host of community-oriented, service programs, including theater training and performances for at-risk and low-income youth and adults.

✈ Ⓢ 6 to Astor Pl. Ⓢ Ticket prices vary from free to cheap. Ⓩ Performance times vary.

SOHO PLAYHOUSE
✈☻ SOHO
15 Vandam St. ☎212-691-1555 🖳www.sohoplayhouse.com
Built in 1826, this 199-seat theater shows productions that require an up-close-and-personal experience between actors and audience members. A mainstage-favorite is the all-female, unscripted sitcom *Naked in a Fishbowl* which has run

arts & culture

for four straight summers. The bar and cabaret downstairs is called the "Huron Club" in reference to the days when the building was a nightclub frequented by the Tammany Hall political machine.

⚡ Ⓢ C, E to Spring St. Walk to Vandam St., between Varick St. and Ave. of the Americas. Ⓢ Mainstage tickets $20-90. Huron Club tickets $10-30. 🕐 Box Office Open Tu-Sa noon-6pm; hours extended on days of shows.

ACTORS PLAYHOUSE
👆⊘❋ GREENWICH VILLAGE

100 7th Ave. ☎212-255-6452 ▪www.nyactorsplayhouse.com

An off-Broadway center since the 1950s, this small theater in the heart of the Village has garnered a reputation for the offbeat by hosting unusual plays and comedians. Its current incarnation began in 2007 after a few years of inactivity due to increased rents.

⚡ Ⓢ 1 to Christopher St. Ⓢ Tickets $25-50. 🕐 Box office open M-F 1-6pm. Showtimes vary; check website for details.

PLAYERS THEATRE
👆⊘❋ GREENWICH VILLAGE

115 MacDougal St. ☎212-475-1449 ▪www.theplayerstheatre.com

The Players Theatre has been busy since the 1940s hosting a wide variety of shows, from musicals to Shakespeare to interactive performances. There are two spaces: an off-Broadway theater holding around 200, and **The Loft,** a small off-off Broadway space that seats 50.

⚡ Ⓢ A, B, C, D, E, F, V to West 4th St. Ⓢ Tickets $25-50. 🕐 Showtimes vary; check website for details.

LUCILLE LORTEL THEATRE
👆♿❋ GREENWICH VILLAGE

121 Christopher St. ☎212-924-8782 ▪www.lortel.org/LLT_theater

One of the Village's premier theaters, the Lucille Lortel has seen productions of *The Threepenny Opera, Steel Magnolias,* and *Seussical* during its nearly 60-year history. Check out the sidewalk in front, where stars emblazoned with famous playwrights' names make for an interesting entrance. Contact the theater in advance if you want to watch a show for free by working as an usher.

⚡ Ⓢ 1 to Christopher St. Ⓢ Prices vary; summer programs often free. 🕐 Showtimes vary; check online schedule for details.

UNION SQUARE THEATER
👆♿❋ UNION SQUARE, GRAMERCY

10 E. 17th St. ☎212-674-2267

Formerly Tammany Hall, the Union Square Theater was founded in 1926 and has since become one of the highlights in Off-Broadway. Plays in the 499-capacity space are generally offbeat; a recent production was an adults-only puppet show.

⚡ Ⓢ 4, 5, 6, L, N, Q, R to 14th St.-Union Sq. Ⓢ Tickets $25-50. 🕐 Box office open Tu-Su 1-6pm.

VINEYARD THEATER
👆♿❋ UNION SQUARE, GRAMERCY

108 E. 15th St. ☎212-353-0303 ▪www.vineyardtheater.org

The Vineyard hosts a variety of new and acclaimed dramas, comedies, and musicals. It's tiny—seating only 120 people—but cozy. This is where 🔖**Avenue Q** began its long and still-popular run, but more recent productions include the award-winning *Scottsboro Boys.*

⚡ Ⓢ 4, 5, 6, L, N, Q, R to 14th St.-Union Sq. Walk uptown to 15th St., between 4th Ave. and Irving Pl. Ⓢ Tickets $25-60. 🕐 Box office open Tu-Th 1-6pm, F 1-8pm.

theater

comedy

COMIC STRIP LIVE
●♿ UPPER EAST SIDE

1568 2nd Ave., between 81st and 82nd St. ☎212-861-9386 ■www.comicstriplive.com

The lobby wall is covered in autographed photographs of comedians such as Jerry Seinfeld, Eddie Murphy, and Adam Sandler who have paid their dues here. The club is also the subject of a new documentary called **EAT DRINK LAUGH** by Chris Rock, who got his start here bussing tables for free. For a club that only features professionals, the prices are great.

⌖ Ⓢ *4, 5, 6, N, R, W to 86th St./Lexington Ave.* ⓘ *2 drink min. 17+.* Ⓢ *M-F $20, Sa-Su $25.* Ⓩ *Shows M-Th 8:30pm; F 8:30, 10:30pm, 12:30am; Sa 8, 10:30pm, 12:30am; Su 8pm.*

GOTHAM COMEDY CLUB
●♿▼ CHELSEA

208 W. 23rd St., between 7th and 8th Ave. ☎212-367-9000 ■www.gothamcomedyclub.com

This is New York City. On the comedy scene, everyone has hosted Jerry Seinfeld and Lewis Black, but not everyone hosts them in a $2.5 million, 1920s-Art-Deco-inspired, 3300 ft. comedy kingdom. Gotham is also the filming location of NBC's "Last Comic Standing" and Comedy Central's "Live at Gotham."

⌖ Ⓢ *F, M to 23rd St./Ave. of the Americas.* ⓘ *First Wednesday of every month is "Homo Comicus," a show featuring gay comedians.* Ⓢ *Cover $10-25, plus 2 drink min.* Ⓩ *Shows nightly. Times vary; call or check website for schedule. Call to make a reservation starting at 10am.*

UPRIGHT CITIZENS BRIGADE THEATRE
◉◉ CHELSEA

307 W. 26th St. ☎ ■www.newyork.ucbtheatre.com

The Upright Citizens Brigade was a group of four Chicago comedians, including SNL's Amy Poehler, who founded a training program for "long improv," one entire show of improvised work, in New York City in 1997. Today the Upright Citizens Brigade Theatre features daily improv, sketch, and stand-up comedy, both in the form of public performances and a full comedy education program. The most rigorous offering within the program is the intense-sounding Improv Guerilla Training Center.

⌖ Ⓢ *1 to 23rd St./7th Ave.; F, M to 23rd St./Ave. of the Americas. Walk uptown to 26th St., between 8th and 9th Ave.* ⓘ *Make reservations online or by telephone.* Ⓢ *Shows up to $10.*

DANGERFIELD'S
●♿ MIDTOWN WEST

1118 1st Ave., between 61st and 62nd. ☎212-593-1650 ■www.dangerfields.com

The only comedy club in New York owned by a famous celebrity, Dangerfield's is also the longest-running comedy club in the world. This funny factory hosts world-famous famous acts such as Jim Carrey, Jay Leno, and Rodney Dangerfield himself.

⌖ Ⓢ *4, 5, 6, N, R, W to Lexington Ave./59th St.* Ⓢ *$15 Su-M, $20 F-Sa.* Ⓩ *Shows M-Th 8:45pm, F 8:30pm and 10:30pm, Sa 8 pm, 10:30pm, 12:30am, Su 8:45pm.*

STAND UP NY
●♿ UPPER WEST SIDE

236 W. 78th St. ☎212-595-0850 ■www.standupny.com

Stand Up NY prides itself on showcasing exclusively local talent. With shows every night of the week, open mike nights are on Monday, Wednesday, and Friday from 5-7pm.

⌖ Ⓢ *1 to 79th St./Broadway. Between Amsterdam Ave. and Broadway.* Ⓢ *M-F $20, Sa-Su $15.* Ⓩ *Shows M-F 8pm; Th-F 10:15pm; F 10:15pm and 12:15am.*

EAST VILLE COMEDY CLUB
EAST VILLAGE

85 E. 4th St., between 2nd Ave. and Bowery ☎212-260-2445 ■www.eastvillecomedy.com

This 130+ seat club features comedians who have been featured in movies or on TV, including Sarah Silverman, Dave Attell, and Jim Gaffigan. Open mikes happen Monday through Friday and a "Rising Stars Showcase" allows some of the most promising new comedians in the area to perform.

⌖ Ⓢ *6 to Astor Pl.* Ⓢ *Tickets M-F $10, Sa-Su $20.*

arts & culture

festivals

▨ RIVER TO RIVER FESTIVAL

VARIOUS VENUES

Venues across Downtown New York   ☎888-391-FEST ▣www.rivertorivernyc.com

Enjoy free music, dance, film, and a variety of other events from the East River to the Hudson during the summer.

🕐 June-August.

▨ LINCOLN CENTER FESTIVAL

❦& UPPER WEST SIDE

Lincoln Center, Columbus Ave.   ▣LincolnCenterFestival.org

Where can you see 12hr. plays, classical Thai dance-drama combined with modern dance, Georgian marionette performances, and hip West African bands all in the same place? Only at Lincoln Center during the Lincoln Center Festival.

⚡ Ⓢ 1 to 66th St. Ⓢ $30-$225, depending on the event. 🕐 Festival runs for two weeks in July. Tickets for all events can be purchased at the Alice Tully box office and Avery Fisher Hall box office M-Sa 10am-6pm, Su noon-6pm and 1hr. before the show. Tickets for events at the Rose Theater may be purchased at the Jazz at Lincoln Center Box Office M-Sa 10am-6pm, Su noon-6pm.

CENTRAL PARK SUMMERSTAGE

CENTRAL PARK

Rumsey Playfield, at 72nd St. near 5th. Ave.   ☎212-360-2777 ▣www.summerstage.org

This local favorite is largely unknown to tourists. The series features a wide range of concerts and events that are free and open to the public. See Central Park (p.73) for complete listing.

⚡ Ⓢ N, W, R to 5th Ave. Ⓢ Free. 🕐 Visit website for information about performance schedules.

CAREFUSION JAZZ FESTIVAL

● CITY FESTIVAL

Venues Throughout the City   ☎212-246-1500 ▣www.nycjazzfestival.com

For nine days in June, the sweet sounds of jazz can be heard at venues throughout the boroughs of New York City. Concerts at **Central Park, Prospect Park,** and **Soundview Park** are free, and most other concert tickets cost $15 or less and occur at jazz-important venues such as the **Louis Armstrong House Museum,** ▨**Flushing Town Hall,** and **Dizzy's Club Coca-Cola.** For a splurge, check out the concerts at **Carnegie Hall.**

Ⓢ Prices vary. 🕐 June.

live television

▨ THE DAILY SHOW

& MIDTOWN WEST

513 W. 54th St.   ☎212-586-2477 ▣www.thedailyshow.com/tickets

Jon Stewart, that prince of political satire can only be better live. To see the action, check the show's website and follow the directions to request tickets. Availability is tight, so plan ahead!

⚡ Ⓢ 1, A, B, C, D to 59th St./Columbus Circle. Ⓢ Free. 🕐 Tapings M-Th 4:30pm.

THE COLBERT REPORT

& MIDTOWN WEST

513 W. 54th St.   ▣www.colbertnation.com/tickets

Tickets to see Mr. Colbert are very difficult to obtain, and are not always available. Check the website as far in advance as possible and follow the instructions to get your tickets.

⚡ Ⓢ 1, A, B, C, D to 59th St./Columbus Circle. Ⓢ Free. 🕐 Doors open at 6pm, people often begin lining up at 4pm.

LATE NIGHT WITH JIMMY FALLON

& MIDTOWN EAST

30 Rockefeller Plaza   ☎212-664-3056 ▣www.nbc.com

You have several options to see the new kid on the late night block. Option 1:

live television

you can call the ticket line to reserve up to four tickets. This should be done around one month in advance. If you are not on top of your game one month ahead of time, do not despair! You can still get standby tickets by lining up outside of 30 Rockefeller Plaza no later than 9am on the day of the taping. Call the ticket line the night before just to make sure there will actually be a show to see the next day. Plus, each taping is a chance to see back-up group **The Roots** in person.

⚲ Ⓢ *B, D, F, M to Rockefeller Center.* **i** *Must be at least 17 to attend.* Ⓢ *Free.* 🕐 *Tapings M-F 5:30pm.*

spectator sports

▨ AQUEDUCT RACE TRACK
ROCKAWAY
110-00 Rockaway Blvd.   ☎718-541-4700 🖳www.nyra.com/aqueduct
For a thoroughbred fun time, head to Aqueduct Race Track from late October to early May.

⚲ Ⓢ *A to Aqueduct.* Ⓢ *Clubhouse and Skyline Club Admission free.* 🕐 *Races W-Su.*

▨ USTA TENNIS CENTER
⚲🚻 QUEENS
Flushing Meadows Corona Park   ☎718-760-6200 🖳wwww.usta.com
Tennis enthusiasts who get their tickets three months in advance can clap politely (that's tennis for "loud, hearty cheering") at the prestigious **US Open**, one of tennis' four Grand Slam events held in late August and early September here at the United States Tennis Association in Flushing Meadows Park, Queens.

⚲ Ⓢ *7 to 111th St. or Willets Point/Shea Stadium.* Ⓢ *Tickets $56-105.* 🕐 *Arthur Ashe box office open M-F 9am-5pm.*

MADISON SQUARE GARDEN BASKETBALL
⚲🚻 MIDTOWN WEST
Between 31st and 34 St., 7th and 8th Ave.   ☎212-465-5800🖳www.thegarden.com
The NBA's **New York Knicks** and WNBA's **New York Liberty** both shoot their home baskets at the Garden. **St. John's Red Storm** in the winter and the **NIT** and **Big East** tournaments in March also go down at MSG.

⚲ Ⓢ *1, 2, 3 to 34th St./Penn Station/7th Ave.; A, C, E to 34th St./Penn Station/8th Ave.* Ⓢ *Tickets from $10.* 🕐 *Tours daily 11am-3pm, every ½hr. Box office open daily 9am-6pm.*

NEW YORK RANGERS AT MADISON SQUARE GARDEN
🚻⚲ MIDTOWN WEST
Between 31st and 34 St., 7th and 8th Ave.   ☎212-308-6977 🖳www.thegarden.com
Watch the NHL's **New York Rangers** put the biscuit in the basket October through April at Madison Square Garden. Also learn more hockey slang.

⚲ Ⓢ *1, 2, 3 to 34th St./Penn Station/7th Ave.; A, C, E to 34th St./Penn Station/8th Ave.* **i** *Tickets go on sale in August; reserve well in advance.* Ⓢ *Tickets from $25.* 🕐 *Tours daily 11am-3pm, every ½hr. Box Office open daily 9am-6pm.*

BELMONT PARK
LONG ISLAND
2150 Hempstead Turnpike Belmont   ☎718-641-4700 🖳www.nyra.com/belmont
Fans seeking equine excitement can watch stallions at the park. The **Belmont Stakes,** run the first Saturday in June, concludes the Triple Crown.

⚲ Ⓢ *F to to 169th street or 179th street then take the N6 or the Q2 bus to Belmont. Or, take the E train to Jamaica Center (Parsons Blvd.) and then take the Q110 bus to Belmont.* Ⓢ *Reserved tickets in clubhouse and grandstand $2 on weekends and holidays.*

arts & culture

leisure sports

SKY RINK AT CHELSEA PIERS
CHELSEA

23rd St. and the Hudson River ☎212-336-6100 🖳www.chelseapiers.com/sr01.htm

Take a break from your Chelsea gallery crawl and hit the ice at this year-round skating rink. Skating novice? Sky Rink has you covered with skate and equipment rental as well as comprehensive classes.

✤ ⑤ C, E to 23rd St. ⑤ $13, youth and seniors $10.50. Skate rental $7.50, helmet rental $4. ⌚ Open summer 12:30-2:20pm, F 12:30-2:20PM, Sa-Su noon-3:50pm; winter M 1:30-5:20pm, Tu-Th 3-5:20pm, Sa-Su 1-3:50pm.

METRO BICYCLE STORES
UPPER EAST SIDE

1311 Lexington Ave., at 88th St. ☎212-427-4450 🖳www.metrobicyclestores.com

Explore the city on wheels. Metro has six other locations throughout the city: 332 E. 14th St., 75 Varick St., 360 W. 47th St., 231 W. 96th St., 546 Ave. of the Americas, and 396 Main St., New Rochelle.

✤ ⑤ 6 to 86th St. i Bikes must be returned 30min before store closes. Credit card required for rental. ⑤ $9 per hour, $45 per day, $55 overnight. Helmets $2.50 per day. ⌚ Open M-Sa 9:30am-6:30pm, Su 9:30am-6pm.

PEDAL PUSHERS
UPPER EAST SIDE

1306 2nd Ave., at 69th St. ☎212-288-5592 🖳www.pedalpushersbikeshop.com

Like ▨**Let's Go,** Pedal Pushers has been around since the 1960s. Unlike ▨**Let's Go,** Pedal Pushers has been renting, selling, and servicing bicycles since that time. The shop also partners with **Bike the Big Apple**, a company that provides bike tours of NYC. Visit 🖳www.bikethebigapple.com for more details.

✤ ⑤ 6 to 68th St. ⑤ Bikes $6 per hr., $25 per day. Helmets and locks $4 per day. No overnight rentals without written notice. i Credit card required for rental. ⌚ Open daily 10am-6pm.

NEW YORK ROADRUNNER'S CLUB
UPPER EAST SIDE

9 E. 89th St. ☎212-860-4455 🖳www.nyrr.org

Gotta run? The NY Roadrunner's Club sponsors training programs and races all over the city, facilitating participation in events such as the **New York City Marathon,** from Verrazano Bridge to Central Park's Tavern on the Green the first Sunday in November. An astounding 22,000 runners participate in the 21.6 mi. race, but only 16,000 actually finish. Call the club or visit the NY Roadrunner's Club website for information about membership, training, and races.

✤ ⑤ 6 to 86th St. Walk uptown to 89th St. between Madison and 5th Ave. ⌚ Open M-F 10am-8pm, Sa 10am-5pm, Su 10am-3pm.

ROCKAWAY BEACH AND BOARDWALK
   ♿ ROCKAWAY

From Beach 3rd St. in Far Rockaway to Beach 149th in the west ☎718-318-4000 🖳www.nycgovparks.org

Rockaway offers 70 blocks and 70 miles of relatively clean city beaches, plus a boardwalk that locals put to good use. The Rockaway area was once known as the "Irish Riviera" for the immigrants living in this part of town. The population is still supposedly over one quarter ▨**Irish-American.**

✤ ⑤ A marked "Far Rockaway" to all stops between Beach 36th St. and Beach 67th St, or A marked "Rockaways" or A, S to all stops between Beach 90th St. and Rockaway Park/Beach 116th St. ⑤ Free. ⌚ Lifeguard on duty Memorial Day through Labor Day 10am-6pm. Swimming permitted only when lifeguard is on duty. Promenade open 6am-10pm.

leisure sports

TRUMP WOLLMAN RINK

⊛ CENTRAL PARK

East side of Central Park, between 62nd and 63rd St. ☎212-439-6900 ▣www. wollmanskatingrink.com

Built in 1949 with $600,000 donated by Kate Wollman, **Trump Wollman Rink** is now, like most things, owned by Donald Trump. Still, you can't get much more romantic than a moonlit skate date in New York's Central Park.

ⓢ *M-Th $9.50, over 59 $4.75, children $4.75; F-Su $12, over 59 8.25, children $5. Skate rentals $5.* ⌚ *Open M-Tu 10am-2:30pm, W-Th 10am-10pm, F-Sa 10am-11pm, Su 10am-9pm.*

ROCKEFELLER CENTER SKATING CENTER

MIDTOWN WEST

5th Ave., between 49th and 50th St. ☎212-332-7654 ▣www.therinkatrockcenter.com

Since the rink opened on Christmas Day of 1936, winter ice skating at Rockefeller Center has become a quintessential New York tradition. During the holiday season, take skating as an opportunity to oooh and aaah at the gigantic 75-90 ft. Christmas Tree in Rockefeller Center.

✚ Ⓢ *B, D, F, M to 47th-50th St./Rockefeller Center/Ave. of the Americas.* ⓘ *Call to confirm hours.* ⓢ *M-Th $15.50-$19, under 11 and seniors $9.50-12; F-Su $19, under 11 and seniors $10.50-12. Skate rentals $9.* ⌚ *Open daily 8am-midnight.*

WEST 4TH ST. COURTS

GREENWICH VILLAGE

Ave. of the Americas and W. 4th St. ☎212-NEW-YORK ▣www.nycgovparks.org

The most intense pick-up basketball around takes place at a sub-regulation-sized court known as The Cage. Some of the city's best amateur players dribble here, and rumor has it that scouts for college and pro teams occasionally drop by to check out new talent.

✚ Ⓢ *A, B, C, D, E, F, M to W. 4th St.* ⓢ *Free.* ⌚ *Open daily dawn-dusk.*

fitness

▧ CRUNCH GYM

⬥ MIDTOWN EAST

1109 2nd Ave., at 59th St. ☎212-758-3434 ▣www.crunch.com

A fun-loving gym famous for its original class schedule, Crunch features an eclectic list of programs, from the conventional to the crazy. The dance schedule, boasting options as uncommon as Bhangra and "Tribal House Party" and as innovative as "Pop Videography" is especially cool. Admit it, you've been dying to learn Britney Spears' hottest moves.

✚ Ⓢ *4, 5, 6, N, R, Q to 59th St./Lexington Ave.* ⓘ *Other Crunch Gym branches throughout the city, but 59th location is the largest.* ⓢ *Enrollment fee $250, monthly membership $90.* ⌚ *Open M-Th 5am-11pm, F 5am-10pm, Sa-Su 8am-8pm.*

MANHATTAN MOTION DANCE STUDIO

⬥⊛ UPPER WEST SIDE

215 W. 76th St. ☎212-724-1673 ▣www.manhattanmotion.com

Offering a wide range of classes, from ballet to hip hop to cardio dance, this studio is well worth the climb to the building's fourth floor.

✚ Ⓢ *1 to Broadway and 79th St. Walk downtown on Broadway and turn right onto 76th St. toward Amsterdam Ave.* ⓢ *$15-20 per class.* ⌚ *Hours vary; call for class schedule.*

92ND STREET Y

⬥♿ UPPER EAST SIDE

1395 Lexington Ave., at 92nd St. ☎212-996-1100 ▣www.92y.org

Six levels plus 125 fitness machines plus more than 400 exercise classes per month plus a 25 yd. pool equals an intense fitness experience. The 92nd St. Y also offers training, instruction, and nutrition counseling.

✚ Ⓢ *6 to 96th St.* ⓢ *1-month membership $92, 2-month summer membership $176, 3-month summer membership $252, annual adult preferred membership $1,275 per year, classes for non-members $180-350.* ⌚ *Open M-Th 6am-10:30pm, F 6am-8pm, Sa-Su 8am-8pm.*

arts & culture

DANCE FORUM NY GRAMERCY PARK

20 E. 17th St., 2nd fl. www.danceforum.org

The instructors at Dance Forum NY use a dancer-developed workout system called BodiBalance™ to improve your health, fitness, and "kinesthetic awareness." No experience necessary for beginners' classes; classes available for the seasoned dancers as well.

[S] L, N, Q, R to Union Square/14th Street Station. Located between 5th and 6th Ave. $ Classes $17-20, 10-class card $150, workshops $98-850 (plus materials and registration fees), private sessions $75. Hours vary depending on class schedule.

INTEGRAL YOGA INSTITUTE CHELSEA

227 W. 13th St., between 7th and 8th Ave. ☎212-229-0586 www.integralyogany.com

This is the mother of all Yoga Institutes. The New York Integral Yoga Institute is just one branch of a global organization founded in 1966 that has its own line of foods and medicinal products. Over 100 classes a week are offered at this location, in rooms with such inviting names as "Lotus," "Gold," and even "Heaven."

[S] 1, 2, 3 to 14th St./7th Ave.; A, C, E, L to 14th St./Eighth Ave. $ Single Class $5-17, 5-class card $80, 10-Class Card $120-150, 20-class card $260. Hours vary depending on class schedule.

NORTH MEADOW RECREATION CENTER CENTRAL PARK

Mid-park at 97th St. ☎212-348-4867 www.centralparknyc.org/visit

Kids in Central Park can never be justifiably bored while the North Meadow Recreation Center is around. Indoor options feature a 20 ft. rock climbing wall, as well as a variety of classes and programs. Outdoor activities include basketball and handball. Make any day Field Day by borrowing a "Field Day kit," free when you give your photo ID as collateral.

[S] B, C to 96th St. $ Free. Open Apr-Jun and Sept-Oct Tu-F 10am-6pm, Sa-Su 10am-5pm; Jul-Aug M-Th 10am-8pm, F 10am-6pm Sa-Su 10am-5pm.

HARLEM YMCA HARLEM

180 W. 135th St. ☎212-912-2100 www.ymcanyc.org/harlem

Pool, exercise equipment, group classes, and a complimentary personal fitness program are all available here at reasonable prices *(day pass $12)*. The Harlem Y also hosts fun fitness events such as the annual golf outing in late August.

[S] 2, 3 to 135 St. Located between Adam Clayton Powell Jr. Blvd. and Malcolm X Blvd. $ $55 per month, 1st month $180, or $12 per day. Open M-F 5:30am-11pm, Sa 6am-8pm, Su 8am-8pm. Pool open M-F 6am-10:30pm, Sa 6:30am-7:30pm, Su 8:30am-7:30pm.

GLEASON'S GYM BROOKLYN

77 Front St., Brooklyn ☎718-797-2872 www.gleasonsgym.net

This legendary boxing training ground began in the 1930s, when Bobby Gleason, who had adopted an Irish name to appeal to boxing's main demographic at the time, founded a gym in the Bronx. The gym helped train several superstars over the next several decades, including Jake LaMotta, Sonny Liston, Mike Tyson, and **Muhammad Ali** himself. After two moves, the gym now resides near the waterfront in Brooklyn. Despite the gym's impressive history, non-professionals frequent the space regularly to take lessons from grizzled trainers.

[S] A, C to High St., F to York St. $ Daily workout fee $20, monthly membership fee $85. Daily spectator fee $10. Open M-F 6am-10pm, Sa 8am-6pm.

EASTERN ATHLETIC BROOKLYN

43 Clark St., 17 Eastern Pkwy. ☎718-625-0500 www.easternathleticclubs.com

These expansive clubs offer a variety of classes, from racquetball to yoga to Pilates to tai chi. The usual strength training is here, of course, along with pools, boxing stations, and spa facilities.

[S] 2, 3 to Grand Army Plaza. $ Day membership pass $25, monthly membership $100. Open M-F 6:30am-11:30pm, Sa-Su 9am-7:30pm.

BODY ELITE

◆ BROOKLYN

348 Court St. (at Union St.)   ☎718-935-0088 🖥www.bodyelitegym.com

Despite its intimidating title, Body Elite is a welcoming gym in the appealing Carroll Gardens neighborhood. Classes and tanning machines complement the weights and cardio equipment. There are four floors, so don't mistake it for a tiny gym on the corner.

🚇 Ⓢ *F, G to Carroll St.* Ⓢ *Day pass $15.* 🕐 *Open M-Th 5:30am-11pm, F 5:30am-10pm, Sa 7:30am-8:30pm, Su 8am-8pm.*

SHOPPING

New York's got the world's largest department stores, fashion's hottest designer boutiques, and the coolest bookstores. Regardless of whether you have the money to actually buy anything, it's a shopper's paradise. Stroll around the city and take a peek into the most stylish windows anywhere around the globe.

greatest hits

- **GET STRANDED** in the Strand (p.190), New York's coolest bookstore.
- **BE NIFTY THRIFTY** at Unique Boutique (p.189), offering great fashion deals on the Upper East Side.
- **SAY CHEESE!** The legendary grocery store Zabar's (p.192) has an entire department devoted to cheese.
- **GLOBAL GLAMOR** hangs on the racks of International Boutique (p.186).

Students looking to spend a day shopping will have better luck in Williamsburg than anywhere in Manhattan. The famously trendy Brooklyn neighborhood is home to New York's best buys for hipsters.

- **WILLIAMSBURG** is obsessed with everything vintage. Walk in to **Beacon's Closet** for a warehouse full of designer clothing at cheap prices. Less decisive shoppers might prefer **Viceversa,** a smaller store with great accessories.

- **SHOW HOW RANDOM YOU ARE AT UGLY LUGGAGE,** which sells every trinket, antique, and wacky furniture piece you might ever want to collect.

- **THE BEST USED AND NEW BOOKS** in Brooklyn are at **Spoonbill and Sugartown.** It makes the medicine go down.

vintage clothing

STELLA DALLAS
218 Thompson St.

GREENWICH VILLAGE
☎212-674-0447

Stella Dallas aims at a small target: the store's entire collection consists of women's wear from the 40s to the 60s. They've mined that narrow niche for all it's worth, however, and this eclectic, treasure-filled shop is the result. Cheap, colorful dresses hang out front in good weather while racks of bags, boots, and designer scarves await you inside, along with more dresses and shirts. Maybe best of all, the small but well-chosen selection of hats is seemingly tailor-made for hip retro fashion. Music from the appropriate decades sets the tone.

✦ Ⓢ A, B, C, D, E, F, V to W. 4th St. Located between Bleecker St. and W. 3rd St. *i* Additional location in Williamsburg, Brooklyn at 281 N. 6th St. Ⓢ Most items $15-40. Dresses $20-40. Hats $40-80. ☼ Open daily 12:30-7:30pm.

INTERNATIONAL BOUTIQUE
500 LaGuardia Pl.

GREENWICH VILLAGE
☎212-677-0705

International Boutique will give you the usual thrift shop array of cheap clothes, from shoes to pants and jackets to many T-shirts. But after all, the store is here to offer you "clothing for body and soul," and on that note, the front of the store is more packed with religious memorabilia and knick-knacks than your grandmother's living room. Many religions are represented: you can get Jesus holograms alongside menorahs and Buddha plates nestled next to crucifixes. It's a strange mixture, but it's stood the test of over 40 years. Must be the neighborhood.

✦ Ⓢ A, B, C, D, E, F, V to W. 4th St. Ⓢ Most clothing items $8-30, jackets $25-70. ☼ Open daily noon-8pm.

ANDY'S NEW AND ANTIQUE CLOTHING
18 W. 18th St.

GREENWICH VILLAGE
☎212-420-5980 ◻www.andyscheepees.com

Andy's packs a lot of vintage into its two floors. "Antique" is pushing it; most items here date from the '50s to the '70s, with a smattering of '80s—we're guessing that the garish AC/DC and Aerosmith T-shirts rep most of that decade. The warm-weather season brings in flowery dresses for the women and polyester shirts for the men. With the cold come military-style coats, flannel, and lots of leather. Out-of-season clothing is kept downstairs, so you can buy patterns whatever the forecast.

✦ Ⓢ N, R to 8th St. Ⓢ Most items $20-60. ☼ Open M-Sa noon-9pm, Su noon-8pm.

HAMLET'S VINTAGE

●✦⊗❊ GREENWICH VILLAGE

162 Bleecker St. ☎218-228-1561 ▬www.hamletsvintage.com

Hamlet's occupies a fairly small and plainly decorated space, but it's packed with heaps of relatively inexpensive items geared to eclectic and wide-ranging tastes. Highlights include the cheap jacket rack and the sizable belt collection. Even indecisive Hamlet could find something he'd like here! Sorry, we had to.

✦ S *A, B, C, D, E, F, V to West 4th St. Located between Thompson St. and Sullivan St.* Ⓢ *Most items $10-80. T-shirts $15. Belts $10-30. Jackets $20-25. Dresses $50-80.* ⏰ *Open noon-8pm daily.*

ENCORE

✦ UPPER EAST SIDE

1132 Madison Ave. and 84th St. ☎212-879-2850 ▬www.encoreresale.com

You can afford clothes on Madison Avenue, you just might have to look a little harder for them. This secret consignment treasure trove is tucked away on the second floor of a store building and protected by a magic buzzer. Press the button to be let in and prepare to go fashion wild.

✦ S *6 to 86th St. Store located on the 2nd fl.* Ⓢ *Discounted designer prices.* ⓘ *July to mid-August closed Su.* ⏰ *Open M-W 10:30am-6:30pm, Th 10:30am-7:30pm, F 10:30am-6:30pm, Sa 10:30am-6:30pm, Su noon-6pm.*

ALLAN AND SUZI

✦ UPPER WEST SIDE

416 Amsterdam Ave., at 80th St. ☎212-724-7445 ▬www.allanandsuzi.net

Whether you're looking for a retro Gucci dress or the perfect silver helmet to go with that purple tutu, no other store comes close to matching the breadth, diversity, or sheer randomness of Allan and Suzi's collection. Go on, get some sequined stilettos to match.

✦ S *1 to 79th St., B, C to 81st St.* ⏰ *Open M-Sa 12:30-6:30pm, Su noon-6pm.*

TOKYO JOE

♿ EAST VILLAGE

334 E 11th St. ☎212-473-0724

Hit this tiny shop for sweet deals on Calvin Klein and Hugo Boss suits *($48-92)* or shirts by Nanette Lepore and Anna Sui *($9-32)*. You may have to splurge a little on your Louis Vuitton or Juicy Couture handbags, though *($28-750)*.

✦ S *6 to Astor Pl. Located between 1st and 2nd Ave.* Ⓢ *Dresses $14-140, shoes $21-96, jeans $18-45.* ⏰ *Open daily noon-9pm.*

ENZ'S

✦♿ EAST VILLAGE

125 2nd Ave., between 7th St. and St. Mark's Pl. ☎212-228-1943 ▬www.enznyc.com

A store that sells 1950s-style, vintage-inspired clothing items and accessories, dipped in a kind of Goth-sauce. This means a lot of blacks, reds, cherries, and checkered patterns. While you're here, you can also pick up your very own copy of the **Burlesque Handbook** *($17)*.

✦ S *6 to Astor Pl.* Ⓢ *T-shirts $28-35, skirts $86-92, dresses $148-178.* ⏰ *Open M-Sa noon-9-pm, Su noon-8pm.*

PATRICIA FIELD

●✦⊗ EAST VILLAGE

302 Bowery, between Bleecker and Houston St. ☎212-966-4066 ▬www.patriciafield.com

A whirlwind of sequins, spandex, and sparkles as well as sundresses with tamer patterns *(items from $5-20)* start at the front; kink (exciting underwear, huge, high-heeled shoes, thigh-high fishnets, and stripper poles) is in the back. In between is all manner of dresses, pants, shirts, jewelry, and other unclassifiable clothing and accessory items.

✦ S *F to Lower East Side/2nd Ave.* Ⓢ *Items $1-840.* ⏰ *Open M-Th 11am-8pm, F-Sa 11am-9pm, Su 11am-7pm.*

BUFFALO EXCHANGE

●✦♿ EAST VILLAGE

332 E. 11th St. ☎212-260-9340 ▬www.buffaloexchange.com

Buffalo Exchange doesn't discriminate between new and used, as long as the clothing is in line with the hottest trends in current fashion. If you need to get rid of some of your old threads, bring them in for 30% cash back or 50% in-store credit. You may be able to get an additional discount by knowing the answers to important fashion trivia (e.g. Who invented the stiletto? Hint: it begins with a "C" and ends with "hristian Louboutin").

⚹ Ⓢ *6 to Astor Pl. Located between 1st and 2nd Ave.* Ⓢ *Women's pants $9-30, women's shirts $6-25, bags $12-60, dresses $10-30, men's shirts $9-30, men's pants $14-40, shoes $9-125.* ⊠ *Open M-Sa 11am-8pm, Su noon-7pm.*

METROPOLIS
43 3rd Ave., between 9th and 10th St.

🍂♿ EAST VILLAGE
☎212-358-0795

A vintage store with a lot of 1990s grunge items and patterned dresses, Metropolis also boasts an impressive T-shirt collection.

⚹ Ⓢ *6 to Astor Pl.* Ⓢ *Prices Vary, mostly low to mid-range vintage prices.* ⊠ *Open M-W noon-9pm, Th-Sa noon-11pm, Su noon-9pm.*

VICEVERSA
241 Bedford Ave.

🍂♿ WILLIAMSBURG
☎718-782-3882 🖥www.viceversavintage.com

It's a tough call to single out any vintage clothing store in this most vintage-obsessed of neighborhoods, but smallish Viceversa is an appealing option. Its bare-bones storage space is filled to the brim with shoes, belts, and a generous selection of both men's and women's wear.

⚹ Ⓢ *L to Bedford Ave.* Ⓢ *Most items $10-25.* ⊠ *Open M-F 1-8pm, Sa-Su noon-9pm.*

BEACON'S CLOSET
88 N. 11th St.

🍂♿ WILLIAMSBURG
☎718-486-0816 🖥www.beaconscloset.com

Beacon's Closet has somehow managed to eke its way to the top of Williamsburg's vintage-clothing totem pole, but its buying policies *(only 35% in cash back)* may be too restrictive for some. Still, you've probably come here to shop—and the time-tested selection is unbeatable. There's also a smaller and more accessible branch in Park Slope.

⚹ Ⓢ *L to Bedford Ave.* *i* *Store selectively buys clothing: 35% cash, 55% store credit.* Ⓢ *Most items $5-25; shirts $7-20, shoes $10-25.* ⊠ *Open M-F 11am-9pm, Sa-Su 11am-8pm.*

fashion week fluctuations

To Fifth-Avenue frequenters, names like Marc Jacobs and Calvin Klein are synonymous with New York fashion as much as Coco Chanel's overly sprayed perfume is with the French. Recently, however, their regular biannual showings in February and September may be threatened by a sweeping trend among New York designers to forgo the elaborate costume and makeup sideshows. Instigated by the faltering economy, many American couturiers including Vera Wang and Betsey Johnson decided to cut models altogether to save on production costs in fall 2009 and opted instead for more intimate private showings. Not only that, but Bryant Park, which has hosted shows for the past 15 years, forced New York Fashion Week out to Lincoln Center for February 2010 due to disputes between designers and local management. As the New York labels scramble to find a new home for their flagrantly theatrical circus acts, some say that this will legitimize them as real artists, not just people obsessed with clothes. Good luck on that one.

thrift shops

◈ UNIQUE BOUTIQUE
⊛ & UPPER EAST SIDE

1674 3rd Ave., between 93rd and 94th   ☎212-427-0077

A thrift store among thrift stores, Unique Boutique offers a broad selection of men and women's clothing, accessories, and furniture, all for prices so low you'll forget you're in a city where you had to pay $5 for a cup of coffee this morning.
⊹ Ⓢ 6 to 96th St. Ⓢ Tops $5-15, dresses up to $20. ⏰ Open M-Sa 10am-9pm, Su 11am-8pm.

ANGEL STREET THRIFT SHOP
◆ & CHELSEA

228 W. 17th St., between 6th and 7th Ave.   ☎212-229-1941 ▦www.angelthriftshop.org

Just because you're thrifty doesn't mean you can't have style. Angel Street Thrift Shop is a fancy boutique store in every sense except for its impact on your finances. You'll find tuxedos (pieces $1-10), designer clothing, and elegant furniture at prices that will make you do double takes. They even provide a section at the front highlighting the season's latest looks.
⊹ Ⓢ F, L, M to 6th Ave./14th St. Ⓢ Men's shirts $10-25, men's pants $17-30, tuxedo pieces $1-10, jeans $10-30, furniture $15-150, skirts $15-80, dresses $15-80, shoes $10-50. ⏰ Open M-F 11am-7pm, Sa 10am-7pm, Su noon-5pm.

HOUSING WORKS
◆ & CHELSEA

157 W. 17th St., between 6th and 7th Ave.   ☎212-366-0820 ▦www.housingworks.org

At Housing Works, you really could get all the necessities of your domicile with everything from clothing, to furniture, to the obligatory piano ($350) and giant scrabble cube ($100). Find the perfect glossy book to plop on that artsy new table in the entertainment section in the back.
⊹ Ⓢ 1 to 18th St. Ⓢ Shoes $10-45, dresses $10-45, men's pants $10-20, jeans from $8, men's shirts $8-25, furniture $50-$420, books $3-12, CDs $1, cassettes and VHS tapes $0.50, records $3. ⏰ Open M-F 10am-7pm, Sa 10am-6pm, Su noon-5pm.

antique stores

UGLY LUGGAGE
WILLIAMSBURG, BROOKLYN

214 Bedford Ave.   ☎718-384-0724

Ugly Luggage packs a random sampling of cool furniture items from 1850 to 2010 into its rather small space. Randomness is compounded by tags with non sequitur phrases above the unpredictable prices.
⊹ Ⓢ L to Bedford Ave. Ⓢ Prices vary. ⏰ Open M-F 1-8pm, Sa-Su noon-7pm.

LAS VENUS LOUNGE 20TH CENTURY POP CULTURE
◆⊗ LOWER EAST SIDE

163 Ludlow St., at Stanton St.   ☎212-982-0608 ▦www.lasvenus.com

When you look at some of the vintage 1960s chairs, lamps, and art at Las Venus you can almost hear the Beatles playing. Specializing in vintage mid-century furniture and art, Las Venus has dozens of funky items that will boost the character factor of your living environment. Be warned: the treasures at this store are not cheap. If you can't afford to spend $175 or more on a lamp, treat it like a museum.
⊹ Ⓢ F, J, M, Z to Delancey St./Essex St. Ⓢ Art pieces $225-1650, chairs $1500-4000, lamps $175-1650, table decorations $45-65. ⏰ Open M-F 11am-8pm, Sa-Su noon-8pm.

ARCHANGEL ANTIQUES
◆⊗ EAST VILLAGE

334 E. 9th St.   ☎212-260-9313

An underground cache of collectibles. Highlights include an extensive collection of vintage eyeglasses and sunglasses, a stock of 2.5 million buttons, and a

antique stores

manager named Michael who knows how every single item in the store fits into the history of fashion.

✼ Ⓢ 6 to Astor Pl. Located between 1st and 2nd Ave. 🕐 Open Tu-Su 3-7pm.

bookstores

▨ STRAND BOOKSTORE
✎♿❄ GREENWICH VILLAGE

Corner of 12th St. and Broadway ☎212-473-1452 🖥www.strandbooks.com

There's little doubt remaining that the Strand is New York's best bookstore—that is, if you're after a store with the most items, the most eclectic collection, and the greatest variety of subjects. Its popularity is attested to by the ubiquitous tote bags, a familiar sight well beyond New York, and by the crowds of people cramming into its sizable, 3 fl. area at seemingly every open hour. A range of new, used, and antique books crowd its 18 mi. of shelves, all well organized into sections (signs indicate which subjects are on which floor). Even unusual groupings—like "Americana"—seem endless. Shelves of antique books populate the first floor, while new books (some offered at half price) are advertised closer to the entrance. It's been around since 1927, and doesn't look to be going anywhere. Make this one of your first downtown stops.

✼ Ⓢ L, N, Q, R, 4, 5, 6 to 14th St.-Union Square. 𝒊 Store buys books M-Sa 9:3am-6pm. Ⓢ Prices vary widely; books on sale outside $1; books inside $5-$30. 🕐 Open daily 9:30am-10:30pm.

▨ SHAKESPEARE AND CO.
✎♿ GREENWICH VILLAGE

716 Broadway ☎212-529-1330 🖥www.shakeadco.com

The New York branch of the famous Parisian English-language bookshop that helped publish Joyce's *Ulysses* lives up to its illustrious pedigree: its two floors of books cater to both the intrigued visitor's and hardcore bibliophile's tastes. A great fiction selection spearheads the collection here; be sure to check out the New York section for a variety of books that go well beyond the usual tourist hustle.

✼ Ⓢ N, R to 8th St. Ⓢ Books $8-40. 🕐 Open M-Sa 10am-9:30pm, Su 11am-9pm.

▨ SPOONBILL AND SUGARTOWN
✎♿ WILLIAMSBURG, BROOKLYN

218 Bedford Ave. ☎718-387-7322 🖥www.spoonbillbooks.com

Williamsburg's premier bookstore offers a mix of new and used, with a focus on the used and a heavier focus on art books, most behind the glass case to the back. The selection is never predictable; you may find new releases here, but they're bound to be unrecognizable. Come for the literature, stay for the adorable cat often seen prowling the grounds.

✼ Ⓢ L to Bedford Ave. 𝒊 Buys used books. Ⓢ Most books $1-30. 🕐 Open daily 10am-10pm.

THREE LIVES AND CO.
✎⊗❄ WEST VILLAGE

Corner of W 10th St. and Waverly Pl. ☎212-741-2069 🖥www.threelives.com

Three Lives is as classy and literate as the quiet neighborhood outside. Titles by highly regarded authors are crammed into a pleasant, wood-lined space; it seems bigger than it actually is, which is a testament to the variety and depth of its selection. Three Lives also hosts notable authors for signing events; check the website for upcoming events.

✼ Ⓢ 1 to Christopher St.-Sheridan Sq. Ⓢ Most items $10-35. 🕐 Open M-Tu noon-8pm, W-Sa noon-8:30pm, Su noon-7pm.

ARGOSY BOOKSTORE
✎ UPPER EAST SIDE

116 E. 59th St. ☎212-753-4455 🖥www.argosybooks.com

Whether you're a book connoisseur looking to spend hundreds of dollars on the newest addition to your collection or just looking for a used novel to read on your trip, you'll find what you're looking for at Argosy Bookstore. Priceless (or rather, highly-priced) treasures from the 16th and 17th century on the ground floor, with an expansive collection of second-hand books in the basement.

✦ Ⓢ N, R, W, 4, 5, 6 to 59th St. Located between Lexington Ave. and Park Ave. ⌚ Open M-F 10am-6pm, Sa 10am-5pm. Closed Sa May-Sep.

bookstores

WESTSIDER BOOKS AND RECORDS
233 W. 72nd St.

●⊗ UPPER WEST SIDE

☎212-874-1588 🖳www.westsiderbooks.com

A literary and audio-visual treasure trove. In addition to the thousands of books, records, CDs and pieces of sheet music they sell, this store will convert your VHS tapes to DVDs and your cassettes to CDs ($25-35).

✦ Ⓢ 1, 2, 3 to 72nd St. Located between Broadway and West End Ave. Ⓢ Books $0.50-$1,000. ⌚ Open M-Th 11am-7pm, F-Sa 10am-9pm, Su noon-6pm.

ACADEMY ANNEX
96 N 6th St.

●♿ WILLIAMSBURG, BROOKLYN

☎718-218-8200 🖳www.academyannex.com

Pile upon teeming pile of used LPs grace the Academy Annex; CDs and DVDs inevitably take a back seat. Selections range from old folk to plain oldies to plain obscure. They also stock new reissue items. New or used, the dirt-cheap records here represent an impressive array of genres.

✦ Ⓢ L to Bedford Ave. 𝒊 Buys used records. Ⓢ Most items $5-15. DVDs $6-9. ⌚ Open M-Th noon-8pm, F-Sa noon-10pm, Su noon-8pm.

BOOKS OF WONDER
18 W. 18th St.

●♿ CHELSEA

☎212-989-3270 🖳www.booksofwonder.net

A children's bookstore so magical you'll wish you were one of the Lost Boys from J.M. Barrie's *Peter Pan*. Along with a stellar collection of new children's books, the store also carries a large quantity of antique books. Events such as art shows, author talks, and workshops are frequent. Savor a cupcake and book at the same time at its irresistibly adorable **Cupcake Cafe** *(cupcakes $2.50-4)*.

✦ Ⓢ F, M to 23rd St./Ave. of the Americas. Located between between 5th and 6th Ave. Ⓢ New books standard bookstore prices. Antique books up to $75,000. ⌚ Open M-Sa 10am-7pm, Su 11am-6pm.

THE DRAMA BOOKSHOP
250 E. 40th St., between 7th and 8th

●♿♟ MIDTOWN WEST

☎212-944-0595 🖳www.dramabookshop.com

Specializing in plays and literature about plays, this one-stop-drama-shop is crawling with acting students looking for monologues, technique help, and agent information. It's also patronized by tourists who tend to buy vintage drama posters and 🎭**Shakespeare dolls.**

✦ Ⓢ 1, 2, 3, N, W, S to 42nd St./Times Square; A, C, E to 42nd St./Port Authority. 𝒊 Complimentary wine and cheese tastings Th 6pm. Ⓢ Prices vary; many books in the $15-$50 range. ⌚ Open M-Sa 11am-7pm.

BLUESTOCKINGS
172 Allen St., between Rivington and Stanton St.

●♿ LOWER EAST SIDE

☎212-777-6028 🖳www.bluestockings.com

An activist center and hipster hangout where genres include Anarchism, Activist Strategies, and Comics/Graphic Novels. The shop also boasts a political pamphlet section *($1-3)*, featuring "On Vegetarianism: The Great Kinship between Humans and Fauna." In the way of non-literary offerings, the bookstore additionally has fair trade coffee and tea available for purchase, as well as a series of pro-bicycle T-shirts.

✦Ⓢ F, J, M, Z to Delancey St./Essex St. Ⓢ Most books $13-$40. Political pamphlets $1-3. T-shirts $15-20. ⌚ Open daily 8am-11pm.

ST. MARK'S BOOKSHOP
31 3rd Ave., at E 9th St.

●♿ EAST VILLAGE

☎212-260-7853 🖳www.stmarksbookshop.com

One of a great but dying breed of independent, non-used bookstores. A corner in the back of the store sells angsty poetry, zines, and cassette tapes self-published on consignment *($2-8)*. The bookstore also has a terrific magazine selection, with a special emphasis on art and literary magazines *($4-30)*.

✚ Ⓢ 6 to Astor Pl. ⌚ Open M-Sa 10am-midnight, Su 11am-midnight.

food shops

🖋 ZABARS
⬦🕭 GROCERY STORE ❷

2245 Broadway, between 80th and 81st. ☎212-787-2000 🖥www.zabars.com

The first thing you'll see when you walk into Zabars is the "Cheese Department." Not just a section, but an entire *department*, filled with more cheese than you've ever seen in your life *($3.79-$23 per lb.)*. You may be tempted to stop right here (it's happened to many a shopper), but press on to the decadent bakery *(items $1.50-$11)*, the deli with freshly prepared packaged meals *($7-8.49)*, the barrels of fresh coffee beans *($7-8 per lb.)*, and the olive bar, offering an abundance of different olive choices for $7 per pound. Next door to the grocery store (slightly more upscale than your average grocery store) is a cafe with a seating area for enjoying sandwiches *($5.50)*, smoothies *($4)*, and pastries*($1.50-$3)*.

✚ Ⓢ 1 to 79th St. Ⓢ Cafe sandwiches $5.50. Quiche $7. Smoothies $4. Coffee $1-3. Pastries $1.50-$3. ⌚ Grocery store M-F 8am-7:30pm, Sa 8am-8pm, Su 9am-6pm; cafe M-F 7am-7pm, Sa 7:30am-7pm, Su 8am-6pm.

BESPOKE CHOCOLATES
⬦🕭 EAST VILLAGE

6 Extra Pl. ☎212-260-7103 🖥www.bespokechocolates.com

Follow the tantalizing scent of freshly made chocolate down a tiny alley for a gourmet treat you will never forget. The shop's specialty is the pretzel-covered sea-salted caramel. They warn that you should pop it all in your mouth at once, lest you lose any of the caramel goodness. Other delectable flavors include the chai spice, hazelnut praline, and white chocolate toasted almond truffle.

✚ Ⓢ 6 to Bleecker St.; or F to 2nd Ave./Lower East Side; or B, D, F, M to Broadway/Lafayette St. Located on E. 1st St and Bond St. Ⓢ Chocolates $2.25. Chocolate hazelnut spread $15. Pretzel bark $4.50. Chocolate almond toffee $7.50. ⌚ Open Tu-F 11am-7pm, Sa-Su noon-8pm.

DEAN AND DELUCA
⬦🕭 SOHO

560 Broadway, at Prince St. ☎212-430-8300 🖥www.deandeluca.com

The original Dean and DeLuca gourmet grocery store (founded 1977) is alive and kicking in SoHo. This is not the place to come for your day-to-day grocery needs, but for a fine cheese or a souvenir tin of Dean and DeLuca Tea, it is worth a stop. High-end dish and cookware can be found in the back, including some pretty surprising items, like Mexican *molinillos ($14)* and dishes made from recycled materials *($7)*. A livestock-shaped cookie labeled "Party Animal" might also tickle your fancy during your visit.

✚ Ⓢ N, Q, R to Prince St. Ⓢ Pastries $2-5. Cheeses $14-42 per lb. Fruit $3-7 per lb. Pasta $4.50-$8 per pack. Breads $4-10. Flowers $9-20 per dozen. ⌚ Open M-F 7am-8pm, Sa-Su 8am-8pm.

liquor stores

New York is a great place to drink beers and cocktails, but if you'd rather drink from a handle there are tons of high-quality liquor stores to help you find exactly what you need.

HEIGHTS CHATEAU
⬦🕭♿❄ BROOKLYN HEIGHTS

123 Atlantic Ave. ☎718-330-0963 🖥www.heightschateau.com

A classy liquor store for a classy neighborhood. The Chateau stocks an enormous collection from all over the world, so you can go from Australia to France without having to seek out specialty stores. The prices can exceed airfare, but luckily the owners keep discount bottles up front—consider it a student deal.

✈ Ⓢ M, R, 2, 3, 4, 5 to Borough Hall. Walk to Henry St. and Atlantic Ave. Ⓢ Discount items $8-15. Other items $10-80. ⓠ Open M-W 10am-9:30pm, Th-Sa 10am-10pm.

BOWERY AND VINE
♿♂ LOWER EAST SIDE
269 Bowery ☎212-941-7943

Whether you're a wine and liquor connoisseur looking for something special or you just like a cheap bottle of wine once in a while, you'll be able to find something here that appeals to your interests and, er, wallet. They place large selections of wines in the $8-25 range separated by country in the middle of the store. Italian vermouth starts at $6, Japanese sake at $10, and there's lots and lots of Stoli starting at $28.

✈ Ⓢ B, D, F, M to Broadway/Lafayette, or F to 2nd Ave./Lower East Side; or 6 to Bleecker St. Located between E. Houston and Stanton. Ⓢ Wines $5-160. ⓠ Open M-Th 11am-10pm, F-Sa 11am-11pm, Su noon-9pm. Tastings Th-Sa.

SAKAYA
♿♂ EAST VILLAGE
324 E. 9th St. ☎212-505-7253 ▣www.sakenyc.com

Sake all the way from the land of Japan. The Kikusi Funaguchi ($7), which comes in a 200mL can and has a high alcoholic content, is a bestseller. For something slightly fancier, check out the more expensive options ($35-40). If you really want to go hard, you can pick up a bottle of Katchou Gesseki ($96).

✈ Ⓢ 6 to Astor Pl. Walk to 9th St. between 1st and 2nd Ave. Ⓢ Sake $7-96. ⓠ Open M-Sa noon-8pm, Su noon-7pm.

hardware stores

If you're just in town for the weekend, you may not need to worry about finding pliers. But if you're living here for a while, here are some places to go for home improvement.

BOWERY HOME SUPPLIES
♿♂ LOWER EAST SIDE
270 Bowery ☎212-505-0022 ▣www.boweryhomesupplies.com

Primarily specializing in lumber, Bowery Home Supplies also has all of the nuts and bolts of home repair. It's also a great place to pick up a broom, a measuring tape, or a tube of Gorilla or Sumo glue.

✈ Ⓢ B, D, F, M to Broadway/Lafayette St.; or F to 2nd St./Lower East Side. Located between Stanton and E. Houston St. 𝒊 Credit card min. $15. Ⓢ Prices vary. ⓠ Open M-F 8am-5pm, Sa 10am-4pm.

SAIFEE HARDWARE
♿♂ EAST VILLAGE
114 1st Ave. ☎212-979-6396 ▣www.saifeehardware.com

Literally anything you could possibly need for your home or garden, you can find at Saifee. They have your standard paints, tools, gardening supplies, etc. but they also have all of those obscure products on which somebody owns a very un-lucrative patent, like shower strainers ($3.75). They also have lots of items for making your living space more pleasing to the senses: candles, flowers, incense and other such embellishments.

✈ Ⓢ 6 to Astor Pl. Located between 6th and 7th St. Ⓢ Paint from $16 per quart. Potted plants from $3. Extension cords from $3. Duct tape from $3. Seeds from $1.69/pack. Gardening shovels from $3.50. Trash cans from $7.49. Incense 5 for $1. Keys $1.39. ⓠ Open M-Sa 8:30am-7:30pm, Su 10am-6:30pm.

furniture

No doubt about it, you can find your Crate and Barrels and your Pottery Barns in New York City. But the City is also a great place to find furniture that has a little more character.

MOMA DESIGN STORE 💳♿ SOHO

81 Spring St. ☎646-613-1367 💻www.momastore.org

Halfway between a museum and a store, this is the place to go if you want to turn your home into a work of art...or at least to fill it with cool, quirky objects. You can pick up an FPE (Fantastic Plastic Elastic) chair designed by Ron Arad *($335)*, a Z Bar LED lamp by Peter Ng *($195-215)*, and Nesting Tables conceived by Joseph Albers in 1926-27 *($1,950)*. You can make your books look like they're hovering in space by using the handy dandy conceal bookshelf designed by Miron Lior *($15)*.

➜ [S] B, D, F, M to Broadway/Lafayette; or 6 to Spring St. Located between Broadway and Crosby St. $ Prices vary by object and designer. Chairs $200-800. Lamps $110-2000. Vases $48-65. M and Co. clocks $52-395. ⏰ Open M-Sa 10am-8pm, Su 11am-7pm.

MUJI ⊗💳 SOHO

455 Broadway, between Grand St. and Howard St. ☎212-334-2002 💻www.muji.us

Furniture at its most space and energy-efficient, the wares at Muji are designed in Japan and available almost exclusively in shades of brown, grey, and off-white. You can purchase a steel pipe side table *($90)* that fits perfectly over your pocket coil mattress with legs *($500-700)* and lay your head on a urethane foam cube *($50)*. Tuck your cardboard, foldable speakers *($40)* in a cotton linen storage box *($50)* and iron your clothing on a steel mesh ironing board *($30-50)*, designed to evaporate steam and absorb heat at a far superior rate than your run-of-the-mill ironing boards.

➜ [S] N, Q, R to Canal St. $ Pillows $20. Beds $400-1100. Comforters $250-$475. ⏰ Open M-Sa 11am-9pm, Su 11am-8pm.

JACQUES CARCANAGUES 💳 SOHO

21 Greene St., between Canal St. and Grand St. ☎212-925-8110 💻www.jacquescarcanagues.com

Remember the masks at the beginning of *Spiderman?* How about the rug the Richard Gere uses to wrap Olivier Martinez's dead body in *Unfaithful?* Both came from SoHo's Jacques Carcanaguas, which carries new and antique furnishings from Southeast Asia.

➜ [S] 1, A, C, E, N, Q, R, 6, J, M, Z to Canal St. $ Furniture pieces $5-20,000. ⏰ Open Tu-Sa 11am-6:30pm.

miscellaneous stores

👍 **ACADEMY RECORDS AND CDS** 💳♿❄ FLATIRON DISTRICT

12 W. 18th St. ☎212-242-3000 💻www.academy-records.com

Unlike many record shops in nearby Greenwich Village, Academy maintains a refreshing, healthy balance of classical music to accompany its still sizable stacks of obscure classic rock and alternative, along with a smattering of more recent indie cuts. You can go for the used LPs *($1-5)*, but Academy has also made the wise choice to truck heavily in CDs as well. Check out their bargain collection *(CDs $1-3)*. Really, it's only a little more than a pirated download, and a lot more legal.

[S] L, N, Q, R, 4, 5, 6 to 14th St.-Union Sq. $ Bargain items $1-8. Most other items $15-50. ⏰ Open M 11am-7pm, Tu-Sa 11am-8pm, Su 11am-7pm.

JAN'S HOBBY SHOP — UPPER EAST SIDE

1435 Lexington Ave. ☎212-987-4765

Enough toy airplanes, ships, and toy soldiers to cause a model apocalypse. Buy pre-fab or do-it-yourself!

[S] 6 to 96th St. Located between 93rd and 94th St. ⏰ Open M-Sa 10am-6:30pm, Su noon-5pm.

BROOKLYN SUPERHERO SUPPLY COMPANY — PARK SLOPE

372 5th Ave. at 5th St. ☎718-499-9884 www.superherosupplies.com

The plethora of text on the Company's sign announces that "dastardly plots will be foiled" while promising "supersonic shipping to select universes." Inside, truth serum, super stretch gels, chin ladders, and of course capes are available at relatively bargain prices. The store is a front for 826 Valencia, a writing and tutoring center for local children, but the retail is real. All proceeds go to the organization, so you can help yourself and others by purchasing quirky gadgets.

[S] F, M, R to 9th St.-4th Ave. $ Most items $8-25. ⏰ Open daily 11:30am-5pm.

REBEL REBEL — GREENWICH VILLAGE

319 Bleecker St. ☎212-989-0778 www.rebelrebelmusic.com

For one, Rebel Rebel's interior is almost impossible to navigate due to the teeming boxes of LPs crowding the floor. But the selection also spills outside, where more records and CDs ensnare innocent bystanders. From the posters on the wall to the records themselves, the emphasis here is on classic rock, with most of the items dating from the '60s to the '80s. But new releases can also be discovered amidst the Bowie and Captain Beefheart. LPs are the focus, though many CDs can be had for great deals.

[S] A, B, C, D, E, F, V to W 4th St. $ CDs $2, 10 for $6, 15 for $10. LPs $10-25. ⏰ Open W noon-8pm, Th-Sa noon-9pm, Su noon-8pm.

VILLAGE CHESS SHOP — GREENWICH VILLAGE

230-234 Thompson St. ☎212-475-9580 www.chess-shop.com

The Village Chess Shop has been insomniac chess addicts' haven since 1972. Yes, you can play chess any time of the day—all week—for the tidy sum of $2.50 per hr. The small interior is filled with tables; there are more outside if the weather's right. The non-profit club also features lectures and tournaments, buys and sells a wide variety of chess materials and books, and offers other classic board games like checkers and backgammon.

[S] A, B, C, D, E, F, V to West 4th St. *i* $5 min. from 2-7am. $ $2.50 per hr. Most items $3-15. ⏰ Open 24hr.

MYERS OF KESWICK — GREENWICH VILLAGE

634 Hudson St. ☎212-691-4194 www.myersofkeswick.com

More than enough cure for the nostalgic Anglophile inside you, Myers stocks up on all things British, from Walker's chips to Union Jacks to Cornish pastries. The bulk of the store is devoted to common grocery items you could find in most London corner shops, but most of the delicious can be had in the fresh foods section—where deli meats, cheeses, and small snack items like steak and kidney, sausage rolls, and curried lamb pies await your fancy.

[S] A, C, E to 14th St./8th Ave. $ Most items $2-10. Fresh foods $3-5. ⏰ Open M-F 10am-7pm, Sa 10am-6pm, Su noon-5pm.

LEATHER MAN — GREENWICH VILLAGE

111 Christopher St. ☎212-243-5339 www.theleatherman.com

The area around Christopher St. has its fair share of gay-themed sex shops, but Leather Man whips them into submission with its large, unique selection. You'll find the expected leather items alongside other costumes, dildoes, books, and DVDs. But they also have perfectly legitimate leather clothes, including belts that may just attract the serious leather customer.

⚡ S *A, B, C, D, E, F, V to West 4th St.* Ⓢ *Prices $6-25.* Ⓩ *Open M-Sa noon-8:45pm, Su noon-7:45pm.*

THE LOST WORLD
⊜⊗ GREENWICH VILLAGE

215 Thompson St. ☎212-388-1466

His Dudeness would have probably dug the Village, so this is his makeshift home: a tiny cubby of a store packed with *Big Lebowski* memorabilia, from T-shirts emblazoned with the all-too-familiar figures of Donny, the Jesus, and the Dude Himself. You can also get life-size cardboard cutouts, paintings and drawings, and bobble heads. The owner stays pretty much in character by walking around all day in a bathrobe. The store's previous lives as a comic-book store and children's bookshop still show in the varied selection on display, while the rest of recent pop culture is represented in a quirky offering of DVDs—including, of course, the Movie itself.

⚡ S *A, B, C, D, E, F, V to West 4th St.* Ⓢ *Prices $10-30.* Ⓩ *Open M-Sa 11am-7pm, Su noon-6pm.*

TENDER BUTTONS
⊜ UPPER EAST SIDE

143 E. 62nd St. ☎212-758-7004

For over 40 years, Tender Buttons has provided the Upper East Side with millions of buttons. If you carelessly lost the button on your Renaissance doublet, you'll find a replacement here.

⚡ S *4, 5, 6, N, R, W to 59th St. Walk uptown to 62nd St. between 3rd Ave. and Lexington Ave.* Ⓢ *Buttons $1-1500.* Ⓩ *Open M-F 10:30am-6pm, Sat, 10:30am-5:30pm.*

BEADS OF PARADISE
⊜Ɫ❄ FLATIRON DISTRICT

16 E. 17th St. ☎212-620-0642 ✉www.beadsofparadisenyc.com

Beads of Paradise rests squarely in the packed-attic retail tradition: African masks, Asiatic souvenirs, religious memorabilia, and miscellaneous toys all stare, dumbfounded, at one another. But the focus here is of course on beads and everything you can do with them. Come here to satisfy all your beaded jewelry needs; pick up a crucifix or miniature Buddha on your way out.

⚡ S *L, N, Q, R, 4, 5, 6 to 14th St.-Union Sq.* ⓘ *Craft classes Su 12:30, 3:30pm.* Ⓢ *Most items $20-60.* Ⓩ *Open M-Sa 11am-7:30pm, Su noon-6:30pm.*

EXCURSIONS

If you've been in fast-paced NYC for some time, you might be dying to trade in sky-scrapers for cottages and pavement for sand dunes. Luckily, there are a number of short excursions from the city that offer respite—but adventurous respite, nonethe-less. Whether you're looking to trace the steps of the Headless Horseman in Sleepy Hollow, camp out on Fire Island, sunbathe at Jones Beach, or savor clams at Oyster Bay, an exciting daytrip is within your reach.

greatest hits

- **CHANNEL TEDDY.** Visit Sagamore Hill (p. 198) in Oyster Bay, the former residence of President Theodore Roosevelt.

- **BEATS ON THE BEACH.** Hit up a concert at the Nikon open-air amphitheater (p. 200) on Jones Beach.

- **BURN, BABY, BURN.** Disco into the wee hours of the night at Ice Palace (p. 202) on Fire Island.

- **GET SPOOKED.** Head to Old Dutch Church (p. 204) in Sleepy Hollow, the old stomping ground of the Headless Horseman.

oyster bay ☎516

ORIENTATION

The silent streets and small-town atmosphere of **Oyster Bay** stand in stark contrast to the energetic metropolis of New York City. Visitors come to the Bay, located at the center of the northern portion of Long Island, for quality seafood and close proximity to the homes of several important American historical figures. It's kind of like **MTV Cribs**, but with American history.

ACCOMMODATIONS

EAST NORWICH INN   ♥ & HOTEL ❸
6321 Northern Blvd., East Norwich   ☎516-922-1500 ✉www.eastnorwichinn.com

A lovely overnight option just a 15min. walk or 5min. drive from Oyster Bay. Rooms include microwaves, refrigerators, free Wi-Fi, cable, and HBO. They are proud of the fact that they sometimes host wedding parties.

⚑ *Take 106 (Oyster Bay Road) South to 25A.* ⓘ *Continental breakfast included.* ⓢ *2 double beds or 1 king-sized bed $117 plus tax, 2 double beds and a living room $230 plus tax, 1 king-sized bed or 2 double beds and a living room $250 plus tx.* ⌚ *Reception 24hr.*

TIDES MOTOR INN   ♥ HOTEL ❷
2 Bayville Ave., Locust Valley, NY   ☎516-671-7070✉www.thetidesmotorinn.com

Slightly farther away than East Norwich (about a 15min. drive), but also slightly more budget-friendly. With an outdoor pool and a location directly across the street from the Long Island Sound, this is the perfect hotel to help you get your water fix. Tennis courts are also on the premises.

⚑ *From Oyster Bay, take W. Main St. northwest until it becomes W. Shore Rd. Turn left onto Bayville Ave.* ⓢ *1 bed $95, 2 beds $125, 2 beds with kitchen $145.* ⌚ *Reception 24hr.*

SIGHTS

SAGAMORE HILL   ♥ HISTORIC RESIDENCE
12 Sagamore Hill Rd.   ☎516-922-4788 ✉www.nps.gov/sahi

The chief reason you might want to visit the quiet town of **Oyster Bay** is to see Sagamore Hill, the residence of dynamic Theodore Roosevelt and the Summer White House from 1902 to 1908. Oyster Rides charges a base fee of $12 and an additional $3 per person for service to Sagamore Hill from Oyster Bay. You can dine on American delicacies such as hot dogs and hamburgers, listen to the **Sagamore Hill Band** play "The Stars and Stripes Forever," and meet a confused-yet-talented man dressed up as Teddy Roosevelt.

⚑ *From 106 North turn right on to Route 25A (Northern Blvd.) and travel 2½ mi. to the Cove Rd. stoplight. Turn left onto Cove Rd. and travel for 1.7 mi. to Cove Neck Rd. Turn right on Cove Neck Rd. and follow the signs for 1.5 mi. to Sagamore Hill Rd. and turn right. Follow Sagamore Hill Rd. to the end and you will see the visitors center.* ⓘ *Continental breakfast included.* ⓢ *Tours $5. Museum and grounds free.* ⌚ *Visitors center open daily 9am-5pm. Park open from dawn to dusk. House tours daily every hr. 10am to 4pm.*

FOOD

BONANZA'S ITALIAN ICE   ⊛& ITALIAN ICES ❶
25 Shore Ave., on Maxwell Ave.   ☎516-922-7796

The Bonanza family has proudly distributed Italian shaved ice to Oyster Bay-ites for 114 years. Although the most popular flavors are the original lemon, chocolate, and strawberry, Bonanza's boasts a flavor list that would put most ice cream shops to shame. If you're feeling adventurous, try the graham cracker swirl, pumpkin, or even peanut butter and jelly. The shop also offers a "fun food" list

including items such as hot dogs (*$2*) and the "Sloppy Bo" (*chili on a bun, $1.75*).
✚ Ⓜ *Oyster Bay. From Train Station, walk Southeast down Shore Ave.* Ⓢ *Small $2, large $2.10. Other food $2-8.50.* 🕘 *Open daily 11am-9pm; closes around 5pm during winter months.*

🖼 CAFE AL DENTE
2 Spring St.

🍷🚻♿ RESTAURANT ❷
☎516-922-2442

An adorable little establishment that is a unique blend of Italian and Oyster Bay—and the mix works well for them. Try the delicious Buffalo Calamari Salad (*$10.50*) or Lobster Ravioli (*$15*). Portions are large enough to feed Roosevelt's Rough Riders.
✚ *From the train station, walk southeast on Shore Ave. until you come to the intersection of Audrey Ave. and Shore Ave.* Ⓢ *Appetizers $5-12.50. Salads $4-12.50. Entrees $13-19. Pasta $7.50-15. Personal Pizzas $7. Burgers and sandwiches $7.25-11. Beer $4.25-$5.75.* 🕘 *Open daily noon-9pm.*

OYSTER BAY FISH AND CLAM BAR
103 Pine Hollow Rd., at Rte. 106

🍷🚻♿ RESTAURANT ❸
☎516-922-5522

A bit of a hike from the center of town and slightly steep price-wise, this restaurant is an option if you feel the need to eat actual oysters in Oyster Bay. They have a "South of the Border Menu," (*$5-22*) and their special "Famous Seafood Platter for Two" (*$80*), which includes a 2-lb. Maine lobster, a shrimp cocktail, steamers, mussels, corn and a salad.
✚ *Take South St. directly south until it becomes Pine Hollow Rd. Restaurant will be on your left.* Ⓢ *Appetizers $8-17. Seafood $24-40. Half-dozen clams $16, dozen clams $28. Desserts $4-8.50.* 🕘 *Open April-mid Sept M-Th 11am-10pm, F-Sa 11am-11pm, Su 11am-10pm.*

ESSENTIALS 🛈

Oyster Bay is fairly small and sights are widely dispersed. For these reasons, it is important to decide which things you want to see and how to get there ahead of time.

Practicalities

- **TOURIST OFFICES:** The **Office of the Town Clerk** (☎*516-624-6333; 54 Audrey Ave.* 🕘 *Open M-F 9am-4:45pm*) has a single pamphlet about the goings-on of Oyster Bay.

- **POST OFFICE:** The beautiful, red-brick post office is located at **1 Shore Ave.** (☎*516-922-8249*) one block away from the LIRR station.

- **HOSPITAL:** **Long Island Jewish Medical Center.** (*26901 76th Ave., New Hyde Park* ☎*516- 470-3293.*)

Getting There ✈

By car, take the Long Island Expressway to Rte. 106N; follow the signs to Oyster Bay. LIRR trains travel from Penn Station to Oyster Bay with a connection in Jamaica. (Ⓢ *$10.75 peak time, $7.75 off-peak.*) For a taxi, call ☎516-921-2141.

Getting Around 🚪

Oyster Rides (*99 Pine Hollow Rd., Oyster Bay* ☎*516-922-2222*) will take you most places in Oyster Bay and the surrounding area for a fairly reasonable price. A taxi is also a viable option for sights that are not within walking distance.

jones beach ☎516

Although Jones Beach State Park is open year-round, things really start to get hot during the summer. While the park is open from sun-up to sundown most of the year, from the end of June through the beginning of September it is open from sun-up to midnight. New Yorkers like to come to Jones Beach to sunbathe, swim, and play sports in the **Game Area** and **Pitch Putt Golf Course.** In addition to all of that fun beach stuff, people flock to Jones Beach for the free concerts in the **Boardwalk Bandshell** (☎*516-679-7222* 🖥*www.jonesbeach.com*) and the less-free (but higher profile) concerts at **Nikon at Jones Beach Theater** *(☎516-221-1000).* Whatever your summer-fun style, Jones Beach can help you make it an awesome season.

ORIENTATION

In 1925, Long Island State Park Commissioner Robert Moses began plans for a beach just south of the main Long Island landmass. This was Moses' first public project in a long career that would shape the New York we know and love. The park's signature landmark is a **brick tower,** which continues to stand today despite the many replacements and remodelings Jones Beach has undergone. Today, the beach Moses designed provides 6½ mi. of fun for New Yorkers and New York tourists alike.

SIGHTS

NIKON AT JONES BEACH THEATER — CONCERT VENUE

1000 Ocean Pkwy. ☎516-221-1000 www.livenation.com/Nikon-at-Jones-Beach-Theater-tickets-Wantagh/venue/237654

A modest wooden theater built as part of a government work program once stood where the Jones Beach Theater is today. Now the venue seats over 14,000 people and is graced with the presence of pop stars ranging from Rihanna to Meat Loaf. A concert at the open-air amphitheater surrounded by water is a coveted entertainment experience indeed.

Take the JB62 bus out of Freeport. From Jones Beach, an underground path near the East Bathhouse leads from the beach across the street to the theater. $ Tickets $26-1502 Box office only open on days of events. Phone box office open all other days.

RECREATIONAL SPORTS AT JONES BEACH — LEISURE SPORTS

1 Ocean Pkwy. ☎516-785-1600 www.nysparks.state.ny.us/parks/10/details.aspx

Tired of lounging in the sun? Feel like doing something more active? Jones Beach offers plenty of sporting options so you can putt, volley, swim, and shuffle. The **Game Area** is located near the West Bathhouse, and offers beach volleyball, paddle tennis, mini golf, a playground, and shuffleboard (complete with instructional signage on the finer points of shuffleboard, in case you've forgotten). A swimming pool also lies behind the West Bathhouse. **Pitch Putt Golf,** a par three golf course, is located between the East Bathhouse and the Central Mall. What are you waiting for? Let's play!

Game Area and Pool near West Bathhouse, Pitch Putt Golf course between East Bathhouse and Central Mall. $ Paddle tennis and shuffle board $2, equipment deposit and $2 per person per 30min.; volleyball $10 per hr.; mini golf $5 per person; pool $3, children $1; pitch putt golf greens fee $7, seniors $4, club rental $2 ($3 deposit), $1 ball deposit. Activities 10am-5pm all year; longer hours during summer months. Call ahead.

FOOD

FRIENDLY'S — RESTAURANT [1]

At West Bathhouse ☎516-826-5979 www.jonesbeachevents.com

Although Friendly's ice cream is available throughout Jones Beach, this is the only spot where you can get their entire menu, including a delightfully unabridged array of ice cream options. Get soft serve *($3.75),* shakes and slammers *($5),* and, if you're feeling particularly excessive, the famous three and five scoop ice cream sundaes *($5.25-$6.50).* Real food options include burgers *($4.25-$8.50)* and Fried Clam Strips *($11.25).*

Upper Level of West Bathhouse. $ Appetizers $4-9.50. Platters $10.75-$11.75. Burgers $4.25-8.50. Ice Cream $3.75-$6.75. May 29-June 25 Sa-Su and holidays noon-6pm; extended hours after June 26.

CAFETERIAS — CAFETERIA [1]

Around Jones Beach ☎516-785-1600 www.nysparks.org

You certainly won't starve at Jones Beach. The cafeterias in the West and East

Bathhouses, Central Mall, and Field #6 are stuffed with everyone's favorite fast foods: mozzarella sticks *($6.75)*, chicken fingers *($4.75)*, personal pizzas *($5.25)*, ice cream *($4.50)*, and the like. A couple of healthier options include wraps *($6.50)*, and fresh fruit cups *($4.50)*. Enjoy your food in one of the many outdoor tables or bring it straight to your towel.

Ⓢ *Sandwiches and burgers $4-7.75, snacks $3.25-$25.25. Personal Pizzas $5.25. Fried clams $11. Fried shrimp $11.75. Ice cream $4.75. Iced coffee $4.* Ⓣ *Central Mall Cafeteria open daily 8am-7pm. East Bathhouse open Sa-Su and holidays 11am-4pm. Field #6 open March 27-May 28 M-F 9am-4pm, Sa-Su 9am-5pm; May 29-June 25 M-F 9am-5pm, Sa-Su and holidays 8am-7pm. Extended hours after June 26.*

ESSENTIALS

Practicalities

- **TOURIST OFFICES: Park Information Center** *(Central Mall* ☎516-679-7222 Ⓣ *Open Apr 30-Sept 1 daily 8am-8:30pm; Sept 2-Apr 29 daily 8am-4pm).*
- **HOSPITAL: Nassau University Medical Center.** *(East Meadow, New York* ☎516-572-6635).*

Getting There

The easiest way to reach Jones Beach is to take the Babylon-bound LIRR to Freeport. A Jones Beach Package *($16.50)* includes round-trip train fare and two rides on the N88 bus. From the Freeport Train Station, take the N88 to Jones Beach. By car, take the Long Island Expwy. E or Grand Central Pkwy. E to Northern State Pkwy. E, Wantagh Pkwy. S, and Jones Beach State Park (about 33 mi.) Parking Lot 4 is open until midnight; all others are open until sundown *($10 May-Sept, $8 Sept-Nov).*

Getting Around

The N88 bus makes three stops at Jones Beach: one at the **West Bathhouse**, one at the **Central Mall**, and one at the **East Bathhouse.** To get from one section of the beach to another, either use the bus *($2.25)* or walk.

fire island ☎631

Stretching beneath Long Island in a thin, 32 mi. strip, **Fire Island** is a relatively short train and ferry ride away from the city. The long beach along most of its southern shore is the main attraction, drawing hordes of daytrippers from the city and nearby areas of **Long Island.** The absence of roads and other infrastructure (you'll have to rely on ferries and water taxis) ensures that peaceful beach atmosphere you've always been referencing in your relationship postings on Craigslist. Fire Island is not just your everyday getaway, though; like Provincetown, it has become synonymous with a vibrant gay culture, which is manifested in exclusively gay communities and a renowned nightlife scene.

ACCOMMODATIONS

Prices are usually sky-high during summer weekends, but if you're interested in more than a quick daytrip, some expensive options are available.

WATCH HILL ⚓ CAMPSITE ❶

Watch Hill Ferry Terminal, Patchogue ☎631-567-6664 ▣www.watchhillfi.com/camping.html
For those willing to work for it, there's a hard-to-reach and very in-demand campsite on Watch Hill, accessible by **Watch Hill Ferry** from Patchogue on Long Island *(*Ⓢ *One-way $8.50, round-trip $16.* Ⓣ *6 per day in summer).* The campsite has running water, baths, showers, and grills.

⚐ *Along the middle of the Great South Bay.* 𝒊 *2-night min. Reserve your spot through a mailed* *reservation form; request processing begins Jan 1. Each site has room for two 2-man tents or one 5-person tent. $ $20 per night. ⏰ Open mid-May to mid-Oct.*

CLEGG'S HOTEL — HOTEL [4]

478 Bayberry Walk ☎631-583-9292 🖥www.cleggshotel.com

Clegg's Hotel in Ocean Beach is the most convenient spot. Its rooms are clean and no-fuss, with light blue walls lending an appropriately aquatic feel.

Right by the ferry terminal. $ M-Th doubles $160, triples $240; F-Sa $395, $595. Su $160, $240.

SIGHTS

ROBERT MOSES STATE PARK AND LIGHTHOUSE — STATE PARK

West Fire Island ☎631-321-7028 🖥www.fireislandlighthouse.com

Walk all the way to the west and you'll reach the Robert Moses State Park, which includes bath houses, a golf course, and the 19th-century **Fire Island Lighthouse** still used as an aid to navigation.

$ Tours $6. ⏰ Open Apr-June 9am-5pm, July-Labor Day 9am-6pm.

FIRE ISLAND NATIONAL SEASHORE AND SUNKEN FOREST — PARK

Seashore ☎631 289-4810 🖥www.nps.gov/fiis

You'll inevitably visit the Fire Island National Seashore, a long and always accessible strip along the island's southern shore. The beach is most crowded by Ocean Beach, but a short walk in either direction will bring you to less spoiled tracts. Just west of Cherry Grove is the **Sunken Forest** (if you're not walking, take the ferry from Sayville to Sailor's Haven), where the endless expanses of sand are replaced by a centuries-old tangle of trees mixed with holly and sassafras. Protection by dunes has allowed this unusual natural feature to develop, and it's a welcome spot of shade if the unrelenting summer sun is getting to you. A 1½ mi. raised boardwalk winds through the forest. At the island's eastern edge is the isolated **Smith Point County Park,** most easily accessible by car from Long Island. A black granite memorial to the victims of the TWA 800, which crashed in 1996 near the shore, sits amidst the dunes.

NIGHTLIFE

Nightlife on the island, a main weekend draw, caters mostly to gay men and is centered around the communities of **Cherry Grove** and **Fire Island Pines.** Parties often spill out onto these villages' boardwalks. The area of beach, dune, and vegetation between the two is known as the Meat Rack, where rampant cruising has led the Gay Men's Health Crisis to hang condoms on the trees.

ICE PALACE — NIGHTCLUB

Grove Hotel, Cherry Grove ☎631-597-6600 🖥www.grovehotel.com

The main nightclub in Cherry Grove is the Ice Palace, attached to the Grove Hotel. A steady stream of DJs and underwear parties throughout the summer keep things moving.

Take Sayville Ferry across Great South Bay to Cherry Grove. ⏰ Open May-Oct daily 9:30am-4am.

BLUE WHALE AND PAVILION — BAR, CLUB

Grove Hotel, Cherry Grove ☎631-597-6600 🖥www.grovehotel.com

Nightlife in Fire Island Pines has an established, decades-old rhythm: "Low Tea" takes place at the Blue Whale on Harbor Walk from about 5-8pm, followed by "High Tea" at the nearby Pavilion from 8-10pm. The Pavilion is a disco, so you can fill in the rest.

Across from ferry. ⏰ Blue Whale open M-Th 6-9pm, F-Su 11am-midnight.

FESTIVALS

THE PINES PARTY AND INVASION OF THE PINES — BEACH PARTIES

Beachside ☎631-597-6060 🖥www.pinesparty.com

Fire Island has its fair share of summer celebrations. The Pines Party is an expensive, all-day beach party held on one day each July near Fire Island Pines. The Invasion of the Pines, held every year on July 4, commemorates an event from Fire Island's more conservative past: a man dressed in drag was refused entry to a restaurant in 1976, sparking a literal boatload of drag queens who "invaded" Fire Island Pines from Cherry Grove on Independence Day in protest. Now, every Independence Day, a huge gathering of drag queens meets in the Ice Palace (see above), parades through Cherry Grove, then repeats the triumphant ferry ride to Fire Island Pines.

West Fire Island. $ Tickets $140-$160.

ESSENTIALS

Getting There

By Train

Long Island Railroad (☎877-LIRR-TSM) stations are near the three mainland ferry terminals for Fire Island. From Penn Station in New York City, you can take the Montauk Branch of the LIRR to get to Bay Shore, Sayville, and Patchogue. You can easily walk from the Patchogue station to the Watch Hill ferry terminal, but a taxi or van may be welcome for the longer distance between the other trains and ferries.

tarrytown and sleepy hollow ☎914

ORIENTATION

Though it's an easy train ride away from the cacophony of New York, the area around quiet Tarrytown provided some of the most recognizable pastoral settings in American literature. **Washington Irving** lived and died near here on his famous estate, Sunnyside. He's the man famous for immortalizing Sleepy Hollow, a village north of Tarrytown, in one of the earliest classic American stories. Today, the area has the usual look of well-to-do Northeastern towns near cities, with an immaculate, retail-heavy main street leading to quiet byways surrounded by forests. Walking to catch all the nearby sights doesn't have to be a chore.

SIGHTS

PHILIPSBURG MANOR

♿ HISTORIC ESTATE

381 North Broadway ☎914-631-3992 🖥www.hudsonvalley.org

The Philipsburg Manor, a colonial-era estate founded in 1693, was a farming and trading center rented out to various tenants from Europe and was home to 23 African slaves—the largest such community in the North. Tours take you around the 18th-century manor house, barn, and grounds, where you'll learn everything you always wanted to know about farm life in New Netherlands.

Walk 1 mi. north of the Tarrytown center along Broadway. $ $12. ⏰ Open Apr-Oct M and W-Su 10am-5pm; Nov-Dec Sa-Su 10am-4pm.

SUNNYSIDE

HISTORIC ESTATE

9 W. Sunnyside Ln. ☎914-591-8763 🖥www.hudsonvalley.org

Washington Irving's beloved Sunnyside estate is now open to tourists. The stately, ivy-covered mansion itself is only accessible through house tours. Costumed guides take you through the rooms, each laden with Irving memorabilia. The grounds themselves, beautiful in nice weather, stretch down to the Hudson River.

From Tarrytown, take a cab or walk south along Rte. 9 for 2 mi. and turn right onto W. Sunnyside Ln., continuing for 1500 ft. $ House and garden tours $12, grounds $5. ⏰ Open Apr-Oct M 10am-5pm and W-Su; Nov-Dec Sa-Su 10am-4pm. Tours leave every 30min. and last 45min. Last tour 4pm.

UNION CHURCH OF POCANTINO HILLS

CHURCH

555 Bedford Rd.   ☎914-631-8200 ▢www.hudsonvalley.org

The Union Church of Pocantino Hills nearby is another beautiful gray-stone structure, but the highlights are the nine stained-glass windows—two of which are by **Marc Chagall** and **Henri Matisse.** The Rose Window was Matisse's last work; you can find it above the altar. Chagall's piece is a memorial to John D. Rockefeller, Jr., Matisse's to his wife Abby, and the rest are tributes to other family members.

 ⚐ *From Tarrytown, walk north along Broadway and turn right onto Bedford Rd., then continue for 1½ mi.* Ⓢ *$5.* ⏰ *Open Apr-Oct M 11am-5pm, W-F 11am-5pm; Nov-Dec M 11am-4pm, W-F 11am-4pm, Sa 10am-4pm, Su 2-4pm. Services Su 8:30, 10am.*

▧ OLD DUTCH CHURCH

CHURCH

420 N. Broadway   ☎914-631-4497 ▢www.olddutchburyingground.org

The Old Dutch Church is New York's oldest church (built in 1685). The small stone building (whose bell was cast in the Netherlands in 1685) is surrounded by its churchyard; most of the graves here were laid before 1849. **Ichabod Crane** and the **Headless Horseman** had some well-known adventures here. Around the church is the far larger **Sleepy Hollow Cemetery,** home to 40,000, including Andrew Carnegie and Irving himself. The church building is now only used for holiday services.

 ⚐ *Travel Rte. 9 through villages of Tarrytown and Sleepy Hollow, about 2½ mi. The Old Dutch Church and its burying ground are on the right side of the highway, across the street from Philipsburg Manor restoration in Sleepy Hollow.*

LYNDHURST

HISTORIC SITE

635 S. Broadway   ☎914-631-4481 ▢www.lyndhurst.org

Built in 1838, Lyndhurst is a stunning Gothic Revival mansion. Today it's associated mostly with railroad tycoon and "robber baron" **Jay Gould,** who owned it as a country house from 1880 until his death in 1892. Tours take you around the obscenely luxurious interior; the 67-acre grounds, which also extend to the river, are predictably gorgeous and include rose and fern gardens, a greenhouse, and a stately carriage house.

 ⚐ *From Tarrytown, walk 1½ mi. south along Rte. 9 and turn left on Lyndhurst Museum Ln.* Ⓢ *Tours $12.* ⏰ *Open daily mid-Apr-Oct 31 10am-5pm; Tu-F six tours per day, Sa-Su 11 tours. Open Nov 1 to mid-Apr Sa-Su 10am-4pm, 6-10 tours per day.*

ESSENTIALS

Getting There

By Train

From Grand Central Station, take the **Metro-North Hudson Line** train to the Tarrytown stop. (Ⓢ*40-50min.; one-way $8.25-11.25.* ⏰ *Trains depart every 15-35min., 5:30am-11:30pm.*) **Main Street** begins from the train station parking lot.

By Car

By car, take I-87 from the city, merge with I-287, take Exit 9, turn left on Rte. 119W, then turn right on Rte. 9 (S. Broadway) and drive up into Tarrytown.

Getting Around

Cabs leave from the train station parking lot; call for one at ☎914-366-0202, ☎914-631-8700, or ☎914-631-2920.

ESSENTIALS

You don't have to be a rocket scientist to plan a good trip. (It might help, but it's not required.) You do, however, need to be well prepared, and that's what we can do for you. Essentials is the chapter that gives you all the nitty-gritty you need to know for your trip: the hard information gleaned from 50 years of collective wisdom (and that phone call to New York City the other day that put us on hold for an hour). Planning your trip? Check. Staying safe and healthy? Check. The dirt on transportation? Check. We've also thrown in communications info, and meteorological charts just for good measure. Plus, for overall trip-planning advice from what to pack (money and as little underwear as possible) to how to take a good passport photo (it's physically impossible; consider airbrushing), you can also check out the Essentials section of ▣www.letsgo.com.

We're not going to lie—this chapter is tough for us to write, and you might not find it as fun of a read as 101 or Discover. But please, for the love of all that is good, read it! It's super helpful, and, most importantly, it means we didn't compile all this technical info and put it in one place for you (yes YOU) for nothing.

greatest hits

- **GET A VISA.** Put it on your spring-cleaning list, since you'll need to apply six to eight weeks in advance (p. 206).

- **BUY AN UNLIMITED METROCARD.** If you're going to be in New York for a week or longer, you'll want to have one (p. 213).

- **SHIP SOUVENIRS HOME BY SURFACE MAIL.** Our scintillating "By Snail Mail" section will tell you how. You'll laugh, you'll cry (p. 214).

- **LOOK SHARP, DON'T PACK SHARP.** Airport security in NYC is extra tight. Your nail clipper is probably harmless, but if you fly into the city, check it (p. 210).

- **BOLT FOR THE BUS.** Ride Bolt Bus from New York City to Boston or Washington, D.C. for $1. Oh, and did we mention the free Wi-Fi? (p. 211).

- **OH, THE HUMIDITY!** New York City gets incredibly muggy in the summer. If your hair is prone to frizz, pack some product (p. 216).

planning your trip

DOCUMENTS AND FORMALITIES

You've got your visa, your invitation, and your work permit, just like *Let's Go* told you to, and then you realize you've forgotten the most important thing: your passport. Well, we're not going to let that happen. **Don't forget your passport!**

entrance requirements

- **PASSPORT:** Required for citizens of all countries, including Australia, Canada, Ireland, New Zealand, and the UK.
- **VISA:** Required for citizens of Australia, New Zealand, Ireland and the UK staying in the US for more than 90 days.
- **WORK PERMIT:** Required for all foreigners planning to work in the US.

Visas

Citizens of most countries need a visa in addition to a valid passport for entrance into the United States; see ▣www.unitedstatesvisas.gov for more information. To obtain a visa, contact a US embassy or consulate. Recent security measures have made the visa application process more rigorous. Apply well in advance of your travel date to guarantee your request will be processed.

Citizens of **Canada** do not need a visa for admission to the US. Citizens of **Australia, New Zealand,** and most **European countries** can waive the US visas through the **Visa Waiver Program.** Visitors qualify if they are traveling only for business or pleasure, are staying for fewer than **90 days,** have proof of intent to leave (e.g., a return plane ticket), possess an I-94 form, and possess a machine-readable passport from a nation of which they are a citizen. See ▣www.travel.state.gov/visa for more information.

If you lose your I-94 form, you can replace it by filling out form I-102, although it's very unlikely that the form will be replaced within the time of your stay. The form is available at the nearest Bureau of Citizenship and Immigration Services office, through the forms request line, or online (☎800-870-3676; ▣www.bcis.gov). Visa extensions are sometimes granted with a completed I-539 form; call the forms request line or get it online at ▣www.uscis.gov/files/form/i-539.pdf.

Work Permits

A passport and visa does not include the right to work, which is authorized only by a work permit. In addition, admittance to the United States as a traveler does not include the right to work, which is authorized only by a work permit. For more information, see the **Beyond Tourism** chapter (p. 225).

TIME DIFFERENCES

New York is 5hr. behind Greenwich Mean Time (GMT) and observes Daylight Savings Time. This means that it is 3hr. ahead of Los Angeles, 5hr. behind the British Isles, 15hr. behind Sydney, and 16hr. behind New Zealand. Note that Australia observes Daylight Savings Time from October to March, the opposite of the Northern Hemispheres. Therefore, it is 14hr. ahead of New York City from March to October and 16 hr. ahead from October to March, for an average of 15hr.

us embassies abroad

- **AUSTRALIA:** *(Moonah Pl., Yarralumla, Canberra, ACT 2600 ☎02 6214 5600 ▪http://canberra.usembassy.gov)*
- **CANADA:** *(Consular Section, 490 Sussex Dr., Ottawa. Mailing address P.O. Box 866, Station B, Ottawa, Ontario K1P 5T1 ☎613-688-5335 ▪http:// ottawa.usembassy.gov)*
- **IRELAND:** *(42 Elgrin Rd., Ballsbridge, Dublin 4 ☎01 668 8777 ▪http:// dublin.usembassy.gov)*
- **NEW ZEALAND:** *(29 Fitzherbert Terr., Thorndon, Wellington. Mailing address: P.O. Box 1190, Wellington ☎04 462 6000 ▪http://newzealand. usembassy.gov)*
- **UK:** *(24 Grosvenor Sq., London W1A 1AE ☎020 7499 9000 ▪www. usembassy.org.uk)*

foreign consulates in new york

- **AUSTRALIA:** *(150 E. 42nd St., 34th fl., New York, NY 10017-5612 ☎212-351-6500 ▪www.australianyc.org)*
- **CANADA:** *(1251 Ave. of the Americas, New York NY 10020-1175 ☎212-596-1628 ▪www.newyork.gc.ca.org)*
- **IRELAND:** *(345 Park Ave. 17th Floor, New York, NY 10154-0004 ☎212-319-2555 ▪www.consulateofirelandnewyork.org)*
- **NEW ZEALAND:** *(222 E. 41st St. Ste. 2510 New York, NY 10017-6702 ☎310-566-6555)*
- **UK:** *(845 3rd Ave., New York, NY 10022 ☎212-745-0200 ▪www.britai- nusa.com/ny)*

money

GETTING MONEY FROM HOME

Stuff happens. When stuff happens, you might need some money. When you need some money, the easiest and cheapest solution is to have someone back home make a deposit to your bank account. Otherwise, consider one of the following options.

Wiring Money

Arranging a **bank money transfer** means asking a bank back home to wire money to a bank in New York City. This is the cheapest way to transfer cash, but it's also the slowest and most agonizing, usually taking several days or more. Note that some banks may only release your funds in local currency, potentially sticking you with a poor exchange rate; inquire about this in advance. Money transfer services like **Western Union** are faster and more convenient than bank transfers—but also much pricier. Western Union has many locations worldwide. To find one, visit ▪www.westernunion.com or call the appropriate number: in **Australia** ☎1800 173 833, in **Canada** ☎800-235-0000, in the **US** ☎800-325-6000, in the **UK** ☎0800 731 1815. To wire money using a credit card in **Canada** and the **US,** call ☎800-CALL-CASH; in the UK, ☎0800 833 833. Money transfer services are also available to **American Express** cardholders and at selected **Thomas Cook** offices.

essentials

TIPPING AND BARGAINING

Tipping is more or less compulsory in the United States. Remember that service is never included on a New York bill, unless you're in a large party at a restaurant (six or more people) and the tip is noted on the bill. As a general rule, tip cab drivers and waiters 15-20%, coat-checkers $1, bellhops around $1 per bag, hotel maids $1 per day, and bartenders $1 per drink.

credit, atm, and debit cards

Where they are accepted, credit cards often offer superior exchange rates—up to 5% better than the retail rate used by banks and other currency exchange establishments. MasterCard and Visa are the most frequently accepted; American Express cards work at some ATMs and at AmEx offices and major airports

The use of ATM cards is widespread in New York City. Almost every major bank has an ATM every few blocks, and there are also machines at many restaurants, hotels, and train stations. Depending on the system that your home bank uses, you can probably access your personal bank account from abroad. ATMs get the same wholesale exchange rate as credit cards, but there is often a limit on the amount of money you can withdraw per day (usually around $500). There is also typically a surcharge of US$1-5 per withdrawal.

Debit cards are as convenient as credit cards but withdraw money directly from the holder's checking account. A debit card can be used wherever it's associated credit card company (usually MasterCard or Visa) is accepted. Debit cards often also function as ATM cards and can be used to withdraw cash from associated banks and ATMs throughout New York City.

TAXES

Quoted prices in *Let's Go* do not include New York's 8.875% sales tax, which applies to hotel rooms (in addition to a 5.875% hotel tax and a $2 room fee per night).

safety and health

GENERAL ADVICE

In an emergency, dial ☎911. Your country's embassy abroad (p. 208) is usually your best resource. The government offices listed in the **Travel Advisories** box (p. 210) can provide information on the services they offer their citizens in case of emergencies abroad.

In any type of crisis, the most important thing to do is **stay calm.** Your country's embassy abroad (p. 208) is usually your best resource in an emergency; registering with that embassy upon arrival in the country is a good idea. The government offices listed in the **Travel Advisories** feature at the end of this section can provide information on the services they offer their citizens in case of emergencies abroad.

Local Laws And Police

The New York City Police force is known as "New York's Finest" for a reason: they are responsible for patrolling the streets 24 hours a day, and are usually a good resource to turn to for help. They can be easily spotted on the street.

Drugs And Alcohol

You must be 21 years old to legally purchase alcoholic beverages in New York State. Most drinking spots and liquor stores do ask for identification. Be aware that using a fake ID can result in serious consequences, including an offense on your record and the suspension of your real driver's license.

Possession of marijuana, cocaine, crack, heroin, methamphetamine, MDMA ("ecstasy"), hallucinogens, and most opiate derivatives (among many other chemicals) is punishable by stiff fines and imprisonment. Attempting to purchase illegal drugs of any sort is a bad idea.

If you carry prescription drugs when you travel, it is vital to have a copy of your written prescriptions readily accessible at US Customs. Check with a US Customs Service for more information before you head out.

SPECIFIC CONCERNS

Terrorism

The September 11th attacks of 2001 revealed the vulnerability of large American cities to terrorist attacks and resulted in the enforcement of stringent safety measures at airports and major tourist sights throughout New York. Allow extra time for airport security and do not pack sharp objects in your carry-on luggage—they will be confiscated. Check your home country's foreign affairs office for travel information and advisories, and be sure to follow the local news while in New York.

PRE-DEPARTURE HEALTH

Matching a prescription to a foreign equivalent is not always easy, safe, or possible, so if you take **prescription drugs,** carry up-to-date prescriptions or a statement from your doctor stating the medications' trade names, manufacturers, chemical names, and dosages. Be sure to keep all medication with you in your carry-on luggage.

travel advisories

The following government offices provide travel information and advisories by telephone, by fax, or via the web:

- **AUSTRALIA: Department of Foreign Affairs and Trade.** (☎+61 2 6261 1111 🖳www.dfat.gov.au)

- **CANADA: Department of Foreign Affairs and International Trade (DFAIT).** Call or visit the website for the free booklet *Bon Voyage...But.* (☎+1-800-267-8376 🖳www.dfait-maeci.gc.ca)

- **NEW ZEALAND: Ministry of Foreign Affairs.** (☎+64 4 439 8000 🖳www.mfat.govt.nz)

- **UK: Foreign and Commonwealth Office.** (☎+44 20 7008 1500 🖳www.fco.gov.uk)

- **US: Department of State.** (☎888-407-4747 from the US, +1-202-501-4444 elsewhere 🖳http://travel.state.gov)

Immunizations and Precautions

Travelers over two years old should make sure that the following vaccines are up to date: MMR (for measles, mumps, and rubella); DTaP or Td (for diphtheria, tetanus, and pertussis); IPV (for polio); Hib (for *Haemophilus influenzae* B); and HepB (for Hepatitis B). For recommendations on immunizations and prophylaxis, check with a doctor and consult the **Centers for Disease Control and Prevention (CDC)** in the US or the equivalent in your home country and check with a doctor for guidance. (☎800-CDC-INFO/232-4636 🖳www.cdc.gov/travel)

getting there

BY PLANE

When it comes to airfare, a little effort can save you a bundle. Tickets sold by consolidators and standby seating are also good deals, but last-minute specials, airfare wars, and charter flights often beat these fares.

Four major airports serve the New York metropolitan region. The largest, **John F. Kennedy Airport (JFK)** (☎718-244-4444) is 15 mi. from midtown Manhattan in southern Queens and handles mostly international flights. **LaGuardia Airport (LGA)** (☎718-533-3400) is 9 mi. from midtown in Queens and the second largest, offering domestic flights as well as hourly shuttles to and from Boston and Washington, D.C. **Newark Liberty International Airport (EWR)** (☎973-961-6000), 16 mi. from midtown in Newark, NJ, offers both domestic and international flights at budget fares often not available at the other airports (though getting to and from Newark is pricey).

BY TRAIN

Though getting in or out of New York by train isn't necessarily cheaper than flying, it is certainly more scenic, and it delivers you directly to the heart of Midtown. You can save a significant amount of money by purchasing tickets in advance, so plan ahead. Amtrak (☎800-USA-RAIL/872-7245; 🖳www.amtrak.com) is the major provider of intercity passenger train service in the United States. The website lists up-to-date schedules, fares, and arrival and departure info. Students with a **Student Advantage Card** or an ISIC (see **By Bus,** below, for how to purchase) save 15% on fares and AAA members save 10%. To be eligible for most discounts, tickets must be purchased at least three days in advance. Weekly specials listed online offer discounts of up to 90%.

Amtrak's trains connect NYC to most other parts of the country through **Penn Station,** 33rd St. and Eighth Ave. (⚡ Ⓢ 1, 2, 3 to 34th St./Penn Station/7th Ave.; A, C, E to 34th St.-Penn Station/8th Ave.) Routes run from **Boston** (Ⓢ One-way from $54. ☒ 4-5hr.), **Philadelphia** (Ⓢ One-way from $42. ☒ 1hr.), and **Washington, DC** (Ⓢ One-way from $63. ☒ 3-4hr.). The Long Island Rail Road and New Jersey Transit both run out of Penn Station. The local MTA Metro-North Railroad runs to upstate New York and parts of New Jersey out of Grand Central Terminal, 42nd St. and Park Ave. (🖳www.grandcentralterminal.com ⚡ Ⓢ S 4, 5, 6, 7, S.)

BY BUS

New York's Port Authority Terminal on 41st St. and Eighth Ave. serves as the hub of the Northeast bus network. (☎212 564 8484 ⚡ Ⓢ A, C, E to 42nd. St./Port Authority.) Port Authority has good information and security services, but the surrounding neighborhood is somewhat deserted at night (particularly towards the west), so it is usually a good idea to call a cab.

Greyhound (☎800-231-2222 🖳www.greyhound.com) operates the largest number of lines, departing from Boston (Ⓢ One-way $35. ☒ 4-6hr.), Montreal (Ⓢ One-way $76.50. ☒ 8-9hr.), Philadelphia (Ⓢ One-way $21. ☒ 2-3hr.), and Washington, D.C. (Ⓢ One-way $37. ☒ 4-6hr.) The fares listed require no advance purchase, but you can save by purchasing tickets in advance. Students ride Greyhound for 15% off with a Student Advantage Card. (☎800-333-2920 🖳www.studentadvantage.com Ⓢ $20.)

The cheapest and most reliable buses to and from New York these days are **Bolt Bus** (☎877-265-8287 🖳www.boltbus.com) and **Megabus** (☎877-462-6342 🖳www.megabus.com), both of which offer $1 tickets if you book far enough in advance (you won't have to pay more than $23 for a ticket). Plus, both companies offer free Wi-Fi on all rides.

A recent phenomenon in budget travel between east coast cities is the so-called **Chinatown bus.** Transporting travelers from one city's Chinatown to the next, these buses attract hordes of budget-minded travelers. Though the reliability and safety of these services can be spotty, they offer frequent departures at unbeatable prices

(often half that of Greyhound and a tiny fraction of a train or plane ticket). The exact names and routes of Chinatown bus companies change frequently, but some of the major players include: to Boston, Fung Wah (🖳*www.fungwahbus.com $15);* and to Washington, D.C., Washington Deluxe (🖳*www.washny.com* $ *One-way $15).* Other possible destinations include Baltimore, Norfolk, VA, and even Atlanta.

metrocards

The MTA fare for one Subway or local bus ride is $2.25, while the fare for an express bus ride is $5.50. Travelers 65 years of age or older can qualify for reduced fare and travel for half fare, and children 44 in. tall and under ride for free when accompanied by a fare-paying adult. If you're under 65 years, above 44 in. and looking for more than one ride, check out these MetroCards you can buy:

- **PAY-PER-RIDE:** Buy as many rides as you want from $4.50 to $80. Put $8 or more on your card and receive a 15% bonus. For example, a $20 purchase gives you $23 on your card. Refill your card to use the balance.
- **1-DAY FUN PASS:** Cost: $8.25, reduced fare not available. Good for unlimited Subway and local bus rides from first use until 3am the following day. Sold at MetroCard Vending Machines and at neighborhood stores. Not available at station booths.
- **7-DAY UNLIMITED:** Cost: $27, reduced fare $13.50. Good for unlimited Subway and local bus rides until midnight, 7 days from day of first use.
- **14-DAY UNLIMITED:** Cost: $51.50, reduced fare $25.75. Good for unlimited Subway and local bus rides until midnight, 14 days from day of first use. This card is protected against loss of theft when purchased at a vending machine with a credit or debit/ATM card.
- **30-DAY UNLIMITED:** Cost: $89, reduced fare $44.50. Good for unlimited Subway and local bus rides until midnight, 30 days from day of first use.
- **7-DAY EXPRESS BUS PLUS:** Cost: $45, no reduced fare. Good for unlimited express bus, local bus, and Subway rides until midnight, 7 days from first use.
- **JFK-AIRTRAIN 30-DAY UNLIMITED:** Good for unlimited JFK-AirTrain trips until midnight, 30 days from first use.
- **JFK-AIRTRAIN 10-TRIP:** Good for 10 JFK-AirTrain trips until midnight six months after use. 1 trip is deducted for each use. Only accepted for AirTrain trips. On sale at AirTrain vending machines, JFK airport, and local merchants.

keeping in touch

BY EMAIL AND INTERNET

Hello and welcome to the 21st century, where you can check your email from anywhere in New York City, though sometimes you'll have to pay a few bucks or buy a drink for internet access. Although in some places it's possible to forge a remote link with your home server, in most cases this is a much slower (and thus more expensive) option than taking advantage of free **web-based email accounts** (e.g., 🖳**www.gmail.com**). For lists of additional cybercafes in New York, check out websites like 🖳www.cybercaptive.com.

Wireless hot spots make internet access possible in public and remote places. Unfortunately, they also pose security risks. Hot spots are public, open networks that use unencrypted, unsecured connections. They are susceptible to hacks and "packet sniffing"—the theft of passwords and other private information. To prevent problems, disable "ad hoc" mode, turn off file sharing and network discovery, encrypt your email, turn on your firewall, beware of phony networks, and watch for over-the-shoulder creeps.

BY TELEPHONE

Calling Home From New York City

Prepaid phone cards are a common and relatively inexpensive means of calling abroad. Each one comes with a Personal Identification Number (PIN) and a toll-free access number. You call the access number and then follow the directions for dialing your PIN. To purchase prepaid phone cards, check online for the best rates; ▧www.call-ingcards.com is a good place to start. Online providers generally send your access number and PIN via email, with no actual "card" involved. You can also call home with prepaid phone cards purchased in New York.

If you have internet access, your best—i.e., cheapest, most convenient, and most tech-savvy—bet is probably our good friend **Skype** (▧www.skype.com). You can even videochat if you have one of those new-fangled webcams. Calls to other Skype users are free; calls to landlines and mobiles worldwide start at US$0.021 per minute, depending on where you're calling.

Another option is a **calling card,** linked to a major national telecommunications service in your home country. Calls are billed collect or to your account. Cards generally come with instructions for dialing both domestically and internationally.

Placing a collect call through an international operator can be expensive but may be necessary in case of an emergency. You can frequently call collect without even possessing a company's calling card just by calling its access number and following the instructions.

Cellular Phones

The international standard for cell phones is **Global System for Mobile Communication (GSM).** To make and receive calls in New York, you will need a GSM-compatible phone and a **SIM (Subscriber Identity Module) card,** a country-specific, thumbnail-size chip that gives you a local phone number and plugs you into the local network. Many SIM cards are prepaid, and incoming calls are frequently free. You can buy additional cards or vouchers (usually available at convenience stores) to "top up" your phone. For more information on GSM phones, check out www.telestial.com. Companies like **Cellular Abroad** (▧www.cellularabroad.com) and **OneSimCard** (▧www.onesimcard.com) rent cell phones and SIM cards that work in a variety of destinations around the world.

BY SNAIL MAIL

US Mail is controlled by the US Postal Service (☎800-275-8777 ▧www.usps.com). Hours vary widely according to the branch; call for details. The city's General Post Office, 421 Eighth Ave., (☎212-330-3002), at between 31st and 33rd St., is open 24hr.

Sending Mail Home From New York City

Airmail is the best way to send mail home from New York. **Aerogrammes,** printed sheets that fold into envelopes and travel via airmail, are available at post offices. Write "airmail" or *"par avion"* on the front. Most post offices will charge exorbitant fees or simply refuse to send aerogrammes with enclosures. Surface mail is by far the cheapest and slowest way to send mail. It takes one to two months to cross the Atlantic and one to three to cross the Pacific—good for heavy items you won't need for a while, like souvenirs that you've acquired along the way.

The **postal rate** for letters under 1 oz. headed anywhere in the US is 44¢, while postcards and aerogrammes cost 28¢. Letters, postcards and aerogrammes to Canada 75¢. For Australia, Ireland, New Zealand, and the UK, rates are 98¢ for letters,

essentials

international calls

To call the US from home or to call home from the US, dial:

1. THE INTERNATIONAL DIALING PREFIX. To call from **Australia**, dial ☎0011; **Canada** or the **US**, ☎011; **Ireland, New Zealand**, or the **UK**, ☎00.

2. THE COUNTRY CODE OF THE COUNTRY YOU WANT TO CALL. To call **Australia**, dial ☎61; **Canada** or the **US**, ☎1; **Ireland**, ☎353; **New Zealand**, ☎64; the **UK**, ☎44.

3. THE CITY/AREA CODE. *Let's Go* lists the city/area codes for cities and towns in the US opposite the city or town name, next to a ☎, as well as in every phone number.

4. THE LOCAL NUMBER.

postcards and aerogrammes. International mail should arrive by air in about four to seven days. A post office clerk (or the official online rate calculator at ▣http://postcalc.usps.gov) will give you other rates.

Sending Mail To New York City

To ensure timely delivery, mark envelopes "airmail" or "par avion." In addition to the standard postage system whose rates are listed below, **Federal Express** handles express mail services from most countries to New York (☎800-463-3339 ▣*www.fedex.com).* Sending a postcard within the United States costs 28¢, while sending letters (up to 1 oz.) domestically requires 44¢.

If you don't have a mailing address in New York, you can still receive mail via **General Delivery** (known as Poste Restante in most other parts of the world). Mail addressed to you at the following address will be held for pick-up for up to 30 days:

General Delivery
General Post Office / James A. Farley Station
42 Eighth Ave.
New York, NY 10001

A photo ID is required for pick-up. For US General Delivery, go to 390 Ninth Ave., at West 30th Street.

The mail will go to a special desk in the central post office, unless you specify a post office by street address or postal code. It's best to use the largest post office, since mail may be sent there regardless. It is usually safer and quicker, though more expensive, to send mail express or registered. Bring your passport (or other photo ID) for pickup; there may be a small fee. If the clerks insist that there is nothing for you, ask them to check under your first name as well. *Let's Go* lists post offices in the **Practicalities** section.

let's go online

Plan your next trip on our spiffy website, ▣www.letsgo.com. It features full book content, the latest travel info on your favorite destinations, and tons of interactive features: make your own itinerary, read blogs from our trusty Researcher-Writers, browse our photo library, watch exclusive videos, check out our newsletter, find travel deals, follow us on Facebook, and buy new guides. Plus, if this Essentials wasn't enough for you, we've got even more online. We're always updating and adding new features, so check back often!

keeping in touch . by snail mail

climate

New York City weather is difficult to predict, so your best bet is to dress for the seasons: falls are cool, winters are cold, springs are breezy, and summers are balmy. There's decent snowfall in the winter months, but the city's plows quickly turn the white powder into to slush and ice. Once summertime rolls around, you'll get all hot and bothered—literally. New York City gets extremely humid in the summer, with muggy conditions stinking up the Subway and messing up your hairdo.

MONTH	AVG. HIGH TEMP.		AVG. LOW TEMP.		AVG. RAINFALL		AVG. NUMBER OF WET DAYS
January	3°C	37°F	-4°C	25°F	94mm	3.7 in.	12
February	3°C	37°F	-4°C	25°F	97mm	3.8 in.	10
March	7°C	45°F	-1°C	30°F	91mm	3.6 in.	12
April	14°C	57°F	6°C	43°F	81mm	3.2 in.	11
May	20°C	68°F	12°C	54°F	81mm	3.2 in.	11
June	25°C	77°F	16°C	61°F	84mm	3.3 in.	10
July	28°C	82°F	19°C	66°F	107mm	4.2 in.	12
August	27°C	81°F	19°C	66°F	109mm	4.3 in.	10
September	26°C	79°F	16°C	61°F	86mm	3.4 in.	9
October	21°C	70°F	9°C	48°F	89mm	3.5 in.	9
November	11°C	52°F	3°C	37°F	76mm	3.0 in.	9
December	5°C	41°F	-2°C	28°F	91mm	3.6 in.	10

To convert from degrees Fahrenheit to degrees Celsius, subtract 32 and multiply by 5/9. To convert from Celsius to Fahrenheit, multiply by 9/5 and add 32.

°CELSIUS	-5	0	5	10	15	20	25	30	35	40
°FAHRENHEIT	23	32	41	50	59	68	77	86	95	104

measurements

Unlike those rational countries that use the metric system, the United States uses standard measurements. The basic unit of length is a foot (ft.), which is divided into 12 inches (in.). Three feet make up a yard (yd.), and 5280 feet make up a mile (mi.). Weight (otherwise known as mass) is measured in pounds (lb.), each of which is divided into 16 ounces (oz.). Fluids are measured in gallons (gal.), which are divided into 128 fluid ounces (fl. oz.). Note: Gallons in the US and those in Britain are not identical: one US gallon equals 0.83 Imperial gallons. Pub aficionados will note that an Imperial pint (20 oz.) is larger than its US counterpart (16 oz.). Chug accordingly.

MEASUREMENT CONVERSIONS	
1 inch (in.) = 25.4mm	1 millimeter (mm) = 0.039 in.
1 foot (ft.) = 0.305m	1 meter (m) = 3.28 ft.
1 yard (yd.) = 0.914m	1 meter (m) = 1.094 yd.
1 mile (mi.) = 1.609km	1 kilometer (km) = 0.621 mi.
1 ounce (oz.) = 28.35g	1 gram (g) = 0.035 oz.
1 pound (lb.) = 0.454kg	1 kilogram (kg) = 2.205 lb.
1 fluid ounce (fl. oz.) = 29.57mL	1 milliliter (mL) = 0.034 fl. oz.
1 gallon (gal.) = 3.785L	1 liter (L) = 0.264 gal.

essentials

NYC 101

Old Blue Eyes so melodiously wanted to "be a part of it," and why shouldn't you? New York City is the most exciting, kinetic, stylish, and diverse metropolis in the United States, and maybe even the world. Upon your visit here, you'll want to know the ins and outs of the city—which newspapers to read, how to tell the boroughs apart, how to eat your over-sized slice of pizza. Not to worry. Even if you can't talk the talk of a New Yorker—please, *don't* try to immitate a Brooklyn accent—we're here to help you walk the walk.

facts and figures

- **SKYSCRAPERS TALLER THAN 656 FEET:** 50
- **YEARLY VISITORS TO CENTRAL PARK:** 30,000,000
- **NUMBER OF SUBWAY ROUTES:** 26
- **UNIVERSITY STUDENTS IN MANHATTAN:** 594,000
- **LANGUAGES SPOKEN:** 70
- **AVERAGE NUMBER OF RAINY DAYS PER YEAR:** 121
- **MILES OF PUBLIC BEACHES:** 14

history

COLONY, CAPITAL, COMMERCE

Giovanni da Verrazzano was the first European explorer to enter New York Harbor in 1524, but usually Henry Hudson gets all the glory. After all, it was not until Hudson's great excursion to the new world that the area was extensively mapped and explored. The region was once inhabited by Native Americans—specifically, the Lenape tribe. The Dutch fur trade was soon established in New Amsterdam, now known as Manhattan. During the 1630s, there was much violence between the Native American tribes and the Dutch, until a peace treaty was drawn up in 1645. The Dutch, however, would not remain in control for long; the English conquered the region in 1664 and named it "New York" after the Duke of York and Albany.

New York was the meeting place of the Stamp Act Congress in 1765, the first organized colonial resistance to British authorities. By the Revolutionary War, the colony of New York had already become a major force in North America, though it was far more Loyalist than Patriot-filled Boston, and was actually the British military and political base of operations. Despite its Loyalist roots, New York City was the first capital of the newly formed United States from 1788-1790. Before Wall Street was all about the Benajmins, the real star of the neighborhood was George Washington; the pathological truth-teller was inaugurated as the nation's first president at Wall Street's Federal Hall. After the war, Alexander Hamilton become the first Secretary of the Treasury. In 1825, Hamilton decided to open up the Erie Canal, connecting New York to the agricultural resources of the nation's interior, and creating a direct trade route across the Great Lakes.

HUDDLED MASSES YEARNING

New York City's great immigration tradition got off to a booming start because of potatoes—yes, potatoes. The Irish Potato Famine brought an influx of Irish immigrants who thanked their 🍀Lucky Charms that they made it to the City; in fact, they comprised a whopping one quarter of NYC's population by 1850. The immigrant influx led to the creation of the Commissioners' Plan of 1811, which created the New York City grid system as a way to sell land in an organized fashion to all the new folks. Most of these immigrants sympathized with the South during the Civil War; they liked conscription even less than New Yorkers today like the Red Sox, and the New York Draft Riots of 1863 were the largest civil uprising in American history, excluding the Civil War. Immigration from Europe continued after the war, and after France's gift in 1886, they were greeted by Lady Liberty herself upon entering the city. Around this time, a slew of African-Americans from the South made their way up to the City, and this Great Migration laid the foundations of the Harlem Renaissance.

Fast forward a few decades to the period following World War I. Immigration to the United States began to wane, as several measures were taken to control the influx of newcomers, including the Immigration Act of 1917. After World War II, New York experienced the "Great Migration," during which more than half a million Puerto Ricans entered the Big Apple. Among other things, this surge in the Puerto Rican population inspired one of the most popular American musicals of all time (thank you, Leonard Bernstein). Whether you're a Shark or a Jet, you can't help but weep a little when the dulcet chords of "Somewhere" begin.

DOOM TO BOOM

Although the skyscrapers constructed in the 1940s seem to tell a different story, New York was hit hard by the Great Depression. Fortunately, the wartime and post-bellum periods led to an eventual economic resuscitation of the city. The millions of new wartime jobs that were created helped NYC get back on its feet, and as more and more WWII veterans returned to the city, it became necessary to expand the amount of housing available. Consequently, a housing development was created in Levittown, Queens to accommodate middle- to upper-class families. This popularized living outside the hustle and bustle of the city, and similar "Levittowns" soon popped up all over eastern Queens, and eventually America.

Thanks to the rebirth of Wall Street in the 1980s and the "dot com boom" that began in the early 90s, New York City has remained one of the major economic centers of the world.

TRAGEDY AND TRIUMPH

On **September 11, 2001,** great tragedy hit New York City. In the worst terrorist attack ever to occur on American soil, members of Al Qaeda flew two planes into the World Trade Center, killing nearly 3000 people, including 343 NYC firefighters. Although the city was shaken by this devastating loss, the event sparked an unprecedented spirit of camaraderie, unity, and patriotism—both citywide and nationwide. Though explicit discussion of 9/11 is rarer in the city today than it once was, the event continues to lurk just below the surface of New York'er's collective consciousness. At Ground Zero, the gaping pit that once housed New York's tallest buildings, construction of the **Freedom Tower** has begun. The project has sparked controversy, but the structure will become the tallest building in the United States. A portion of the ruins from the Twin Towers will be preserved as a memorial to the victims.

the city

New York City is governed by a mayor elected to a four-year term; Mayor Michael Bloomberg currently rules the roost. The New York City Council is composed of 51 members from different geographic districts who are also elected for four year terms. Although the five boroughs—the Bronx, Brooklyn, Queens, Staten Island, and Manhattan—each have their own district attorney, they are still under the rule of the centralized New York City Government.

MANHATTAN

Manhattan is what you were thinking of when you decided to take a vacation to New York City. Although technically all five boroughs are "the city", many people are specifically referring to Manhattan when they use this term. Famous for its skyscrapers, Manhattan is home to most of the major tourist sights of New York City. There's the Upper East Side, where most TV shows about spoiled, jaded NYC teenagers take place. Think ➡Gossip Girl. Then there's Greenwich Village, known for funky cafes, artsy boutiques and experimental theater. Little Italy and Chinatown give Manhattan an ethnic flair, while Central Park provides an idyllic place to exercise off all that carb-loaded ethnic food. And of course, no traveler goes to New York without a visit to Times Square to observe the local culture of...the other tourists. Be sure not to get run over by a yellow cab while you're snapping your photo.

BROOKLYN

Home to the infamous "tough guy" accent, Brooklyn is New York City's most populous borough. Because of the rising price of real estate in Manhattan, Brooklyn has become the new hot place to live, particularly for young pre-professionals who partake in the ever-growing hipster culture. Many once dangerous areas of Brooklyn have been converted into artsy, gentrified hotspots, such as Williamsburg. It's not uncommon to find Orthodox Jews living beside Hispanic families and young college students in other parts of Brooklyn, and no trip is complete without a visit to 🏖Coney Island in the south. A playground for the rich in the 20th century, the park now caters to a more pedestrian crew. Who cares if its glamour has dissipated? It's the host of the annual Nathan's Hot Dog Eating Contest!

QUEENS

The largest of the five boroughs, Queens covers 37% of the city's total area. Although large, it lacks extensive Subway and bus transportation, and tends to have a more residential feel than Manhattan. Queens is a melting pot in the true sense of the word; with recent immigrants from all over the world, it is perhaps the best place to find authentic international cuisine. Queens boasts Long Island, as well as the infamous Levittown, home to the 📖Great Gatsby.

BRONX

Dubbed by some as "the home of hip-hop," by others as "the home of the Bronx Cheer," the Bronx contains such attractions as the Bronx Zoo, the Botanical Gardens, Yankee Stadium and the birthplace of John Gotti. Some areas—particularly South Bronx—have a reputation for gangs and violence. Although several neighborhoods in the Bronx are low-income, there are also wealthy spots, like Riverdale.

STATEN ISLAND

Hop on the Staten Island Ferry from Manhattan so you can ogle at some of New York's most famous sights: the Statue of Liberty and Ellis Island. Staten Island is the most suburban of the boroughs, and is the only one without an extensive grid system. Its four Democratic sister boroughs are somewhat miffed with Republican Staten Island: it has only voted for a Democratic presidential nominee three times since 1952.

eating

New York City offers any cuisine your heart could desire—or your stomach could fit—whether you're craving Glatt kosher sushi, Ethiopian fare at 2am, or a meal served by an entirely ninja wait staff. Ethnic neighborhoods like Chinatown in Queens and Little Italy in Manhattan are home to many immigrants who brought their native flavors to the United States—which means you can get the *real thing*.

The stereotypes associated with distinctive New York cuisine tend toward the lowbrow. Start your day with a **bagel**, with lox or a "schmear" of cream cheese. At lunchtime, businessmen and construction workers alike crowd at the city's fast-food carts, which offer deceptively delectable fare: New York **hot dogs** can come doused in ketchup, mustard, onions, sauerkraut and chili, while **pizza** is thin, greasy, and meant to be folded and consumed like a sandwich. **Falafel, shawarma, burritos,** and **knishes** (Eastern European Jewish dumplings with fillings like mashed potatoes, meat, cheese, or spinach) are just some of the ethnically inflected street-cart delicacies. For snackin', grab a **pretzel** or a handful of **hot nuts** from street vendors.

New York street food has certainly been democratized, but restaurant dining in the city can be elitist. Securing a table at a hip new bistro, a sexy sushi bar, or a gastronomic temple (à la Carrie, Samantha, Charlotte, and Miranda) can be a blood sport. The level of decadence at the pinnacle of the New York restaurant world soars ever skyward. NYC is home to four Michelin 3-star restaurants—an extremely rare distinction granted to only the highest quality establishments world wide. Among these all-stars is Thomas Keller's **Per Se;** the menu here may look simple, but dishes like "Macaroni and Cheese" and "Bacon and Eggs" actually include items ranging from expensive caviar to butter-poached lobster.

But between these two extremes lies an enormous and delicious middle ground waiting to be explored and devoured. The city overflows with cafes specializing in brunch, designer bistros, sedate business-oriented rooms, and every type of ethnic restaurant you can imagine. The popular website **Fresh Direct** (www.freshdirect.com) offers next-day delivery of high quality groceries throughout the city, and gourmet grocery stores like **Dean and DeLuca** in SoHo and **Zabar's** on the Upper West Side are a feast for the eyes, even if your wallet can't afford such a feast for your taste buds. A cheaper alternative is the massive Whole Foods in the basement of the Time Warner Center in Columbus Circle. The streets of Chinatown abound with fishmongers, butchers, and produce dealers. Farmers' markets set up weekly in 28 locations throughout the five boroughs, with an enormous market four days weekly at Union Square.

sports and recreation

SPORTS

New York City is a sports lover's dream, with teams in every major sports league, and two in the MLB. The Mets—short for Metropolitans—are in the National League, while the good ol' Yankees play in the American League. From time to time, the two New York teams square off in the World Series in what is dubbed a "Subway Series." The only thing that evokes more baseball enthusiasm than a Subway Series is the event of a Yankees/Red Sox face-off. If you're planning to wear a Boston Red Sox shirt on game day, you should fughettaboutit.

PARKS

A handful of parks throughout the city serve as welcome respite from the concrete jungle. By far the largest and most famous park in New York City is Central Park, which spans from 59th St. to 110th St. in Manhattan, dividing the borough into East and West. Enjoy a picnic lunch in the idyllic setting, or coax your sweetie into taking a jaunt in a horse-drawn carriage. Central Park also hosts several outdoor festivals and concerts, particularly during the summer. After the park, monkey around at the Bronx Zoo (p. 93), or get a good whiff of the flowers at the ■New York Botanical Gardens (p. 94).

media

New York is the largest media market in North America, and feature's most of the world's top advertising agencies, record labels, and media conglomerates such as Time Warner, the Hearst Corporation and Viacom.

If you need some good reading to facilitate any of your daily activities, not to worry: New York is home to four of the ten largest papers in the United States. *The Wall Street Journal* is distributed to over 2.1 million readers a day. Cha-ching! *The New York Times* is New York City's other national newspaper, and has been proudly circulating "All the News That's Fit to Print" since 1851. *The Village Voice* is a free weekly newspaper that highlights arts and culture, complete with listings of events that will satiate any liberal appetite. Perhaps you'll get the biggest hoot from ■The Onion, a free satirical newspaper as vital to the Internet as it is to New York City.

New York City is also home to tons of heavy-hitters in the magazine publishing world. Perhaps no publication captures the witty, intellectual spirit of the city as well as the *New Yorker*, a weekly magazine of the arts, literature, journalism, and coffee shop discussion fodder. Of course, New York City's huge music scene is not without its own magazine: *Rolling Stone* has been not-so-subtly reminiscing about the late 60s since the late 60s.

arts

ARCHITECTURE

Kurt Vonnegut once described New York City's architecture as "Skyscraper National Park." Meanwhile, ■Godzilla once referred to New York City's architecture as "my little playthings." Primarily concentrated in Midtown and the Lower Side, there are 50 completed skyscrapers taller than 656 ft. in New York City, only second to Hong Kong. The tallest of these is the Empire State Building, which measures a soaring 1250 ft. Legend, albeit a false one, has it that a penny dropped from the top of the Empire State Building could kill a passerby below. Nearly as famous are the Brooklyn Brownstone residences, notable for their color and their stoops leading onto the street. They are immortalized in pop culture by their prominent role on ■Sesame Street.

FINE ARTS

New York City has more pieces of fine art than taxi cabs—and the greatest collections are parked in two major museums. The exhibits at these museums represent a global gamut of aesthetic tastes and trends. The ■Metropolitan Museum of Art has over two million items in its permanent collection and 19 different curatorial departments. The ■Museum of Modern Art, known as "MoMA," is perhaps the most famous modern art museum in the world. Though sometimes outlandish, the pieces at MoMA offer an intellectually stimulating experience unlike any other.

Besides the major museums, there are over 500 smaller art galleries throughout the city, most heavily concentrated in Chelsea between Sixth Ave. and Tenth Ave., from 14th St. to 34th St. In general, Chelsea and SoHo galleries tend to feature up-and-coming artists, whereas Midtown galleries focus on established artists and Upper East Side Galleries contain many antiques and art of historical significance.

LITERATURE

Some of America's greatest literary rockstars worked in the Big Apple, including Willa Cather, Henry James, Herman Melville, Edgar Allen Poe, and Edith Wharton. It's no surprise that the frenetically creative atmosphere of NYC has given rise to some of the most influential movements in American literature. The Algonquin Round Table, a collection of literary New Yorkers who met for lunch at the Algonquin Hotel in New York City, was established in 1919. The big celebrities of the crew included Harpo Marx and Dorothy Parker. Following World War I, the Harlem Renaissance helped transform Harlem into a cultural Mecca. It was Langston Hughes, the iconic figure of the Harlem Renaissance, who asked, "What happens to a dream deferred? Does it dry up Like a raisin in the sun?... Or does it explode?" Of course, the literary atmosphere of NYC exploded once more in the 1950s and 60s with the Beat generation of Jack Kerouac and Allen Ginsberg. And that's no lie, daddy-o.

FILM

Lights, camera, and more action than you can imagine. New York City was the original center of American filmmaking before studios relocated to California in pursuit of better shooting weather. Although most major studio productions are now based in Hollywood, New York City still serves as a hub for independent films, and is home to the **Tribeca Film Festival.**

SOME FAMOUS FILM AND TV LOCATIONS

- **SEX AND THE CITY.** Carrie Bradshaw's Apartment at 66 Perry St.

- **GHOSTBUSTERS.** Ghostbusters Headquarters, 8 Hook and Ladder, 14 North Moore St., Tribeca

- **BREAKFAST AT TIFFANY'S.** Tiffany's jewelry shop at Fifth Ave. and 58th Street.

- **SUPERMAN.** The Daily Planet at 220 E. 42nd St., between Second and Third Ave.

- **WHEN HARRY MET SALLY.** Katz's Delicatessen at 205 E. Houston, where Sally "faked it" for Harry.

holidays and festivals

New York City is already the biggest ▧**party in the USA.** Still, there are several noteworthy celebrations throughout the year that make it even more of a ball.

- **MACY'S THANKSGIVING DAY PARADE.** Every year on Thanksgiving people line the streets as early as 6:30am to watch a tangled orgy of large ▧**balloons** and floats glide through Manhattan.

- **NEW YEAR'S BALL DROP.** Millions of viewers tune in annually at 11:59PM EST to watch the ball drop over Times Square. It's not that exciting to watch on TV, but nonetheless an American tradition.

- **ROCKEFELLER CENTER CHRISTMAS TREE.** This gigantic tree in the middle of

Rockefeller center is lit every year on the Wednesday after Thanksgiving. The New York City Rockettes generally accompany the tree-lighting with their ⬛**world-class high-kicks**.

- **NEW YORK CITY MARATHON.** An annual event dubbed "one of the world's great road races." Thousands of volunteers and over two million spectators gather on the first Sunday of November to watch over 35,000 athletes run 26.2 miles. We're sweating just thinking about it.

- **RESTAURANT WEEK.** Occurs bi-annually in January and June. Some of the finest New York City restaurants serve their cuisine at a fraction of their usual cost. Great for ▢**foodies,** detrimental to waistlines.

BEYOND TOURISM

If you are reading this, then you are a member of an elite group—and we don't mean "the literate." You're a student preparing for a semester abroad. You're taking a gap year to save the trees, the whales, or the dates. You're an 80-year-old woman who has devoted her life to egg-laying platypuses and figuring out what the hell is up with that. In short, you're a traveler, not a tourist; like any good spy, you don't observe your surroundings—you become an active part of them.

Your mission, should you choose to accept it, is to study, volunteer, or work in New York City as laid out in the dossier—er, chapter—below. More general wisdom, including international organizations with a presence in many destinations and tips on how to pick the right program, is also accessible by logging onto the Beyond Tourism section of ▣www.letsgo.com. We leave the rest (when to go, whom to bring, and how many changes of underwear to pack) in your hands. This message will ▧**self-destruct** in five seconds. Good luck.

greatest hits

- **HIT THE BOOKS.** Bring an apple for teacher in the Big Apple, and study at one of the city's great institutions (p. 226).

- **KINDLE CREATIVITY.** Provide arts education for abused and underprivileged urban youth (p. 230).

- **BE AN AU PAIR EXTRAORDINAIRE.** If you like kids, it's a great way to make some dough while trying to make it big in NYC (p. 233).

- **STAR IN A FEATURE FILM.** Okay, so you'll actually just be making a cameo, but you've got to start somewhere (p. 234).

studying

It's hard to dread the first day of school when New York City is your campus and exotic restaurants are your meal plan. Study-abroad programs range from basic language and culture courses to university-level classes, often for college credit. For accommodations, dorm life provides a better opportunity to mingle with fellow students, but there is less of a chance to experience the local scene. If you live with a family, you could potentially build lifelong friendships with New Yorkers and experience day-to-day life more in-depth, but you might also get stuck sharing a room with their pet iguana. Conditions can vary greatly from family to family.

visa information

Three types of visas are available: the **F-1,** for academic studies, the **J-1,** for those interested in participating in an exchange program, and the **M-1,** for nonacademic and vocational studies. To secure a study visa, you must already be accepted into a full course of study at an educational institution approved by the **Immigration and Naturalization Services (INS).** F-1 applicants must also prove they have enough readily available funds to meet all expenses for the 1st year of study, and that adequate funds will be available for each subsequent year of study; J-1 applicants must agree to return to their home country for a period after studying in the UNited States; and M-1 applicants must have evidence that sufficient funds are available to pay full tuition and living costs for the entire period of intended stay. Be prepared to show transcripts and standardized test results, and make sure your passport is valid for at least 6 months after entry. See 🖥www.unitedstatesvisas.gov or travel.state.gov/visa for more information. Applications should be processed through the American embassy or the consulate in your country of residence.

UNIVERSITIES

The Big Apple has more institutions of higher education than any other city in the world, and many of its schools offer summer or extension programs. **NYU** and **Columbia,** for instance, greet visiting students with open arms during summer months. Institutions like the **Cooper Union for Advancement of Science and Art** offer respected adult-education programs.

BARNARD COLLEGE

3009 Broadway, New York, NY, 10027 ☎212-854-5262 🖥www.barnard.edu

Barnard is an all-female college that welcomes degree candidates from other universities to come and study for a semester or a full year. Visiting students have access to the college's more than 3000 courses. In the spring semester only, Barnard also has a Visiting International Students Program.

$ Semester $19,434. ⏰ Semester or year-long exchanges within the US; international exchanges last through spring only.

COLUMBIA UNIVERSITY CONTINUING EDUCATION

203 Lewisohn Hall, 2970 Broadway ☎212-854-9666 🖥www.ce.columbia.edu

Columbia's 35 acre campus boasts one of the largest library collections in the nation. The university has continuing-education options for those not enrolled in degree programs, which include Auditing Programs and Summer Sessions. A whole slew of courses is available from creative writing to international and public affairs.

$ Summer $1,270 per credit; prices vary for special courses. Auditing Programs tuition $500-1,800 per course. ⏰ Summer sessions last 6 weeks

THE COOPER UNION FOR THE ADVANCEMENT OF SCIENCE AND ART

30 Cooper Square, New York, NY, 10003　　　　☎212-353-4100 ■www.cooper.edu

The Continuing Education department at Cooper Union offers noncredit classes in art, green building design, history, languages, writing, and professional development.

Ⓢ*Tuition varies by course.* Ⓩ *Semester classes last 10 weeks; summer classes last 8-9 weeks.*

FORDHAM UNIVERSITY

Rose Hill Campus, Bronx, NY 1045　　　　☎718-817-1000 ■www.fordham.edu

Fordham College of Liberal Studies offers part- and full-time bachelors programs for adults. Through Fordham's Summer Sessions, students can participate in several Special Programs, including a Pre-College Program, an NYC Summer Internship Program, and a Summer Actors Workshop.

Ⓢ *Pre-College Program $2,025-2,700; NYC Summer Internship Program $1,700; Summer Actors Workshop $2,700.* Ⓩ *Pre-College Program July-Aug; NYC Summer Internship Program 10weeks; Summer Actors Workshop 5 weeks.*

HOFSTRA UNIVERSITY

Hempstead, N.Y. 11549-1000　　　　☎516-463-6600 ■www.hofstra.edu

Hofstra's Continuing Education Program offers courses, certificate programs, and other events. Life-long learning and professional development courses available for both adults and youth.

Ⓢ *Fees vary.* Ⓩ *Courses offered throughout the year.*

THE NEW SCHOOL

66 West 12th St., New York, NY. 10011　　　　☎212-229-5620 ■www.newschool.edu

Continuing education programs are offered through **Parsons The New School for Design, Mannes The New School for Music,** and The New School for General Studies, with courses in business, English, foreign languages, and Food Studies, among others.

Ⓢ *Non-credit tuition varies.* Ⓩ *Summer or semester programs.*

NEW YORK UNIVERSITY (NYU)

70 Washington Square South, New York, NY, 10012　　　　☎212-998-1212 ■www.nyu.edu

Students from other colleges and universities and adults who want to earn college credit can take summer classes at this Greenwich Village institution. Graduate programs also available through NYU Steinhardt and Tisch School of the Arts at NYU.

Ⓢ *Tuition $1,137-1,148; graduate tuition $970-1,447.* Ⓩ *Most summer courses last 6 weeks.*

SCHOOL OF VISUAL ARTS

209 E. 23rd St., New York, NY, 10010　　　　☎212-592-2000 ■www.schoolofvisualarts.edu

Offers continuing education courses, program, and workshops. Courses cover the whole gamut of visual arts, from advertising to interior design. In addition to visual arts courses, the institution has liberal arts classes in art history, humanities, English as a second language, and cinema studies. The school also has Arts Abroad and Arts for Kids programs.

Ⓢ *Courses $120-510. Special programs vary in price.* Ⓩ *1-day workshops to semester-long workshops.*

LANGUAGE SCHOOLS

As renowned novelist Gustave Flaubert once said, "Language is a cracked kettle on which we beat out tunes for bears to dance to." While we at *Let's Go* have absolutely no clue what he was talking about, we do know that the following are good resources for learning English.

EUROCENTRES

56 Eccleston Sq., London, UK, SW1V 1PH　　　　☎+44 20 8297 1488 ■www.eurocentres.org

Study English at Columbia University through the American Language Program (ALP). Must be at least 18 years old to enroll.

Ⓩ *Programs last 4-13 weeks.*

LANGUAGE STUDIES INTERNATIONAL NEW YORK CITY

75 Varick St., Ste. 1203-B, New York, NY 10013 ☎212-965-9940 🖥www.lsi-america.com

Located at the Manhattan campus of the Metropolitan College of New York, the New York branch of this global organization boasts small class sizes and flexible start times.

$ *Course prices $245-810.* ⏰ *Courses last 1-20+ weeks.*

SPRACHCAFFE

75 Varick St., Ste. 1203-B, New York, NY 10013 ☎212-965-9940 🖥www.lsi-america.com

Learn English in the heart of Manhattan at Sprachcaffe's English School in New York. Arrange a stage at Sprachcaffe accommodations for the duration of your courses, or live with a host family.

$ *Courses $510-1430; with residence $1070-3080; with host family stay $1,510-2,655.* ⏰ *Courses last from 1-4 weeks, with the option of an additional week with charge.*

STUDY ABROAD EXPO

1746 E. Winchcomb Dr., Phoenix, AZ 85022 ☎602-942-6734 🖥www.studyabroadexpo.org

Presented by the International Partners for Study Abroad Consortium (IPSA), this organization sponsors schools around the country, with two campuses for the English Language School of New York.

$ *Intensive courses $230-510 per week.* ⏰ *Courses last from 1-20+ weeks.*

FILM, THEATER, AND MUSIC SCHOOLS

Do you dream of seeing your name in lights? Well, start spreading the news: New York, New York is the place to go for education in the performing arts. Unfortunately, most of the city's prestigious performing arts schools are for full-time students only. Such schools include the **Columbia University School of the Arts** *(Film ☎212-854-2815 🖥www.columbia.edu/cu/arts/film)*, **The American Musical and Dramatic Academy** *(☎212-787-5300 or 800-367-7908 🖥www.amda.edu)*, and the **New York University Department of Film and Television** *(☎212-998-1600 🖥www.filmtv.tisch.nyu.edu/page/home)*. Still, these schools often cast non-students for short films and provide valuable networking opportunities. The following schools offer short-term programs:

AMERICAN ACADEMY OF DRAMATIC ARTS (AADA) IN NEW YORK

120 Madison Ave., New York, NY, 10016 ☎800-463-8990 🖥www.aada.org

The Academy has provided stage, film, and television training for 125 years.

$ *6-week summer intensive course $2100.* ⏰ *2- or 6- week summer intensive acting courses.*

CIRCLE IN THE SQUARE THEATRE SCHOOL

1633 Broadway, New York, NY, 10019 ☎212-307-0388 🖥www.circlesquare.org

In addition to its two-year professional acting workshop, offers a seven-week summer program with a professionally oriented curriculum of acting and musical theater classes.

$ *Summer course $2600-2750.* ⏰ *7 weeks, July-Aug.*

THE JUILLIARD SCHOOL EVENING DIVISION

60 Lincoln Center Plaza, New York, NY, 10023-6588 ☎212-799-5000 🖥www.juilliard.edu

The Juilliard School Evening Division affords adults the opportunity to pluck their strings with the best of 'em. The school gives the public access to top-notch musical and dramatic training. Be aware that performance and for-credit courses require an audition or interview.

$ *For-credit courses $400 per credit; non-credit fees vary by course.* ⏰ *Fall, spring, and summer evening courses available.*

THE SCHOOL FOR FILM AND TELEVISION

39 W. 19th St., 12th fl., New York, NY 10011 ☎888-645-0030 🖥www.filmandtelevision.com

A fully accredited educational institution, the School for Film and Television offers professional training programs in Film and Television Performance, as well as in Theater, Film, and Television Performance. The school's summer program allows high school and college students to earn college credits while learning cutting-edge performance techniques.

Ⓢ *Summer courses $4670.* 🗓 *4 weeks, June-July or July-Aug.*

volunteering

Though New York is often portrayed as a city of opulence and opportunity, it also is home to substantial disadvantaged populations that lie hidden beneath the city's bright lights. As a result, New York is a city rich with volunteer opportunities—so you, too, can be a part of it in old New York. Most people who volunteer in New York City do so on a short-term basis at organizations that make use of drop-in or once-a-week volunteers. There are two main types of volunteer organizations—religious and nonsectarian—though there are rarely restrictions on participating in either. The **Volunteer Referral Center** (☎212-889-4805 🖳*www.volunteer-referral.com*) places individuals in volunteer positions at organizations throughout the city based on detailed personal interviews. **New York Cares** (☎212-228-5000 🖳www.newyork-cares.org) also specializes in public service placements. **The Mayor's Volunteer Center** (🖳*www.nyc.gov/html/mvc*) has an extensive list of community service organizations. **United Way of New York City** (☎*212-251-2500* 🖳*www.unitedwaynyc.org*) directs both corporate partners and individuals toward volunteer opportunities. As always, read up before heading out.

Those looking for longer, more intensive volunteer opportunities usually choose to go through a parent organization that takes care of logistical details and often provides a group environment and support system—for a fee. Websites like 🖳**www.volunteerabroad.com**, 🖳**www.servenetorg**, and 🖳**www.idealist.org** allow you to search for volunteer opening both in your country and abroad.

HOMELESSNESS

Homelessness is one of New York City's major social challenges. In any given year, some 100,000 New Yorkers experience homelessness for at least one night, and every night of the year, the city's shelters fill with 32,000 people, including 12,000 children. New York has many organizations seeking to fight homelessness, and you can always provide much-needed support.

- **COMMON GROUND COMMUNITY:** Through a three-pronged strategy of affordable housing, outreach, and prevention, Common Ground seeks to provide permanent residences to the homeless. (☎212-389-9360 🖳*www.asylum-welcome.org*)

- **COVENANT HOUSE NEW YORK:** Provides food, shelter, health services, counseling, job training, and 24hr. crisis assistance to homeless, abused, or at-risk youth. Locations in Brooklyn, Queens, Staten Island, and the Bronx. Wide variety of opportunities. (☎212-613-0300 🖳*www.covenanthouseny.org*)

- **HABITAT FOR HUMANITY NEW YORK CITY:** Through volunteer labor and donations, Habitat builds and rehabilitates simple homes with the help of the future homeowners. (☎212-991-4000 🖳*www.habitatnyc.org*)

- **NEIGHBORHOOD COALITION OF SHELTER:** Offers a variety of services to New York's needy, including housing, 24hr. support, shelter, counseling, and job and education specialists. A variety of volunteer opportunities available, including weekly and as-needed positions. (☎212-537-5100 🖳*www.ncsing.org*)

- **PARTNERSHIP FOR THE HOMELESS:** Dedicated to breaking the cycle of homelessness through a variety of programs geared toward families, the elderly, those affected by HIV/AIDS, and several other at-risk groups. Volunteers staff shelters throughout the city and assist with Partnership's many programs. (☎212-645-3444 ▇www. partnershipforthehomeless.org)

FOOD ASSISTANCE

In a city as wealthy as New York, hunger is a daily concern for an astonishing number of people. More than one million New Yorkers require food assistance annually, and one in four New York City children live below the poverty line. New York has more than 1000 food banks, yet they continually struggle with cutbacks in governmental and charitable support.

- **CITY HARVEST:** Founded in 1981, City Harvest is the world's first food-rescue organization. Committed to feeding hungry people in NYC using innovative, practical, and cost-effective methods, they rescue food that would otherwise be wasted from restaurants, grocers, corporate cafeterias, manufacturers, and farms and deliver it to those who serve the hungry. Volunteer opportunities vary in nature and time commitment. Possible tasks include picking up food donations from the city's vendors and markets or providing administrative support. (☎917-351-8700 ▇www.cityharvest.org)

- **FOOD BANK FOR NEW YORK CITY:** Supplies over 50 million pounds of food to more than 1,000 food assistance programs annually. Volunteer opportunities include assisting at one of its 1000 community food programs; volunteers might serve hot meals at the Community Kitchen in Harlem or assist at fundraising events. (☎212-566-7855 ▇www.foodbanknyc.org)

- **GOD'S LOVE WE DELIVER:** Prepares and delivers fresh, nutritious meals to those living with AIDS, cancer, and other serious illnesses, who cannot shop and cook for themselves. Several volunteer opportunities available, as the organization takes on 1,400 volunteers monthly. (☎212-294-8100 ▇www.godslovewedeliver.org)

- **YORKVILLE COMMON PANTRY (YCP):** Weekly on Thursdays, Fridays, and Saturdays, Yorkville Common Pantry delivers food to 1600-1800 families. In addition to food distribution, services include nutrition education, hygiene services, and homeless support. YCP's programs focus on East Harlem and other underserved New York City communities. Volunteer opportunities include preparing and serving meals, in addition to several off-site options.(☎917-720-9700 ▇www.ycp.org)

YOUTH AND COMMUNITY AND PROGRAMS

All five of New York City's boroughs boast exciting tourist attractions. The unfortunate truth, however, is that there is a great disparity in resources and opportunities from neighborhood to neighborhood. Many poorer communities lack strong educational and recreational programs, support services, and career counseling. Contributing to a community support organization can make a tremendous difference.

- **CITY YEAR:** Volunteers participate in a broad range of public service programs in high-need New York neighborhoods. Service work focuses primarily on youth development, enrichment, and mentoring. Participants must be US citizens. (☎212-675-8881 ▇www.cityyear.org)

- **EAST HARLEM TUTORIAL PROJECT (EHTP):** This nonprofit program offers Harlem children lessons in areas like math and reading. Volunteers needed for tutoring, homework help, arts programs, and more. (☎212-831-0650 ▇www.ehtp.org)

- **QUEENS COMMUNITY HOUSE:** Volunteers are encouraged to participate in the organization's wide range of programs, which include tutoring, employment support, homelessness prevention, early childhood development, and youth outreach. (☎718-592-5757 ▇www.queenscommunityhouse.org)

- **THE POINT COMMUNITY DEVELOPMENT CENTER:** A nonprofit organization operating in Hunts Point that is committed to promoting youth development and cultural and economic revitalization. It offers South Bronx residents after-school programs,

beyond tourism

music instruction, visual arts workshops, community leadership projects, and much more. (☎718-542-4139 ▣www.thepoint.org)

- **UNION SETTLEMENT ASSOCIATION:** An organization dedicated to fostering leadership and self-sufficiency among the immigrant population in Harlem. The Union Settlement Association's after-school, childcare, summer job placement, nutrition, and economic development programs have an impact on more than 13,000 people each year. (☎212-828-6000 ▣www.unionsettlement.org)

ART AND CULTURE

The New York Alliance for the Arts has created ▣www.nyckidsarts.org as a resource for finding arts and culture events throughout the city. The website lists a range of volunteer opportunities with New York's museums, theaters, opera companies, and more. Also see the following organizations for ways to be artsy and humanitarian all in one!

- **ARTISTS STRIVING TO END POVERTY (ASTEP):** An organization that brings arts education to communities of children with little exposure to this kind of creative learning. By bringing them together with volunteer artists, ASTEP educates children on topics including self-empowerment, creative problem-solving, HIV/AIDS awareness, and positive future-building.(☎212-921-1227 ▣www.asteponline.org)

- **ARTSTART:** Connects NYC's artists with at-risk youth to engage in the visual, performance, and media arts, declaring that "art saves lives." Volunteers can contribute in many ways, but the main opportunity is to be a Workshop Volunteer, which requires committing to a weekly session. (☎212-460-0019 ▣www.art-start.org)

- **FREEARTSNYC:** Dedicated to bringing creative arts programs to low-income, homeless, abused, and neglected children. FreeArtsNYC partners with facilities like shelters and schools to develop programs that encourage children's creativity and foster communication and trust. (☎212-974-9092 ▣www.freeartsnyc.org)

- **GUGGENHEIM MUSEUM:** Several volunteer positions, including Family Programs gallery assistant, artist's assistant, department assistant, and information technology support. Volunteer opportunities depend on availability of positions and applicant qualifications. (☎212-423-3500 ▣www.guggenheim.org)

OTHER CONCERNS

- **CITY OF NEW YORK PARKS AND RECREATION:** Volunteers can participate in recreational programs, join community groups, or work to maintain local parks. (☎212-NEW-YORK ▣www.nycgovparks.org)

- **NEW YORK CIVIL RIGHTS COALITION:** College, law, and graduate students participate in the Coalition's effort to defend civil rights and improve race relations through its *Unlearning Stereotypes* program. Groups of two volunteers teach semester-long courses. (☎212-563-5636 ▣www.nycivilrights.org)

- **SANCTUARY FOR FAMILIES:** With nine locations throughout New York City, Sanctuary for Families provides shelter, support, and clinical and legal services to victims of domestic violence and their children. Volunteers can participate in projects like tutoring, holiday helping, and translation. (☎212-974-9092 ▣www.freeartsnyc.org)

volunteering . other concerns

working

New York may be a "concrete jungle where dreams are made of," but a stay in this dreamy city can come at a price. Fortunately, there are some opportunities to earn a living and travel at the same time. To find long-term or short-term employment, start by checking the **classifieds** of New York's newspapers, particularly in *The Village Voice*, *New York Press*, and the Sunday edition of the *New York Times*. Also check bulletin boards in local coffee shops, markets, libraries, and community centers for help-wanted posters. In addition, all of New York's colleges and universities have **career and employment offices;** even if you can't get into the office itself (some may require a school ID to enter), they may have bulletin boards with helpful information outside (for a list of colleges and universities in New York, see **Studying,** p. 226).

LONG-TERM WORK

If you're planning on spending a substantial amount of time (more than three months) working in New York City, search for a job well in advance. Although they are sometimes only available to college students, **internships** are a good way to ease into working. Be wary of advertisements for companies claiming to be able to get you a job for free—often the same listings are available online or in newspapers. For foreigners looking to find work in New York, the **Council on International Educational Exchange (CIEE)** is a reputable organization. CIEE offices are located at 300 Fore St., Portland, ME 04101 (☎1-207-553-4000 🖳www.ciee.org). **Craigslist** (🖳www.newyork.craigslist.org), **Monster** (🖳www.www.monster.com), and Yahoo Hotjobs (🖳www.hotjobs.yahoo.com) are also worth a look.

more visa information

A work permit is required for all foreigners planning to work in the US. In typical bureaucratic style, there are dozens of employment visas, most of which are difficult to get. There are three general categories of work visas or permits: employment-based visas, generally issued to skilled workers that already have a job offer in the US; temporary worker visas, which have fixed time limits and very specific classifications; and cultural exchange visas, which allow for employment by participants in fellowships or reciprocal work programs with the aim of promoting cultural exchange. For more on these requirements, visit 🖳www.unitedstatesvisas.gov or travel.state.gov/visa.

Teaching

While some elite private American schools offer competitive salaries, teaching in the United States tends to offer more personal satisfaction than monetary incentives. Perhaps this is why volunteering as a teacher instead of getting paid is a popular option. In almost all cases, you must have at least a bachelor's degree to be a full-fledged teacher, although college undergraduates can often get summer positions teaching or tutoring.

New York requires teachers to obtain one of a number of different types of certificates, including Initial, Provisional, and Professional, which are all valid for different length of time. Complete information can be found at the New York Department of Education website (🖳http://schools/nyc.gov/TeachNYC). You may still be able to find a teaching job without a certificate, but certified teachers often find higher-paying positions. Placement agencies or university fellowships programs are

beyond tourism

the best resources for finding teaching jobs. The following organization is extremely helpful in placing teachers in New York City.

- **TEACH NYC:** Sponsored by the New York Department of Education, this service provides the most comprehensive information on how to obtain a teaching position. (☎718-935-4000 📧www.schools.nyc/teachNYC)

Au Pair Work

Au pairs are typically women aged 18-26 who work as live-in nannies, caring for children and doing light housework in exchange for room, board, and a small spending allowance or stipend. One perk of the job is that it allows you to get to know New York City without the high expenses of traveling. However, drawbacks can include mediocre pay and long hours. The average weekly salary for an au pair in the United States (roughly 40-45 hours) is around $140. The agencies below are a good starting point for looking for employment.

- **INTEREXCHANGE:** A nonprofit organization that promotes cross-cultural awareness, offering volunteer and work opportunities. The "Au Pair USA" work provides helpful information for both families looking to hire au pairs, and young people looking to go into this line of work. (☎212-924-0446 📧www.interexchange.org)

- **CHILDCARE INTERNATIONAL:** A service based in London that matches au pairs with prospective host families. With its partner Au Pair in America, Childcare International offers many Stateside opportunities. (☎+44 20 8906 3116 📧www.childint.co.uk)

- **THE BABY SITTERS' GUILD:** Established 70 years ago to provide trustworthy part-time, full-time, and emergency childcare for families. (☎212-682-0227 📧www.babysittersguild.com)

Food Service

The highest paid food-service employees tend to be **waiters** and **waitresses.** Food service employees often make less than minimum wage, but their salary is supplemented with tips, which can average around $15 per hour. Since tipping is 15-20% of the bill, the more expensive the restaurant, the more tips for the wait staff (although higher-class restaurants want experienced staff). If you are working as a **cashier** or **host,** you probably won't make much in tips and your salary will be close to minimum wage. **Bartenders** make great tips, but they work late and usually need certification and previous experience. The **American Bartending School,** 68 W. 39th St., NY 10018 (☎212-768-8460 📧www.newyorkbartendingschool.com) provides a one- to two-week 40hr. bartending course, as well as job placement. For food-service jobs, check out the search engines listed under **Long-term work** (see p. 232).

SHORT-TERM WORK

Traveling for long periods of time can become expensive. Many travelers try their hand at odd jobs for a few weeks at a time to help pay for another month or two of touring around. One of the easiest ways to earn money is as a temp worker. Offices often hire employees for short periods (anywhere from a few days to several months) through New York's many temp agencies. Most jobs are secretarial in nature: data entry, filing, answering phones, etc. The **Red Guide to Temp Agencies** (📧www.panix.com/~grvsmth/redguide) provides great reviews of the city's temp agencies. Another popular option is to work for several hours a day at a hostel in exchange for free or discounted room and/or board.

Most often, these short-term jobs are found by word of mouth or by expressing interest to the owner of a hostel or restaurant. Due to high turnover in the tourism industry, many places are eager for help, even if it is only temporary. *Let's Go* lists temporary jobs of this nature whenever possible; look in the **Essentials** chapter of this book or see below.

- **ATRIUM:** With its corporate headquarters in New York City, Atrium is a talent-solutions firm that specializes in Office Support, Finance, IT, Healthcare, Scientific, and Fashion and Retail staffing. (☎212-292-0550 📧www.atriumstaff.com)

- **WORKEVOLVED:** Claiming to "understand the business behind the creative," WorkEvolved is an expert in freelance and permanent staffing. (☎646-254-4380 📧www.workevolved.com)

- **SNELLING STAFFING SERVICES:** An organization that matches employers and employees, specializing in such areas such as Administrative and Clerical, IT, Finance and Medical staffing. (☎800-411-6401 📧www.snelling.com)

- **THE SUPPORTING CAST:** Directs job-seekers to open temp, temp-to-hire, and direct hire positions. (☎212-532-8888 📧www.supportingcast.com)

Acting and Movie Extra Opportunities

New York boasts tons of small theaters and low-budget independent film companies that offer opportunities for unknown actors. **Backstage** (📧www.backstage.com) posts **casting notices** for features, stage, indie film, and TV productions. Keep in mind, though, that the entertainment industry is fickle: look for a day job as well if you want to be able to eat and live in New York City.

Many film producers select **extras** from a casting agency's album of headshots; registration fees at casting agencies are usually around $25. You don't have to belong to a union to land a gig, but union members do earn considerably more than non-union extras. The **Screen Actors Guild** office is located at 360 Madison Ave., 12th fl., New York, NY, 10017 (☎212-944-1030 📧www.sag.org). Still, non-union members might be able to pick up $50 a day. Below is a list of agencies that cast background actors in New York.

- **ACTORS REPS OF NEW YORK:** Supplies extras, bit parts, and speaking roles for TV, feature films, commercials, musical videos, and industrials. Invites all performers age 5 and above to audition. (☎212-391-4668 📧www.actorsreps.org)

- **IMPOSSIBLE CASTING:** Presents opportunities for actors, models, personalities and entertainers. (☎212-255-3029 📧www.impossiblecasting.org)

- **KEE CASTING:** An organization that casts for film, television, commercials, and industrials. Opportunities for both union and non-union performers. (☎212-725-3775 or 201-854-6396 📧www.keecasting.biz)

tell the world

If your friends are tired of hearing about that time you saved a baby orangutan in Indonesia, there's clearly only one thing to do: get new friends. Find them at our website, 📧www.letsgo.com, where you can post your study-, volunteer-, or work-abroad stories for other, more appreciative community members to read. There's also a Beyond Tourism section that elaborates on non-destination-specific volunteering, studying, and working opportunities. If you liked this chapter, you'll love it; if you didn't like this chapter, maybe you'll find the website's more general Beyond Tourism tips more likeable, you non-likey person.

INDEX

index

index

MAP APPENDIX

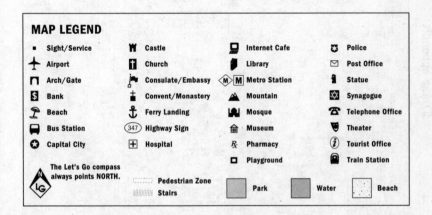

MAP LEGEND

▪ Sight/Service	♖ Castle	🖥 Internet Cafe	♥ Police
✈ Airport	🏛 Church	📙 Library	✉ Post Office
⊓ Arch/Gate	⚑ Consulate/Embassy	Ⓜ M Metro Station	🗿 Statue
$ Bank	✝ Convent/Monastery	▲ Mountain	✡ Synagogue
🏖 Beach	⚓ Ferry Landing	☪ Mosque	☎ Telephone Office
🚌 Bus Station	(347) Highway Sign	🏛 Museum	♣ Theater
✪ Capital City	✚ Hospital	℞ Pharmacy	🛈 Tourist Office
		▢ Playground	🚂 Train Station

The Let's Go compass always points NORTH.

⬡ LG

┈ Pedestrian Zone

▥ Stairs

▨ Park   ▨ Water   ⬚ Beach

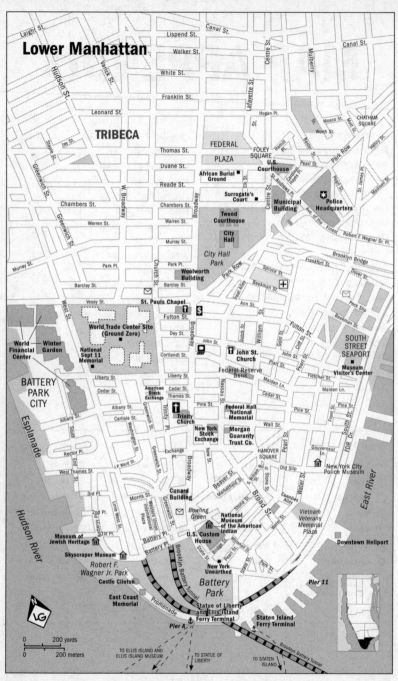

Lower Manhattan

TRIBECA

Canal St.
Lispend St.
Walker St.
White St.
Franklin St.
Leonard St.
Laight St.
Hudson St.
Varick St.
Centre St.
Mulberry
Canal St.

CHATHAM SQUARE
Hogan Pl.
Mosco St.
Worth St.
Henry St.
Park Row

FEDERAL PLAZA
FOLEY SQUARE
U.S. Courthouse

Thomas St.
Duane St.
Reade St.
Chambers St.
Warren St.
Murray St.
Park Pl.
Barclay St.
Vesey St.

African Burial Ground
Surrogate's Court
Tweed Courthouse
City Hall
Municipal Building
Police Headquarters

Broadway
W. Broadway
Greenwich St.
Hudson St.

Chambers St.
Warren St.
Murray St.
Park Pl.
Barclay St.

City Hall Park
Brooklyn Bridge
Robert F. Wagner Sr. Pl.
Ave. of the Finest

Woolworth Building
St. Pauls Chapel
Fulton St.

World Trade Center Site (Ground Zero)
National Sept 11 Memorial

Spruce St.
Beekman St.
Ann St.
Frankfort St.
Dover St.
Peck Slip
Beekman St.

World Financial Center
Winter Garden

BATTERY PARK CITY

Esplanade

Dey St.
Cortlandt St.
Liberty St.
Cedar St.
Albany St.
Carlisle St.

John St.
John St. Church
Federal Reserve Bank
Platt St.
Maiden Ln.
Cedar St.

SOUTH STREET SEAPORT
Museum Visitor's Center
Fulton St.
Gold St.
William
Dutch St.
Nassau St.

American Stock Exchange
Thames St.
Trinity Church
Trinity Pl.

Pine St.
Federal Hall National Memorial
Wall St.

Maiden Ln.
Front St.
South St.
Pine St.

Hudson River

New York Stock Exchange
Morgan Guaranty Trust Co.
HANOVER SQUARE

Exchange Pl.
J.P. Ward St.
West Thames St.
3rd Pl.
2nd Pl.
1st Pl.

Cunard Building
Bowling Green
National Museum of the American Indian
U.S. Custom House

Morris St.
Beaver St.
Stone St.
Broad St.
Coenties Alley
Gouverneur Ln.
Old Slip

New York City Police Museum

Vietnam Veterans Memorial Plaza

Downtown Heliport

East River
EDR Dr.
South St.
Water St.

Museum of Jewish Heritage
Skyscraper Museum
Robert F. Wagner Jr. Park
Castle Clinton
East Coast Memorial

Battery Park
New York Unearthed
Statue of Liberty and Ellis Island Ferry Terminal
Staten Island Ferry Terminal
Pier 11

Pier A
Promenade

Brooklyn Battery Tunnel

0   200 yards
0   200 meters

TO ELLIS ISLAND AND ELLIS ISLAND MUSEUM
TO STATUE OF LIBERTY
TO STATEN ISLAND

map appendix

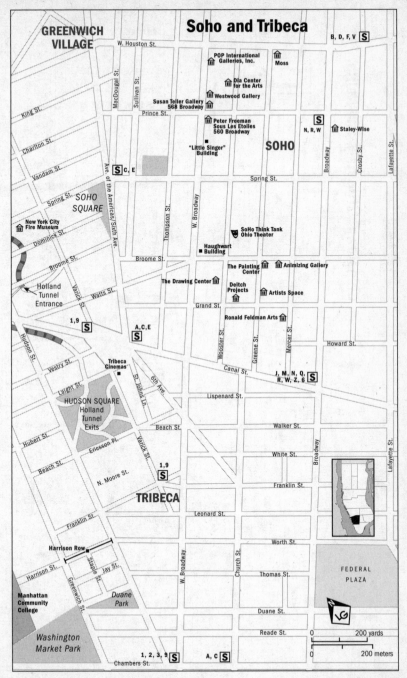

Soho and Tribeca

GREENWICH VILLAGE

W. Houston St.

POP International Galleries, Inc.

Moss

Dia Center for the Arts

Westwood Gallery

Susan Teller Gallery 568 Broadway

Prince St.

Peter Freeman Sous Les Etoiles 560 Broadway

N, R, W

Staley-Wise

SOHO

"Little Singer" Building

B, D, F, V

King St.

MacDougal St.

Sullivan St.

Charlton St.

Vandam St.

Spring St.

SOHO SQUARE

Ave. of the Americas/Sixth Ave.

C, E

New York City Fire Museum

Dominick St.

Broome St.

Spring St.

Thompson St.

W. Broadway

SoHo Think Tank Ohio Theater

Haughwart Building

Broome St.

The Painting Center

Animizing Gallery

The Drawing Center

Deitch Projects

Artists Space

Holland Tunnel Entrance

Watts St.

Varick St.

Grand St.

Ronald Feldman Arts

1, 9

A, C, E

Wooster St.

Greene St.

Mercer St.

Howard St.

Canal St.

Vestry St.

Tribeca Cinemas

St. John's Ln.

6th Ave.

Lispenard St.

J, M, N, Q, R, W, Z, 6

Hudson St.

Laight St.

HUDSON SQUARE Holland Tunnel Exits

Ericsson Pl.

Beach St.

Walker St.

Hubert St.

Varick St.

White St.

Beach St.

1, 9

Franklin St.

Broadway

Lafayette St.

N. Moore St.

TRIBECA

Leonard St.

Franklin St.

Worth St.

Harrison Row

Staple St.

Jay St.

FEDERAL PLAZA

Harrison St.

W. Broadway

Church St.

Thomas St.

Manhattan Community College

Greenwich St.

Duane Park

Duane St.

Washington Market Park

Reade St.

0   200 yards

1, 2, 3, 9

A, C

0   200 meters

Chambers St.

map appendix

Chinatown, Little Italy, and Nolita

Ludlow St.

Orchard St.

Allen St.

Rivington St.

Eldridge St.

Broome St.

Grand St.

Forsyth St.

Sara Delano Roosevelt Park

Delancey St.

Chrystie St.

B, D **S**

Stanton St.

Bowery

S J, M, Z

Elizabeth St.

Elizabeth St.

NOLITA

Mott St.

LITTLE ITALY

Mott St.

Prince St.

DeSalvio Playground

Kenmare St.

Broome St.

Mulberry St.

Mulberry St.

Grand St.

Pack Building

Jersey St.

Spring St.

Cleveland Pl.

Police Headquarters

Lafayette St.

Lafayette St.

S 6

S N, R, W

Prince St.

Crosby St.

Grand St.

Broadway

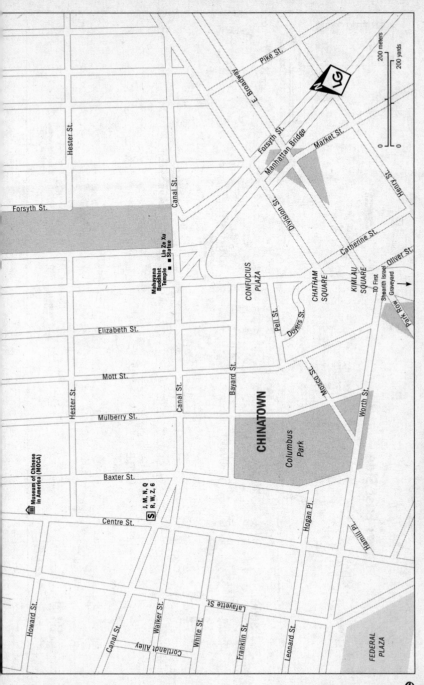

CHINATOWN

Columbus Park

FEDERAL PLAZA

Museum of Chinese in America (MOCA)

Mahayana Buddhist Temple

Lin Ze Xu Statue

CONFUCIUS PLAZA

CHATHAM SQUARE

KIMLAU SQUARE

10 First Shearith Israel Graveyard

Park Row

Forsyth St.

Hester St.

Canal St.

Elizabeth St.

Mott St.

Mulberry St.

Baxter St.

Centre St.

Hester St.

Canal St.

Bayard St.

Pell St.

Doyers St.

Mosco St.

Worth St.

Hogan Pl.

Baxter St.

Howard St.

Canal St.

Cortlandt Alley

Walker St.

White St.

Lafayette St.

Franklin St.

Leonard St.

Pike St.

E. Broadway

Forsyth St.

Manhattan Bridge

Market St.

Division St.

Catherine St.

Oliver St.

Henry St.

S J, M, N, Q R, W, Z, 6

200 meters
200 yards

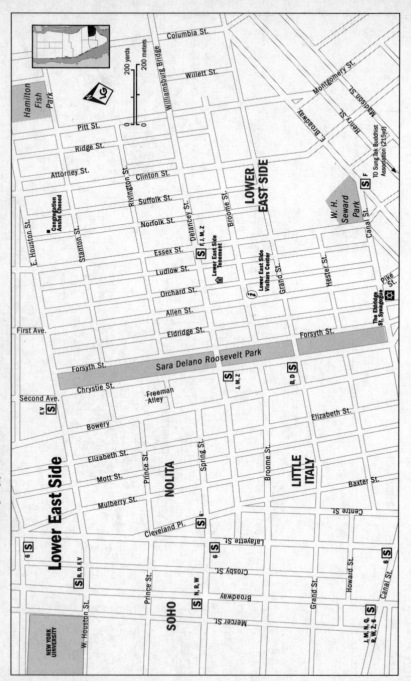

Columbia St.

Willett St.

Williamsburg Bridge

Hamilton Fish Park

Pitt St.

Ridge St.

Attorney St.

Clinton St.

Rivington St.

Suffolk St.

Norfolk St.

Congregation Anshe Chesed

E. Houston St.

Stanton St.

Delancey St.

Broome St.

LOWER EAST SIDE

Montgomery St.

Madison St.

Henry St.

E. Broadway

S F

To Sung Tak Buddhist Association (215yd)

Canal St.

W. H. Seward Park

Hester St.

Grand St.

S F, J, M, Z

Essex St.

Lower East Side Tenement

Ludlow St.

Orchard St.

i Lower East Side Visitors Center

Allen St.

Pike St.

The Eldridge St. Synagogue

First Ave.

Eldridge St.

Forsyth St.

Forsyth St.

Sara Delano Roosevelt Park

Forsyth St.

Chrystie St.

Second Ave.

Freeman Alley

S J, M, Z

S B, D

S F, V

Bowery

Elizabeth St.

Elizabeth St.

Prince St.

Spring St.

NOLITA

Mott St.

Broome St.

LITTLE ITALY

Baxter St.

Mulberry St.

Centre St.

Cleveland Pl.

S 6

Lower East Side

S 6

S B, D, F, V

S 6

Lafayette St.

S 6

W. Houston St.

Prince St.

Crosby St.

Broadway

SOHO

Grand St.

Howard St.

S 6

Canal St.

NEW YORK UNIVERSITY

S N, R, W

Mercer St.

S J, M, N, Q, R, W, Z, 6

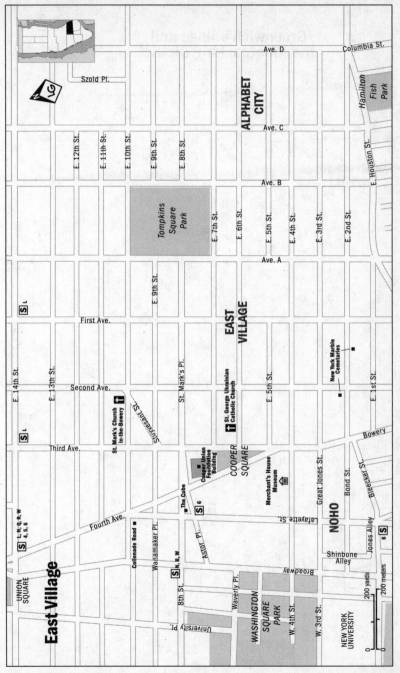

East Village

map appendix

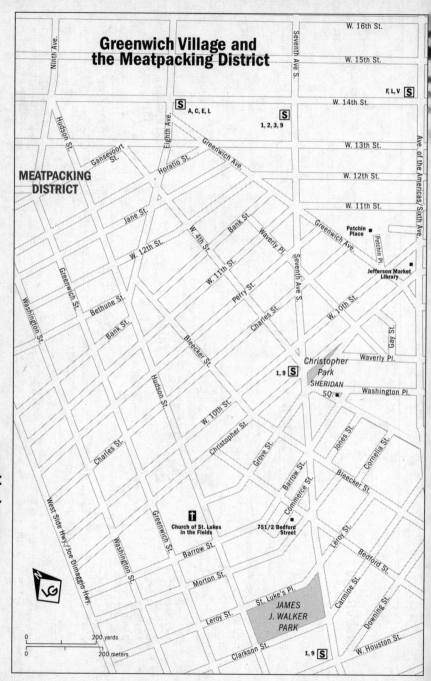

Greenwich Village and the Meatpacking District

E. 16th St.

UNION SQUARE

Fifth Ave.

E. 15th St.

Union Sq. W.

L, N, Q, R, W, 4, 5, 6 Ⓢ

E. 14th St.

E. 13th St.

Broadway

Rorbes Magazine Galleries ▪

E. 12th St.

New School for Liberal Arts (Eugene Lang College) ▪

E. 11th St.

Fourth Ave.

✝ Grace Church

W. 10th St.

E. 10th St.

W. 9th St.

E. 9th St.

Fifth Ave.

University Pl.

W. 8th St.

E. 8th St.

N, R, W Ⓢ

MacDougal Alley

Washington Mews

GREENWICH VILLAGE

Washington Sq. N.

Waverly Pl.

A, B, C, D, E, F, V Ⓢ

WASHINGTON SQUARE PARK

Washington Sq. E.

Greene St.

Mercer St.

Broadway

West 4th St. Basketball Courts ▪

Washington Sq. S.

E. 4th St.

W. 3rd St.

ⓘ

Minetta Ln.

Great Jones St.

NEW YORK UNIVERSITY

LaGuardia Pl.

Bond St.

Minetta St.

Bleecker St.

Mercer St.

MacDougal St.

Sullivan St.

Thompson St.

▪ Picasso

Crosby St.

Lafayette St.

W. Houston St.

E. Houston St.

W. Broadway

Wooster St.

Greene St.

Mercer St.

Broadway

Lincoln Tunnel

Chelsea

Jacob K. Javits
Convention Center

W. 39th St.
W. 38th St.
W. 37th St.
W. 36th St.
W. 35th St.
W. 34th St.

Eleventh Ave.

Twelfth Ave.

0   500 yards
0   500 meters

W. 33rd St.
W. 32nd St.
W. 31st St.
W. 30th St.
W. 29th St.

A, C, E
S

General Post Office
(James A. Farley Building)

Chelsea Park

Cheim & Read
Kashya
Hilderbrand
Gallery

Gagosian
Gallery
Matthew Marks

To The Museum of
the Fashion Institute
of Technology

Ninth Ave.

Eighth Ave.

525 W. 22nd St.
Max
Protetch

Chelsea Art
Museum
Sonnabend

Dia Art
Foundation

529 W. 20th St.

Anton Kern

David Zwirner

West Side Hwy.

Chelsea
Piers

CHELSEA

W. 23rd St.
C, E   S
W. 22nd St.
W. 21st St.

General Theology
Seminary

W. 20th St.
Cushman Row

St. Peter's
Episcopal Church

W. 19th St.
W. 18th St.
W. 17th St.
W. 16th St.

Chelsea Market

W. 15th St.
W. 14th St.
A, C, E, L   S
W. 13th St.

Eleventh Ave.

Washington
St.

Hudson
River

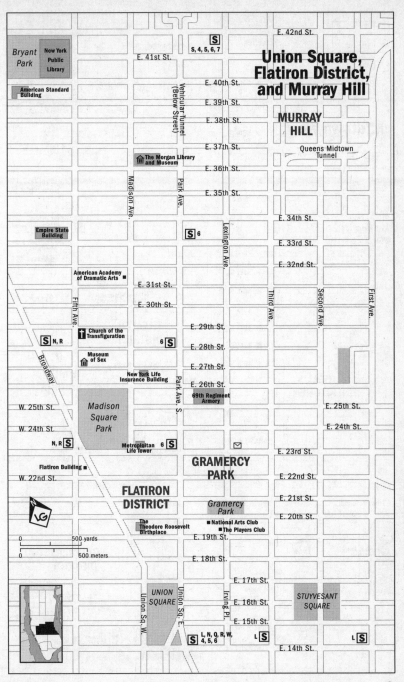

Union Square, Flatiron District, and Murray Hill

MURRAY HILL

Bryant Park

New York Public Library

American Standard Building

E. 42nd St.

S S, 4, 5, 6, 7

E. 41st St.

E. 40th St.

E. 39th St.

E. 38th St.

Vehicular Tunnel (Below Street)

E. 37th St.

Queens Midtown Tunnel

The Morgan Library and Museum

E. 36th St.

E. 35th St.

Madison Ave.

Park Ave.

E. 34th St.

Empire State Building

S 6

E. 33rd St.

E. 32nd St.

Lexington Ave.

American Academy of Dramatic Arts

E. 31st St.

E. 30th St.

Fifth Ave.

Third Ave.

Second Ave.

First Ave.

E. 29th St.

S N, R

Church of the Transfiguration

6 **S**

E. 28th St.

Museum of Sex

E. 27th St.

Broadway

New York Life Insurance Building

E. 26th St.

Park Ave. S.

69th Regiment Armory

W. 25th St.

Madison Square Park

E. 25th St.

W. 24th St.

E. 24th St.

N, R **S**

Metropolitan Life Tower

6 **S**

✉

E. 23rd St.

Flatiron Building

GRAMERCY PARK

E. 22nd St.

W. 22nd St.

FLATIRON DISTRICT

E. 21st St.

Gramercy Park

E. 20th St.

The Theodore Roosevelt Birthplace

■ National Arts Club
■ The Players Club

E. 19th St.

0   500 yards

E. 18th St.

0   500 meters

E. 17th St.

UNION SQUARE

STUYVESANT SQUARE

Union Sq. W.

Union Sq. E.

Irving Pl.

E. 16th St.

E. 15th St.

S L, N, Q, R, W, 4, 5, 6

L **S**

L **S**

E. 14th St.

map appendix

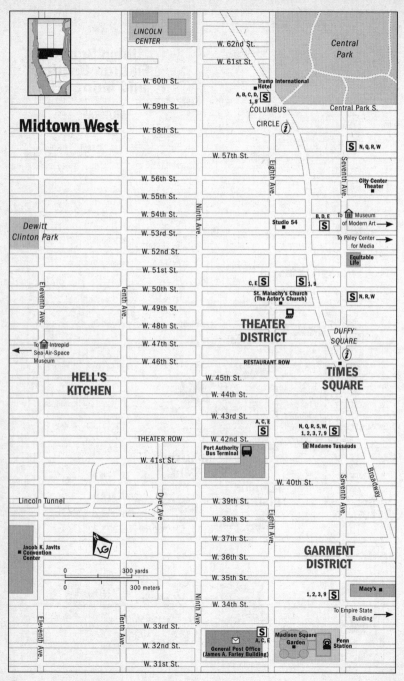

LINCOLN
CENTER

W. 62nd St.

W. 61st St.

Central
Park

Trump International
Hotel

A, B, C, D, S
1, 9

COLUMBUS
CIRCLE (i)

Central Park S.

W. 60th St.

Midtown West

W. 59th St.

W. 58th St.

S N, Q, R, W

W. 57th St.

Eighth Ave.

Seventh Ave.

City Center
Theater

W. 56th St.

W. 55th St.

W. 54th St.

*Dewitt
Clinton Park*

W. 53rd St.

Studio 54

B, D, E
S To 🏛 Museum
of Modern Art →

W. 52nd St.

To Paley Center
for Media →

Ninth Ave.

W. 51st St.

Equitable
Life

W. 50th St.

C, E S

S 1, 9

Eleventh Ave.

St. Malachy's Church
(The Actor's Church)

S N, R, W

W. 49th St.

Tenth Ave.

W. 48th St.

**THEATER
DISTRICT**

*DUFFY
SQUARE*

To 🏛 Intrepid
Sea-Air-Space
Museum ←

W. 47th St.

W. 46th St.

(i)

**HELL'S
KITCHEN**

RESTAURANT ROW

**TIMES
SQUARE**

W. 45th St.

W. 44th St.

W. 43rd St.

A, C, E
S

N, Q, R, S, W
1, 2, 3, 7, 9 S

THEATER ROW

W. 42nd St.

Port Authority
Bus Terminal 🚌

🏛 Madame Tussauds

Broadway

W. 41st St.

W. 40th St.

Seventh Ave.

Lincoln Tunnel

Dyer Ave.

W. 39th St.

W. 38th St.

Eighth Ave.

W. 37th St.

VG

Jacob K. Javits
Convention
Center

W. 36th St.

**GARMENT
DISTRICT**

W. 35th St.

0   300 yards

0   300 meters

W. 34th St.

1, 2, 3, 9 S

Macy's ■

To Empire State
Building →

W. 33rd St.

Eleventh Ave.

Tenth Ave.

Ninth Ave.

W. 32nd St.

S
A, C, E
✉
General Post Office
(James A. Farley Building)

Madison Square
Garden

Penn
Station

W. 31st St.

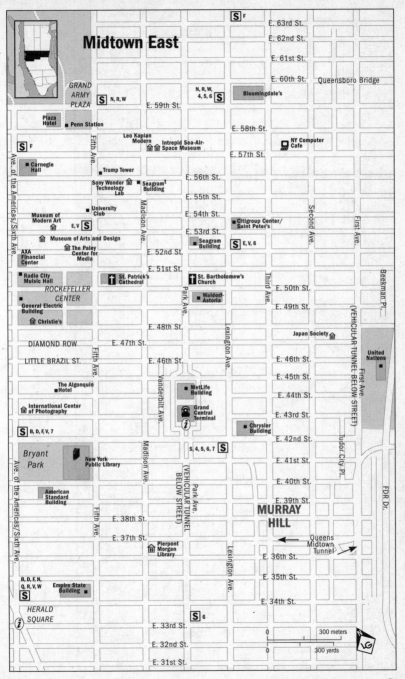

Midtown East

GRAND ARMY PLAZA

Queensboro Bridge

S F

E. 63rd St.
E. 62nd St.
E. 61st St.
E. 60th St.

S N, R, W

N, R, W, 4, 5, 6 **S**

Bloomingdale's

E. 59th St.

E. 58th St.

Plaza Hotel

Penn Station

S F

Leo Kaplan Modern

Intrepid Sea-Air-Space Museum

NY Computer Cafe

E. 57th St.

Carnegie Hall

Trump Tower

Sony Wonder Technology Lab

Seagram Building

E. 56th St.

E. 55th St.

University Club

E. 54th St.

Citigroup Center/ Saint Peter's

Museum of Modern Art

E, V **S**

E. 53rd St.

Seagram Building

S E, V, 6

Museum of Arts and Design

The Paley Center for Media

E. 52nd St.

AXA Financial Center

E. 51st St.

Radio City Muisic Hall

St. Patrick's Cathedral

St. Bartholomew's Church

ROCKEFELLER CENTER

E. 50th St.

Waldorf-Astoria

General Electric Building

E. 49th St.

Christie's

E. 48th St.

Japan Society

DIAMOND ROW

E. 47th St.

LITTLE BRAZIL ST.

E. 46th St.

United Nations

The Algonquin Hotel

MetLife Building

E. 45th St.

International Center of Photography

E. 44th St.

Grand Central Terminal

E. 43rd St.

S B, D, F, 7

Chrysler Building

E. 42nd St.

Bryant Park

New York Public Library

S, 4, 5, 6, 7 **S**

E. 41st St.

E. 40th St.

American Standard Building

E. 39th St.

MURRAY HILL

Fifth Ave.

E. 38th St.

E. 37th St.

Queens Midtown Tunnel

Pierpont Morgan Library

E. 36th St.

B, D, F, N, Q, R, V, W **S**

Empire State Building

E. 35th St.

E. 34th St.

HERALD SQUARE

E. 33rd St.

S 6

0   300 meters

E. 32nd St.

0   300 yards

E. 31st St.

Fifth Ave.

Madison Avenue

Park Avenue

Lexington Avenue

Third Ave.

Second Ave.

First Ave.

Vanderbilt Avenue

Ave. of the Americas/Sixth Ave.

Beekman Pl.

Tudor City Pl.

FDR Dr.

(VEHICULAR TUNNEL BELOW STREET)

map appendix

Upper West Side

W. 111th St.

Cathedral Pkwy.

1 S

Broadway

W. 104th St.
W. 103rd St. **S** 1
W. 102nd St.
W. 101st St.
W. 100th St.

W. 99th St.
W. 98th St.

W. 97th St.
W. 96th St.

1, 2, 3 S

Broadway

Amsterdam Ave.

Columbus Ave.

Riverside Park

Soldiers and
Sailors Monument

Hudson River

Henry Hudson Pkwy.

Riverside Dr.

West End Ave.

Cathedral of St.
John the Divine

W. 109th St.
W. 108th St.
W. 107th St.
W. 106th St.
W. 105th St.

W. 95th St.
W. 94th St.
W. 93rd St.
W. 92nd St.
W. 91st St.
W. 90th St.
W. 89th St.

W. 88th St.
W. 87th St.
W. 86th St.
W. 85th St.
W. 84th St.
W. 83rd St.
W. 82nd St.

W. 81st St.

W. 80th St.

W. 79th St.
W. 78th St.
W. 77th St.
W. 76th St.
W. 75th St.

W. 74th St.
W. 73rd St.

1 S

The Children's
Museum of Manhattan

79th St.
Boat Basin

S 1

The Ansonia
Apartments

SHERMAN
S SQ.
1, 2, 3

W. 72nd St.
W. 71st St.
W. 70th St.

W. 69th St.
W. 68th St.
W. 67th St.

S 1

W. 66th St.
W. 65th St.

Broadway

Freedom Pl.

West End Ave.

Juilliard
School

LINCOLN
CENTER

Damrosch
Park

Dante
Park

FORDHAM
UNIVERSITY

W. 60th St.

W. 59th St.

Manhattan Ave.

Central Park N.
(W. 110th St.)

B, C S

B, C S

B, C S

B, C S

Central Park W.

B, C S

B, C
S

Theodore
Roosevelt
Park

Hayden
Planetarium

American Museum
of Natural
History

New York
Historical Society

Dakota Apartments

B, C S

Columbus Ave.

Central Park W.

Central Park

W. 64th St.
W. 63rd St.
W. 62nd St.
W. 61st St.

Trump
International
Hotel

**A, B, C,
D, 1** S COLUMBUS
CIRCLE
M

Warner Center

0   300 yards
0   300 meters

map appendix

Upper East Side

E. 113th St.

Thomas Jefferson Park

E. 112th St.
E. 111th St.
E. 110th St.
E. 109th St.
E. 108th St.
E. 107th St.
E. 106th St.

Footbridge

Wards Island Park

El Museo Del Barrio
Frick Collection

E. 105th St.
E. 104th St.
E. 103rd St.
E. 102nd St.
E. 101st St.
E. 100th St.
E. 99th St.

Mt. Sinai Hospital

Metropolitan Hospital Center

St. Nicholas Russian Orthodox Cathedral

E. 98th St.
E. 97th St.
E. 96th St.

CARNEGIE HILL

E. 95th St.
E. 94th St.
E. 93rd St.
E. 92nd St.
E. 91st St.

The Jewish Museum
Cooper-Hewitt National Design Museum
Museum of the City of New York (MCNY)
Guggenheim Museum

E. 90th St.
E. 89th St.
E. 88th St.
E. 87th St.

Gracie Mansion

The Church of Holy Trinity

The Neue Gallery

4, 5, 6

E. 86th St.
E. 85th St.
E. 84th St.
E. 83rd St.
E. 82nd St.
E. 81st St.
E. 80th St.

Henderson Place Historic District

Carl Schurz Park

Metropolitan Museum of Art

Aquavella Gallery

E. 78th St.
E. 79th St.

Leo Castelli Gallery
Gagosian Gallery
Whitney Museum of American Art

E. 77th St.
E. 76th St.
E. 75th St.
E. 74th St.
E. 73rd St.

Church of St. Jean Baptiste

East River

Central Park

Hirschl & Adler Galleries
The Asia Society

E. 72nd St.
E. 71st St.
E. 70th St.
E. 69th St.
E. 68th St.
E. 67th St.
E. 66th St.
E. 65th St.

Sotheby's

West Channel

East Channel

Roosevelt Island

Frick Collection

M. Knoedler & Co., Inc.
Lotos Club

New York Presbyterian Hospital

Rockefeller University

Temple Emanu-El
St. Nicolas Russian Orthodox Cathedral

E. 64th St.
E. 63rd St.
E. 62nd St.

Knickerbocker Club

Museum of American Illustration

Metropolitan Theater
Henderson Place Historic District

N, R, W
4, 5, 6

E. 61st St.
E. 60th St.

Roosevelt Island Tramway

To Southpoint Park Area

GRAND ARMY PLAZA

N, R, W

Queensboro Bridge

map appendix

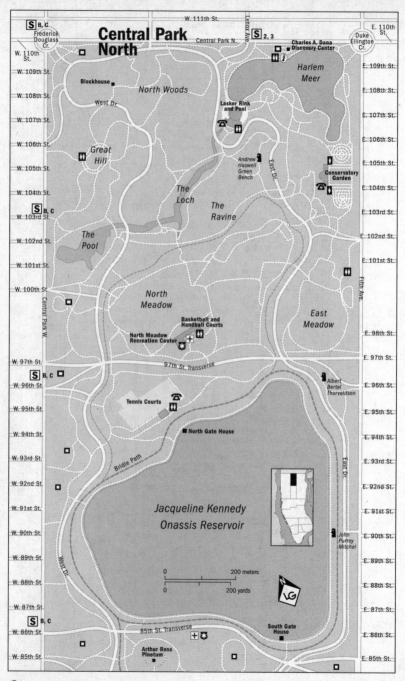

Central Park North

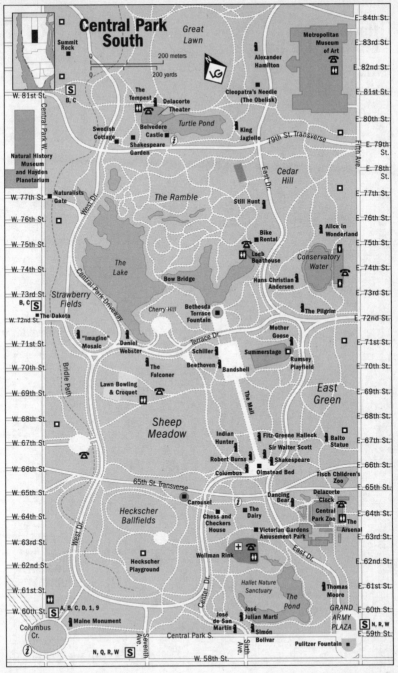

Central Park South

Great Lawn

Summit Rock

Metropolitan Museum of Art

Alexander Hamilton

Cleopatra's Needle (The Obelisk)

The Tempest

Delacorte Theater

Swedish Cottage

Belvedere Castle

Shakespeare Garden

Turtle Pond

King Jagiello

79th St. Transverse

Natural History Museum and Hayden Planetarium

Naturalists Gate

Cedar Hill

The Ramble

Still Hunt

Alice in Wonderland

Bike Rental

East Dr.

The Lake

Loeb Boathouse

Conservatory Water

Bow Bridge

Hans Christian Andersen

Strawberry Fields

Central Park Driveway

Cherry Hill

Bethesda Terrace Fountain

The Pilgrim

The Dakota

"Imagine" Mosaic

Daniel Webster

Schiller

Mother Goose

Terrace Dr.

Summerstage

Beethoven

The Falconer

Bandshell

Rumsey Playfield

Bridle Path

Lawn Bowling & Croquet

East Green

The Mall

Sheep Meadow

Indian Hunter

Fitz-Greene Halleck

Balto Statue

Sir Walter Scott

Robert Burns

Shakespeare

Columbus

Olmstead Bed

Tisch Children's Zoo

65th St. Transverse

Heckscher Ballfields

Carousel

Dancing Bear

Delacorte Clock

The Dairy

Central Park Zoo

Chess and Checkers House

West Dr.

Victorian Gardens Amusement Park

The Arsenal

Heckscher Playground

Wollman Rink

Hallet Nature Sanctuary

Thomas Moore

Center Dr.

The Pond

GRAND ARMY PLAZA

Maine Monument

José de San Martin

José Julian Martí

Simón Bolívar

Seventh Ave.

Columbus Cr.

Central Park S.

Sixth Ave.

Pulitzer Fountain

N, Q, R, W

W. 58th St.

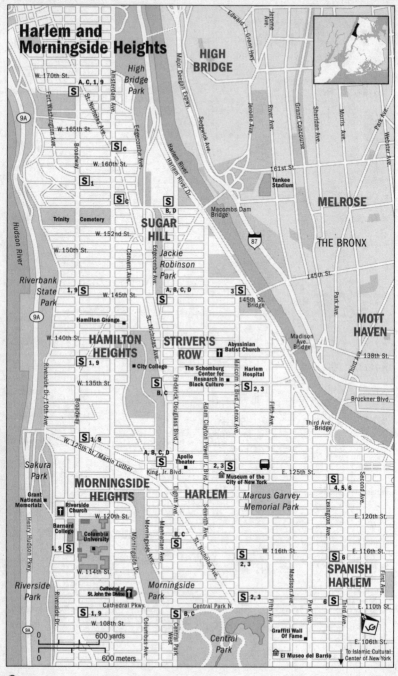

Harlem and Morningside Heights

HIGH BRIDGE

High Bridge Park

W. 170th St.

A, C, 1, 9 Ⓢ

W. 165th St.

Ⓢ C

W. 160th St.

Ⓢ 1

Ⓢ C

B, D Ⓢ

Trinity Cemetery

SUGAR HILL

W. 152nd St.

Jackie Robinson Park

W. 150th St.

Riverbank State Park

1, 9 Ⓢ W. 145th St.

A, B, C, D Ⓢ

3 Ⓢ

145th St. Bridge

Hamilton Grange

W. 140th St.

HAMILTON HEIGHTS

Ⓢ 1, 9

STRIVER'S ROW

Abyssinian Batist Church

City College

W. 135th St.

The Schomburg Center for Research in Black Culture

Harlem Hospital

Ⓢ 2, 3

Ⓢ B, C

Ⓢ 1, 9

W. 125th St./Martin Luther

A, B, C, D Ⓢ

Apollo Theater

King, Jr. Blvd.

2, 3 Ⓢ

Sakura Park

MORNINGSIDE HEIGHTS

Grant National Memorialz

Riverside Church

Barnard College

Columbia University

W. 120th St.

HARLEM

Museum of the City of New York

Ⓢ 4, 5, 6

Marcus Garvey Memorial Park

E. 120th St.

Ⓢ B, C

1, 9 Ⓢ

W. 114th St.

Riverside Park

Cathedral of St. John the Divine

Morningside Park

Ⓢ 2, 3

W. 116th St.

Ⓢ 6

E. 116th St.

SPANISH HARLEM

Cathedral Pkwy.

Central Park N.

Ⓢ 2, 3

Ⓢ 1, 9

W. 108th St.

Ⓢ B, C

Central Park

6 Ⓢ

E. 110th St.

Graffiti Wall Of Fame

E. 106th St.

To Islamic Cultural Center of New York

0 600 yards

0 600 meters

El Museo del Barrio

HIGH BRIDGE

Edward I. Grant Hwy.

Jerome Ave.

River Ave.

Grand Concourse

Sheridan Ave.

Morris Ave.

Park Ave.

Webster Ave.

161st St.

Yankee Stadium

MELROSE

THE BRONX

145th St.

MOTT HAVEN

Madison Ave. Bridge

138th St.

Third Ave. Bridge

Bruckner Blvd.

Fort Washington Ave.

Amsterdam Ave.

St. Nicholas Ave.

Edgecombe Ave.

Harlem River Dr.

Broadway

Convent Ave.

Henry Hudson Pkwy.

Riverside Dr./10th Ave.

Frederick Douglass Blvd.

Adam Clayton Powell Jr. Blvd.

Malcolm X Blvd./Lenox Ave.

Fifth Ave.

Madison Ave.

Lexington Ave.

Park Ave.

Third Ave.

Second Ave.

First Ave.

Columbus Ave.

Central Park West

Hudson River

Harlem River

Macombs Dam Bridge

Major Deegan Expwy.

Sedgwick Ave.

map appendix

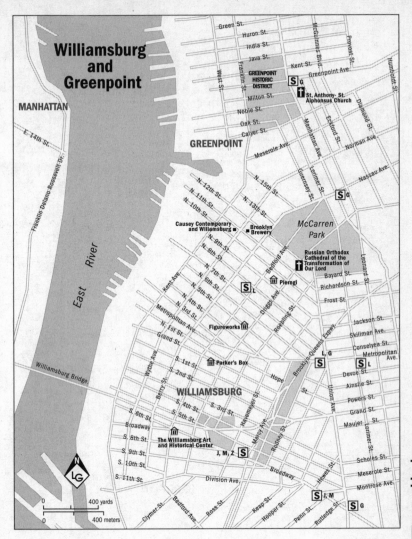

Williamsburg
and
Greenpoint

MANHATTAN

Green St.
Huron St.
India St.
Java St.
GREENPOINT HISTORIC DISTRICT
Kent St.
Greenpoint Ave.
McGuiness Blvd.
Provost St.
Humboldt St.
S G
✝ St. Anthony- St. Alphonsus Church
Milton St.
Noble St.
Oak St.
Calyer St.
Meserole Ave.
Manhattan Ave.
Eckford St.
Diamond St.
Norman Ave.
Nassau Ave.
Guernsey St.
Lorimer St.

GREENPOINT

West St.

East River

Franklin Delano Roosevelt Dr.

E. 14th St.

N. 12th St.
N. 11th St.
N. 10th St.
N. 13th St.
N. 15th St.
S G

Causey Contemporary and Williamsburg ■
■ Brooklyn Brewery
McCarren Park
N. 9th St.
N. 8th St.
Bedford Ave.
Russian Orthodox Cathedral of the Transformation of Our Lord ✝
Leonard St.
N. 7th St.
N. 6th St.
N. 5th St.
Bayard St.
Richardson St.
Kent Ave.
S L
🏛 Pierogi
Frost St.
N. 4th St.
N. 3rd St.
Metropolitan Ave.
N. 1st St.
Grand St.
Figureworks 🏛
Driggs Ave.
Roebling St.
Jackson St.
Skillman Ave.
Conselyea St.
Metropolitan Ave.
Wythe Ave.
Berry St.
🏛 Parker's Box
S. 1st St.
S. 2nd St.
L, G
S
S L
Devoe St.
Ainslie St.
Powers St.
Grand St.
Mauier St.
Union Ave.
Brooklyn-Queens Expwy.
Hope St.
Lorimer St.

WILLIAMSBURG

Williamsburg Bridge

S. 3rd St.
S. 4th St.
S. 5th St.
S. 6th St.
Broadway
S. 8th St.
S. 9th St.
S. 10th St.
S. 11th St.
Havemeyer St.
Marcy Ave.
Rodney St.
The Williamsburg Art and Historical Center 🏛
J, M, Z **S**
Scholes St.
Meserole St.
Montrose St.
Hewes St.
Broadway
Division Ave.
Clymer St.
Bedford Ave.
Ross St.
Keap St.
Hooper St.
Penn St.
Rutledge St.
S J, M
S G

N
L G

0 ____ 400 yards
0 ____ 400 meters

map appendix

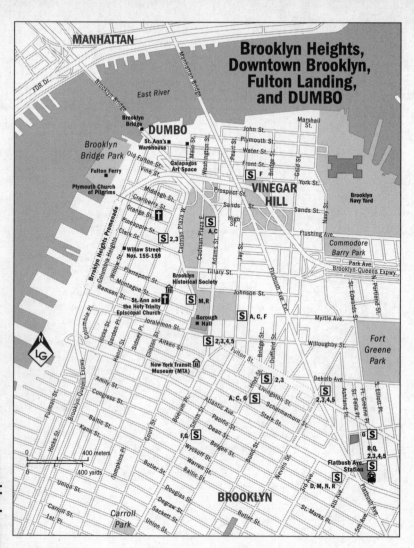

Brooklyn Heights,
Downtown Brooklyn,
Fulton Landing,
and DUMBO

MANHATTAN

East River

Brooklyn Bridge

FDR Dr.

Brooklyn Bridge

Brooklyn Bridge Park

Fulton Ferry

Plymouth Church of Pilgrims

Brooklyn Heights Promenade

Columbia Heights

DUMBO

St. Ann's Warehouse

Galapagos Art Space

VINEGAR HILL

Brooklyn Navy Yard

Commodore Barry Park

Park Ave.
Brooklyn-Queens Expwy.

Old Fulton St.

Vine St.

Middagh St.

Cranberry St.

Orange St.

Pineapple St.

Clark St.

Willow Street Nos. 155-159

Pierrepont St.

Montague St.

Remsen St.

St. Ann and the Holy Trinity Episcopal Church

Joralemon St.

Brooklyn Historical Society

Borough Hall

Aitken St.

New York Transit Museum (MTA)

John St.

Plymouth St.

Water St.

Front St.

Prospect St.

Sands St.

High St.

Sands St.

Flushing Ave.

Marshall St.

York St.

Jay St.

Bridge St.

Gold St.

Navy St.

St. Edwards St.

Portland St.

Fort Greene Park

Myrtle Ave.

Johnson St.

Tillary St.

Willoughby St.

Dekalb Ave.

Washington St.

Cadman Plaza W.

Cadman Plaza E.

Adams St.

Flatbush Ave. Ext.

Bridge St.

Fulton St.

Duffield St.

Livingston St.

Schermerhorn St.

State St.

Ashland Pl.

St. Felix St.

Ft. Greene Pl.

S. Elliott Pl.

Hicks St.

Henry St.

Garden Pl.

Sidney Pl.

Clinton St.

Court St.

Boerum Pl.

Smith St.

Hoyt St.

Bond St.

Nevins St.

3rd Ave.

4th Ave.

Flatbush Ave.

Atlantic Ave.

Pacific St.

Dean St.

Wyckoff St.

Bergen St.

Warren St.

Baltic St.

Douglas St.

Degraw St.

Sackett St.

Union St.

St. Marks Pl.

Butler St.

BROOKLYN

Fulton St.

Furman St.

Brooklyn-Queens Expwy.

Columbia Pl.

Willow St.

Amity St.

Congress St.

Baltic St.

Kane St.

Tompkins Pl.

Union St.

Carroll St.

1st Pl.

Carroll Park

Hicks St.

S F

A, C

2, 3

M, R

A, C, F

2, 3, 4, 5

2, 3

A, C, 6

F, G

2, 3, 4, 5

G S

B, Q, 2, 3, 4, 5

Flatbush Ave. Station

D, M, N, R

0   400 meters
0   400 yards

N LG

map appendix

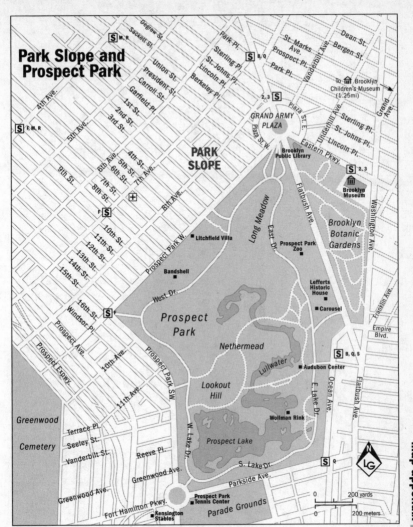

Park Slope and Prospect Park

Degraw St.
Sackett St.
Union St.
President St.
Carroll St.
Garfield Pl.
1st St.
2nd St.
3rd St.

Park Pl.
Sterling Pl.
St. Johns Pl.
Lincoln Pl.
Berkeley Pl.

4th Ave.

S M, R

S B/Q

St. Marks Ave.
Prospect Pl.
Park Pl.

Dean St.
Bergen St.

Vanderbilt Ave.

To Brooklyn Children's Museum (1.25mi)

Grand Ave.

S F, M, R

5th Ave.

4th Ave.
5th Ave.
6th Ave.
7th Ave.

4th St.
5th St.
6th St.
7th St.
8th St.

9th St.

10th St.
11th St.
12th St.
13th St.
14th St.
15th St.
16th St.

8th Ave.

PARK SLOPE

2, 3 **S**

GRAND ARMY PLAZA

Plaza St. E.
Plaza St. W.

Brooklyn Public Library

Eastern Pkwy.

Plaza St.

Sterling Pl.
St. Johns Pl.
Lincoln Pl.

S 2, 3

S 2, 3

Brooklyn Museum

Washington Ave.

Prospect Park W.

■ Litchfield Villa

Bandshell ■

West Dr.

Long Meadow

East Dr.

Flatbush Ave.

Prospect Park Zoo ●

Lefferts Historic House ●

● Carousel

Brooklyn Botanic Gardens

Franklin Ave.

F **S**

S

Prospect Park

Nethermead

Lullwater

Lookout Hill

Prospect Park SW

10th Ave.

11th Ave.

Windsor Pl.

Prospect Ave.

Prospect Expwy.

W. Lake Dr.

E. Lake Dr.

● Audubon Center

Ocean Ave.

S B, Q, S

Empire Blvd.

Wollman Rink ●

Prospect Lake

S. Lake Dr.

Greenwood Cemetery

Terrace Pl.
Seeley St.
Vanderbilt St.

Reeve Pl.

Greenwood Ave.

Greenwood Ave.

Fort Hamilton Pkwy.

Parkside Ave.

Prospect Park Tennis Center ■

■ Kensington Stables

Parade Grounds

S Q

Flatbush Ave.

N
LG

0   200 yards
0   200 meters

map appendix

Carroll Gardens
and Red Hook

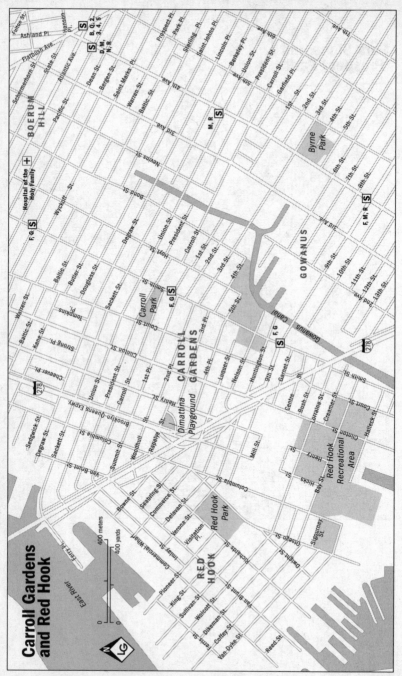

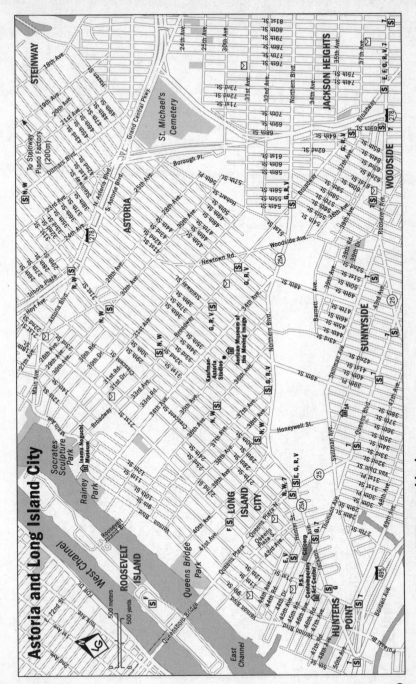

Astoria and Long Island City

STEINWAY

To Steinway Piano Factory (200m)

St. Michael's Cemetery

ASTORIA

JACKSON HEIGHTS

WOODSIDE

SUNNYSIDE

American Museum of the Moving Image

Kaufman-Astoria Studios

LONG ISLAND CITY

Socrates Sculpture Park

Rainey Park

Isamu Noguchi Museum

ROOSEVELT ISLAND

Queensboro Bridge

Queensbridge Park

East Channel

West Channel

HUNTERS POINT

P.S.1 Contemporary Art Center

500 meters
500 yards

map appendix

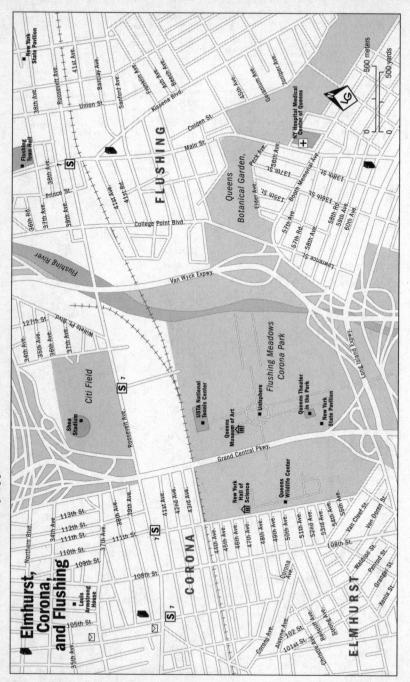

Elmhurst, Corona, and Flushing

FLUSHING

New York State Pavilion

Roosevelt Ave.
41st Ave.
38th Ave.
Barclay Ave.
Union St.
Sanford Ave.
Franklin Ave.
Ash Ave.
Beech Ave.
45th Ave.
Geranium Ave.
Juniper Ave.

NY Hospital Medical Center of Queens

Flushing Town Hall
38th Ave.
36th Rd.
37th Ave.
Prince St.
35th Ave.
39th Ave.
41st Rd.
41st Ave.
College Point Blvd.
Kissena Blvd.
Colden St.
Main St.

Queens Botanical Garden

Peck Ave.
56th Ave.
Elder Ave.
137th St.
136th St.
138th St.
136th St.
57th Ave.
57th Rd.
58th Ave.
58th Rd.
60th Ave.
Lawrence St.

Flushing River

Van Wyck Expwy.

Long Island Expwy.

127th St.
34th Ave.
35th Ave.
36th Ave.
37th Ave.
Willets Pt. Blvd.

Citi Field

Shea Stadium

Roosevelt Ave.

USTA National Tennis Center

Flushing Meadows Corona Park

Queens Museum of Art
Unisphere
Queens Theater in the Park
New York State Pavilion

Grand Central Pkwy.

New York Hall of Science
Queens Wildlife Center

113th St.
112th St.
111th St.
110th St.
109th St.
108th St.
37th Ave.
38th Ave.
39th Ave.
41st Ave.
42nd Ave.
43rd Ave.
111th St.
34th Ave.

CORONA

44th Ave.
45th Ave.
46th Ave.
47th Ave.
48th Ave.
49th Ave.
50th Ave.
51st Ave.
52nd Ave.
53rd Ave.
54th Ave.
55th Ave.
Van Cleet St.
Van Doren St.
108th St.

Louis Armstrong House

Northern Blvd.
105th Ave.
35th Ave.

Corona Ave.
Alstyne Ave.
102 St.
101st Ave.
Chester Ave.
Radnitz St.
Sidon Ave.

ELMHURST

Waldron St.
Penfold St.
Granger St.
Xenia St.

500 meters
500 yards

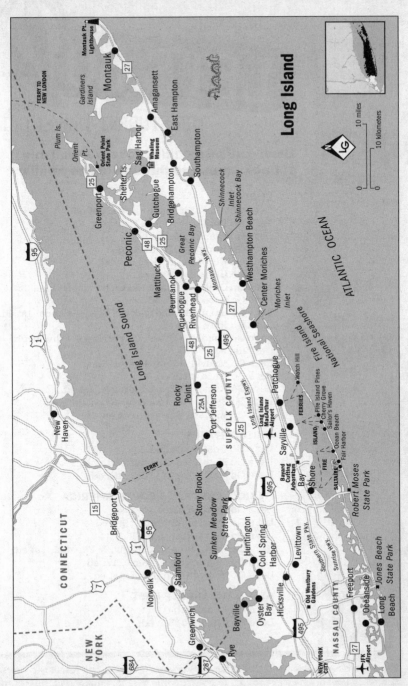

Long Island

map appendix

THE STUDENT TRAVEL GUIDE

These Let's Go guidebooks are available at bookstores and through online retailers:

EUROPE

Let's Go Amsterdam & Brussels, 1st ed.
Let's Go Berlin, Prague & Budapest, 2nd ed.
Let's Go France, 32nd ed.
Let's Go Europe 2011, 51st ed.
Let's Go European Riviera, 1st ed.
Let's Go Germany, 16th ed.
Let's Go Great Britain with Belfast and Dublin, 33rd ed
Let's Go Greece, 10th ed.
Let's Go Istanbul, Athens & the Greek Islands, 1st ed.
Let's Go Italy, 31st ed.
Let's Go London, Oxford, Cambridge & Edinburgh,
    2nd ed.
Let's Go Madrid & Barcelona, 1st ed.
Let's Go Paris, 17th ed.
Let's Go Rome, Venice & Florence, 1st ed.
Let's Go Spain, Portugal & Morocco, 26th ed.
Let's Go Western Europe, 10th ed.

UNITED STATES

Let's Go Boston, 6th ed.
Let's Go New York City, 19th ed.
Let's Go Roadtripping USA, 4th ed.

MEXICO, CENTRAL & SOUTH AMERICA

Let's Go Buenos Aires, 2nd ed.
Let's Go Central America, 10th ed.
Let's Go Costa Rica, 5th ed.
Let's Go Costa Rica, Nicaragua & Panama, 1st ed.
Let's Go Guatemala & Belize, 1st ed.
Let's Go Yucatán Peninsula, 1st ed.

ASIA & THE MIDDLE EAST

Let's Go Israel, 5th ed.
Let's Go Thailand, 5th ed.

ACKNOWLEDGMENTS

MEAGAN THANKS: Matt for his unwavering dedication and fresh-to-deathness, even when Rocky ate my life; you're the best RM an Ed could ask for. Our fearless RWs for their tireless work and adventurous spirits. DBarbs for MEdits and chop-busting. Marykate for calming my crazy. Sara and DChoi, who kept me rollin' on the RIVER. Joe for his marketing prowess, but mostly his smiles. Nathaniel for flawless editorial and ticket management. Ashley for teaching Meags how to make moves in the roughest times. Joey G. for hugs and *Glee*. I'm not really tryna forget Colleenie Bear and Sarah for making Fun Pod the best. Thanks to Betty White, Leslie Uggams, Cher, Meryl, Marge, and all the other deeves; to HRST 2010 for Tater Tots and fishnet therapy. Matt and Chris for being so sweet when Maj had to edit. Megabus, DUMBO, MTG, and dramaturgy. Thank you to Mrs. O'Brien and Nicole. Finally, thank you, mom, for your constant support.

MATT THANKS: Our RWs, for their phenomenal work in the big city. Meg, for being a friend, a grandma, and a wordsmith. Daniel, for his multilingual motivational speaking. Marykate, for answering my XV hourly questions. Colleen, for being the best. Colleen, for being not the worst. Sarah, for sharing my favorite corner of 67 Mt. Auburn. Maybe she's born with it; maybe it's Fun Pod. Ashley, for helping me lock it up by day and rip it up by night. Nathaniel and Sara, for all the late-night help and snack foods. Molimock, for making marketing moves. DChoi, for his technological wizardry. Joe Gaspard, for assisting my caffeine addiction. Hasty Pudding Theatricals 163. Not floods. Anybody who brought me from homeless to Harvard. Elisandre, for starting the week off right. Drake. Snuggies. BoltBus. Mom and dad, who gave me the best possible job training by raising me in Manhattan. Rachel, Edna, and the rest of my incredible family. And of course, New York City, my hometown, which I hope all of our readers will enjoy discovering.

ABOUT LET'S GO

THE STUDENT TRAVEL GUIDE

Let's Go publishes the world's favorite student travel guides, written entirely by Harvard students. Armed with pens, notebooks, and a few changes of clothes stuffed into their backpacks, our student researchers go across continents, through time zones, and above expectations to seek out invaluable travel experiences for our readers. Because we are a completely student-run company, we have a unique perspective on how students travel, where they want to go, and what they're looking to do when they get there. If your dream is to grab a machete and forge through the jungles of Costa Rica, we can take you there. If you'd rather bask in the Riviera sun at a beachside cafe, we'll set you a table. In short, we write for readers who know that there's more to travel than tour buses. To keep up, visit our website, www.letsgo.com, where you can sign up to blog, post photos from your trips, and connect with the Let's Go community.

TRAVELING BEYOND TOURISM

We're on a mission to provide our readers with sharp, fresh coverage packed with socially responsible opportunities to go beyond tourism. Each guide's Beyond Tourism chapter shares ideas about responsible travel, study abroad, and how to give back to the places you visit while on the road. To help you gain a deeper connection with the places you travel, our fearless researchers scour the globe to give you the heads-up on both world-renowned and off-the-beaten-track opportunities. We've also opened our pages to respected writers and scholars to hear their takes on the countries and regions we cover, and asked travelers who have worked, studied, or volunteered abroad to contribute first-person accounts of their experiences.

FIFTY-ONE YEARS OF WISDOM

Let's Go has been on the road for 51 years and counting. We've grown a lot since publishing our first 20-page pamphlet to Europe in 1960, but five decades and 60 titles later, our witty, candid guides are still researched and written entirely by students on shoestring budgets who know that train strikes, stolen luggage, food poisoning, and marriage proposals are all part of a day's work. Meanwhile, we're still bringing readers fresh new features, such as a student-life section with advice on how and where to meet students from around the world; a revamped, user-friendly layout for our listings; and greater emphasis on the experiences that make travel abroad a rite of passage for readers of all ages. And, of course, this year's 16 titles—including five brand-new guides—are still brimming with editorial honesty, a commitment to students, and our irreverent style.

THE LET'S GO COMMUNITY

More than just a travel guide company, Let's Go is a community that reaches from our headquarters in Cambridge, MA, all across the globe. Our small staff of dedicated student editors, writers, and tech nerds comes together because of our shared passion for travel and our desire to help other travelers get the most out of their experience. We love it when our readers become part of the Let's Go community as well—when you travel, drop us a postcard (67 Mt. Auburn St., Cambridge, MA 02138, USA), send us an email (feedback@letsgo.com), or sign up on our website (www.letsgo.com) to tell us about your adventures and discoveries.

For more information, updated travel coverage, and news from our researcher team, visit us online at www.letsgo.com.

THANKS TO OUR SPONSORS

- **HOTEL WOLCOTT.** 4 West 31st Street, New York, NY 10001. ☎212 268 2900. ▧www.wolcott.com.
- **AMERICAN MUSEUM OF NATURAL HISTORY.** 79 Street And Central Park West, New York, NY 10024. ☎212 769 5100. ▧www.amnh.org.
- **CHELSEA SAVOY HOTEL.** 204 W. 23rd Street, New York, NY 10011. ☎212 929 9353. ▧www.chelseasavoy.com.
- **NEW YORK INNS HOTEL GROUP.** ▧www.nyinns.com.
- **HOTEL 99.** 244 W. 99th St., New York, NY 10024. ☎212-222-3799. ▧www.hotel99.com.
- **CENTRAL PARK HOSTEL.** 19 West 103rd St. near Central Park West, New York, NY 10025. ☎212-678-0491. ▧www.centralparkhostel.com.

notes

HELPING LET'S GO. If you want to share your discoveries, suggestions, or corrections, please drop us a line. We appreciate every piece of correspondence, whether a postcard, a 10-page email, or a coconut. Visit Let's Go at **www.letsgo.com** or send an email to:

feedback@letsgo.com, subject: "Let's Go New York City"

Address mail to:

Let's Go New York City, 67 Mount Auburn St., Cambridge, MA 02138, USA

In addition to the invaluable travel advice our readers share with us, many are kind enough to offer their services as researchers or editors. Unfortunately, our charter enables us to employ only currently enrolled Harvard students.

Distributed by Publishers Group West.
Printed in Canada by Friesens Corp.
Maps © Let's Go and Avalon Travel
Design Support by Jane Musser, Sarah Juckniess, Tim McGrath

ISBN-13: 978-1-59880-708-0
Nineteenth edition
10 9 8 7 6 5 4 3 2 1

Let's Go New York City is written by Let's Go Publications, 67 Mt. Auburn St., Cambridge, MA 02138, USA.

Let's Go® and the LG logo are trademarks of Let's Go, Inc.

quick reference

YOUR GUIDE TO LET'S GO ICONS

☎	Phone numbers	⊘	Not wheelchair-accessible	❄	Has A/C
▣	Websites	((ᵖ))	Has internet access	⇌	Directions
💳	Takes credit cards	☁	Has outdoor seating	*i*	Other hard info
⊛	Cash only	▼	Is GLBT or GLBT-friendly	Ⓢ	Prices
♿	Wheelchair-accessible	⚲	Serves alcohol	⏰	Hours

PRICE RANGES

Let's Go includes price ranges, marked by icons ❶ through ❺, in accommodations and food listings. For an expanded explanation, see the chart in How To Use This Book.

NEW YORK CITY	❶	❷	❸	❹	❺
ACCOMMODATIONS	under $75	$75-120	$120-200	$200-300	above $300
FOOD	under $8	$8-15	$15-25	$25-40	above $40

IMPORTANT PHONE NUMBERS

EMERGENCY: POLICE ☎911, FIRE ☎911			
Crime Victims Hotline	☎212-577-7777	EMS Main Office	☎718-999-2770
Rape Crisis Hotline	☎212-227-3000	Western Union	☎800-325-6000
Center for Disease Control and Prevention	☎800-232-4636	Bureau of Citizenship and Immigration Services	☎800-870-3676

MAKING INTERNATIONAL CALLS

DIAL ☎011 FOLLOWED BY THE COUNTRY CODE...			
Australia	☎61	New Zealand	☎64
Ireland	☎353	United Kingdom	☎44

CURRENCY CONVERSIONS

AUS $1 = US $0.88	US$1 = AUS $1.13	NZ $1 = US $0.72	US $1 = NZ $1.40
CDN $1 = US $0.95	US $1 = CDN $1.05	UK £1 = US $1.53	US $1 = UK £0.65
EUR €1 = US $1.39	US$1 = EUR €0.77	US$1 = US$1	WHOA!

TEMPERATURE CONVERSIONS

°CELSIUS	-5	0	5	10	15	20	25	30	35	40
°FAHRENHEIT	23	32	41	50	59	68	77	86	95	104

MEASUREMENT CONVERSIONS

1 inch (in.) = 25.4mm	1 millimeter (mm) = 0.039 in.
1 foot (ft.) = 0.305m	1 meter (m) = 3.28 ft.
1 mile (mi.) = 1.609km	1 kilometer (km) = 0.621 mi.
1 pound (lb.) = 0.454kg	1 kilogram (kg) = 2.205 lb.
1 gallon (gal.) = 3.785L	1 liter (L) = 0.264 gal.